CAMBRIDGE STUDIES IN AMERICAN LITERATURE
AND CULTURE

Ezra Pound and Italian Fascism

Cambridge Studies in American Literature and Culture

Editor
Albert Gelpi, Stanford University

Advisory board
Nina Baym, *University of Illinois, Champaign-Urbana*
Sacvan Bercovitch, *Harvard University*
David Levin, *University of Virginia*
Joel Porte, *Cornell University*
Eric Sundquist, *University of California, Berkeley*
Tony Tanner, *Cambridge University*
Mike Weaver, *Oxford University*

For a list of books in the series, see page 289.

Ezra Pound and Italian Fascism

TIM REDMAN

The University of Texas at Dallas

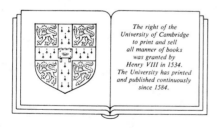

The right of the
University of Cambridge
to print and sell
all manner of books
was granted by
Henry VIII in 1534.
The University has printed
and published continuously
since 1584.

CAMBRIDGE UNIVERSITY PRESS

Cambridge
New York   Port Chester   Melbourne   Sydney

Published by the Press Syndicate of the University of Cambridge
The Pitt Building, Trumpington Street, Cambridge CB2 1RP
40 West 20th Street, New York, NY 10011, USA
10 Stamford Road, Oakleigh, Melbourne 3166, Australia

First published 1991

Printed in Canada

Library of Congress Cataloging-in-Publication Data
Redman, Tim.
Ezra Pound and Italian fascism / Tim Redman.
p.   cm. – (Cambridge studies in American literature and
culture)
Originally presented as the author's thesis – University of
Chicago, 1987.
Includes bibliographical references.
ISBN 0-521-37305-0
1. Pound, Ezra, 1885–1972 – Political and social views.   2. World
War, 1939–1945 – Literature and the war.   3. Fascism and literature –
United States.   4. Fascism – Italy.   I. Title.   II. Series
PS3531.082Z794   1990
811'.52 – dc20   90-1627

British Library Cataloguing in Publication Data
Redman, Tim
Ezra Pound and Italian fascism. – (Cambridge studies in
American literature and culture).
1. Poetry in English. American writers. Pound, Ezra, 1885–
1972. Influence of right-wing political movements
I. Title
811.52

ISBN 0-521-37305-0   hardback

For my parents,
William Charles and Eileen Keenan Redman

Contents

Acknowledgments

This book began as a dissertation for the Committee on Comparative Studies in Literature at the University of Chicago. I am grateful to Edward Wasiolek, whose vision of the potential of comparative literature was so beneficial at the beginning of this project, and to his successor as Chair of Comparative Literature at Chicago, Anthony Yu, who was so helpful as I concluded the dissertation.

I would like to thank the members of my committee for their aid with this project. Philippe Schmitter provided useful advice on Chapters 4 and 8 before he left the University of Chicago to accept an appointment in political science at the European Economic Community University in Florence. Paolo Cherchi has been consistently helpful. I owe to him my first encounter with Dante, and his dual expertise in medieval philology and Gramsci, as well as his deep knowledge of Italian culture, has greatly benefited this work.

Robert von Hallberg directed this study in its dissertation form. An early remark of his, that Pound more than almost any other poet must be approached inductively, set me on the right track and has proved its wisdom a number of times. After the dissertation was completed, he guided its metamorphosis into a book. His confidence in the value of this study, his patience throughout the long period of its maturation, and the tact and perceptivity of his comments have all been exemplary. Mary de Rachewiltz, A. Walton Litz, and James Machor have read this book at various stages in its development, and all provided helpful advice. All four of these individuals have made significant contributions to the final form of this study, and I am grateful to them.

I have been helped at various times in the lengthy process of researching and writing this book, and I would like to acknowledge the aid of Paolo and Carla Ameglio, Lynne Babcock, James Bode, Susan Brown, George and Evelyn Cunningham, Gerard Dullea, Ada and Amedeo Fravili, Carlo Fravili, Donald Gallup, Sylvia Garay, Ervene Gulley, John Hellmann,

Reverend Thomas Hogan, S.J., James Laughlin, William McNaughton, Kevin Oderman, the late Louis D. and Ann Rosinski Redman, Mary Margaret Richards, Barry Spergel, Judy Von Blon, Peter Way, and Pat Willis.

The editors at Cambridge University Press, a bicoastal and transatlantic group, have all been splendid. I would like to thank in particular Andrew Brown, Pamela Bruton, Albert Gelpi, Julie Greenblatt, Russell Hahn, and Terence Moore. I would also like to thank the Mrs. Giles Whiting Foundation for providing a fellowship to support this work at a crucial time in its evolution as a dissertation.

James S. Biddle, former Dean and Director of the Ohio State University at Lima, started a program to allow time off and summer support for junior faculty to further their research, and this book benefited from that help. Finally, Dean Robert Corrigan and my students and colleagues at the University of Texas at Dallas have all been generous with their time and advice as I completed this book. They, in particular Charles Bambach, Milton Cohen, Zsuzsanna Ozsvath, Jeffrey Perl, and Frederick Turner, have my thanks.

A writer's reputation often reaches a point... where what he actually said is falsified even when he is correctly quoted. Such falsification... is very likely the result of some single aspect of a man's work serving as a convenient symbol of what other people want to think.

– Lionel Trilling

Introduction

I

"Why read Pound?" a physicist, a friend of my father, once asked me. "Wasn't he a fascist, anti-Semitic, and insane?" I read Pound because he has written some of the most astonishing poetry in English, yet for many the perception of Pound as a crazed, right-wing bigot blocks any desire to approach the poetry. Add to that perception the admittedly difficult nature of Pound's art, and many among his potential audience are lost through distaste and discouragement.

The central problem of any Pound biography must certainly be the events surrounding his indictment (in July 1943) and arrest (in May 1945) for "radio treason." As a result of that charge, he was confined without trial in St. Elizabeths Hospital in Washington, D.C., for more than twelve years. The Pound case has so entered the cultural discourse of this century that we do ourselves a disservice by ignoring the frightening aspects of his allegiances or by attempting to somehow partition his life and work into the acceptable and the taboo. This book explores inductively the evolution of Pound's political thought, beginning with the First World War. It focuses on Pound's relation to Italian fascism from the early thirties to the end of the Second World War in Europe.

In particular, I propose to determine to what extent the common notion of his political activity is correct. That a vague, stereotypical understanding of Pound's achievement persists could be seen during the centenary year of his birth. When James Laughlin wrote a tribute to Pound in the *New York Times*, giving a sensitive account of the compelling qualities to be found in the *Cantos*, the outraged letters quickly followed.[1] All but one addressed Pound's fascism, his anti-Semitism, and his supposed psychosis. The only letter to focus on his art theorized that modern poetry

---

[1] Laughlin, 58–9.

originated in poor typing, "technical incompetence subsequently enshrined as a technique." Exasperated, Laughlin could only reply, quoting Pound: "'READ THE BOOKS!' "

Many critics hold to this common perception of Pound; some have repeated it in their writing, without taking the trouble to examine the matter more closely. Even for critics who have pondered it, however, the Pound case presents difficulties because of the critical vocabularies framing discussion. Since the time of the Romantics, the common conception of the poet as inspired genius (with its concomitant exaltation of poetics over rhetoric) has meant that in discussing Pound critics have faced a nearly impossible dilemma from the start. To avoid this dilemma, New Critics divorced Pound's work from his life: The fallible man was ignored, the transcendent work of art admired. Critics who do consider Pound's life will sometimes split it into the portion representing the true, sympathetic Pound, generous and kind to others, and the false, fascist Pound, full of hate and bigotry.[2] Others have split Pound's work, with some, such as Julia Kristeva, maintaining that the poetry of the *Cantos* undermines and overcomes the fascist ideology, and others, such as Massimo Bacigalupo, holding that the fascist ideology irremediably contaminates the poetry.[3] These fictive critical fissions result in irresolvable logical difficulties.

In fact, the Pound case calls into question the rather curious separation of poetics from rhetoric that has held sway since the Romantic period, occasioned presumably by a hunger for transcendence left by the decline of religious faith. The view that poetry offers wisdom to a nation, that the poet is a seer, was exploited by Pound and the Moderns to gain acceptance for their difficult art. Take as the major premise of poetic faith that the Poet as Genius offers guidance to the tribe. Add to that the minor premise that the Poet Pound embraced fascism, and the conclusion that we should also embrace fascism seems to follow. Since few can accept such a conclusion, critical contortions ensue, all focused on the second term of the syllogism: Pound was not really a poet; Pound was not really a fascist; Pound was a fascist, but his poetry is not fascistic; the good, essential Pound was not a fascist, but the evil, insane Pound

---

[2] Flory's first book, *Ezra Pound and the Cantos: A Record of Struggle,* though illuminating in its reading of the poetry, tries to separate the good Pound, the friend of Gaudier-Brzeska, from the bad Pound, the associate of Wyndham Lewis.

[3] Julia Kristeva advances this position in an interview for *L'Espresso,* 10 Apr. 1977. Bacigalupo, in *The Formed Trace: The Later Poetry of Ezra Pound,* maintains that the *Cantos* "are, among other things, the sacred poem of the Nazi-Fascist millennium which mercifully never eventuated" (p. x). Hatlen agrees with Kristeva that "however 'closed' and regressive the political system to which Pound committed himself, *The Cantos* remains an 'open' text. . . . *The Cantos* may set out to affirm fascism, but in fact the poem 'deconstructs' fascist ideology" (158–9).

was; Pound's fascism was not really fascism. As Conor Cruise O'Brien has asked about Yeats, how do you reconcile the poetry that you love with the politics that you loathe?[4]

This book is not an account of Italian fascism; rather, it is the story of one man's support of the fascist regime. Those critics who have written on Pound and fascism have seemed to me all too sure that they knew what fascism was. I thought it more appropriate to examine in detail Pound's political and economic thought and his responses to events from the beginning of the First through the end of the Second World War instead of proposing some theoretical relation between Pound and an ideology so nebulous that the term *fascism* has lost much of its meaning, if indeed it ever represented any coherent political philosophy at all.[5] Of the many explanations of Italian fascism that I have read, only the work of A. James Gregor and his description of Italian fascism as a "Marxist heresy" offer any useful insight into Pound's political beliefs.[6]

The problem in Pound studies has not usually been one of finding the political implications of Pound's writings but rather of escaping them. Pound's activity as an apologist for Mussolini has been an embarrassment for a whole generation of Pound scholars, who have responded, understandably, by largely ignoring that period of his life. Their reaction began with the controversy over the award of the Bollingen Prize to Pound in 1949. It is well summarized in Dwight Macdonald's comment in *Politics* in 1949:

> By some miracle the Bollingen judges were able to consider Mr. Pound the poet apart from Mr. Pound the fascist, Mr. Pound the anti-Semite, Mr. Pound the traitor, Mr. Pound the funny-money crank, and all the other Mr. Pounds whose existence has properly nothing to do with the question of whether Mr. Pound the poet had or had not written the best American poetry of 1948.[7]

This separation of life from poetry was to become the dominant critical approach to Pound for the next forty years.

Despite the central position Pound's involvement with Italian fascism occupies in his story, until recently Pound critics have avoided it altogether. In his summary essay in the companion volume for the PBS series on American poetry, Hugh Kenner, the dean of Pound studies, cogently reiterates his lifelong critical position by concluding:

---

[4] O'Brien, 273.

[5] In his famous postwar essay "Politics and the English Language," George Orwell notes that "the word *Fascism* has now no meaning except in so far as it signifies 'something not desirable' " (83).

[6] Gregor, *Italian Fascism and Developmental Dictatorship* and *Young Mussolini and the Intellectual Origins of Fascism*.

[7] Cited in Raffel, 117.

I have said nothing about the political controversies that stormed round the last third of Pound's life: the rant of the wartime broadcasts, the indictment, the imprisonment near Pisa and in a Washington madhouse. The emphasis belongs where I keep it, on the continuities of the life of the mind and on the pleasures of his craggy texts.[8]

Although I can understand the reluctance of a critic who belongs to the generation that lived through the Second World War to engage this aspect of Pound's life and work, I think that it is no longer a tenable position. Antimodernism has resulted, in great part, from a reaction against this kind of formalism. If Pound is to be legible, his politics must be confronted.

As a consciously epic poet, Pound has chosen a genre of great historical authority and durability. Consider the case of another epic poet involved in the politics of his time. How many readers today believe that the Guelphs were correct to exile Dante or that the Ghibellines were wrong? The Guelphs supported the Church and the papacy; the Ghibellines supported the Empire and the emperor. Since Dante was a Ghibelline, we assume without further thought that they were correct. The epic poet frequently gets the last word in these disputes, or at least the benefit of the doubt, and so will Pound, unless we fully face his support for Italian fascism.

Fascism, in Walter Benjamin's influential and illuminating dictum, is the aestheticization of politics. Since the time of the Bollingen controversy, Pound scholarship has engaged in an aestheticization of fascism. Only recently has the climate changed, as the New Critics have given way to critics more sympathetic to the study of the political implications of literature (and too young to have experienced the war). These younger critics have turned their attention to the political aspects of Pound's work. As I note, two critics in particular, Robert Casillo and Wendy Flory, have recently reopened serious discussion of Pound's anti-Semitism, his support for Italian fascism, and his supposed insanity.

In tracing Pound's support of Italian fascism, I have also had occasion to examine in some detail his anti-Semitism, though that important subject is not the principal focus of this work and awaits a more complete, historical account elsewhere.[9] Pound *was* anti-Semitic, and I think it useless for Pound scholars to pretend otherwise or to see in his distinction

---

[8] Vendler, 241.

[9] Casillo's book on Pound's anti-Semitism, *The Genealogy of Demons,* is psychoanalytic rather than historical in approach, although it does contain a brief, historical account of the four stages of Pound's developing anti-Semitism (5). Goldensohn has also treated this subject, in his "Pound and Antisemitism" 399–421. Flory's most recent book, *The American Ezra Pound,* has some good material on the historical background of Pound's anti-Semitism, though it, too, is largely a psychoanalytic reconsideration of the Pound case.

between "big jews" and "poor yitts" some basis for exoneration. Pound grew up during a period that witnessed a resurgence of anti-Semitism in the United States. His wife, Dorothy, as was common for the English of her class and time, was anti-Semitic. The distinctions that Pound attempts to make – the confused statements, qualifications, and evasions that make up those portions of his writings that are anti-Semitic – represent to some degree an intermittent recognition that his attitude is morally and intellectually wrong; nonetheless, the statements are there, and they cannot be explained away.

It should be emphasized that Pound was not aware of the horror that the Germans were perpetrating at the same time he was making his broadcasts. I have not seen any evidence to indicate that Pound was aware of the death camps.[10] This does not make Pound's anti-Semitism blameless, but we should at least try to see it in a historical context, difficult as that may be. The specific, historical event of the Holocaust has so decisively altered our view of the evils of anti-Semitism that it is nearly impossible to recover, and understand, the view of a period when, at least in some circles, anti-Semitism was an acceptable form of bigotry, without the terrifying associations it now has. Such a time and such a view did exist, and Pound did participate in them; at the same time he sporadically recognized their error.

II

Several critics have used Pound's supposed insanity as a way of excusing his activities during World War II. I reject the claim that Pound was insane during this time for several reasons. First, although his writings of this period are at times eccentric, excessive, or even momentarily incomprehensible, they are ultimately consistent and reveal an understandable system of political and economic beliefs. However mistaken we may think these beliefs are, they do cohere if considered carefully and they deserve a fair and open-minded hearing. Furthermore, Dr. Jerome Kavka, who during his residency at St. Elizabeths examined Pound, has stated categorically on several occasions that Pound was not insane and would not have been confined to a mental institution had it not been for the treason charge hanging over him.

Moreover, Dr. E. Fuller Torrey, in his book *The Roots of Treason: Ezra Pound and the Secret of St. Elizabeths*, has examined the records relating to Pound's medical case and has stated that there was no evidence of psychosis. In a popular account of his work, Torrey summarizes:

---

[10] Critics mistakenly continue to insist the opposite. For example, David Bromwich recently implied, quite wrongly, that Pound advocated the Holocaust (326).

"Hospital records of the Pound case that have recently been released and my own interviews with key people involved in the case persuade me that Pound was never insane and he was never unfit to stand trial." According to Torrey, Pound's insanity plea was concocted by his friends (with his agreement) and by Dr. Winfred Overholser, the director of St. Elizabeths, to avoid the necessity of Pound's coming to trial.[11] Torrey also claims that Overholser made Pound's stay pleasant and comfortable. Although I do not agree that there was a conspiracy among Pound's friends, Torrey's conclusion does accord with the available medical diagnoses, which, while admitting that Pound had suffered a physical breakdown in Pisa that adversely affected his mental condition, did not find him insane.

These diagnoses are extensively summarized by Humphrey Carpenter in the most recent Pound biography. While confined at Pisa, Pound was examined on 15 and 16 June 1945 by two psychiatrists, Captain Richard W. Fenner and Captain Walter H. Baer. Fenner reported:

> No paranoia, delusions nor hallucinations. . . . Patient is oriented as to place and person. . . . Memory for remote events is good. Memory is also good for recent events. . . . No evidence of emotional instability. . . . very superior intelligence. No evidence of disease of the central nervous system, and no notable personality defect.[12]

Baer reported:

> No evidence of psychosis, neurosis, or psychopathy. He is of superior intelligence, is friendly, affable, and cooperative. . . . Due to his age and loss of personal resilience, prolonged exposure in present environment may precipitate a mental breakdown, of which premonitory symptoms are discernible.[13]

Pound was also examined at the Disciplinary Training Camp at Pisa on 17 July by Major William Weisdorf, who reported that

> speech is on the whole relevant and coherent. . . . There is no evidence of hallucinations or delusions. . . . no evidence of depression. . . . Intellectual powers . . . are superior. . . . The prisoner apparently developed transitory anxiety state, as the culmination of several weeks of close confinement. . . . These manifestations cleared up rapidly as the prisoner was made more comfortable physically. He shows no evidence of psychosis or neurosis at the present time.[14]

[11] Torrey, "The Protection of Ezra Pound," 57.
[12] Carpenter, 663.
[13] Ibid., 663–4.
[14] Ibid., 668.

Carpenter cites another psychiatrist who examined Pound, Dr. Addison
Duval, who concluded: "I couldn't elicit any symptoms of psychosis at
all. There were no delusions, no thought disorder, and no disturbance
of orientation. He definitely did not seem to be insane."[15] Carpenter
summarizes: "The evidence is that in November 1945, in the DC Jail,
Ezra was not 'mad' in any clinical sense; he was simply his usual highly
eccentric self."[16] Thus we cannot fall back upon the convenient explanation of pathology or aberration when we consider Pound's behavior
during this time: Such an evasion ends discussion at a point where discussion should begin.

Pound wanted to be treated seriously as an economic and political
thinker, and whatever our final judgment about his case, he must be
heard as one. Pound's support for Italian fascism was not the result of
psychosis but was consistent with and developed from his thought about
social and economic issues. Certainly there were flaws in his character
and in his judgment, but they are not sufficient to explain his support
of Mussolini's regime. To do this we must look carefully at Pound's
own ideology and his belief that Mussolini's regime would put into effect
the economic reform for which Pound hoped.

Aside from the ethical and medical issues presented by the Pound case,
there are legal questions as well. These are explored by Judge Conrad
L. Rushing in " 'Mere Words': The Trial of Ezra Pound." Rushing
proposes in his article to determine whether a jury in 1947 or 1948 would
have found Pound guilty of treason. He concludes:

> Pound's case should have been brought to trial within one or two years
> after his commitment to St. Elizabeths because he had a reasonable
> chance of being found not guilty of treason; even if found guilty, the
> circumstances in mitigation of a long prison term would have been so
> evident that he would have likely spent considerably less time in prison
> than he spent locked up at the mental institution.[17]

"Moreover," Rushing states, "Pound would have emerged as a man
who had repaid his debt, a person who, having committed a wrong,
restored the moral balance by submitting to the appropriate punishment
of his society."[18] Drawing on the work of the legal philosopher Herbert
Morris (*On Guilt and Innocence*), Rushing sees a fundamental injustice in
the way Pound was treated by the legal system. His case was handled
in a way that deprived him of his right to be punished. This idea may
strike us as somewhat paradoxical, but Rushing cites Morris in arguing

[15] Ibid., 729.
[16] Ibid., 704.
[17] Rushing, 112.
[18] Ibid., 131.

that a person's right to be punished is the same as the right to be treated as a human being. Although the argument for Pound's incompetence to stand trial was a correct strategem to delay the proceedings, a tactic that was in Pound's best interest, he should have been brought to trial. Because this did not occur, his punishment for a crime of which he may or may not have been found guilty was excessive.

Rushing does not share Torrey's view of the pleasant life led by Pound in St. Elizabeths Hospital:

> St. Elizabeths was a scandal awaiting discovery. It had never met the standards of the American Psychiatric Association. . . . Overholser, St. Elizabeths' director, was one of the most sued men in the District of Columbia [for abuses his patients suffered].[19]

Rushing does, however, share Torrey's belief that Pound was not insane. He contends that the incompetency plea was not the consequence of a conspiracy among Pound's friends and Dr. Overholser and that the acceptance of the plea resulted from the attitudes of the judge and the government prosecutors to the case against Pound.[20] Rushing hypothesizes that the government probably lacked confidence in its case and so did not raise any strong objection to the insanity defense. He believes the judge, seeing that the prosecutor had no objection and knowing the nature of confinement in St. Elizabeths, did not attempt to block the plea on his own. Rushing surmises that the judge knew St. Elizabeths to be a place "far worse than any prison."[21]

Apart from the legal considerations of the case, the issue of Pound's moral culpability remains to be addressed. Although I have tried to eschew a moralizing tone in the course of the book, it is not because I believe that moral judgments about Pound's activity before and during the Second World War should be avoided. Judgment should be based on full and fair consideration of the facts, and until now, no scholar has attempted this kind of inductive approach to Pound's support of fascism. To understand all is not to forgive all; understanding should be the basis of decision and even of condemnation, where appropriate. Law, religion, and medicine have all recognized the restorative powers of the second halves of dichotomies such as remorse and expiation, guilt and punishment, confession and penance, defect and rehabilitation, illness and cure, but only when the first terms are fully understood. Pound is too important a figure for us to rush to judgment. After considering his work during this period in detail, we should be able to arrive at some conclusion about the degree of his moral guilt or innocence.

[19] Ibid., 124.
[20] Ibid., 122.
[21] Ibid., 124.

What moral standards should we use to judge Pound's actions? What are the ethical responsibilities of intellectuals, and how do they meet or fail to meet them? These questions have received renewed attention recently. At a conference marking the twentieth anniversary of the quarterly *Salmagundi,* a panel consisting of Conor Cruise O'Brien, George Steiner, and Leszek Kolakowski spoke on the duties of thinkers, particularly in the political realm.[22] Certainly intellectuals have a duty to truth and, I believe, a concomitant duty to clarity of expression. The panelists took the discussion further. O'Brien, a former member of the Irish Parliament, noted that lying was "required by the nature of the political process" and that it sickened him and he was glad to get out of it. He expressed his own goals in Confucian terms:

> I care, in circles going out, about my family, my city, my country, people with whom I identify . . . in other countries. . . . I would like at least that my own intellectual activity should not make things worse or more dangerous for those people and, preferably, that it would make things by a tiny margin a little bit better, a little bit clearer, a little bit more rational, even a little bit more compassionate. . . . I don't set myself any larger goal than that, and I'm not sure that I'm going to achieve that.

Certainly this is an agenda for our times, one whose modesty derives from experience in the political realm as well as from our current reluctance to make large claims for the truth of our convictions. Pound would have recognized and agreed with the Confucian concept of degree of responsibility moving in concentric circles outward from self to family to village, but his own ambition was far greater in scope and encompassed, in his economic program, at least all of Western society. One should not fault him for his ambition, though the grand scale of it certainly calls into question his political judgment. In fact, as we shall see, Pound was a political naïf, with an idealized conception of how political systems functioned.

George Steiner spoke of the "answerability of the intellectual" and of the necessity to live our convictions:

> I think the person who lives the risks of his conviction, of his passion – maybe they're a dangerous person, maybe a terribly mistaken person – I think he won't sizzle at the last judgment. . . .
> I would say that the definitions of the irremediable (the unpardonable) came out of the Dreyfus affair, when the intellectual and the intelligentsia, as concepts, were developed, and one of those is that you leave any city rather than sacrifice to it what bit of truth possesses you or

what you believe to be the truth. And no city, no nation, no loyalty is worth a lie.

Although paid for his propaganda work for the Italian fascist government, Pound was not merely a hired broadcaster; he engaged in those activities out of conviction that Mussolini would put into effect desirable economic reforms. Pound did take risks for his convictions, and although he committed many errors in judgment, I have no sense that his beliefs were anything other than firmly held. His activities were not self-serving but were directed at his perception of the general good.

Leszek Kolakowski sees the specific responsibility of the intellectual in Flaubertian terms with which Pound would certainly have agreed:

> It's not political, it's a responsibility for the proper use of words, for a not misleading use of words. And that's all. There is not specific political responsibility, because intellectuals are not wiser or better guided in their minds in political choices, as we know very well. What I want to point out is that there are people among intellectuals who are openly racist, anti-Semites, Communists or supporters of terrorism. They are wrong, of course, morally and intellectually. But it's apart from the question of specific responsibility.

As the Nicaraguan poet Pablo Antonio Cuadra put it: "Love things for their true name; that's one of a writer's duties."[23] Pound departed on many occasions from his responsibility to le mot juste during his radio broadcasts for Rome Radio, and by taking on the job of propagandist he abrogated his vocation as poet. In fact, the period of the radio broadcasts coincided with a period of sparse poetic activity in Pound's life. Poets forsake that duty to precise definition when they engage, as Pound consciously did, in propaganda, no matter how well intentioned or in support of whatever worthwhile goal.

III

Pound's activity on behalf of Italian fascism needs to be understood historically and with a great deal of specificity. I have pursued this goal by examining primary documents from this time: Pound's letters, articles, and books, as well as archival materials. Most of these documents are located at Yale's Beinecke Library, but in addition I have studied material at the Humanities Research Center at the University of Texas at Austin; Pound's personal library at the Humanities Research Center and at Schloss Brunnenburg in Italy; the Archivio Nazionale dello Stato in EUR, Italy; the archives of the Department of Justice and the State

---

[23] Goldman, section 6, 50.

Department in Suitland, Maryland, and Washington, D.C.; the Italian national libraries in Rome, Florence, and Milan; the library of the University of Genoa, Italy; and the municipal library in Alessandria, Italy.

Pound proposes several models for the historian: Varchi, the man wanting all of the evidence; Confucius, who remembers the time "when the historians left blanks in their writings, / . . . for things they didn't know" (C, XIII, 60).[24] In the Exile he writes that "it is the historian's function to leave the record and to leave the record as accurate as he can."[25] My attempt here is to contextualize Pound's writings and actions during this period, to re-create the political, economic, and social background from which they emerged and the contemporary problems to which they responded. My guiding principle in this endeavor has been non lego non credo: If I have not read something, I do not believe it; and I have restricted myself to an examination of documents from the period prior to May of 1945. Oral accounts and written material from the period after Pound's arrest are frequently too unreliable and potentially too self-serving to provide a trustworthy guide to such a controversial subject.

There has been no lack of material to study. Pound was a prolific writer and sent an average of well over a thousand letters a year during the period between 1930 and 1945 ("and you must work day and night / to keep up with your letters," C, XLI, 203). They are frequently repetitious, a characteristic reassuring to historians because important matters are mentioned frequently, providing an internal means of verification. My approach has been inductive and chronological. I have read extensively in Pound's writings (including a great deal of unpublished and previously unexamined material) during the period between the early thirties and the end of the Second World War. This close look at documentary evidence makes up the second part of this book.

The first part of the book is also chronological, though less detailed. It provides the conceptual background necessary for an understanding of the material in the second part. Chapter 1 starts with Pound's political education at the New Age office in London during the years of the First World War, a period that saw him change from aesthete to politically engaged poet. Chapter 2 considers Pound's conversion to the economic thought of Major C. H. Douglas and his doctrine of Social Credit. Chapter 3 treats Pound's literary activity and growing reputation in Italy in the early thirties. Chapter 4 describes his conversion to fascism, his meeting with Mussolini, and his book Jefferson and/or Mussolini. Chapter 5 discusses his discovery of the work of Silvio Gesell, who completed

---

[24] All quotations of Pound's poetry are from the standard editions of his works: Personae, indicated with a "P" followed by a page number; and The Cantos of Ezra Pound, indicated with a "C" followed by the canto number in roman numerals and the page number.
[25] No. 3 (Spring 1928): 60.

Pound's economic education. Although some readers will be dismayed at a second chapter on economics, the chapter on Gesell is necessary for two reasons. First, a detailed description of Gesell's thought, so vital for Pound, is not to my knowledge available elsewhere.[26] Second, the emphasis on Douglas in Pound scholarship instead of on Gesell (a far more considerable figure in the history of economics) has tended to reinforce the notion that Pound was an economic crank, despite Leon Surette's splendid groundbreaking work to the contrary.[27]

The second part of the book considers in great detail the years of Pound's enthusiastic support for Italian fascism. Chapter 6 covers the period from 1933 until the start of the Second World War in 1939. Chapter 7 treats the years of the Second World War up to the invasion of Italy. Chapter 8 considers the period from the fall of Mussolini and the founding of the Salò Republic until Pound's surrender to Allied authorities in May of 1945. For the most part, then, this work takes the form of an intellectual biography of Pound, focusing on politics and economics and using a historical approach, during the period of what has been called (to emphasize its unity) "The Second Thirty Years' War," 1914–45.

This study of Pound and Italian fascism can be justified solely on the basis of Pound's importance as a poet. But I believe that it raises questions that have broader implications for literature, questions about the relation between poetry and society, about the poet's political obligations, and about the ethical responsibilities of intellectuals. In particular, the Pound case has eroded the claim poets have made in previous centuries to address authoritatively the largest concerns of their cultures.

Some pages back, I made explicit the logical contradictions resulting from the Pound syllogism and how critics have tried to evade them by challenging or qualifying the minor premise in various ways. In the larger view, however, the Pound case has challenged the major premise of that syllogism, the *religio poetae* inherited from the Romantics. Perhaps poetry is not to be taken seriously in the public, political realm; perhaps poetry, as Auden said, "makes nothing happen"; perhaps poets offer lyrical solace or decorative speech, nothing more.[28]

Donald Davie commented years ago that awarding the Bollingen Prize to Pound meant recognizing the "absolute discontinuity between the life of the poet and the life of the man."[29] The serious consequence of that decision has been the loss of poetic authority. Because of Pound, the

---

[26] Eva Hesse has recognized the importance of the Proudhon–Gesell–Pound connection and considered it in her *Ezra Pound: Metodo e follia*, 115–20.
[27] Particularly in the economics chapter of Surette's book *A Light from Eleusis* and in his article "Ezra Pound and British Radicalism."
[28] Rorty's recent book, *Contingency, Irony, and Solidarity* argues for this kind of separation of a private, aesthetic realm of self-creation from a public, ethical realm of justice.
[29] Davie, *Ezra Pound: Poet as Sculptor*, 242.

poet is no longer considered exalted or wise: Society treats him "from the first as pathologically irresponsible in everything beyond mere connoisseurship and expertise in his craft."[30]

Davie continues, correctly I believe, that "Pound has made it impossible for anyone any longer to exalt the poet into a seer."[31] In other words, the combination that we find in Pound of undoubted poetic mastery and questionable political beliefs has contributed to the widespread retreat of American poets from political engagement. Whether this is a result of the public perception that "the poet cannot truthfully see or investigate public life"[32] or the result of a private crisis of confidence among poets is not presently germane. What is germane, even vital, is the fact that since Pound our culture has been without strong poetic guidance.[33]

The turn to the lyrical and away from the political in American poetry is widely acknowledged. Richard Jones questions "why poets have chosen to put themselves in a kind of prison of the self," engaging only in "a sort of propaganda of the self."[34] Turner Cassity believes that "meditation and the first person have rather paupered English poetry. The hermetic lyric of personal emotion and its sloppier successor, the psychological self-search, account for an appalling percentage of all verse."[35] Terrence Des Pres put the matter most succinctly: "For poetry . . . there is as yet, in America, no poetics equal to the import of politics in language or in life."[36]

I would suggest that this retreat into subjectivity, this radical loss of bardic consequence, can be attributed to a large extent to the case of Ezra Pound. The vehemence with which his work is discussed indicates that the debate is not just about Pound but about the very nature and source of written authority, as it was conceived both during the previous century and now. The question is not, Why read Pound? but, rather, Why read poetry? If poetry is ever again to assert the kind of moral authority it claimed in the nineteenth century, and if the poet is ever to recover the role of cultural preceptor, we must come to terms with Ezra Pound. For Pound was the last poet to have assumed the role of discerning guide for Western society. He was fully conscious of the poet's claim to au-

---

[30] Ibid., 243.
[31] Ibid.
[32] Ibid., 244.
[33] Wendell Berry and Gary Snyder are two exceptions. I do not consider the poetry of protest to be political, because it is of necessity reactive, though it frequently serves as the chrysalis for political poetry. I treat in detail these and related issues in a book in progress, *Ecopoetics*.
[34] Jones, 11–12.
[35] Cassity, 133.
[36] Des Pres, xviii.

thority. He put on the poet's mantle himself, invoking the epic tradition of his predecessors. Because of egregious mistakes in judgment, he may have indelibly stained the mantle. If poetry is going to reassert its claim to cultural consequence, we must come to a resolution about the case of Pound that encompasses his whole life – not just those periods with which we are comfortable – and all of his work, the strident and the lyric alike.

Part I. "A Moralist and Thence an Economist"

1

A. R. Orage and the Education of a Poet

I

Like his later hero, Mussolini, Pound began his conversion to fascism through the pages of a socialist newspaper. For Pound, that newspaper was the *New Age;* his contributions to its pages continued over a period of ten years, from 30 November 1911 to 13 January 1921 (with a fifteen-month gap between October 1913 and January 1915, when only one Pound piece appeared). More particularly, Pound first encountered the linking of anti-Semitism and usury in that British intellectual milieu, not in the Italian milieu he later inhabited. I wish to show here how misleading it is to single out Pound as extraordinarily culpable, vicious, or insane. His attachment to Italian fascism followed naturally from his involvement in the London literary and intellectual scene of 1911–20. Pound's political views were not so anomalous as they are sometimes made to appear.

Noel Stock notes that as a regular contributor, Pound began to frequent the paper's small editorial offices and would attend the Monday afternoon teas for its writers "in the basement of the ABC restaurant in Chancery Lane."[1] There were other regular gatherings at other cafes and restaurants, and Pound was introduced to a lively group including such writers as Cecil Chesterton, S. G. Hobson, J. M. Kennedy, Beatrice Hastings, H. G. Wells, Arnold Bennett, F. S. Flint, Katherine Mansfield, T. E. Hulme, and Ramiro de Maetzu.[2] Wallace Martin observes: "Many whose interests were purely literary (Ezra Pound among them) received their first political and economic education in the Chancery Lane ABC. [A. R.] Orage hoped that each contributor would be led to see his objectives as part of the whole magazine's policy."[3]

[1] Stock, *The Life of Ezra Pound,* 105. I am much indebted to this reliable biography though I agree with Stock's own assessment that it is not definitive.
[2] Martin, 43–4. Much of the material in this section depends on Martin's account.
[3] Ibid., 44.

17

The *New Age* was purchased in 1907 by the Fabian Arts Group, an outgrowth of the Fabian Society. The first issue under new management (the joint editorship of Holbrook Jackson and A. R. Orage) appeared on 2 May 1907; it displayed the new subtitle "An Independent Socialist Review of Politics, Literature, and Art."[4] By the time Pound began writing for it, the *New Age* was edited solely by Orage and had acquired a reputation as one of the most important weekly papers of its time. Margaret Cole, recalling that period, wrote to the *New Statesman* in 1959: "*The New Age,* particularly just before and in the early part of the first world war, was *the* left-wing paper, which everybody who was anybody read."[5] The *New Witness* in June of 1917 called it "the most intelligent and independent paper of our time." C. K. Ogden, in a contemporary article, indicated its importance in shaping the policies of the Labour Party.[6] Although it never acquired a large circulation (Orage reported weekly sales of 2,000 in a column of 10 October 1918), its radical, lively, and eclectic approach exerted a great deal of influence in the intellectual and artistic circles of London at that time.[7]

During its early years, such writers as Shaw, Wells, Chesterton, and Belloc discussed the cultural meaning of socialism in the pages of the *New Age.* Starting in 1912, the paper advocated what Martin terms "an ingenious synthesis of political Socialism and industrial Syndicalism"[8] known as Guild Socialism. This was not the radical syndicalism of continental Europe but a variant deriving from the English craft tradition advocated by such writers as William Morris and John Ruskin. Still, a mix of socialism and syndicalism was precisely what Benito Mussolini was inventing in Italy at about the same time, and it is easy to see why Pound, through Odon Por, would later find in fascism many congenial and already familiar ideas.

The paper was eclectic in approach. It included a regular column, "Foreign Affairs," by "S. Verdad" (a pun on the Portuguese "it is true"); articles on Guild Socialism; various series by Pound; art, music, and drama criticism; book reviews; a great deal about current affairs, with extensive commentaries about parliamentary and cabinet action in Orage's regular lead column, "Notes of the Week"; and a fair amount of original literary work, criticism, short fiction, poetry, and translation. Regular columns included "Press Cuttings" and "Current Cant," favorable excerpts and mocking quotations from contemporary journal-

---

[4] Ibid., 21–4.
[5] Ibid., 5.
[6] Ibid., 120.
[7] Flory provides further evidence of Orage's stature: "Shaw judged him to be the most brilliant editor of the past century and Eliot 'the finest critical intelligence of our day' " (*The American Ezra Pound,* 44).
[8] Martin, 208.

ism, and Orage's own literary column, "Readers and Writers" by "R. H. C."

Until the First World War, the *New Age* exhibited a lively sense of humor and would frequently run light satiric pieces. For example, "Lionel de Fonseka" wrote "Futurism in Food" for the issue of 5 June 1913, detailing a visit to the new "Futurist Restaurant," where "every emotion may be rendered gastronomically" and the diner introspected before ordering: "You inform the chef of your emotion of the moment, and he sends up the corresponding dish" (148–9). Not even Guild Socialism was exempt from this spirit of fun. In "The Guild System in West Africa" R. E. Dennet spoke of the economic effects of devils, spirits, and deities in mock-solemn tones.

Equally spirited in tone was the *New Age* circle that Orage gathered around him. Several of his contemporaries would later recall him as the most brilliant talker of his day.[9] In addition to the regulars, visitors such as Yeats, Epstein, Augustus John, Upton Sinclair, and R. S. Crane would occasionally drop by to share in the stimulating conversation.[10] We should recall that Pound was quite young in those days, that he had not yet established himself as a writer, that he was eager for a reputation, and that his work for Orage constituted one of the principal means of his support. He was impressionable and, as his letters from the time show, somewhat in awe of the writers whom he was meeting. Thus it is not surprising that the Pound of this time was receptive to the influence of Orage and to the integration of the arts with the political concerns of society advocated by the *New Age*. These *New Age* gatherings also formed the basis of Pound's education in economics. As Martin summarizes: "Bechhofer-Roberts spoke for scores of writers when, on being asked where he was educated, he replied, 'On *The New Age*.' "[11]

Pound's position with the *New Age* did not come easily. In "Readers and Writers" of 13 November 1913, Orage remarked: "Mr. Pound – I say this with all respect – is an enemy of *The New Age*" (51). In fact, Orage and Pound seldom agreed about literature, and an examination of the literary columns of the *New Age* during the decade of their collaboration reveals how modernism, far from being the inevitable and dominant poetic movement we now take it to be, had to struggle for recognition. Pound observed their differences after Orage's death: "For twenty-three years I don't think that either of us ever took the other seriously as a critic of letters."[12] Pound's earliest attempt at political

[9] Ibid., 46–7.
[10] Ibid., 43.
[11] Ibid., 56.
[12] Pound, "In the Wounds (Memoriam A. R. Orage)" (Apr. 1935). Reprinted in *Selected Prose*, 450.

commentary, on the Balkan War ("The Black Crusade"), was met with scorn by regular contributors to the paper in letters to the editor: "Your correspondent, Mr. Ezra Pound, writes as one who, knowing nothing of a subject, cannot endure to hear a word about it." "As an absolutely regular occasional contributor, may I be allowed to differ from my colleague, Mr. Ezra Pound, on the subject of this most cowardly war" (28 Nov. 1912, 93).

Even Pound's literary efforts were mocked. His seven-part series on French poetry, begun in September 1913, soon attracted a series parodying it that Orage chose to run simultaneously. Although Orage respected Pound's accomplishments in *Cathay* and "The Seafarer," he frequently took him to task in public. In his "Readers and Writers" column of 5 August 1915, "R. H. C." had this to say:

> Mr. James Douglas has half accused *The New Age* of inventing Mr. Ezra Pound. . . . However often we have mentioned Mr. Pound's name, it is at least certain that we have never countenanced his theories. But then Mr. Pound is so much better than his theories that to dispose of them is by no means to dispose of him. . . . I would part Mr. Pound from his theories as often as I found him clinging to one, for they will in the end be his ruin. . . . It is noteworthy that all the movements, without exception, with which Mr. Pound has identified himself are of foreign extraction, like himself, and are seeking like him to become naturalised. (332–3)

Orage was a perceptive critic. His remarks about Pound's theories will strike readers as prescient; his remarks about Pound's attempts to become naturalized are no less so. Pound's endeavors to win approval and acceptance from the London literary world have been well documented elsewhere. His passage from aesthete to politically engaged poet, from frequent target of criticism to frequent contributor (one who could later remark that, with Orage, "for one period we seemed almost to get out the old *New Age* between us"[13]), is a remarkable journey of a decade, resulting in a decisive conversion, one that is the foundation for Pound's later support of Italian fascism. Although those many conversations in the *New Age* office survive only as scattered fragments in autobiographies and memoirs, we can reconstruct their themes in great detail through a careful examination of the editorial policy and political thought of that most remarkable man, A. R. Orage, during Pound's involvement with the paper from autumn 1912, when "Patria Mia" first was serialized in the *New Age,* to autumn 1920, when, just after the serialization of "Indiscretions," Pound prepared to leave London.

---

[13] Pound, "Obituary: A. R. Orage" (Nov. 1934), in *Selected Prose,* 437.

II

Jackson and Orage began the *New Age* to examine the relation of socialism to art and philosophy.[14] This attempt to enrich political theory through a systematic examination of the implications of socialism for the arts, literature, and philosophy made for a lively journal that never lost its focus even as it went beyond economics to regard all of culture. Orage consciously tried to bring together diverse elements of European life, in both the arts and the social sciences. Pound too would espouse such a syncretic program in the thirties under the misleading rubric of "totalitarianism." Martin observes:

> It was Orage's conscious and declared intention to integrate these forces so that culture would have an intelligible structure and direction. His assumption that political and economic problems were inseparable from the problems of culture as a whole was part of his nineteenth-century heritage, in the tradition of Carlyle, Ruskin, and William Morris.[15]

These nineteenth-century traditions were particularly noticeable in the work of Arthur J. Penty, who envisioned the restoration of the guild system, an organization of craftspeople banded together to determine standards of workmanship and price. Orage and such *New Age* contributors as S. G. Hobson intermixed those earlier ideas with Fabian concerns to create the movement of Guild Socialism that dominated political debate in the paper until the First World War. Leon Surette has commented upon the pervasive importance of John Ruskin's work on economics, especially *Unto This Last,* for the climate of opinion of the time: "Ruskin's strongest appeal – at least within *The New Age* circle – was that he provided an economic justification for expenditure on the arts."[16] The guild model of slow, careful craft rather than cheap, mass production was bound to attract support from the *New Age* group, especially when framed in the traditional political vocabulary of socialism. Orage outlined his concerns in the unsigned series "National Guilds":

> The commodity theory is at the root of the present discontent. However this theory may sincerely be held by profiteers and economists, it remains a trick by which labour is defrauded. . . . when the vast mass of the wage-earners perceive the inherent dishonesty of a system that robs them of two-thirds of the value of their labour, from that moment not only is that system doomed, but its destruction is at hand. . . . the new revolution must be based upon an aesthetic and ethical proposition – the certain demonstration that the value and significance of human labour are not in the same category as the inanimate elements that go into wealth production. A commodity is something that has exchange

[14] Martin, 21.
[15] Ibid., 15.
[16] Surette, "Ezra Pound and British Radicalism," 440.

value; labour is priceless, and, therefore, its value cannot be expressed.
(4 Dec. 1913, 134)

Despite this talk of destruction, doom, and revolution, the *New Age*,
though tirelessly taking the side of labor, was more representative of an evolutionary, rather than revolutionary, socialism.[17] Its later advocacy of Social Credit was also indicative of its reformist bent. As Surette has correctly
pointed out, "the political appeal of Social Credit was, of course, that it
promised the resolution of economic problems without any significant al-
teration of prevailing political and social structures."[18] Pound's political
and economic thinking in the thirties and forties followed a similar path. He
advocated Social Credit (and Gesellist) monetary reforms because they
provided mechanisms by which to correct an unjust economic system.
Moreover, as we will see later, Pound always maintained that the Fascist
and the Bolshevik revolutions, both of which he admired, were suitable
only for Italy and Russia, and that a lesser amount of political energy ex-
pended in either Britain or the United States would successfully revitalize
their parliamentary and republican systems through reform.

Orage's attempt to incorporate politics, economics, literature, and the
arts all within one comprehensive editorial policy led him to judge severely those who imagined that such subjects might be considered sep-
arately. Martin reminds us that Orage's "opinion of those who concerned
themselves exclusively with the arts was no less harsh than his opinion
of those interested only in politics."[19] His eclecticism would explain many
of his early differences with Pound. But despite the apparent equality of
these intermingled activities, the one guiding principle of their treatment
in the *New Age* and the prevailing theme of the journal during the decade
of Pound's involvement was the idea that "economic power precedes
political power." That conviction dominated Orage's weekly column.
It obviously echoes orthodox Marxism, though Orage took pains to note
that he adhered to *an* economic interpretation of history but not *the*
Marxist economic interpretation. Orage's constant attempt to seek an
economic explanation behind the apparently political events of the period
before, during, and after the First World War led him to gradually aban-
don his Guild Socialism, advocate greater confrontation of capital by
labor, and ultimately embrace C. H. Douglas's Social Credit movement.
Since so much of Orage's growth (and Pound's transformation) in
thought is directly attributable to the shattering experience of the war,
it should be considered next.

---

[17] The classic statement of this doctrine is Eduard Bernstein's *Evolutionary Socialism*. On
the connection between the Fabians and Bernstein see Gay, 93–8.
[18] Surette, "Ezra Pound and British Radicalism," 444.
[19] Martin, 235.

III

In issue after issue of the *New Age* Orage blasted the inequality of the sacrifice being made in the war by the British working class: the conscription of men, but not of capital; the sacrifice of lives, but not of profit. It is difficult for us to imagine the horror experienced by the average soldier on the front line, though Fussell conveys it vividly:

> The trenches were always wet and often flooded. . . . rats also gave constant trouble. They were big and black with wet, muddy hair. They fed largely on the flesh of cadavers and on dead horses. . . . One can understand rats eating heartily there. It is harder to understand men doing so. The stench of rotting flesh was over everything, hardly repressed by the chloride of lime sprinkled on particularly offensive sites. Dead horses and dead men – and parts of both – were sometimes not buried for months and often became simply an element of parapets and trench walls. You could smell the front line miles before you could see it.[20]

The average front-line life span of an infantryman, Fussell tells us, was only six weeks.[21] By the autumn of 1918, near the end of the war, more than half of the British infantry were younger than nineteen.[22]

An occasional columnist for the *New Age,* W. Mears, was able to express savage indignation at the human costs and unequal sacrifices of the war by employing Swiftian satire. One such piece, "The Disposal of Disabled Soldiers: A Few Suggestions towards the Solution of This Problem, Addressed to the Governing Class," began: "The disposal of the human debris created by the war is a question that demands the serious attention of the best minds in this country. Unfortunately, the whole matter has been obscured by a sentimental agitation"; and ended: "Whatever solution they adopt they can rest assured that there are plenty of journalists and others ready to persuade the public that the interests of the profiteers are the interests of all true patriots" (29 June 1916, 208). Mears's remark upon the mendacity of the mainstream press reflected Orage's own view of "the carefully taught parrot Press" (9 Oct. 1919, 385) found in the pages of the *New Age* repeatedly throughout the decade.

International socialism was an early casualty of the Great War. Throughout Europe, national loyalty superseded class loyalty as the national socialist parties, instead of cooperating in the great general strike that socialist theorists had foreseen, found some way to accommodate

[20] Fussell, 47–9.
[21] Ibid., 124.
[22] Ibid., 18.

themselves to the war aims of their nations. The Second International had stressed the duty of the working class to international solidarity against capitalist and imperialist war, but once the war started, no international opposition to it emerged. In Great Britain, the Fabian Society was actually in favor of the war. The *New Age,* though highly critical of government policy throughout the duration of the conflict, also supported the war. Orage rationalized this stance in his "Notes of the Week" of 6 August 1914, saying: "We believe that England is necessary to Socialism, as Socialism is necessary to the world" (313). His justification was that only in England could the socialist experiment of changing the wage system be tried in practice. Since England was the hope of civilization, England had to be defended.

Throughout the First World War the two continuing themes in Orage's "Notes of the Week" were the inequality of the burden of the war for the working and privileged classes and the methods and impossibility of paying for it. Orage stated his position clearly at the outset:

> In England, the rich intend to remain at home and at business while the poor are to ruin themselves at home and abroad. *That* is what the cry of conscription means on our plutocracy's lips. It means compelling the poor to fight for the rich in war as they sweat for the rich in peace. (3 Sept. 1914, 411)

He would continue his vehement opposition to the unequal share shouldered by the laboring class for the duration of the war. Although specific issues changed, Orage's championing of the rights of workers never did. At least during the first stages of the war, Orage had the ability to be thoughtful, critical, and solicitous of the interests of the working class, yet not in any way defeatist or treasonable:

> It is not true that the working classes disapprove of the war; it is not true that the working classes are not anxious to serve their country; it is not true that the working classes, greatly as they sacrifice themselves now for the profiteers, are not prepared to sacrifice themselves even more for the sake of the nation, incredible and impossible though this may seem. But it is a fact that the workmen resent, and very properly resent, the treatment which, apparently, is to be meted out to themselves and to their dependents when they have offered everything they possess for their country. The soldier's pay will amount to half a sovereign per week. If he be married his wife will have about seven shillings a week during his absence, with the absurdly small allowance of twopence per child per diem. . . . We wish, as we have said before, that we could see the same spirit of self-sacrifice among the people of the middle class and the upper class. (17 Sept. 1914, 466)

The *New Age* from the beginning argued strongly for decent pay for soldiers and against conscription. Orage vehemently denied the charge that he was fomenting class warfare in his columns, asserting that the "wage system" by its nature was responsible for division between classes. Press censorship was in effect in England during the war; surprisingly, however, it was never used against the *New Age,* perhaps because the censorship dealt primarily with the way in which battles were reported.

As a part of his opposition to the conscription of soldiers, Orage began a campaign for what he called "the conscription of capital" in order to pay for the war. In "Notes of the Week" of 2 December 1915, he wrote: "The conscription of men for the war has proved impossible, as we said it would, in the absence of the concurrent conscription of capital which our wealthy classes were unwilling to allow" (99). But pressures on the government to supply soldiers for the war were great. As the inevitability of conscription loomed nearer, Orage became more strident:

> This, we say, is an accurate account of the situation as it stands in our democracy at this moment: a people of a trustworthiness unparalleled in history, and a governing class of unequalled incompetence and corruption. And this is the moment chosen for making a demand upon us for the abandonment of our last birthright of liberty. . . . Another circumstance that adds to the vileness of the present proposal to conscript men is the absence of the correlative, and, we should have thought, the precedent conscription of capital. (6 Jan. 1916, 218)

The conscription bill passed shortly thereafter, over the opposition of the Labour Party.

IV

Pound's own view about the war, and about the poet's position in society, underwent a transformation during his decade of association with the *New Age.* Surette has noted that Pound's initial response to the First World War was very conventional: "He repeatedly took his countrymen to task for their tardiness in joining it. He even attempted to enlist."[23] In his "American Chaos I" Pound wrote: "It is deep chagrin to me that my country is not at this moment England's ally in war." But he then went on to qualify his opinion:

> And on the whole, *mes amis,* what do you expect of us? You have not said you wanted us to fight. You cannot expect our Socialists to be enthusiastic over a conscription urged *not by military authority,* but by Brunner, Mond and Co. [British alkali firm] and their like. . . . You cannot expect us to be interested in Earl So-and-so's interest or Lord So-and-so's shares. . . . And, thanks to the hatred of realist letters in

[23] Surette, "Ezra Pound and British Radicalism," 441.

both countries, nearly all that is finest in either is hopelessly obscured from the other. (9 Sept. 1915, 449)

Although this passage shows the influence of Orage, it also contains an early version of what would later be a fairly common theme in Pound's work: that a nation's literature was its foreign office and that better understanding of literature could prevent war. In a similar vein, Pound urges America's entry into the war in his article "This Super-Neutrality," at one point "writing as a citizen of a country which has quite possibly disgraced itself" and at another stating "people like myself. . . believe that America's place is with the Allies" (21 Oct. 1915, 595). He criticizes Wilson ("a man incapable of receiving thought") and then goes on to a more sinister comment, which will be echoed in an anti-Semitic vein almost thirty years later: He is "firmly convinced that the slaughter of one or two dozen carefully selected inhabitants of this city would be of advantage to the race at large."[24]

Pound's attempt to join up was met by the *New Age* with its usual spirit of fun. In "Observations and Reflections," "A. B. C." remarks:

> An American poet, not unknown unfavourably [!] to *New Age* readers, remarked that he would volunteer for the war if he might join a company of intellectuals. He was told by one person that he asked too much even of war; and by another that he should argue the war with a German poet and so rid each country of the same nuisance. (13 Aug. 1914, 354)

That was written shortly after the war began, but soon the paper's tone would change. The *New Age* sense of humor was another casualty of the war.

In his series of the time, "Affirmations," Pound attempted to define his position as an artist in the midst of turmoil. Although he had sought to enlist, he was opposed to war. He wrote in "Affirmations II": "The political world is confronted with a great war, a species of insanity" (14 Jan. 1915, 277). His general opposition to war remained the same more than two years later; in "Provincialism the Enemy II" he wrote again: "Nothing 'matters' till some fool starts resorting to force. To prevent that initial insanity is the goal, and always has been, of intelligent political effort" (19 July 1917, 268).

Continuing his series "Affirmations," he sketched his position in a way that maintained the superiority of the artist's calling over the political realm but that included some hints of ambivalence that may indicate the

---

[24] After the start of the Second World War, this suggestion of violence would be specifically directed at Jews: "Of course if some man had a stroke of genius and could start pogrom UP AT THE top, there might be something to say for it" (no. 32, 30 Apr. 1942, 115). "Don't go for the little Jews, go for the big Jews" (no. 94, 1 June 1943, 329). See Pound, *Ezra Pound Speaking.*

beginning of political interest. Using language that he would reprint in
Gaudier-Brzeska: A Memoir, he observed:

> Neither America nor England cares enough to elevate great men to
> control. . . . It is the artist's job to express what is "true for himself."
> In such measure as he does this, he is a good artist, and, in such measure
> as he himself exists, a great one. (21 Jan. 1915, 312)

Continuing in "Affirmations VI. Analysis of This Decade" Pound wrote:
"I do not wish to become entoiled in the political phases save in so far
as they are inextricably bound in with literature. . . . For when words
cease to cling close to things, kingdoms fall, empires wane and diminish"
(11 Feb. 1915, 410). He would expand on these thoughts in the late
twenties and early thirties, in "How to Read" and *ABC of Reading,* when
he again began to consider seriously the role of the artist in politics.

Without choosing to become "entoiled," the artist can be affected
nonetheless. Pound anticipates the worst at the close of "Affirmations V":

> And if the accursed Germans succeed in damaging Gaudier-Brzeska
> they will have done more harm to art than they have by the destruction
> of Rheims Cathedral, for a building once made and recorded can, with
> some care, be remade, but the uncreated forms of a man of genius
> cannot be set forth by another. (4 Feb. 1915, 382)

His words proved prophetic. The death of his friend Henri Gaudier-
Brzeska on 5 June 1915 moved Pound greatly. He wrote: "His death in
action at Neuville St. Vaast is, to my mind, the gravest individual loss
which the arts have sustained during the war."[25] Pound's book *Gaudier-
Brzeska: A Memoir* bears ample witness to the effect on Pound of the
death of the young sculptor. It contains some of Pound's best prose;
Chapter V is certainly one of his finest prose pieces, and the depth of
his emotion (not just the usual Poundian rage) reveals the extent of his
personal loss: "He was certainly the best company in the world, and
some of my best days, the happiest and most interesting, were spent in
his uncomfortable mud-floored studio when he was doing my bust."[26]

Pound's attitude toward society in 1915 was that of an artist convinced
of the superiority of his calling over those more common in society, and
he was determined to play this role to the fullest. "There are few real
men, the rest are sheep," he quoted from Niccolò Machiavelli in the
epigraph to *Gaudier-Brzeska.* In the same volume, he wrote: "The man
who tries to express his age, instead of expressing himself, is doomed

[25] Pound, "Preface to the Memorial Exhibition, 1918," 136.
[26] *Gaudier-Brzeska,* 47.

to destruction."[27] But the age had intervened and killed Gaudier-Brzeska, Pound's best hope for a new artistic era. The combination of his friend's death and Orage's persistent efforts to understand why certain groups benefited from the war while other groups suffered disproportionately acted gradually to change Pound's idea of the duty of an artist to society.

V

Pound's shift from aloofness to social engagement is discernible in his poetry. In his two most important poetic works of this period, we can see the gradual erosion of Pound's confidence that the artist should ignore or disdain society and its problems and that the individual artist would triumph despite society's impositions. From "Homage to Sextus Propertius" (1917) to "Hugh Selwyn Mauberley" (1920) his treatment of the same subject undergoes a transformation that reflects Pound's own changing ideas about the role of the artist.

In "Homage to Sextus Propertius" Pound adopts a persona whose calm detachment and quiet irony indicate his certainty that the poet's own artistic vocation will prevail over the exigencies of empire. Its pages contain an awareness of the demands of the state, but they reject those demands:

> Annalists will continue to record Roman reputations,
> Celebrities from the Trans-Caucasus will belaud
>   Roman celebrities
> And expound the distensions of Empire,
> But for something to read in normal circumstances?
> For a few pages brought down from the forked hill
>   unsullied? (*P*, 207)

Propertius feigns acquiescence to the poetic industry sponsored by Maecenas for the imperial Roman court but insists on following a different path from that of Virgil and Horace:

> The primitive ages sang Venus,
>   the last sings of a tumult,
> And I also will sing war when this matter of a girl is
>   exhausted. (*P*, 216)

When this matter of a girl is exhausted? This will not be very soon, as Propertius immediately indicates:

> If she goes in a gleam of Cos, in a slither of dyed
>   stuff,

[27] Ibid., 102.

> There is a volume in the matter; if her eyelids sink
>   into a new sleep,
> There are new jobs for the author;
> And if she plays with me with her shirt off,
>   We shall construct many Iliads. (*P*, 217)

As late as 1917, Pound is still confident about the artist's ability to remain aloof.

In his poem "Hugh Selwyn Mauberley" the subject is the same, the relation of the artist to society, but the perspective of Pound's persona has shifted in the three years that separate the two works. In "Homage" the demands of the state are in the background: "I should remember Caesar's affairs . . . for a background" (*P*, 218). In "Mauberley" the demands are in the foreground, seriously impinging on artists' success with their work. The personae in "Mauberley," E. P. and Mauberley, are more at the mercy of the society to which they belong and they lack the ironic confidence of Propertius. These two personae, instead of outwitting the empire, succumb to it. The first section of "Mauberley," which concerns E. P., starts with the morbid subtitle "E. P. Ode pour l'Election de Son Sepulchre." The oblivion suffered by this character and the fact that the ode is written in preparation for his death do not bolster our confidence that E. P. has chosen well or rightly his life's course of action. But instead of rising above or ignoring society's demands, as had Propertius, E. P. begins a critique of society in the subsequent sections of the poem, focusing his wrath on literary institutions and, in one of the most powerful anti-war statements in world literature, on the madness of World War I. In a restricted way, because it is an emotional reaction and not an attempt at critical analysis, this Poundian persona has started to engage with the problems of the society in which he lives.

The second persona of the poem also fares badly. The picture of the perfect aesthete, Mauberley's epigraph is "mouth biting empty air."[28] His life and vocation are perfectly described in the section entitled "The Age Demanded":

> Thus, if her colour
> Came against his gaze,
> Tempered as if
> It were through a perfect glaze
>
> He made no immediate application
> Of this to relation of the state

---

[28] The phrase is from Ovid, "vacuos exercet in aera morsus." Espey points out that the reading most frequently given, however, is "vanos exercet in aera motus" ("leaps at empty air") but allows that the image of the mouth snapping is more effective (104).

> To the individual, the month was more temperate
> Because this beauty had been. (*P, 201*)

Pound clearly has sympathy for Mauberley; his vocation as an artist is pure and he will not compromise it. But it is also clear that he rejects Mauberley and the role of the artist that Mauberley represents. Mauberley dies before the end of the poem. He expressed himself, not his age, and is doomed. "Hugh Selwyn Mauberley" was Pound's farewell to the self-sufficient, self-justifying poet whom Pound was superseding in his own life. It is an affectionate farewell, to be sure, but a farewell nonetheless.

Pound's drift toward political interest and involvement was also echoed in some of his prose pieces for the *New Age*. In "Provincialism the Enemy II" Pound shows the influence of Belloc's *The Servile State* in the following attempt to articulate his political position:

> I think the work of the subtlest thinkers for the last thirty years has been a tentative exploration for means to prevent slavery to a "State" or a "democracy," or some such corporation. . . . Undoubtedly we must have something at least as good as socialism. . . . The arts, explorative, "creative," the "real arts," literature, are always too far ahead of any general consciousness to be of the slightest contemporary use. (19 July 1917, 268)

This statement is clearly a turn to the political, if only to establish the place of the arts outside the political realm. In "Provincialism the Enemy IV" he wrote: "Fundamentally, I do not care 'politically,' I care for civilisation, and I do not care who collects the taxes, or who polices the thoroughfares" (2 Aug. 1917, 308). A year later, in "What America Has to Live Down," he offered some further political considerations:

> AT PRESENT the intellectual sees himself threatened by bolshevism on one side and the Y.M.C.A. on the other. . . . He does not want labouring men and their families mowed down by the machine-guns of militia subsidised by the capitalist. He does not want labour to bulldoze civilization. . . . He does not want his papers suppressed. He does not want a censorship of literature and the arts placed in the hands of the ignorant and of fanatics. We must devise new forms of moderation. . . . All violence is in the end futile. It is of use only against other violence. Violence defeats its own purpose, and, in the end, perishes under the counter-violence it has aroused. (12 Sept. 1918, 314)

Pound's essentially libertarian beliefs show through clearly here. He wishes to be left alone to do his work, but he cannot ignore the turmoil around him.

Pound's move from aloofness to commitment paralleled his country's political movement from isolationism to involvement. With the entry of the United States in the First World War, America and Woodrow

Wilson began to receive a great deal of attention in the pages of the *New Age*. There was a growing curiosity about the new political figure, and about the newly allied nation. Pound, the resident alien journalist, was in a position to benefit from this new attention to his native land. Two years later, in his "Revolt of Intelligence II" he gave, for the first time, an extended political commentary on the United States:

> Few men having been once elected U.S. President have shown them-selves so incompetent or so nonchalant as not to be re-elected. . . .
> America likes enthusiasm for its own sake, and loathes all forms of discrimination, literary or political. . . . the elector in that fateful year was too busy fleeing from the adipose tissue of Taft and the stark terror of "Teddy." (11 Dec. 1919, 90)

The article went on to explain "Senator Lodge's 'torpedoing' of the Treaty." In the same series ("Revolt of Intelligence VII") Pound noted:

> At no time in its history has *The New Age* been so hard up or short handed as to ask me to take charge of its economic discussion; and I have no intention of trespassing on the domains of technical economics in this article. I am searching, as usual, for a quality of intelligence, or, if you like, for a quality of stupidity; I happen to find it in what is alleged to be an article on economics. (22 Jan. 1920, 186)

This statement offers clear evidence of his shift in interest to economics. Further evidence is found in his next article of the series ("Revolt of Intelligence VIII"), in which he wrote of "the triumph of Major Douglas' profound attack on usury" (4 Mar. 1920). A year later, Pound renounced his previously held view of the artist's separation from society in his review of C. H. Douglas's *Credit Power and Democracy:*

> The symbolist position, artistic aloofness from world affairs, is no good now. . . . "*Pour la Patrie, comme tu veux, mais pour une société anonyme de Petrole: mourir! Pourquoi?*" In a world politically governed by imbeciles and knaves, there remain two classes of people *responsible:* the financial powers and the men who can think with some clarity.
>
> (Don't imagine that I think economics interesting – not as a Botticelli or Picasso is interesting. But at present they, as the reality under political camouflage, are interesting as a gun muzzle aimed at one's own head is interesting; when one can hardly see the face of the gun holder and is wholly uncertain as to his temperament and intentions.)[29]

Through Orage, the devastating effect of the war, and the influence of the *New Age* milieu, Pound had undergone conversion.

---

[29] In *Contact* 4 (Summer 1921): 1.

VI

Since so much of what we will encounter in Pound's political
and economic writings of the thirties and forties has its base in Orage,
it is useful to continue tracing Orage's growing awareness of the power
of finance and his other characteristic concerns as the war progressed, as
he became acquainted with C. H. Douglas, and as the aftermath of the
war brought further shocks. Orage never lost his patriotism, but his
fundamental loyalty to the British working class and his increasing sense
of outrage at its victimization throughout the war by government, finance, and industry caused Orage to look very deeply into the economic
consequences and causes of modern war and to pass on his conclusions
in print to his readers and in conversation to Pound and his other
colleagues.

As we have observed, Orage was sensitive from the outset to the charge
that in time of war, his journalism for the *New Age* was open incitement
to class warfare. In "Notes of the Week" for 19 November 1914, he
wrote:

> Another charge is that, in a time when the nation both ought to be and
> is united, we persist in our endeavour to set class against class. If this
> was true either in its assumption or its conclusion, we would cheerfully
> submit to be shot as traitors. Perish ourselves and perish *The New Age*
> rather than England upon whom the hopes of civilisation rest should
> be imperilled by our misdemeanours! But again we have to say that
> not only is the charge unjust, but nobody in possession of his five senses
> can believe it. It is certainly not we who have either created or even
> discovered the fact that, while the wage system is in existence, every
> nation under it is divided class against class. (57)

Orage was never shot as a traitor, never indicted for treason, nor was
his paper ever shut down. Yet he persisted, throughout the war and its
aftermath, in leveling telling criticisms and charges at the political, financial, and industrial leadership of Great Britain. Pound must have
absorbed this lesson on how to practice political and economic criticism
in the midst of a war from Orage, as well as the lesson that the war was
not an isolated event but part of a system that led inevitably to wars and
the victimization of workers.

The pages of the *New Age* provided space for consideration of the
most recent socialist theories. For example, J. A. Hobson's influential
thesis, that the imperialistic system led inevitably to war, was known
and discussed in the pages of the *New Age*. One of its regular columnists,
Joseph Finn, in "Capitalism and the World Market" (6 Mar. 1913),
cogently explained that a capitalist country could never be a market for
all of the goods it manufactured, because the working class could only

buy about a third of what a country produced, and that a cycle of worsening depressions and class conflict would be the inevitable result:

> When the market gets clogged up, then we have unemployment, commercial crises, panic, and hard times generally. When, after much suffering by the poor, the world market has digested the accumulated surpluses, a new commercial and industrial activity sets in, and lasts till the world market becomes again clogged up. (424)

A week later in a further article, "The Death of Old Capitalism," Finn showed how the cycles would become ever more severe, causing the ultimate collapse of capitalism:

> The class war . . . will reach the acutest stage. The workers will then make their last and greatest effort to gain political power, and to right matters by constitutional means. The propertied classes, in their fury and blindness, will then throw off the mask of constitutionalism. . . . organised force will be on the side of the propertied classes. . . . universal war is bound to break out. (448)

Such a view was representative of the socialist heritage that Orage gradually, during the decade, transmitted to Pound.

At first, the war seemed like an opportunity to educate the British public about the rapacity of the commercial and financial classes. In "Notes of the Week" for 28 January 1915, Orage wrote hopefully: "the nation is now in the same position, relatively to our profiteers, that Socialists like ourselves always are. *Now* the world in general may know what we in particular have had to suffer and what undoubtedly we shall have to suffer long after the war is over" (331). But in answer to the question What can we do? Orage advocated only higher taxation: "The legal instrument of taxation, in fact, is there ready to our hand, and should be employed to extract from the profiteers every penny of illegitimate profit they have made out of the war" (331). Orage (and Pound) preferred a peaceful and legal solution to the problem, not a revolutionary one.

Orage throughout the war acted as an impassioned defender of the interests of the working class. He accused the trade unions signatory to the agreements with the government (the Shells and Fuses Agreement and the Treasury Agreement) of having given away more than necessary to Lloyd George (the minister of Munitions). He blamed the unions for agreeing "to the suspension of Trade Union rights during the war for the vague and empty promise to restore them when the war is over" ("Notes of the Week," 1 July 1915, 193). Orage leveled this criticism along with his customary charge that industry was engaging in rampant profiteering: "It will be observed that while the abolition of profiteering is partial, the corresponding concession of the Unions to forgo the right to strike is total" (194). In fact, the Munitions of War Act passed in July of 1915 gave the government wide powers over labor. By declaring factory essential to the war effort, the government gained the power to control wages and bind the workers to their places of employment. Profits were also partially controlled, limited to 20 percent above the average of the two years preceding the war.[30]

Another intrusion into the life of the working man came with the introduction of compulsory military service in Great Britain. Paul Fussell gives a vivid sense of the British army's growing need for soldiers by remarking that the height requirement for volunteers went from five feet eight inches at the beginning of the war to five feet five inches in October of 1914 to five feet three inches a month later.[31] At first the government, with the support of the unions, held firm to the idea of an all-volunteer army. During the first half of 1915, 20,000 men volunteered each week, though it was estimated that 30,000 per week were needed.[32] The problem was that the war had evolved into a battle of attrition in the trenches. Fussell writes, illuminating a famous line of Pound's ("Wastage as never before"): "And in these holes and ditches extending for ninety miles, continually, even in the quietest times, some 7000 British men and officers were killed and wounded daily, just as a matter of course. 'Wastage,' the Staff called it."[33] The shortfall meant the inevitability of conscription, which came about with the Military Service Act of January 1916. For Orage, who had repeatedly argued that a corresponding conscription of capital was the only way to level the burdens of the war, that law came as a bitter event.

Recurring statements of outrage at the inequality of the sacrifices being demanded by the war were frequent in the pages of the *New Age*. Orage, in his "Notes of the Week" of 9 November 1916, observed of both England and Germany: "The outstanding economic fact in both countries is the contrast between the sacrifices of the people engaged in war and war-work and the luxurious living and rapid enrichment of the class that owns the means of production" (25). In many of the belligerent nations there was widespread criticism of the profiteering engaged in by industry, but attempts by governments to curtail excess profits were ineffectual. Legal measures were passed to expand the powers of the state to control industry, but they were sparingly applied. In Great Britain, as Hardach notes, "the word, 'control' meant in practice nothing more than governmental coordination of private business activities and the limitation

---

[30] Hardach, 83.
[31] Fussell, 9.
[32] Hardach, 189–90.
[33] Fussell, 41.

of private profits, or at all events an attempt in that direction."[34] In his "Notes of the Week" for 10 May 1917, Orage remarked on the government's excess profits tax:

> The surprising thing, indeed, is not that our employing classes should have made so little complaint, but, next to their impudence in making any at all, that a far greater complaint than theirs should not have been made by the people at large. In a war such as this, when millions are risking and thousands are losing all that is dear to them, the employers first procure and afterwards make a merit of accepting not just their ordinary profit, but an excess, a surplus, something more than usual. And Mr. Bonar Law congratulates them on their patriotism! The opportunities, moreover, for evading the tax, or, at any rate, for mitigating its severity, are numerous, and our employers have not hesitated to use them all. (27)

Pound would absorb Orage's justifiable outrage. The war and the governments were in fact being used for the benefit of business. Industry profited enormously from the war, and industrialists brought into government were, consciously or not, always solicitous of their own interests. As Hardach concludes: "Government decisions depended upon business interests. . . . [The] findings point, not so much to the harnessing of big business to the machine of state, as to the reverse."[35]

VII

Orage, editor of a small, independent journal, was well aware of the power of the press. His view is summed up in his "Notes of the Week" for 9 March 1916, shortly after a time during which his proposal for the conscription of capital had seemed to gain some ground:

> The power of daily journalism is enormous. By its means (consisting largely of repetition), not only are lies and half-truths concerning public affairs put and kept in circulation, but simple and beneficent truths of the utmost value to the nation are, by the easy means of never mentioning them twice, denied any circulation at all. We are all aware of the sudden spasm that seized the Press a few weeks ago to popularise the notion of the Conscription of Capital for the purposes of the war. We are all now aware of the equally sudden silence. . . . The explanation in our own case, however, is rather sinister than naive. The power of the Daily Press is the power of the rich men who own and control it. It follows, therefore, that however beneficent nationally any truth may be, its circulation will be impeded if it threatens at the same time the interests of the privately wealthy. (433)

[34] Hardach, 82.
[35] Ibid., 107.

That Pound assimilated this idea becomes abundantly clear when we consider his writings from the thirties and forties. Hilaire Belloc also enlarged upon this theme in a series he contributed to the *New Age* entitled "The Present Position and Power of the Press." In that series, on 28 December 1916, Belloc wrote: "This Capitalist Press has come at last to warp all judgment. The tiny oligarchy which controls it is irresponsible and feels itself immune. It has come to believe that it can suppress any truth and suggest any falsehood. It governs, and governs abominably" (198). Belloc did not despair entirely, though, since he went on to remark upon the growth of an independent press made up of small-circulation journals, "the free Press" (199), that he saw as having a potentially salutary influence.

Obviously, the British press conveyed at home a picture of the war very different from what was actually experienced in the trenches. Under its publisher Lord Northcliffe, the *Times* emphasized the healthful activity and hearty food of a soldier's life on the front, as well as the soldiers' patriotism, sportsmanship, and general good luck at being there. Northcliffe, who ultimately was put in charge of government propaganda, was a frequent target of the *New Age,* as was the servility of the press in general. In his "Notes of the Week" for 14 December 1916, Orage remarked upon "the guttersnipings of the Northcliffe Press" (146). In "Notes" for 22 November 1917, he gave a more detailed account of Northcliffe's influence:

> The fact remains that our national policy, internal and external, military, economic, political, and diplomatic, is liable at any moment to be deflected from its course, not only (which would be natural) by the turn of events, but still more by the whims and fancies, the assumptions and presumptions, of Lord Northcliffe. We are not exaggerating in the very least when we say that at any moment, with or without plausible reason, Lord Northcliffe can create a "crisis" of no matter what kind. Not a person or a policy or a Government or the nation is safe from him for two weeks running. . . . From the beginning of the war, with scarcely a single exception, no Minister, Government, or policy has been allowed to act without the consent of Lord Northcliffe. . . . Parliament has no longer any sovereign rights. Its power has been usurped by Lord Northcliffe, who alone can determine who shall or shall not be a Minister. . . . What will be done is what Lord Northcliffe wishes to be done. (62–3)

Given the tone of the above, Pound's constant criticism of the English press in the thirties and forties (e.g., in Chapter IX of *Jefferson and/or Mussolini*) seems considerably less surprising. Orage was not alone in his views. Remarking upon the very prompt delivery of newspapers and magazines to the front line[36] and taking into account the chasm that separated a soldier's daily experience of trench warfare and the way it was reported to the public, Fussell concludes that "a lifelong suspicion of the press was one lasting result of the ordinary man's experience of the war."[37] It was certainly one result of that war for Pound.

VIII

Orage's stand on the conscription of both men and capital reflected his other principal concern during and immediately after the First World War: the question of how the war was to be paid for. At the outset, from his frequent discussion of these subjects in "Notes of the Week," we gain the impression that Orage did not understand the nature of money or the role that banking played in financing the war. By early 1915, we see his growing realization of the importance of finance to the war and of the partnership between the banks and the government in keeping the monetary system functioning. In the same way that Pound, through constantly returning to these subjects in the thirties, developed a growing understanding of them, Orage, through his weekly commentary, acquired and deepened his economic knowledge. By the time of his first meeting with C. H. Douglas toward the war's close, he was ready for conversion to the evolving theories of Social Credit (considered in detail in the next chapter). Although Pound was later to go beyond his teacher in his understanding of the nature of currency, Orage's self-education in economic matters during this time, and his conversion, formed the basis for Pound's.

The first casualty of the Great War was the international gold standard. Already in the days preceding the war the international monetary system was in a state of crisis. Prior to the war, English currency had consisted almost entirely of gold and paper that, for all practical purposes, was convertible to gold. In the tense days just before the actual declaration of war, the bank rate in England rose precipitously to 10 percent per annum in one day. The English banks, anticipating a run by depositors, suspended payment for several days and obtained from the Treasury the issue of several hundred million pounds of paper currency in the form of one-pound and ten-shilling Treasury notes, which were made legal tender.[38] Thus the de facto gold basis of currency collapsed in days, though in England the convertibility of currency into gold persisted throughout the war as a legal fiction. A series of regulations, however,

---

[36] Fussell, 66–7.
[37] Ibid., 316.
[38] The war broke out on 4 August 1914; the proclamation regarding currency and bank notes was issued on 6 August.

made it nearly impossible for the public to exchange its paper. Similarly, although gold in theory was still exportable, in practice its export was most difficult, because the Bank of England would not aid transactions between individuals and because the danger and subsequent insurance costs of wartime shipping made international exchange prohibitive.[39]

At the beginning of the war, Orage wrote as one who still believed in the gold basis of money and in the orthodox socialist position that the primary class conflict was between capital and labor. His constant preoccupation was the cost of the war and how it was to be financed. In "Notes of the Week" he laments that "we are carrying on the war on borrowed money. . . . Between three and four millions a day is the amount we are spending on the war; every penny of it is borrowed" (9 Sept. 1915, 441). For a considerable time, Orage was conceptually tied to the notion that only through increased taxes or war loans could the ongoing costs be covered. In fact, there is (and was) a third way to pay for government expenditures, what a contemporary economist would refer to as "monetizing the debt," but since money, to Orage, was tied to gold, he did not at first understand the transaction that actually took place between the Bank of England and the Treasury to enable the government to cover the enormous costs of the war.

Surette has accurately pointed out that both before and after the First World War,

> the popular superstition was that gold was money, and paper currency merely a certificate for gold. Economists all knew that money was merely a conventional substitute for gold, but finance ministers were constrained to act as if the supply of money was an invariable function of the supply of gold.[40]

By the end of the war, Orage and Pound were disabused of this superstition, but it remained a belief in the popular mind until well after the Second World War. The information about the real basis of currency had been available before the war; in fact Arthur Kitson, president of the British Banking and Currency Reform League and an occasional contributor and letter writer to the *New Age,* frequently pointed it out. His league had predicted that the gold standard was overdue for collapse, and when in fact at the outset of the war the banks suspended payment and the Treasury was forced to issue notes, he wrote to the *New Age:*

> The fraud of the gold standard now stands fully exposed. The gold credit system is now superseded by the National Credit system. . . .

[39] Hardach, 140.
[40] Surette, "Ezra Pound and British Radicalism," 447.

Our credit can now stand securely upon the wealth of the nation instead of on the very illusive commodity – gold – which vanished the moment danger is [*sic*] scented. What the people of this country must be out on the look-out for, however, is that the bankers and money-lenders do not deprive them of this invaluable system after the war is concluded. (3 Sept. 1914, 429)

Kitson was prophetic, but few at the time understood what he was saying. He was also anti-Semitic, and his economic articles for the *New Age* occasionally evidenced an English anti-Semitism that was endemic in some circles at the time. In his article "The 20th Century Napoleon," he wrote:

The world's masters of to-day are not found wearing epaulettes, swords, and cocked hats, riding at the head of armies. These men are merely the puppets who move at the command or by the permission of those who control the financial affairs of the world. The world's rulers are men mainly conspicuous by their noses, who occupy quiet offices at the backs of the great banking houses of London, Paris, New York, Berlin, and Vienna. . . . Your modern Napoleon is a moneylender, a credit dealer, a direct descendant of those whom Christ drove from the Temple! The conquest of the world . . . has been achieved by a small group of otherwise insignificant persons who deal in gold and credit. . . . by the imposition of the gold standard – which the Jew moneylenders have fastened upon the world within the past 40 years – trade has completely changed in character, and has degenerated into a merciless struggle for gold. (24 July 1913, 357, 359)

This kind of offensive rubbish could be found from time to time in the *New Age* and, unpleasant as it is, it merits brief discussion here because it too was part of the milieu influencing Pound.

The *New Age* was not an anti-Semitic journal, but Orage did not censor his contributors' material, even when he objected to some of it. A rejoinder to the above was printed the next week in the form of a letter from Joseph Finn, a regular contributor to the journal:

Mr. Kitson's article in *The New Age* deserves not only criticism but also a little bit of admonition. What relationship can there be between political economy and anti-Semitism? Apparently none whatever. Still, Mr. Kitson managed to combine the two in his article. . . . Mr. Kitson, in comparison with some orthodox authorities on finance, is a wise man; he ought, therefore, to know that by holding up the Jew as the universal financial octopus he diverts the attention of the reader from the iniquities of the system, and directs his hatred to the Jew. Moreover, whilst the rich Jew snaps his fingers at anti-Semitism, the poor Jew receives the blows. (31 July 1913, 403)

To make the position of the *New Age* completely clear, an unsigned article (thus, presumably, by Orage himself) appeared three weeks later. Entitled "The Folly of Anti-Semitism," it began:

> From time to time we see ominous indications of an anti-Semite agitation. . . . We repeat that such a movement would be disastrous. Disastrous to whom? And why? It would be a disaster to democracy in its struggle for economic freedom, because it would divert our attacks upon private capitalism into attacks upon a group of individuals, most of whom are not only innocent of usury, but hate it as much as we do ourselves. (14 Aug. 1913, 449)

Twenty years before the beginning of the Holocaust, the occasional anti-Semitism that appeared in the pages of the *New Age* probably was considered relatively harmless and adequately met by this kind of response.

Kitson had a fundamentally sound insight into the nature of currency, the effectiveness of which, like Pound's insight later, was vitiated by his anti-Semitism. He had earlier offered a scheme for repealing the British legal tender laws and adopting an imperial paper money system that would be legal currency throughout the British Empire. Such a plan would have worked, but it would not have been accepted by the vast majority of the population, who equated gold and money. It took the rupture in the system brought about by the war to expose the actual nature of money, and even then achieving such insight was not easy, because the British government took steps to preserve the illusion that the nation continued on the gold standard.

What actually took place was the following. Although England was nominally on the gold standard, at no time was there on hand a sufficient backing of gold to cover bank deposits, nor did there need to be for internal circulation. Only for the settling of balances between nations was gold actually necessary. When the war broke out, a national currency had to be issued to cover depositors' demands, and the regulations governing convertibility had to be changed. Whenever the government needed money to pay for the war, the Treasury arranged with the Bank of England to borrow money on the strength of future taxes. The overdraft granted by the Bank of England enabled the government to meet its debts for munitions and the like, paying for its purchases with money that was literally made out of nothing other than the government's future credit. However, the money paid out also created an increase in demand deposits on the banks by those firms and employees holding government contracts. To allow the banks to meet the demands on those deposits caused by payments by the government, it was necessary for the Treasury to issue more notes, which it did. As already stated, this solution to government indebtedness is called monetizing the debt, and it results in inflation.

IX

Orage gradually began to unravel the tangle. In "Notes of the Week" for 3 February 1916, he commented upon the issuing of Treasury notes at the beginning of the war, calling it a two hundred million pound "loan" to the banks, and then went on to observe that the banks had been making unprecedented profits:

> Look at the Banking Reports published last week. Every great Bank, without a single exception, announced a year of unparalleled prosperity. ... It is against nature, we say, that a nation can become poorer and richer as a nation at the same moment. But it is not against the nature of Capitalism that the nation can become poorer while its moneylenders and profiteers grow richer. (315)

That column represented a conceptual breakthrough for Orage and a change in direction for the *New Age*. On 9 March 1916, a bit more than a month later, he continued with an attack on the banking system:

> For the present, however, not only is the subject taboo in the Press, but, by reason of its association with the word Money, it is largely taboo in general society. ... its secret is, of course, the secret of Plutocracy. ... we have only to ask whether if the City [the English banking industry] were ruined (as we should like to see it), our own nation would carry on the present war, to grasp the fact that not money, but goods and services, are alone necessary to war as to peace. (434)

He adds, in a rush of insight that takes him almost all of the way to C. H. Douglas's soon-to-be-born Social Credit movement:

> But if this agent [money] is in the hands of private financiers who insist upon taking ruinous toll for the national use of it, every service and commodity we produce will cost us, over and above the exertion necessary to its production, a sum, in what is called interest, at least equal to the labour cost. *That* is what capitalism means. ... Nationalise credit, mobilise money, confiscate capital, conscript wealth, and the nation has in its hands not only goods and services, but the means of their exchange. (435)

With his discovery of the role of finance, Orage's previous conception of the class war between owner and worker would be expanded to acquire a new dimension, finance, and a new villain, the banker.

Arthur Kitson gained prominence in the *New Age* as his earlier observations about the nature of currency proved correct. In "Views and

Reviews" for 20 December 1917, "A. E. R." (A. E. Randall, who wrote a great deal for the journal) reviewed Kitson's book *A Fraudulent Standard* using language that, except for its clarity, foreshadowed Pound's:

> We are fighting in this war for political and industrial freedom; but if the gold basis is restored, industry will be the slave of finance. . . . And finance means cosmopolitan finance. . . . The bullion brokers are brothers in usury, and the only way to destroy their power is to withdraw their privileges. These privileges have been established by Acts of Parliament; the remedy therefore is to repeal them. The Bank Charter and the Legal Tender Gold Act must be annulled. We must nationalise the whole of our banks, and substitute Treasury and bank notes for our former gold currency by issuing them against the national wealth. . . . the real enemy to civilization [is] Usury. (155–6)

The review goes on to sound the alarm about the contemplated return to the gold basis, pointing out that the war loan had been subscribed in cheap pounds as the result of inflation (already at 100 percent since 1914), and if there were a return to gold, it would be paid back in the dear pounds of 1914. In fact, such a transition was already in the works, as Arthur Kitson pointed out in a letter of 24 January 1918:

> Do the Labour leaders know that the cosmopolitan financiers are already preparing to bowl over all their little plans by controlling output under the reign of the gold standard which they are determined to set up again as soon as peace is declared?. . . . Already a Currency Commission has been appointed by the Treasury. . . . The intention is to destroy the National Treasury notes which saved the country from panic and ruin at the beginning of the war, and to restore the gold currency, which, with Free Trade, will enable the bankers to regain their strangle-hold on trade and industry. (258)

In fact, the British government was already contemplating a return to gold convertibility at the old par rate and had appointed a Committee on Currency and Foreign Exchange under the leadership of Lord Walter Cunliffe to examine the question.

Randall, who wrote articles on psychology as well as the paper's drama criticism under the pseudonym of John Hope Francis, continued to sound the alarm about a bankers' conspiracy in his weekly "Views and Reviews" column. In that column for 31 January 1918, entitled "The Bankers' International," he concluded: "To that problem Labour must turn its attention unless it is content to let the bankers govern the world" (276). There had recently been a bank amalgamation in Britain, continuing a trend that since 1891 had seen the number of joint-stock banks decrease from 106 to 34 while the number of private banks decreased from 37 to 6. In his "Views and Reviews" column for 23 May 1918, entitled "Cui

Bono?" Randall pointed to the damaging consequences of the amalgamation of the American banks engineered by J. P. Morgan and asked: "The question is not whether a certain bank did or did not give its provincial branches adequate support, but whether the whole banking organisation is to be the servant, or the master, of industry, and through industry, of the whole national life and government" (59).

It was toward the end of the war that Orage began to realize fully the nature and organization of credit and the British credit system, and its effect on the public welfare. He criticized the bank amalgamations and pointed out that the Treasury committee appointed to inquire into them consisted mainly of bankers. "How did the amalgamation come about?" Orage asked in his "Notes of the Week" for 30 May 1918:

> How were they to encourage the process of amalgamation, so profitable to themselves, even to the degree of a monopoly, without awakening public hostility and provoking the demand for the nationalisation of money? Nothing easier when you have a public opinion to consider that is proud of its ignorance of the monetary system. (67)

Whereas previously Orage had proclaimed that economic considerations determined political and historical ones, he now progressed to a further refinement of that view, stated in his "Notes of the Week" for 8 August 1918, that "credit is really the dominant form of economic power" (229). By 1918 he had come to subscribe to a political and economic view that stops little short of an outright conspiracy theory, which includes the collusion of the press. In "Notes of the Week" for 3 October 1918, we see evidence for that:

> The recent Bank amalgamations are now a fait accompli and no wishes of ours can alter it. But that they constitute the most formidable menace to democratic government yet devised we have no doubt whatsoever. It appears, however, that with their transition from discussion to actuality their character, in the opinion of the "Times," has completely changed. Not only are the amalgamations now to be regarded as designed solely in the interests of the public, but the apprehensions of the formation of a "Money Trust," which the "Times" was one of the first journals to express, are, we learn, now entertained only by "those dominated by a sort of Bolshevist creed." The transformation scene, even for the "Times," is a little sudden; and we can only suppose the machinery connecting the Banks with the Press to be unusually efficient. (359)

That these opinions form the basis for many of Pound's later beliefs should be already clear to those familiar with his political and economic writings during the thirties and forties. To those not so familiar, the connections will become clear as we consider those writings in later chapters. Pound had already absorbed some of these ideas, as is evident from his article "Hapsburgiana":

> In England and even more in America, a vast amount of power, un-controlled and subject to no popular influence, resides in banking rings. . . . Obviously the banking rings do not want England to get out of her present financial difficulties so long as they maintain a government which will listen to Prof. Pigou's suggestion that the best remedy is to let the bankers levy a higher tax on loans than is already permitted them. (22 Apr. 1920, 400)

The difference between the views of Orage and Pound and the views of Kitson and C. H. Douglas on the banking rings was that the latter believed that the banks were dominated by Jews, an opinion that Orage rejected and that Pound had not come to yet.

Pound's writing at the time contained almost no anti-Semitism. The only instance that I could find appeared in an article in his "Regional" series entitled simply "Regional XVI":

> There is no greater curse than an idea propagated by violence. The African savage invokes his "Ju" when he wants to bash the next tribe successfully; his god is an assistant of his worst instincts; the Jew, however, received a sort of roving commission from his "Jhv" to bash all and sundry. . . . The chief and almost the sole function of government is to maintain order, to prevent appeals to violence. . . . We note, in support of our proposition *re* the futility of violence, that since the lions of Judah gave up the sword, "beat it" metaphorically into the pawn-shop, their power has steadily increased; no such suave and uninterrupted extension of power is to be attributed to any "world-conquering" bellicose nation. Those of us who live in immaterial things, in art, in literature, "owe more" to Greece and Rome; the rest of the world "owes," or is alleged to owe, to the Jews. (6 Nov. 1919, 16)

The very next week, in response perhaps to criticism from Orage, Pound explained in "Regional XVII": "My last antithesis sprang from no an-tisemitism. I point out simply the practicality of avoiding needless coer-cions, strifes, and combustions. Inasmuch as the Jew has conducted no holy war for nearly two millennia, he is preferable to the Christian and the Mahomedan" (13 Nov. 1919, 32). That Pound possessed a latent anti-Semitism at this time is probable. And for at least some of his acquaintances the words *bankers* and *Jews,* and *international bankers* and *Rothschilds,* were interchangeable.

Orage was critical of the Cunliffe committee's recommendations. In "Notes of the Week" for 7 November 1918, he attacked the composition of the committee: "not only was there no Labour member, but, with the exception of Professor Pigou, its personnel consisted entirely of bankers and the Treasury colleagues" (2). In keeping with his new view about the nature of the credit process, their recommendation for return to gold convertibility came as no surprise: "The report of such a Committee was of necessity a foregone conclusion. The restoration of the gold-basis of currency was naturally recommended, since gold is the bankers' peculiar monopoly guaranteed them by the State for nothing" (3).

C. H. Douglas's first article for the *New Age* appeared on 2 January 1919; he and Orage had been meeting to discuss economics frequently during the previous year. As has already been seen, Orage had come to realize a great deal about the real basis of credit during the course of the war, and so he was ready for the crystallization of his beliefs offered by Douglas. The importance of their meeting and the extent of Douglas's influence are indicated by the fact that Orage, ill, allowed Douglas to write his "Notes of the Week" column for both 6 and 13 February 1919. Orage comments succinctly on the impact of Douglas in his "Readers and Writers" column for 6 November 1919 by "R. H. C.":

> Major Douglas' ideas are by no means subversive of our former economic opinions and theories. On the contrary, they are the fulfillment of them; and they are destined, so I believe, to transform from theory into reality the splendid conception of National Guilds with which *The New Age* will always be inseparably associated. (12)

As a matter of fact, Orage had already moved far beyond many of the schemes, if not the aspirations, of the Guild Socialism movement, and the *New Age* would become increasingly associated with the nascent Social Credit movement in the next few years. Pound was quick to follow this new direction.

X

Although the victorious conclusion of the war must have cheered Orage, the postwar period abounded with examples of the stupidity of the government and the continued victimization of the working class. As early as 14 November 1918, in his "Notes of the Week," Orage wrote of the coming Versailles peace conference: "The next world-war, if unhappily there should be another, will in all probability be contained within the clauses and conditions attaching to the present peace settlement" (19). The *New Age* pointed out several times in 1919 the unrealistic nature of the indemnities demanded of Germany, as well as the prospects for large-scale unemployment in Great Britain. The consequences of the method found to finance war costs became clear as inflation rose and the high cost of living became a frequent topic. To show the helplessness of orthodox economists in dealing with these problems, Pound recounts a conversation he and Douglas had with John Maynard Keynes:

> And C.H. said to the renowned Mr. Bukos:
> "What is the cause of the H.C.L.?" and Mr. Bukos,
> The economist consulted of nations, said:
> > "Lack of labour."
> And there were two millions of men out of work.
> And C.H. shut up, he said
> He would save his breath to cool his own porridge,
> But I didn't, and I went on plaguing Mr. Bukos
> Who said finally: "I am an orthodox
> Economist." (*C*, XXII, 101–2)

By the end of the war, then, Orage had come fully to believe that the manipulation of the currency system by the banks and the government was the real cause of the economic hardships faced by British workers. In his "Notes of the Week" for 18 September 1919, he built on some remarks by Ernest Bevin that he found congenial:

> "Not an industry existed," said Mr. Bevin, "in which production was not regulated to the last degree by the banking system"; and not an industry exists, we may point the inevitable conclusion, that is not "controlled" and "governed" by the financial oligarchy. Such power as this, situated, as it is, at the very apex of the pyramid of power, is clearly inconsistent with the "democratic control" of industry. (339)

Yet in the same column Orage rejected Bevin's recommendation of the nationalization of finance, since he had no more confidence in British Treasury officials than in bankers. In a remark that anticipated Pound's later complaint about public ignorance of the nature of money, Orage stated in "Notes of the Week" for 25 September 1919: "The capitalist conspiracy to ignore the problem of currency or to treat it as if it were only a remote, over-intricate, or academic problem . . . cannot, however, be much longer carried on in complete silence" (355). That Pound was absorbing these lessons can be seen in his "Revolt of Intelligence. IX." where he wrote:

> A quarter of an hour's talk with a Continental and international financier is almost enough to turn a thoughtful man into a Bolshevik. . . . The modern banker is a less pleasing spectacle than the fat Medici pontiff; he is as debonairly and as naively anxious to tax the hoaxable "many" by wangles of exchanges, by floatings, and re-collectings of paper money, by juggling of credits, as was ever a wide-hatted cardinal. . . . He occasionally runs art as a side line; but he does not even pay lip-service to literature. (11 Mar. 1920, 301)

Pound's attempt to explain the problem of currency to a wider audience, and to enlarge upon these ideas, would take a great deal of his energy during the thirties and the forties.

By 1920, Orage believed that the difficulty of attracting public attention to the currency question was a result of conscious conspiracy. In his "Notes of the Week" for 15 July he wrote: "We should be the first to admit that the subject of Money is difficult to understand. It is *intended* to be, by the minute oligarchy that governs the world by means of it" (162). Pound again was picking up Orage's view and expounding it as his own when, in the "Revolt of Intelligence. X." he wrote:

> With a few more endowed Chairs of Economics, we shall soon have the subject made much too complicated for the man in the street to grasp, which is exactly what every gang of exploiters, religious, despotic, economic, have always tried to do with their particular monopoly. Truly, the real history of our time would be very interesting, though probably unhealthy for its aspiring author.... If, as some of my colleagues have said, real control is financial control, one of the phenomena of our time is the very retiring nature of our controllers. ... There is a curious heat in the manner wherewith some men deny the very existence of a financial lining to present politics. (18 Mar. 1920, 319)

Pound in that column is starting to sound very much like Orage in his "Notes of the Week," both occasional and political. The reference to the "aspiring author" of the "real history of our times" gives credence to the view that his conversion to the economic views of Douglas (and, as I think is clear, Orage) and the real beginning of the *Cantos* are linked. About to write his epic, a poem containing history, he was in the process of discovering a method to explain history.

Pound also agreed with Orage as to the necessity of explaining the whole question of finance to the public. In his article "Masaryk" he wrote:

> The national heritage of England is the dogged belief that power resides in the people.... The hope of England economically is that what has long since become an instinctive attitude towards "political" rights must ultimately become operative toward economic rights as soon as these are understood, as soon as they are seen and felt as having a bearing upon, or being of one nature with "political" rights. The right to credit-control is implicit in English custom, in the English attitude toward life. (1 Apr. 1920, 320)

The currency question, despite its difficulty, had important consequences. Inflation was rampant in the postwar period and caused great hardship; the cost of food had risen almost 140 percent between 1914 and 1920. The inflation was a direct result of one method of paying for the war, the issuing of Treasury notes on the strength of future tax revenue. The government called for increased productivity on the part of labor as a means of meeting inflation. For Orage, this was just another demand that the working class shoulder unfairly the burden of the war. The Cunliffe committee recommendation for return to the gold standard was another indication of how the moneyed classes would benefit from the hardship of the people. In his "Notes of the Week" for 22 July 1920, Orage succinctly indicates how his beliefs had changed since the war:

> The line of conflict to-day, the real trench warfare, is no longer between Capital and Labour; it is between Finance, on the one side, and Capital and Labour, more or less in the same army, on the other side. It is a hard saying, no doubt, but the world has not stood still since Marx wrote; and, in effect, his doctrines are as dead as himself. (179)

Pound would come to share this view, and encountered it first in Orage. Pound's views had also changed. In "Regional XVII" he wrote:

> We are always being told, as Gaudier by the old French captain in 1914, "*La Patrie n'est pas en danger.*" Even De Gourmont leaned towards the symbolistic error of detachment; the man of letters need not, perhaps, go "down into the forum" – i.e., the House of Commons – or take up a detailed answer to all the editorials in the Press, but he must have some concern for public affairs, recognising the impossibility of his works having any immediate effect, but trying to conserve at least a free corner, a "lighted spot," a "sound core," somewhere in the gehenna. (13 Nov. 1919, 32)

Almost two years before, Pound had apologized in "Studies in Contemporary Mentality XVIII" for writing on political topics: "These are the thoughts of an amateur in these matters, of one who has turned from the, to him, far more serious matter, that of making poetry" (3 Jan. 1918, 193). Now he was convinced, as he wrote in "Regional XVIII," that "universal peace will never be maintained unless it be by a conspiracy of intelligent men" (20 Nov. 1919, 48). Mauberley was dead.

Orage emerged from the war and the inflationary aftermath with a profound sense that a swindle had been perpetrated on the British public. Although the potential for the Social Credit movement to induce needed changes would engage his hopes and attention for several more years, he was disillusioned over his lack of effect and left England in the fall of 1922 to study with Gurdjieff.[41] Pound himself had clearly changed also. His move to Paris was undoubtedly motivated by a need to get on with

---

[41] Martin, 289. Philip Mairet described this as "complete submission to a will not his own," perhaps foreshadowing Pound's later turn to a charismatic leader (94).

his work; it may have also been motivated by a desire to escape political commitment, to retreat to the aesthete's noninvolvement. Certainly there were monetary considerations. The *New Age* was again experiencing financial hardships and on 19 August 1920 was cut from sixteen to twelve pages an issue, which may have meant a cut in income for Pound. Since Pound was having difficulty getting published anywhere else, and since the exchange rate made living inexpensive in Paris, Pound's move is understandable.

After considering Pound's long exposure to Orage's social thought, the surprise is not that Pound turned to politics and economics but that it took him so long to do so. Because so many of Pound's opinions in the thirties and forties were anticipated by opinions in the *New Age,* it is fair to say that Orage's thinking on these matters formed the base for Pound's and that frequently, when he later wrote about these subjects, Pound was remembering conversations with Orage. This influence holds not only for the fundamentally socialist thrust of the *New Age* and Orage's views on banking, currency, and the press but also for many particular judgments – for example, those on the League of Nations and Winston Churchill, as we shall see. Beyond these convergences of theme, attitude, and subject, there were influences of form. In the roles he assumed in the thirties and forties, roles of political commentator, editor, and later broadcaster, Pound consciously or unconsciously imitated Orage (Orage died shortly after giving a radio broadcast on economics, a broadcast that Pound heard). Pound even adopted some of Orage's journalistic methods. A regular feature of the *New Age* was the column entitled "Press Clippings," which displayed quotations from other newspapers and journals that confirmed Orage's viewpoints. For years Pound kept a similar scrapbook, and he occasionally tried to interest the Italian government in a periodical that he proposed to edit consisting of quotations from the foreign press. Even Orage's reputation as the most persuasive talker of his time was later to pass to Pound.

Orage taught Pound that economic power preceded political power, that political reform was useless without economic reform. He awakened in Pound a sense of outrage at collusion between bankers and government officials, aided by the press, to favor private over national interests. For some pages of the *New Age* and from the London milieu, Pound absorbed the Edwardian and Georgian anti-Semitism that claimed to link usury with the Jews. Although because of their difference in background Pound lacked his teacher's profound affinity for the working class, he would later advocate such programs as public works, national dividends, and full employment through shortened work days, all of which were meant to benefit ordinary workers. Without question, Pound's turn to the political started and was decisively influenced at the office of the *New Age.*

Recently more attention has been given to the profound impact of Orage on Pound's thinking, and more needs to be done.[42] I would go so far as to suggest that during his decade-long association with Orage and the *New Age,* Pound received, even while resisting it and trying to insist on the purity of his vocation of poet, a complete political and economic education, including doctrine, rhetoric, and attitudes, that will show up, time and again, in his political and economic writings and in his poetry throughout the thirties and forties. This is not to say that Pound himself did not achieve his own original insights and syntheses. He did, in particular with his discovery of the economist Silvio Gesell and in his devotion to *il Duce.* But to a surprising degree, the themes and even methods of Pound's own later political and economic journalism and correspondence represent imperfect recollections of the *New Age* under Orage.

[42] I refer to Leon Surette's article, already cited, and to Coyle's " 'A Profounder Didacticism': Ruskin, Orage and Pound's Reception of Social Credit," Flory's *The American Ezra Pound* also notes the importance of Orage (43–52).

2

C. H. Douglas and Social Credit

I

In the autobiographical preface to the New Directions edition of his *Selected Poems,* Pound wrote in 1949: "1918 began investigation of causes of war, to oppose same."[1] His "investigation" was sparked by his meeting with Major C. H. Douglas that year in the office of Orage's *New Age.*[2] Douglas was beginning to formulate the economic theories that eventually would form the basis for a political movement known as Social Credit, but at that time his ideas were inchoate and his prose worse. Orage helped Douglas with his writing style, and the *New Age* began to serialize Douglas's first two books, *Economic Democracy* and *Credit Power and Democracy.* Both appeared in book form in 1920. Pound and Orage were thus present at the birth and during the early development of an influential political and economic movement of the twenties and thirties. Although it never gained power in England, the Social Credit movement had electoral successes in both New Zealand and the Canadian province of Alberta during the thirties.

Because Pound's first interest in economics coincided with Orage's (and therefore Pound's) conversion to the doctrines of C. H. Douglas, it is appropriate that we consider Douglas's thought next. Although Douglas's Social Credit movement fits into the broader context of the failure of liberalism and liberal economics in the last quarter of the nineteenth century, it was most immediately influenced by the changes in the British economy wrought by the First World War. Because Douglas came upon his "discovery" during the war, and because Pound, too, was driven to the study of economics by the First World War, a brief consideration of the British wartime economy gives important background.

[1] Pound, *Selected Poems,* viii.
[2] Stock, 221.

As we saw in the last chapter, the Great War required a total national commitment to the war effort that was previously unknown. To achieve victory, the British government was forced to intervene in every aspect of the national economy. This was particularly true in the areas of prices and production, which fell largely under government control by 1915. Although it succeeded in mobilizing wartime industrial capacity and, to some degree, in preventing profiteering, the government was less successful in financing the war. Along with Orage, many felt that the method used to raise capital was "dishonest or unduly favorable to certain classes" and that there were advantageous insider deals for "fortunately placed institutions and individuals."[3] A climate of opinion suspicious of banking and finance gradually predominated.

The success of the British government in managing the wartime economy contrasted markedly with the disastrous period of depression after the 1918 victory. Many argued

> that government measures had actually *caused* the postwar slumps.... Not only the man in the street but the professional economist accused the government of bringing about disaster by a policy of extreme deflation. At a time when the economy needed a careful helping hand to guide the transition from war to peace the authorities acted with unjustifiable rigor.[4]

Having just seen what could be achieved by strong government intervention in the economy and with centralized planning, people thought the same should continue in peacetime.

Two other factors would contribute to the increasing popularity of Social Credit doctrines during this period after the war. The first was the widespread recognition that the means and possibilities for production had altered radically and that an age of plenty, powered by electricity and mass production, had arrived. Simultaneously, though, it seemed that the working class would not share in the benefits of this new age of plenty and that instead what was transpiring was increasing poverty in the midst of plenty.[5]

The second factor was a growing awareness of the arbitrary nature of money. The British government's action in removing the pound from the gold standard during the war and then restoring the gold standard after the war's conclusion certainly added to this realization. If money could suddenly and successfully be freed from its tie to gold, then that tie was not as necessary as most people had believed. People were no longer sure that they understood just what constituted money.

[3] Finlay, 9. As the ensuing discussion demonstrates, I have relied a great deal on this work.
[4] Ibid., 13–14.
[5] Ibid., 11.

Actually, suspicion of the banks and the critique of the economy offered by Douglas and Social Credit had a number of precedents in the nineteenth century. The Bank Act of 1844 had restricted the loan-making ability of local banks by limiting to one central bank the power to issue notes. This started a gradual trend toward concentration of power in the British banking industry. There were 273 British banks in 1890, 157 in 1903, and only 40 in 1918.[6]

Part of the criticism directed at financial institutions was an attack on the gold standard, prominent in the U.S. presidential election of 1892, but a recurring theme in the economic writings of the latter part of the nineteenth century. Some suggested that the mints be opened to any substance, "tin, iron, anything," and blamed a system where it was possible to profit from currency manipulation. As we have seen, a reformer later favored by Pound, Arthur Kitson, was active in this cause. Kitson, who was born in 1862 in London, had an active career as an engineer and an inventor and was a colleague of Edison and Bell. He was a lifelong opponent of the gold standard and of the banking system and served as president of the British Banking and Currency Reform League. He believed that the possibilities for plenty inherent in the industrial age were being thwarted by the monetary system and its manipulation by financiers, a view that he disseminated in the pages of the New Age.[7]

Patrick Geddes and Victor Branford were two other forerunners of the Social Credit movement. They believed that bankers were making use of public credit for private profit and demanded that this misfeasance be acknowledged and regulated. Maintaining that the ultimate source of credit was in the community, they thought that credit should be used for socially beneficial investments without the need for paying interest. Reacting to the manipulation of currency during the First World War, Geddes and Branford attacked "the gold bugs and the fact that in the war manpower but not moneypower had been conscripted.... If the credit system was so well adapted to finance the war," they asked, "may it not now be adapted to the eutopian finance of militant peace?"[8] Although it is not clear that Pound knew directly of their work, their thinking forms a background to the emergence of the Social Credit movement in the period following the war. He was certainly aware of some of these ideas from Orage and the New Age.

A further awareness of the arbitrary nature of credit was one result of these debates. A distinction was beginning to be made between real and nominal capital, real and financial credit. Orage was one who saw this

[6] Ibid., 18–19.
[7] Ibid., 23–5.
[8] Ibid., 38.

early. Nominal credit was represented in monetary terms, whereas real capital consisted of tools of production, "not only the actual tools, but the credit men establish for themselves that the tools will be usable and will be used."[9] "The notion that capital was real only when it reflected productive capacity which consumers wished to set in motion"[10] became important for Pound and Social Credit. That argument would gain force during the difficult times after the Great War and again during the deflation of the Depression and would lead to statements like that of the Italian Marshall Pietro Badoglio, cited by Pound: "A government that said, 'we can't build roads because we don't have any money' would be as ridiculous as a government that said 'we can't build roads because we don't have any kilometers.'" As Pound said, "The state HAS credit, and does not need to rent it from banks."[11]

The belief that credit had a social base was, of course, what gave Douglas's movement its name and was one of the two ideas that attracted Pound (through Orage) in the beginning. The other was Douglas's belief in the primacy of the free individual. As Pound explained it in an early essay:

> Fabianism and Prussianism alike give grounds for what Major Douglas has ably synthesized as "a claim for the complete subjection of the individual to an objective which is externally imposed upon him; which is not necessary or even desirable that he should understand in full. . . . The danger which at the moment threatens individual liberty far more than any extension of individual enterprise is the Servile State."[12]

Pound went on to give Douglas's definition of the Servile State (a phrase introduced by Belloc in his book of that title): "the erection of an irresistible and impersonal organisation through which the ambition of able men, animated consciously or unconsciously by the lust of domination, may operate to the enslavement of their fellow men."[13] To Pound, still the artist in 1920, these were worthwhile ideas, and he admired Douglas for the ethical base upon which he constructed his economic theory. Certainly the observations were prescient, given what was to evolve over the twenty-five (and more) years that followed. By the time Pound wrote *Jefferson and/or Mussolini,* thirteen years later, this matter of the Servile State was no longer so prominent in his thoughts. Moreover, Pound probably did not think of fascist Italy as a Servile State.

But the major point was economic: Douglas's (and Orage's) perception "that the ultimate control of industry is financial control. These are the

[9] Orage, 9. This book, like so many others, first appeared as a serial in the *New Age.*
[10] Finlay, 43.
[11] Pound, *Social Credit,* 14.
[12] Pound, "Probari Ratio" (1920), in *Selected Prose,* 207, 209.
[13] Ibid., 209.

makers of credit."[14] Douglas's solution was to take control out of the hands of the banker and return it to the community, the real source of credit: "The State should lend, not borrow. . . . in this respect, as in others, the Capitalist usurps the function of the State."[15]

II

The primary problem addressed by economists in the post– World War I years was the reestablishment of the international monetary scheme and the payment of war debts and reparations.[16] Social Credit does not address those problems; it stops at the border. Those issues are also skirted by Pound and Gesell.

The First World War made the United States, which had suffered from it least and profited most, into the leading economic power of the world. Although the United States underwent a severe depression in 1920 and 1921 (at its worst, almost 12 percent of the labor force was out of work), the setback was short lived. After recovery, and throughout the period from 1922 to 1929, the American economy enjoyed a period of sustained growth and optimism. Worldwide curiosity about the United States meant that there was a demand for journalism explaining its economic and social conditions, a trend that must have certainly been of some benefit to Pound.

The war had completely destroyed the fragile mechanism of international finance; in order for the United States to collect its war debts from allies and its reparations from Germany, that mechanism had to be restored. It is understandable, then, that "pressure from New York bankers and the U.S. State Department . . . over objections from the British, French, and Italians, who were not yet back on the gold standard," led to the decision to return Germany to the gold standard in March of 1921 (60). By 1925, "with much League and central bank assistance, most continental European nations returned to the gold standard" (70).

The Baldwin government adopted the recommendation of the Cunliffe committee (in two reports of 1918 and 1919), and under Chancellor of the Exchequer Winston Churchill's leadership, put Great Britain back on the gold standard in 1925. This move was subsequently considered a blunder,[17] although Davis argues that it was not the gold standard per

[14] Ibid., 207.
[15] Ibid., 208.
[16] Joseph S. Davis, *The World between the Wars.* As will be clear from the ensuing discussion, I have relied heavily upon this exhaustive study. In this section, numbers in parentheses refer to pages in Davis.
[17] There was contemporary opposition to the move by Keynes, and later economists such as D. E. Moggridge and P. A. Samuelson have considered it a decision with disastrous consequences for the British economy. The decision was one basis for Pound's hatred

se that was at fault but the fact that the pound was set at the prewar parity of $4.8665, "about 10 to 12 percent too high in relation to the dollar" (74). D. E. Moggridge has concluded that this decision was disastrous and "represented a triumph of shortrun interests and conventional assumptions over longterm considerations and hard analysis."[18] In fact, Great Britain was in an industrial depression (from which it never fully recovered) throughout the late twenties. Only the dole, a system of public assistance, made high unemployment in British basic industries somewhat tolerable.

With the exception of an occasional lone voice warning of overextension of credit, no recognized economist anticipated a worldwide depression of the magnitude seen in the early thirties. Without entering into a full discussion of its causes, it is enough to note that three factors worsened an already serious situation. Banks, in an effort to strengthen their reserve position, called in their demand loans and refused to extend maturing commercial loans. This "led to distress selling of goods and materials by debtor concerns, which hastened declines in commodity prices" (231). Further, "the almost universal multiplication of trade barriers in the early 1930s, through tariff measures and many other devices, figured significantly in throttling down international trade, accelerating price declines, and curtailing economic activity all over the world" (241).

Finally, the adoption of the gold standard in the middle twenties meant that the drop in both commodity prices and income spread from country to country. The economic decline in the United States, which consumed almost 40 percent of the world's primary goods, meant serious setbacks in other countries (234). "By the spring of 1933 the volume of world trade was at best one-fourth, and its value only one-third, of the respective 1929 levels" (308). World trade and the international currency system had collapsed. Things seemed hopeless in the trough of the Depression in 1932 and 1933. Davis sums up the general feeling:

> It is hard to overstate the profound and far-reaching distrust of businessmen, financiers, economists, forecasters, and statesmen which pervaded this country and others in the depths of the depression. . . . Thus the stage was set for the rise of charismatic political leaders [and] . . . bold or even rash experimentation was welcome. (296)

This was the world situation to which Pound was responding when he took up his active study of economics and propaganda for economic reform.

---

of Churchill, who supported the move, although at least one biographer, Martin Gilbert, believes that Churchill had some genuine doubts about the wisdom of the change. See Kindleberger's *A Financial History of Western Europe*, 339–41, for further discussion.
[18] Cited in Joseph S. Davis, 422.

The United States, of all the major industrial nations, was hit hardest by the Depression, and the number of unemployed grew from over four million workers in 1930 to over eight million in 1931 and over twelve million in 1932 (364). Although the Roosevelt policies had a positive effect, the consequences of the Depression were not overcome until the outbreak of the Second World War; in fact, after four years of recovery, the United States suffered a short but drastic eight-month depression in 1937 and 1938, cured only when the administration "reluctantly returned to heavy spending" (316). It was only after the war started and vast expenditures were made for defense that full recovery was achieved; unemployment remained above 4 percent until the United States actually entered the war (226).

Pound's quarrel with Roosevelt was not that recovery was slow but that the president did not understand a fundamental principle of economic reform, that the basis of credit is in the state. Pound wrote: "*TWO sorts of nations exist: those which control their finances and those which 'are financed'.*"[19] This idea explains his preference for the economic systems that he thought were being put into effect in Italy and Germany over the solution adopted in the United States by FDR. According to Pound: "The American New Deal to date (December 1934–January 1935) has shown no comprehension of fundamentals, no perception of the basic relations of the currency system, money system, credit system to the needs and purchasing power of the whole people."[20] This lack of comprehension was demonstrated by the fact that the United States borrowed money to put people back to work on public projects, instead of reforming the currency or issuing dividends as Gesell and Douglas advocated. For Pound, using his system of dichotomies, this put Roosevelt on the side of private exploitation of the crisis, instead of on the side of the state solution for it:

> In contrast to the idiotic accumulation of debt by Roosevelt, observe that if such government expenditure be necessary or advisable, the direct payment of workers, etc., in stamp scrip would in eight years consume itself, and leave the next decade *free* of all debt. The Roosevelt system is either a fraud or a selling of the nation's children into slavery without the ghost of an excuse.[21]

Although his criticism of Roosevelt would become more virulent, that is its essential basis.

In Great Britain, in response to the Wall Street crash, a fourteen-member Committee on Finance and Industry, chaired by Hugh P. Mac-

[19] Pound, *ABC of Economics* (1933), in *Selected Prose*, 250.
[20] Pound, *Social Credit*.
[21] Pound, "The Individual in His Milieu" (1935), in *Selected Prose*, 280.

millan and including Keynes as a member, was appointed on 5 November 1929. Its report was published on 13 July 1931 and "was unanimous that there could be no question of Great Britain departing from the gold standard" (396). On 20 September, nine weeks after the firm recommendation of the committee, the Bank of England suspended gold payments. This "abrupt abandonment of the gold standard astounded and shocked the world" (269). Pound read the report and wrote to Senator Bronson Cutting on 11 February 1932: "the Macmillan Report (old stuff.) I only read a few weeks ago because I supposed it wd. be BUNK, and it was. Interest mainly in old Bradbury's final note of dissent." Davis notes that Keynes reversed his position when Britain left the gold standard and adds that the Macmillan committee's "contribution to recovery policy was negligible" (396).

The rapid onset of the Depression did much to discredit the economics profession. Attesting to that, Davis recalls that in the spring of 1933, "a mock-trial of 'the economists' was staged at the London School of Economics; Robert Boothby, M.P., representing 'the state of the popular mind,' charged the economists with 'conspiring to spread mental fog' " (386). The inability of the profession to agree on remedies did little to help its reputation. Interestingly enough, at a series of lectures on the crisis, one presenter stated that "only a world dictator could break his way out now" (397).

Those details may give some idea of the climate of opinion that saw the rise of Hitler and the unprecedented actions taken by Roosevelt. Keynes, advocating increased expenditures, expressed the hope that the world would not need to wait for another war but could find some way to spend money on "the enterprises of peace. . . . to discover *some* object which is admitted even by deadheads to be a legitimate excuse for largely increasing the expenditures of someone on something" (317). Surette has made the same point in an even stronger fashion, noting that "the only socialized [state financed] form of consumption known in the 1920s [was] the market for military hardware. . . . War was therefore an almost inevitable consequence of the economic structures of Western nations."[22] Pound would probably have agreed with Keynes (and Surette) on that, though he would have insisted that the government did not have to borrow the money to wage war and that economic recovery could be achieved through Douglas's and Gesell's proposals and expenditures on public works or the arts.

III

The problem faced by the British economy in the twentieth century, according to Douglas, was that although the miracles of in-

[22] Surette, *A Light from Eleusis*, 91.

dustrial modernization should have raised everyone's standard of living, in fact they had not. Douglas, an engineer, was determined to find out why the expected improvement did not occur. The most obvious manifestation of the problem lay in the business cycle, those periodic waves of prosperity and poverty that worried European and American economies throughout the nineteenth century and before. In thinking about the causes of these cycles, Douglas was influenced early on by another economic "heretic," John A. Hobson, an occasional contributor to the *New Age*. Hobson's views form an essential background to Social Credit, a background that was only twice acknowledged by Douglas.

According to Hobson (and his colleague A. F. Mummery) the primary fault in capitalism was its inherent inability to distribute enough purchasing power to clear its markets, that is, to buy all the goods it produces. That problem was continually aggravated by oversaving, which was the direct consequence of the unequal distribution of wealth in the capitalist system. The rich do indeed get richer and the poor poorer, but hidden within that rather inert bromide was an element that would fatally corrode industrial society.

Put simply, the working poor did not have enough money to consume all that was produced, and the rich, having too much money, did not have the ability or the need to consume all that was left. The result was that the rich invested their money in further capital ventures: more factories and further improvements in the means of production, which led in turn to an increased quantity of goods to be sold. The problem, then, was not in the production of wealth but in its consumption or distribution. Oversaving, and the concomitant investment of capital, led to underconsumption. Hobson explored a further consequence of this in his 1902 book *Imperialism*. Because markets at home do not suffice, capitalist nations are forced to compete for markets abroad. The resulting competition and exploitation leads to war.[23]

Douglas quoted Hobson's book *Democracy after the War* toward the beginning of *Economic Democracy*. Douglas agreed that modern industry left the home market with "inadequate power to purchase and consume," and he spoke further about the "practical limitation of the expansion of markets for goods" throughout the world.[24] Douglas also mentions Hobson in *Social Credit* (the only other time he acknowledges his debt), saying that Hobson

> attributes the general lack of purchasing-power (the *fact* of which he most properly emphasizes) to the undue investment of savings, on the part of the more fortunate members of Society, in what are termed

[23] Heilbroner, 198–203.
[24] Douglas, *Economic Democracy*, 26.

capital undertakings, with the result that the production of capital goods is in excess of the amount required.[25]

But Douglas finds Hobson's explanation of this occurrence inadequate, for reasons he does not give. Social Credit seeks to offer a better explanation.

After the disaster of World War I, Hobson's argument could be refined by Douglas. He believed that one cause of the war was the need "to prevent the supply of goods from outrunning the supply of money by too great a margin."[26] War accomplishes this through massive destruction of manufactured armaments. Scarcity could also be maintained, according to Douglas, by dumping abroad and by advertising and sabotage. Advertising increases demand; sabotage restricts supply so that it is always less than demand.[27]

For Douglas, Pound, and others, full employment necessitated competition for overseas markets, a major cause of the First World War.[28] Another economist who wrote for the *New Age,* Arthur James Penty, argued that Germany had been forced into the war because it lacked colonial outlets for her overproduction. He called for an end to the continual reinvestment of capital in industry and "advocated the medieval solution, the spending of surplus wealth on art."[29] This is a valid analysis and represents the kind of solution to which Pound would be drawn. Attempting to clarify terminology, Pound would later point out that the problem was not overproduction in itself: "Dissociation 2. Overproduction did not begin with the industrial system. Nature habitually overproduces. Chestnuts go to waste on the mountain side, and it has never yet caused a world crisis."[30] Certainly Pound and Douglas were correct in maintaining that the lack of adequate purchasing power, or "underconsumption, was a cause of depression in modern industrial economies."[31]

IV

We should next consider what solution Douglas proposed and what he saw as the underlying cause of the problem. For answers he went to an analysis of credit and finance.

Douglas received his essential clue to the underlying cause of underconsumption from the First World War, with its imperatives "superior

[25] Douglas, *Social Credit,* 82.
[26] Surette, *A Light from Eleusis,* 91.
[27] Douglas, *Social Credit,* 45.
[28] Ibid., 112, 115.
[29] Finlay, 48.
[30] Pound, *ABC of Economics* (1933), in *Selected Prose,* 233.
[31] Surette, *A Light from Eleusis,* 84.

to all questions of legal and financial restriction."[32] British society quickly reorganized itself after the war began. Douglas observed:

> In order to maintain a connection between finance and production, finance has to follow production instead of, as in the normal case, production having to follow finance. The extension of production to its utmost intrinsic limits, therefore, involves an extension of finance at a rate out of all proportion to that which obtains in the normal course of events, and this extension at once reveals the artificial character of normal finance. . . . the Gold Standard, on which British finance was supposed to be based, broke down within a few hours of the outbreak of the war.[33]

The war required optimal production for victory to be achieved. This increase in production was secured by arbitrarily changing the nature of credit, in effect reversing the normal relation between finance and production. Douglas saw this being done during the war and naturally he asked himself why the same methods should not be used during peace.

The highly organized wartime economy needed to produce goods at nearly 100 percent efficiency because of society's will to survive. During the war, this efficiency was brought about by a restructuring of British finance. There could be no underconsumption in a war, since the materials produced were quickly destroyed. What would happen after the transition to a peacetime economy? Presumably, society would be forced to scale back to a less efficient rate of production. With the return of soldiers and after a burst of pent-up consumer demand, massive unemployment would result.

Douglas proposed that Britain not retreat from the managed economy of wartime. Unemployment, according to Douglas, was a sign of economic progress – the progress of freeing men from labor – not a sign of industrial breakdown.[34] But the unemployed should not be left in misery by society; instead, through the device of a national dividend, they too could benefit from industrial progress. The answer to underconsumption, the plague of all industrial societies, was simply to "create enough money to purchase all the goods and services the nation was capable of delivering."[35] In today's terminology, we would say that Douglas advocated an expansionary monetary policy.

Douglas differs from Hobson in that instead of seeing the problem of underconsumption as the fundamental contradiction in global capitalism, he thinks that he "discovered" it from his experience in studying cost

---

[32] Douglas, *Social Credit*, 134.
[33] Ibid., 135.
[34] Ibid., 10.
[35] Surette, *A Light from Eleusis*, 90.

accounting for a single factory. This discovery led to his A + B theory, explained by Pound:

> A factory
> has also another aspect, which we call the financial aspect
> It gives people the power to buy (wages, dividends
> which are power to buy) but it is also the cause of prices
> or values, financial, I mean financial values
> It pays workers, and pays *for* material.
> What it pays in wages and dividends
> stays fluid, as power to buy, and this power is less,
> per forza, damn blast your intellex, is less
> than the total payments made by the factory
> (as wages, dividends, AND payments for raw material
> bank charges, etcetera)
> and all, that is the whole, that is the total
> of these is added into the total prices
> caused by that factory, any damn factory
> and there is and must be therefore a clog
> and the power to purchase can never
> (under the present system) catch up with
> prices at large,
> and the light became so bright and so blindin'
> in this layer of paradise
> that the mind of man was bewildered. (*C, XXXVIII*, 190)

That canto, first published in the *New English Weekly* of 28 September 1933, offers a reasonably clear exposition of the Douglas A + B principle. However, it does not address an objection that immediately springs to mind, namely, that factories shut down and businesses fail, selling much inventory well below cost, a common situation that would tend to operate against the "clog." Douglas's A + B theory stated simply that the prices of factory goods outrun a society's ability to pay for them, owing to the need for profit. He wrote that when "the book value of the world's stocks is always greater than the apparent financial ability to liquidate them . . . the creation of subsidiary financial media [what we today call "near money"], in the form of further bank credits, becomes necessary. . . . The effect of this is, of course, to decrease progressively the purchasing power of money."[36] Here Douglas brings up an objection that would later be raised against him, that the addition of credit to keep the system in motion results in inflation. Yet he endorses controlled inflation as one of the possible remedies to the problem. The question was, who would add that money, the private banks or the government, and to whose advantage?

[36] Douglas, *Economic Democracy*, 29.

As Keynes did later, Douglas was attacking two fundamental laws of the orthodox economics of his day: Say's Law of Markets and the law of supply and demand. That attack explains his reputation as a heretic among university economists who were his contemporaries. Douglas believed that only the upper limit of the price of an item was governed by the law of supply and demand and that the important limit was the lower limit, where there was an unacknowledged floor. That was "the ruling limit, being fixed by the cost plus the minimum profit which will provide a financial inducement to produce."[37] To that extent he resembled the orthodox economists of the thirties, who, in the face of the massive oversupply of labor during the Depression, believed that there was an unacknowledged floor to wage price. The requirement for a minimum profit meant that the prices demanded by manufacturers would clog the system by removing needed purchasing power. As Surette has pointed out, this concept violates Say's law, the foundation of classical economics.[38] Say's law essentially states that "products are paid for by products," or that supply creates its own demand. "Production increases not only the supply of goods but, by virtue of the requisite cost payments to the factors of production, also creates the demand to purchase these goods."[39] Say's law implies that the capitalist system will always be able to absorb increases in productivity; Douglas (and later Keynes, vigorously and in great detail) did not agree.

Critics of Douglas attacked him using Say's law and common sense to point out that money spent on wages, capital investment, interest charges, and dividends reentered the economy and that therefore a clog was not possible. To counter this, Douglas came up with his notion of rate of flow:

> Let not the patient reader allow himself to become confused by the fact that B has at some previous time been represented by payment of wages, salaries, and dividends. While this is of course true, it is quite irrelevant – it is the rate of flow which is vital. The whole economic system is in ceaseless motion – purchasing power is constantly flowing back from individuals into the credit system from which it came.[40]

The last sentence rather hazily begs the question, and Douglas does not offer any clearer explanation of the concept. Finlay, who made a careful and sympathetic study of the Social Credit movement, has better elucidated this idea of rate of flow, which he considers central to the A + B theorem and thus to Social Credit.

[37] Ibid., 52.
[38] Surette, *A Light from Eleusis*, 83.
[39] Blaug, 153.
[40] Douglas, *Credit Power and Democracy*, 24–5.

Douglas had to meet the objection that "money taken off the market in price is simultaneously and just as quickly reentering the market as wages."[41] He did so by noting that in late industrial economies an ever-expanding number of machines are employed. These require an increasing investment in capital assets:

> The nature of advanced industrial technique meant that an ever-growing number of projects were intricate undertakings which could only begin to produce wealth after a long period of time.... In the meantime, however, the wages and salaries... and the cost of the materials... were being paid.... none of this extra money was on hand to pay for the extra goods when eventually they came onto the market. It was this point which was the basis of the Douglas analysis.[42]

Even though this explanation, with its underlying assumption that what applies to one plant would hold true for all plants in a complex, interdependent society, does not entirely convince, Douglas's principal point has some validity. The crux is not that the system must eventually clog or come to a halt but that in its nature it would demand an increasing amount of credit from some source and that whatever group or groups were providing the loan capital, they would come to hold more and more power within an industrial economy. To what extent should this power remain in the traditional realm of banking, and to what extent should the power be transferred to the state?[43]

Douglas did not want to change or abolish the monetary system, which he considered "the correct estimate of the capacity of society with its plant, culture, organisation, and morale, to deliver goods and services desired by individuals."[44] Money allowed the full distribution of society's goods and services, if it functioned properly. Money was not the measure of value but rather served as an efficient means of allocating a nation's priorities. "*The proper function of a money system is to furnish the information necessary to direct the production and distribution of goods and services,*" Douglas wrote.[45] Pound shared this view, although he was more willing than Douglas to conceive of different forms of money to suit the different purposes of circulation and saving.

Douglas's solution to the underconsumption resulting from his A + B dilemma was twofold. First, he wished to create enough money to make up the shortfall and distribute it by means of a national dividend. Each citizen had a right to that dividend because, as Pound was fond of pointing out, the wealth of society was as much a product of the cu-

[41] Finlay, 110.
[42] Ibid., 108–9.
[43] Ibid., 107, 111.
[44] Douglas, *Credit Power and Democracy*, 132.
[45] Douglas, *Social Credit*, 62.

mulative inventiveness of all humanity, the cultural heritage, as it was of living individuals and accumulated capital. Second, Douglas revived the medieval notion of the "Just Price," which would also help resolve the problem. The price of each item would be fixed. What would that price be? Douglas wrote:

> The answer to this is a *statement of the average depreciation of the capital assets of the community, stated in terms of money released over an equal period of time, and the correct price is the money value of this depreciation in terms of the cost of the article.* In other words, the Just Price of an article, which is the price at which it can be effectively distributed in the community producing, bears the same ratio to the cost of production that the total consumption and depreciation of the community bears to the capital production.[46]

There is no evidence that Pound (or anyone) understood this line of argument; it was probably enough for him to hear the term *Just Price,* with its origin in medieval canon law, for him to support the idea enthusiastically. I am not convinced that Douglas himself was entirely clear about what he meant. He proposes a relationship involving two ratios – Just Price is to the cost of production as consumption plus depreciation is to capital production – though he does not clarify the terms of the ratios. As nearly as I can guess, Douglas believed that the profit made on any item should be limited to direct costs plus the accrued costs resulting from a straight-line depreciation of plant. In other words, Douglas seems to have been well on his way to discovering (or realizing) the difference between cash-based and accrual accounting and to recognizing the need to provide for the cost of replacing capital goods in one's price structure. Reynolds alludes to this briefly, without explanation, when he states that "Douglas's idea ... grew out of his experience with business accounting."[47] Douglas believed that it would be a simple enough task to come up with the figures involved.

V

Douglas's revision in 1933 of the first (1924) edition of *Social Credit* contains a lot of broad political and social theorizing (what he was best at); it also enables him to remind his readers, caught in the trough of the Depression, that he had warned of an impending breakdown in

---

[46] Douglas, *Economic Democracy*, 124. An earlier version of this is found in his correction of an article for the *New Age*: "Prices are arranged so that they bear the same relation to cost that consumption does to production" (18 Sept. 1919, 350).
[47] Reynolds, 386.

the system nine years before, and even earlier. His "I told you so" is understandable; more relevant for our study of Pound is Douglas's tendency to see conspiracies among bankers and financiers, a tendency also present in Orage. One does not necessarily have to hold on to a conspiracy theory of history to recognize that men do combine their efforts to achieve selfish ends, but to focus exclusively on conspiracies means ultimately to look for individual villains. In the preface Douglas quotes approvingly

> Mr. William Jennings Bryan in his famous election speech: "The money power preys upon the nation in times of peace, and conspires against it in times of adversity. It is more despotic than monarchy, more insolent than autocracy, more selfish than bureaucracy. It denounces as public enemies all who question its methods, or throw light upon its crimes. It can only be overthrown by the awakened conscience of the nation."[48]

Douglas had suffered political disappointments and setbacks both from inside his party and from the outside, so it is easy to understand his bitterness. But in those times of crisis he had forsaken the role of economist and engineer for one of politician and polemicist:

> The position into which money and the methods by which it is controlled and manipulated have brought the world arises, not from any defect or vice inseparable from money (which is probably one of the most marvellous and perfect agencies for enabling co-operation that the world has ever conceived), but because of the subordination of this powerful tool to the objective of what it is not unfair to call a hidden government.[49]

Pound shared this tendency of Douglas and Social Credit to see conspiracy and manipulation at work in economics, partly owing, no doubt, to his nineteenth-century American background, where these views were common. This notion of conspiracy was to involve him more and more deeply, and cause him great trouble.

From the start, Pound was aware of some of the problems with the Douglas plan. Commenting upon Douglas's prose and the way his solutions were presented, Pound wrote that the "formula is certainly not framed to stir streetcorner enthusiasms, it is proposed in very moderate if not very comprehensible terms . . . the author is not very definite about the composition of his 'decentralized local authority.' "[50] This remark is about as kind as one can get toward Douglas's muddy prose. Douglas's recommendations for enactment of his proposals are neither specific nor clear.

[48] Douglas, *Social Credit*, vi.
[49] Ibid., 25.
[50] Pound, "Probari Ratio" (1920), in *Selected Prose*, 208.

Others responded more negatively to the Social Credit programs. In 1922 "the Labour party committee set up to examine Social Credit . . . rejected the proposals. Douglas and Orage were invited to testify before the subcommittee and refused,"[51] believing they would not receive a fair or sympathetic hearing. The English Communist party also rejected Social Credit, but with more specific strictures: "The Douglasites cannot have it both ways. *They cannot both inflate credit and deflate prices.*"[52] Though both issuing a national dividend (inflating credit) and establishing a Just Price (deflating prices) are not logically exclusive, the communists were correct in pointing out a certain lack of direction to the Social Credit plan.

Political figures frequently have more problems with their supporters than with their detractors, and C. H. Douglas was no exception. In England an outgrowth of the Boy Scout movement, the Kindred of the Kibbo Kift, adopted Social Credit in 1929.[53] During the early thirties, this group evolved into the Green Shirts, a militant wing of Social Credit that gave a fascist sheen to the whole movement. The leader of this group, which was recognized by Douglas, was John Hargrave, a charismatic figure with rather vague notions. His book, *The Great War Brings It Home* (London, 1919) begins: "All Life is Life. There is no Life but Life. Everything is Everything and we are part of It all." As Finlay notes, this contains "a hint of eclecticism."[54]

The link between the Green Shirts and Social Credit has been used as evidence that the latter was a fascist movement. It appears that to some extent the Green Shirts imitated fascist tactics. At the height of their influence they had sixteen local groups across Britain and sold seven thousand copies a week of *Attack,* their journal. Yet they rejected both fascism and communism, preferring to see themselves and their philosophy as "the third resolvent factor."[55] Nonetheless, association with the Green Shirts did little to help the reputation of Social Credit among a majority of the English.

After the economic crisis of 1929, Social Credit flourished. With a number of nations facing disaster, its critique of the capitalist system drew many adherents. Nevertheless, with the single exception of a major electoral victory in the Canadian province of Alberta in 1935, Social Credit never really succeeded as a political movement. Much of the blame rests with Major Douglas.

[51] Finlay, 122, 198. A record of the correspondence can be found in the *New Age* (18 Aug. 1921, 191–2).
[52] Finlay, 193–4.
[53] Earle Davis, 106.
[54] Finlay, 150, 158–9.
[55] Ibid., 158–9, 162–3.

The movement had always been more political than economic, as Pound recognized:

> So much has been written recently of Social Credit as if it were a mechanism for use of merely ECONOMIC man, *homo economicus,* a creature of abstract thought, that we might appear to have forgotten the nature of "Economic Democracy" (First Edition 1920). . . . The surprise in RE-reading is that Douglas here seems to deal so little with economics and so greatly and generally with the philosophy of politics.[56]

Part of the impact of Pound's rereading must certainly have come from his own change in perspective in the intervening years. The practical problem for Social Credit lay in Douglas's own ambivalence about his political role.

In his defense, it can be pointed out that Douglas was an unlikely politician. He was an engineer and a plant manager who believed that he had discovered a basic problem with capitalism and a technique to solve it. Douglas believed that his scheme "owed nothing to faction and was capable of being implemented by any party. Thus his rejection of politics."[57] Yet he retained a central role in the Social Credit movement, as its founder and ideologue. Finlay relates that it was difficult to work with Douglas because "he could not rest content until he had pointed out all the difficulties and snags in any proposed course of action."[58] Pound also complained about this rigidity and about Douglas's inability to integrate converging movements into an effective political whole. Critics are agreed that Social Credit could not function with Douglas ("Douglas was not a good practical leader and showed few signs of political intelligence in action"[59]) and yet could not function without him ("Douglas always retained too crucial a position, and independent Social Credit developments never acquired a healthy life of their own"[60]). Thus the movement's failure.

VI

What about Social Credit economics, its diagnoses and cures? How do they stand up to scrutiny? The principal problems lie in the implementation of its two suggested remedies. To put the doctrine of Just Price into practice in a complex industrial society would require an enormous governmental bureaucracy. The number of calculations required is bewildering. Although theoretically possible, that remedy does

---

[56] Pound, "The Return of the Native," *New English Weekly,* 2 Apr. 1936.
[57] Finlay, 191.
[58] Ibid., 93.
[59] Earle Davis, 107.
[60] Finlay, 88.

not seem practical. A national dividend in some form would be much easier to implement and would have the desired beneficial effects. Its inflationary tendency, however, would have to be checked.

Douglas's diagnosis of a fundamental problem in capitalist societies of his day was basically sound. His assertion, that the capitalist industrial system did not distribute enough money to purchase all of the goods and services it produced, offers as valid an explanation of the Great Depression as any. But Douglas owes this insight to John A. Hobson. Nor was Hobson himself entirely original. His analysis paralleled those of the German economist J. K. Rodbertus and the German revolutionary Rosa Luxemburg. Interestingly enough, Hobson's view of imperialism was taken up by another of Pound's heroes, a theoretician who did have talent as a political leader, V. I. Lenin.[61]

As to Douglas's idea that the basis of credit is social, not private, the debate continues today in many guises. The issue of political versus private control of credit is fundamental and its implications are vast. The fact that Douglas articulated some of these problems is worthy of serious attention.

Unfortunately, Douglas's confidence in his "discovery," and his opposition to private banks pushed him to the edge of paranoia:

> Since the greater part of the real purchasing-power of the world is in a potential form which is not represented by any figures anywhere, but can be materialized by those in possession of the secret of the process, as and when required, taxation of *visible* purchasing-power is exactly what is most valuable in maintaining the power and supremacy – the power to reward and punish – of the money "makers."[62]

Besides the conspiracy theories, there are echoes of anti-Semitism in this passage, echoes from a previous section of the same book. Using the same phrase, Douglas had claimed earlier that "rewards and punishments," "finance and law," and "unchecked collectivism" in prewar Germany and postwar Russia were Jewish in origin.[63] He went on to say: "It should in any case be emphasized that it is the Jews as a group, and not as individuals, who are on trial, and that the remedy, if one is required, is to break up the group activity."[64] Like Pound later, Douglas approaches and then veers away from out-and-out anti-Semitism. Douglas even brings the notorious anti-Semitic tract *The Protocols of the Learned Elders of Zion* into his argument. That book, a forged document of nineteenth-century Czarist Russia, purports to show the means by which

[61] Heilbroner, 205.
[62] Douglas, *Social Credit*, 91.
[63] Ibid., 29.
[64] Ibid., 30.

a group of Jews, using currency manipulation to create boom and bust cycles and wars, controls the world. Douglas says it describes

> a Machiavellian scheme for the enslavement of the world. . . . The authenticity of this document is a matter of little importance; what is interesting about it, is the fidelity with which the methods by which such enslavement might be brought about can be seen reflected in the facts of everyday experience.[65]

What Douglas says here is that although its attribution to a secret group of Jewish elders is in doubt, the document does present a convincing explanation of how the economy is, or might be, manipulated to the public detriment. Pound, too, would later echo this view. Douglas's final assessment of the book was that it is "quite possible that this document is inductive," written by a single person of "great but perverted talents."[66] The villainy has been correctly analyzed; only the villain remains in doubt. Douglas's hedging probably represented real anti-Semitism on his part or an attempt to appeal to English anti-Semitism of the time, but the fact that he could give some credence to such a malicious book does not increase our confidence in his analytical powers.

VII

One of Douglas's ideas that undoubtedly attracted Pound to these economic and political theories, at least initially, was the emphasis that Douglas placed on the importance of leisure time in the economic life of a culture and the desirability of freeing the time of the more creative members of society so they are able to contribute to the high level of innovation and invention that a civilization needs to make progress. That idea appealed to Pound, the artist; moreover, he was intrigued by the fact that Douglas claimed to have found the causes of war rooted in the capitalistic economic system. But Pound's concern for economic and social issues during the twenties stemmed specifically from his concern for the problems "facing the artist in the modern world."[67] This focus came directly from his own artistic interests and from his belief that society should allow artists maximum independence for their work. These concerns were not yet the more general social concerns of a political crusader. Pound did crusade during the twenties, but for policies that would favor his own rather restricted self-interest.

This can readily be seen by examining the social issues with which Pound involved himself during that time: the "passport nuisance," the

---

[65] Ibid., 146.
[66] Ibid., 147.
[67] Ibid., 225.

inadequate copyright laws of the United States, and article 211 of the U.S. Penal Code. Each involved an impingement of the state upon the rights of its citizens (read artists), and each was intolerable to Pound. Passports were anathema to Pound, especially troublesome owing to his frequent travels. Introduced during the war, they represented governmental interference of the wrong kind, and he campaigned vigorously against them, chiefly through the letters-to-the-editor columns of the *New York Herald* and the Paris edition of the *Chicago Tribune*. More directly troublesome to Pound the artist, particularly because of his sponsorship of James Joyce's *Ulysses,* were the antiquated copyright laws of the United States and the even more pernicious subsection 211 of the U.S. Penal Code. Writing to Senator Bronson M. Cutting on 8 November 1930, Pound stated that article 211 "confuses smutty postcards, condoms, and Catullus" and added: "Article 211 of the Penal code was, as I have had occasion to remark 'obviously made by gorillas for the further stultification of imbeciles.' The late Chief Justice Taft was somewhat shocked at this expression, but I see no reason to soften it." (Pound, in the same letter, went on to ask Cutting, in confidence, for a list of the literate members of the Senate).[68] Cutting was a publisher before being appointed to fill the seat vacated in the U.S. Senate by the death of Andrius A. Jones and was known for his defense of First Amendment rights. He thus might have been sympathetic to Pound's complaint. Joyce's book had been banned by the U.S. Postal Service, and an unscrupulous American publisher, Samuel Roth, took advantage of American copyright laws and began publishing an unauthorized version of *Ulysses* in 1926. Hemingway and Joyce tried to draw Pound into a protest against Roth, but Pound declined, stating that it was not Roth's fault but the fault of the American law, and that the trouble should be attacked there.[69] This is a significant statement, for it shows that Pound was beginning to focus his attention on civic, rather than individual, virtue.

VIII

Pound's "Mauberley," apart from indicating his changing attitudes toward the role of the artist in society, was also "distinctly a farewell to London" (*P*, 185). It is clear from the poem that there was friction

[68] Unless otherwise indicated, all letters quoted are from the Pound Archive at the Beinecke Library of Yale University. Those marked "(ddp)" can be found in the typescript prepared by D. D. Paige for his 1950 edition of Pound's *Selected Letters* but were left out of the final selection. Those marked "(fbi)" were received from the Department of Justice under a Freedom-of-Information request, though I understand that many of them have been sent by now to the Beinecke. The letters are, for the most part, filed by correspondent.

[69] Pound, *Selected Letters*, 206, letter to James Joyce dated 25 Dec. 1926.

between Pound and many members of the London literary establishment, difficulties indicated by his satiric portrait of Nixon and strictures upon British society scattered throughout "Mauberley." Pound was a blunt man, who spoke his mind freely. He was later to state in an article for *L'Indice*: "The hatred for Pound in London was caused principally by the fact that he always distinguished between first and second rate writers."[70] This may seem self-serving, but it has been confirmed by several of Pound's contemporaries. Orage wrote in the *New Age*:

> Mr. Pound, like so many others who have striven for the advancement of intelligence and culture in England, has made more enemies than friends. Much of the Press has been deliberately closed by cabal to him; his books have for some time been ignored or written down; and he himself has been compelled to live on much less than would support a navvy. (13 Jan. 1921, 125–7)

Pound's move to Paris in 1921 was motivated as much by his dislike of artistic conditions in England as by his interest in the artistic and literary scene in postwar Paris. His fascination with nineteenth- and early twentieth-century French poetry was already in evidence in 1913 with his series of articles "Approach to Paris" (they were later reprinted in Italian translation as a series for the "Supplemento Letterario" of *Il Mare* of Rapallo in 1932 and 1933). In addition, there was the presence of a thriving American expatriate colony with Hemingway, Stein, and others. Paris must have seemed an excellent alternative to London, and although Pound initially planned on staying there for one year, he ended up staying for more than three. He moved again, according to Malcolm Cowley, because he found the Paris literary scene too frenetic. Pound was thirty-nine and he felt that he was becoming too involved with the careers of others and not getting on with his own work. Pound told Cowley that he needed more quiet to proceed with the *Cantos* and that he had found an ideal spot, where he had stayed before. That spot was Rapallo.[71]

Rapallo was a logical choice for the Pounds. At the time of their move, in 1924, it was one of the most beautiful seacoast towns in Italy, sharing the Bay of Tigullio with Santa Margherita Ligure and Portofino, and located only twenty-six kilometers from Genoa, itself a much underrated city. The olive trees, flowers, and seacoast of Rapallo began to make their appearance in the *Cantos,* in the idealized Mediterranean land-scapes, which become more frequent. Life was inexpensive in Italy, and Mussolini's new government seemed orderly and progressive. The climate was temperate, and of course Pound always loved Italy and had vacationed there many times. These were all good reasons to move, and

---

[70] *L'Indice,* (Genoa, Italy), Sept. 1930.
[71] Cowley, 122.

I agree with Noel Stock that politics was not what attracted Pound to Rapallo in 1924.[72] The attractiveness of Rapallo drew the Yeats family there in 1928, and that same year Pound's parents, Homer and Isabel, also decided to settle there, after a visit.

During the twenties, after his move to Rapallo and with his increasing interest in political affairs, Pound became an admirer of both Lenin and Mussolini. Although the appearance of this pair in the Pound pantheon may seem odd, it is typical of Pound, and a historian of this period becomes accustomed to the frequent juxtaposition of both fascist and Marxist references in Pound's writing, not a contradiction to Pound in his search for the ideal economic doctrine, "a new synthesis." As we shall later see, in 1944 Pound attempted to convince the German–Italian government of the Republic of Salò to publish what he considered to be the essential works of Marxism. Not surprisingly, it was not initially receptive to the idea.

In the first issue of his magazine the *Exile,* Pound said that "both the Fascio and the Russian revolution are interesting phenomena," although he continued to insist that the artist was always well ahead of any political revolution.[73] About the same time (in the spring of 1927) the American communist journal *New Masses* published a letter from Pound asking for certain books and complimenting the editors on their publication. This letter, which they entitled "Pound Joins the Revolution?" was followed shortly by an article by Pound ("Workshop Orchestration") on Antheilian music and the rhythms of factories. Pound was genuinely interested in any kind of suggestion for improvement in the economic system and welcomed all constructive new ideas without regard to their provenance. He believed that a consensus could be reached on economic reform without necessarily entailing a consensus about politics. The more ideological movements of his time rejected his attempts to absorb the best from each of them (another theme we will see repeated through the thirties), and *New Masses* printed Pound's last article for them, "The Damn Fool Bureaukrats" (June 1928), with the following note appended:

> (NOTE: The *New Masses* disagrees violently with the following statement, but prints it because it is important. Ezra Pound is the leader of the most vital wing of the younger American writers. He formulates the unformed political creed in their minds.
>
> (Mr. Pound is irritated by all forms of the parliamentary system – by prohibition laws, copyright laws, bureaucracy and other minor eruptions. But like most literary men he has no solid knowledge of the disease: Capitalism. . . .

---

[72] Stock, 256.
[73] *Exile* 1 (Spring 1927).

(The most tough-minded of the capitalists are as weary of the bureaucrats as is Mr. Pound. In Italy, for instance, the industrial barons rule with a club named Mussolini, instead of the slapstick named Parliament. Does this completely satisfy Mr. Pound? Does he want Mussolini, and a more efficient capitalism in America?

(Yes, there are some bureaucratic lice left in the Soviet Russia, left with the filth and disorder of the old tenants. But the disinfecting squads are on the job day and night. . . .

(Or does he think that the literary man has no concern with the economic problems of the American "boobs," but ought to work in his own garden – at prohibition and copyright laws?)

These strictures upon Pound's limited interest in larger economic issues ("his own garden") were valid in 1928 but were not to remain so for long. The hostility of the *New Masses* toward Pound was to increase. Shortly after the Second World War there was a symposium in *New Masses* on Pound, "in which all of the contributors declared that he should be executed forthwith, some favoring hanging, some shooting."[74]

In the *Exile* (no. 2, Fall 1927) Pound quoted both Mussolini – "We are tired of government in which there is no responsible person having a hind-name, a front-name and an address" – and Lenin – "The banking business is declared a state monopoly. The interests of the small depositors will be safeguarded." Part of his enthusiasm for Mussolini may have been due to the fact that Pound's companion, Olga Rudge, a violinist, had given a private concert for the Italian leader on 19 February 1927. Mussolini was an extremely charismatic man, and he made a favorable impression on Ms. Rudge. In the *Exile* (no. 4, Fall 1928) Pound spoke of Lenin: "Apart from the social aspect he was of interest, technically, to serious writers. He never wrote a sentence that had any interest in itself, but he evolved almost a new medium, a sort of expression halfway between writing and action." It is clear that Pound himself was attracted to this "new medium" and that he was evolving toward what would be the dominant interest of his work during the thirties.

IX

Although political and economic themes appear occasionally in the first thirty cantos, they by no means predominate as they do in the middle cantos, XXXI–LXXIII. The first extended presentation of economic themes occurs in Canto XII, where we encounter a grudging admiration expressed in the story of Baldy Bacon, who cornered the market for copper centavos in Cuba, as well as an account of a bankers' meeting, "usurers in excelsis." The bankers complain about "the general

[74] Norman, *The Case of Ezra Pound*, 11.

uncertainty of all investment / Save investment in new bank buildings, / productive of bank buildings, / And not likely to ease distribution" (C, XII, 55). We can clearly see the influence of Douglas in these lines, but the tone of the canto is humorous, ending as it does with the "Tale of the Honest Sailor" (C, XII, 55), a juxtaposition of usury and sodomy borrowed from Dante. Among the early cantos there are other occasional references to economic and political subjects. The Hell Cantos (XIV and XV) contain politicians, profiteers, financiers, the press gang, and usurers, all villains from the First World War. The Purgatorio Canto (XVI) mentions the war and also the Russian Revolution. Canto XVIII reveals the secret of coinage in China (paper currency issued by the state) as related by Marco Polo and condemns Basil Zaharoff ("Zenos Metevsky"), the arms merchant. Cantos XIX, XXI, and XXII all contain mention of economic topics, as do Cantos XXIV, XXV, and XXVI, though these cantos tell of a begrudging economic relation between a government and an individual artist, in sharp contrast to the same relation under the more generous, though often impecunious, patron, Malatesta, in Cantos VIII–XI. In the first thirty cantos, these scattered economic references are well integrated into the greater variety of themes that Pound treats.

Pound's life and thought underwent many changes in the period between the First World War and 1930. He and his wife, Dorothy, moved twice: from London to Paris in 1921 and from Paris to Rapallo, Italy, in 1924. His companion, Olga Rudge, bore him a daughter in 1925, and his wife bore a son in 1926. And Pound started to reevaluate his ideas concerning the artist's place in society, a reevaluation that began during the Great War, continued during the twenties, and went through its most radical changes during the tumultuous decade of the thirties, as we shall see.

3

The Writer–Critic, 1930–1931

I

An interview with Pound by Francesco Monotti, published in the magazine *Belvedere* in March 1931, sheds some light on his move to Rapallo but is even more revealing about his thoughts on the state of Italy in 1931:

> "But why ever," I ask him, "you who lived in Paris and London for so long, did you come several years ago to make camp in Italy?"
>
> Ezra Pound gives a glance at the Gulf of Tigullio and at Rapallo which are stretched out below our eyes infused with the fading light of sunset, and seemed to look to them for the answer to my question.
>
> "The thing that most interests me in the world," he finally told me, "is civilization, the high peaks of culture. Italy has twice civilized Europe. No other country has done that even once. Each time a strong, live energy is unleashed in Italy, a new renaissance comes forth. I have written many times that after the war England was reduced to the point of abandoning its corpses in the streets. Intellectual France is tired, very tired, but at least it summoned the strength to bury the corpses of its dead ideas. I am fed up equally with English stupidity and French imbecility, even if they affect different areas. . . . "
>
> "You have mentioned Italy and the person who governs it. Which man from your own country would you compare to Mussolini?"
>
> "Comparisons of this kind are not easy. I will only say that the American historical character who comes to mind when I consider the part of Mussolini's effective program which includes land reclamation, the 'battle for grain,' and the mobilization of the nation's internal credit is Thomas Jefferson. . . . "
>
> "Do you believe that Italy is on the right path?"
>
> "Italy is the only country in the world . . . that can't be governed better than it already is. Italy is headed toward power. Without a strong Italy, I don't see the possibility of a balanced Europe. I dream for you the return of an epoch which, *mutatis mutandis,* is a bit similar to the

fifteenth century. An age in which the possibilities of science and culture are made to function at their maximum. In the fifteenth century, the summit of power coincided exactly with the summit of intelligence. You also find this idea in Confucius (Kung fu Tseu)."

"Fascism is involved here, up to a certain point. It's Italy's new virility and continual growth which is so impressive. Today's England is suffocated by the most blatant idiocy. Its press is nothing but the orchestration of lies, the most arrogant and subtle that humanity has ever seen. Even in America the newspapers fib from time to time, but at least they don't all sing the same tune. The unanimity of the English press is one of the wonders of the century."

"Would this by any chance be the first sign of English decadence?"

"A 'first' sign of decadence? Holy Christ! England was in full decadence in 1908. But it was a dignified decadence, an armchair padded with comforts. And it at least allowed for a few foreigners, American, Irish, etc., to do a bit of art and literature."[1] (tr)

I have quoted most of this interview, which was later reprinted by Pound in his own edition of his Italian journalism (*Orientamenti*, 1944), because it contains the beginning of several themes that will recur in Pound's writing during the next decade. There is the hatred for the English press and the conviction that it was under the control of a group determined to subvert the truth, a view, as we have seen, taken from Orage and the *New Age*. Along with this there is the conviction that England was finished as a world power and as a cultural force. Pound shows the same attitude toward France although his hatred is not nearly as virulent.

Pound's hope for Italy and admiration for Mussolini are equally extreme and equally exaggerated. Although his rather effulgent praise for both may have resulted from Pound's playing to a new audience, another factor is involved. Pound needed to believe that Italy was on the verge of a new renaissance, partly because of his need to be at the center or vortex of any new movement. He wanted to help create it, which will explain much of the programmatic writing that we will see when we examine his articles for *L'Indice* (Genoa) and the impatience and energy with which he exhorted his Italian audience.

Pound was reading the edition of the works of Thomas Jefferson, which forms the basis for Cantos XXXI–XXXIII. He believed that both Mussolini and Jefferson were *polumetis*, "of many devices," the epithet

---

[1] This can be compared to what Stravinsky said in an interview that took place earlier than this one, just before his 1930 meeting with Mussolini: "I don't believe that anyone venerates Mussolini more than I. To me, he is the *one man who counts* nowadays in the whole world. . . . I have an overpowering urge to render homage to your Duce. He is the savior of Italy and – let us hope – of Europe" (cited in a review of Harvey Sachs, *Music in Fascist Italy* [New York: W. W. Norton, 1988]). "(tr)" following a quotation indicates that I have translated it from Italian.

used by Homer for Odysseus and Hephaestus, and he would extend that comparison in his book *Jefferson and/or Mussolini,* finished in 1933. What should be highlighted here is Pound's conviction that the Italian dictator was mobilizing "the nation's internal credit," in other words, that he was pursuing economic reform along the lines suggested by Douglas and Orage. That belief was largely responsible for Pound's admiration of Mussolini, and it is a dominant motif in Pound's writing during this period.

Finally, the allusion to Confucius is very important. Confucius was to provide Pound with an entire system of ethics, upon which he based his idea of the societal importance of art, and Pound's interest in classical Chinese was to absorb more and more of his time during the next twenty years.

At the beginning of the decade, though, in 1930 and 1931, this transition was not yet apparent. His meeting with Mussolini and his discovery of Gesell's work in economics were still ahead of him. Pound himself marked the change as occurring in 1932: "From 1932 continual polemic in two languages, moving from Social Credit to Gesellism."[2] His writing in 1930 and 1931 was primarily concerned with literature. Pound's identity in 1930 and 1931 was primarily that of a poet and literary critic who also happened to be a loyal supporter of C. H. Douglas and the Social Credit movement. The change would come later.

II

Pound was very active, both as a writer and in an editorial capacity, in the pages of the bimonthly Genoese literary newspaper *L'Indice* during 1930 and 1931. Although his involvement with *L'Indice* stops abruptly at the end of 1931, for reasons I have not been able to determine, while it did continue Pound wrote a number of very important critical articles and he had a strong impact on the paper's editorial environment. Pound's writing and editing for *L'Indice* were exclusively literary, of a kind very familiar to a student of his career in London and Paris.

Two statements by Pound, one in *L'Indice* at the beginning of the decade and one on the same subject in an interview at the decade's end, will show how radically Pound's thought changed during the thirties. In an article published in September 1930 and entitled "Joyce, Historically (and Censorship)," Pound said of his friend: "HE is a realist. He doesn't believe that 'life' would be completely charming if we outlawed vivisection or instituted a new economic system. He presents things as they *are*." At the end of the decade, Pound would sometimes refuse to talk

[2] Pound, *Selected Poems,* viii.

to people unless they were willing to discuss economics. In a shipboard interview that Pound gave upon arriving in New York on 20 April 1939, he stated: "The men who are worth anything today are down on money – writing about money, the problem of money, exchange, gold, silver."[3] He went on to criticize Joyce's *Finnegan's Wake* as "retrogression." In the intervening years, Pound had decidedly changed his views.

But in 1930 he was still the complete man of letters: writer, instigator, poet, critic, editor, journalist, and propagandist. His reputation in Italy was at that time exclusively literary, as was his activity. In the *Belvedere* interview, Francesco Monotti had introduced him as follows:

> Ezra Pound, without doubt the greatest contemporary American poet, is gifted with prodigious energy. Besides his many volumes of poetry . . . he was also the dominant element in the formation of two artistic–literary schools which had fame and worldwide influence: that of the "vorticists" and that of the "imagists." T. S. Eliot and James Joyce are only the most famous writers who owe him their initial discovery.

A translation of Pound's article "How to Read" was printed in the 20 February and 20 March 1930 issues of *L'Indice*. Apart from being recognized as a literary *pezzo grosso* ("big shot") by the Italians, his views were gaining acceptance in Italian literary circles. Pound's praise in that article of the forcefulness and modernity of early Italian poetry of the *dolce stil nuovo* evidently had some impact. In the 20 April 1930 issue of *L'Indice,* in the cartoon feature "Letteratissimi d'Oggi" (roughly "superwriters of today"), there is a drawing of three men sitting around a table and the caption: "Have you heard? There's no difference between us and the 'Stil Nuovo.' " – "As for me, I would never write a nasty little sonnet as simple as the one of Dante for Beatrice"(tr).

Apart from his direct contributions to the paper, Pound's opinions were starting to influence several of its contributors, and *L'Indice* became the first journal to introduce British and American modernism systematically to Italy. Francesco Monotti's regular column, "Semaforo" ("Stoplight"), began in 1931 to concern itself with James Joyce, Richard Aldington, George Antheil, and Wyndham Lewis. Articles by Pound disciples Louis Zukofsky and Basil Bunting started to appear that same year in translation in *L'Indice*. One by Bunting "Contemporary English Writers" expressed the opinion that as long as Eliot had remained American, he had been the most influential and, in a limited sense, perhaps the best English language poet, but since the day he became an English gentleman, afraid of offending the sensibilities of other English gentlemen, he had published nothing of value. Bunting went on to say that Pound's *Cantos* and Joyce's *Ulysses* were the most important literary

---

[3] Norman, *Ezra Pound*, 358.

events in years. Robert McAlmon wrote a satirical piece on Gertrude Stein that began: "Gertrude Stein, monument of ancient Sumeria" and went on to quote both Miss Stein – "Yes indeed, jews have given Humanity only three creative geniuses: Christ, Spinoza, ME" – and her brother Leo – "I discovered Picasso and kept his pictures in the studio for a good two years before Gertrude began to think that a certain quality emanated from them" (tr). Pound may have left London and Paris, but it was business as usual, literary and otherwise, and his feuds continued, if only by proxy.

Other articles by or about his friends appeared in *L'Indice*. The tactics of literary propaganda that had served Pound so well in London and Paris were brought into play in Genoa: gaining editorial influence with a small magazine, securing writing assignments for his friends, encouraging *les jeunes,* promoting the work he felt to be important, and getting his circle to promote his own work. His methods are familiar. Edmondo Dodsworth, who, along with Lina Caico, was a new Italian disciple, wrote on Henry Adams, a recent Pound enthusiasm. There was a two-part article on Picasso by Jean Cocteau, an article, "Memory of W. H. Hudson," by Ford Maddox Hueffer, and translations of Hudson, Henry James, and some of Pound's poetry, including a version of Canto VIII by F. Carnevali. Occasional conversations with Pound were also recorded in the paper. When asked about Sinclair Lewis, who had just been awarded the Nobel Prize for literature, Pound remarked: "The books of Sinclair Lewis are realistic portraits of bourgeois life in thousands of American towns." "We weren't able to drag even a half word more out of him," reported the columnist.

Pound's ambition for *L'Indice* and Italy can be seen in an exchange between him and editor Gino Saviotti that was printed in full in the issue of 10 May 1931. Saviotti began:

> Given that in matters of foreign art I am much less competent than you, I'll make you an offer. I'll completely entrust you with the guidance of *L'Indice* in all that concerns foreign contributions. Do you accept? We'll start a special section (a page, a half-page), we'll call it what you want, you'll fill it as you wish, inviting the writers and contributors yourself. (tr)

Pound's response was printed right below that invitation, along with a notice asking for volunteers for the rather grand project he had in mind:

> I accept. I cannot produce a fortnightly bulletin of foreign writing all by myself, but I can at least insist on a little seriousness. . . .
> I do not know how much work you are asking of me. . . . There are, or there must be, young men (or kind young women, beautiful or ugly) to help.

If you cannot find translators, it will be a bad sign, not to be taken lightly, for contemporary Italy (or Genoa). Anyway, let's openly insert an advertisement:

EZRA POUND asks for the help of 25 translators with foreign news that he judges useful for the development of cheer or acceleration of Italian literary life of this year, year IX, or 1931 old calendar. They can write directly to E.P., via Marsala 12 apartment 5 Rapallo, indicating how much work they are willing to do, and which languages they know. (tr)

Translation had always played an important role in Pound's theory of literature.[4] It was a way of "conquering" another country's literature for your own, and it was a form of literature in its own right, as he emphatically states in "How to Read." Pound was following a familiar pattern here, almost by rote. He was attempting to create a vortex in Genoa, trying to ensure that the most important works of contemporary English, American, and French literature gained currency in Italy. He was replaying his part of missionary and preceptor of modernism and final arbiter of international literary standards, the part he had played before in London and Paris. And he plunged into the task with all of his very considerable energy. A note appended to the above announcement indicates that the type had not been set before Pound was off to Paris to round up writers:

Like the dynamic man he is, while waiting for responses, Pound took the train for Paris where he is already gathering material. He wrote us that he has already secured the collaboration with L'Indice of the principal writers "not corpses" of today, among whom are Joyce, Cocteau, De Chirico, etc. Needless to say, we are very satisfied with this. (tr)

The vortex had moved to Rapallo.

Clearly, not everyone would react well to Pound's brashness. His friend Manlio Dazzi advised him in a letter shortly thereafter that what he was in effect saying was that " 'you Italians do not know what is good, I will inform you, I will go to Paris and find out, 15 unknowns will help me, I do not know who they are, but we will create masterpieces.' I confess that this does not go over very well, neither with me nor with many others" (tr). Dazzi's advice was good. Pound had already started to make enemies in Italian literary circles.

---

[4] Translation was also important to the New Age. Orage wrote: "I cannot help thinking that it is better for a nation to 'import' art than to go without it altogether; and, in fact, it is the duty of its critics to stimulate homeproduction by importing as many as possible of the best foreign models (New Age, 30 Sept. 1920, 319).

III

Pound's own original contributions to *L'Indice* form an important segment of his literary criticism. They are wholly literary – Pound did not begin his Italian political and economic polemics until 1937 – and contain valuable reminiscences of his days in London and Paris, as well as a record of his then-current concerns. They are also audacious, in a way that only Pound could be. For Pound had decided that he was going to teach the Italians to write their own language! This despite the fact that his own Italian, though good, used English rather than Italian sentence structure. He also decided that Italian literature needed to become more international in ambition but that at the same time it needed to avoid overdependence on French literature. All very bold for a man who had lived in Italy for only six years.

Pound began his series of "Jottings" ("Appunti") for *L'Indice* with an article, "Le Mystere Cocteau" (5 May 1930), that called for international standards in art. He stated: "Fear or envy of a foreigner comes from an inferiority complex. . . . There is a kind of supremacy in literature. The dominant race is that which absorbs. I say *absorb*, I don't say digest." He praised Cocteau as "worth all of the French Academy in 1930" and called Paul Valery a "so-so writer." The key to an English translation of French, he said, was "to eliminate 10–30% of the words" (tr).

Pound's first numbered "jotting" was entitled "Letter to a Translator" (October 1930). In it he compared Italian and English and attempted to encourage in Italian the concision he championed in English prose. All of this was according to a familiar program, to which some local variations were added. He was full of advice for writing effective Italian prose:

> When translating me, do not look for elegance. Do not be afraid of harshness. . . .
> It is not enough to say that the English language is more "concise" than Italian. Every translation must be more concise than the original. . . . There are ways of condensing proper to Italian. Naturally a foreigner cannot conduct such a reinvigoration of the language: there is need for a native speaker. (tr)

He insisted that to produce a vigorous Italian prose, Italian had to stay away from French, which he felt was overly manipulated. From these articles it is clear that Pound had great hopes for the future of Italian writing and wished to have the same impact in literary Italy that he had already enjoyed in London and Paris. His criticism alternates between castigation of Italian cultural isolation and recollection of the glories of the Italian literary and cultural past. Since Pound did have a thorough grounding in Italian literary history, he was able to speak with some authority:

> I believe that every reinvigoration of Italian must come from Latin: Caesar, Tacitus, Ovid (not Horace, whose writing is contorted).
>
> I was reading some selections from d'Annunzio last year in a magazine that I have only seen once. There one discovered the mature d'Annunzio, abandoning the exuberance and Africanism of his famous works, searching for the *latinitatem,* arousing envy in whoever writes in a language more distant from Latin.

Pound's writings for *L'Indice* are too numerous and important to be discussed exhaustively here, but some indication of their range is useful. They contain prescriptions for a contemporary fiction, the history of *moeurs contemporaines* that he valued in Henry James. They also contain strictures about the interminable sentences of Italian prose style: "Dear fellows and colleagues, 93% of the printed matter in Italy is completely unreadable because it is all written in a dead cadence, but DEEEAAAD, dead in the tradition. Even brave and clever futurists fall back into this grey mud from time to time" (tr). Finally, they often contain reminiscence:

> Of the burlesque songs that Joyce used to sing, one stanza in particular is worthy of memory:
>
> Are judges on the bench compelled to wear
> A night gown and a bag wig made
> Of someone else's hair?
> They got that toilet
> From Pontius Pilate
> Said Mr. Dooley, etc.

Pound's criticism for *L'Indice* was very much the kind that he advocated in his essay "How to Read," but with an Italian accent. It provided a kind of workshop for putting his advice in "How to Read" into practice.

"How to Read" first appeared as a series for the *New York Herald Tribune Books* in 1929 and was reprinted as a booklet in London in 1931. Along with its expanded version, the *ABC of Reading,* which appeared as a book in 1934, it is Pound's most influential critical work. It had considerable impact on American New Criticism and is still widely read. "How to Read" marks a transition in Pound's activity, the transition from Pound the poet and critic to Pound the pamphleteer.

Although the essay claims to be the distillation of "twenty-seven years' thought on the subject" of various literatures and indeed focuses on the results of that thought, it is remarkable from our viewpoint in that it represents Pound's first systematic attempt to define the role of art in a well-ordered state, based upon a Confucian model.[5] Pound states that "the individual cannot think and communicate his thought, the governor and legislator cannot act effectively or frame laws, without words, and the solidity and validity of these words is in the care of the damned and despised *litterati*."[6]

The basis of the social order for Pound's Confucius is in precise verbal definition. When language becomes imprecise, according to Pound, society disintegrates. Conversely, when language, polished by the genius of Homer or Dante or Shakespeare, reaches a maximum of clarity, the particular society in which such writers live will thrive. This idea marks an important turning point for Pound. He had previously felt some obligation to justify his activity as an artist, but only in terms that provided a clear space in which to pursue his work. Now he felt a need to explain how the writer contributes to the functioning of the state. And the justification he arrived at, with the help of Confucius, was one that took as its highest good the well-regulated state. Although Pound still insisted that the method of study he recommended in "How to Read" "would be entirely independent of consideration as to whether the given passage tended to make the student a better republican, monarchist, monist, dualist, rotarian, or other sectarian"[7] (in other words, that the method had no partisan ideological aim), he had abandoned his previous belief that art was a self-justifying activity. Confronted by the war and his response to it, Pound could no longer maintain his belief in the individual genius, "favored of the gods," who was superior to the society in which he lived.

IV

Pound's discovery of the work of Leo Frobenius in 1929 aided his transition from the world of art to the world of politics and economics. Frobenius's concept of *paideuma,* the total (or, in Pound's usage, totalitarian) expression of any culture manifested in all of its forms, gave Pound an intellectual underpinning for his new inquiries into economics. In a statement that reveals the new direction his own interests were taking, Pound remarked sarcastically about Frobenius that "his most annoying tendency is to believe that bad art indicates something more than just bad art."[8] In other words, by analyzing the art of a given time and culture

---

[5] Pound, "How to Read" (1929), in *Literary Essays,* 39.

[6] Ibid., 21. Orage had written in a similar way about the social function of writers in the *New Age:* "A democracy is governed by words, all human government, in fact, is logocracy" (2 Mar. 1916, 421).

[7] Pound, "How to Read" (1929), in *Literary Essays,* 19.

[8] Pound, "Murder by Capital" (July 1933), in *Selected Prose,* 227.

one can also discern the nature of that culture's economic system; in a period in which good art prevails, good economics will also prevail, and, conversely, in a period during which bad economic thought and practice prevail, bad art will also prevail. The study of Frobenius allowed Pound to unify his two chief concerns, synergistically augmenting the psychic energy he was able to devote to both. Pound thus arrived at a new understanding of the notion of taste, a unity of the aesthetic and the economic, as represented by the following remark, commixing the two fields: "In that barocco was lost the distinction between usury and par-taggio [a fair interest rate, a share]."[9] We find a clearer expression of this in the *Cantos*:

> you have seen a good deal of
> the evidence, not knowing it evidence, in monumentum
> look about you, look, if you can, at St. Peter's . . .
> Wanting TAXES to build St. Peter's, thought Luther beneath
> civil notice,
> 1527. Thereafter art thickened. Thereafter design went to
> hell,
> Thereafter barocco, thereafter stone-cutting desisted. (*C*, XL, 234)

This idea of *paideuma,* although of use as a heuristic, is of dubious validity as the basis of a prescription for social action; nevertheless, it was of great utility to Pound. That unity of culture he discerned, although it may have been true for the Renaissance court at, say, Urbino, cannot be said to be true for larger and more complex cultures, except at the highest level of abstraction, for example, when we speak of the unity of a culture during a decade such as the twenties in the United States.

Pound's *Cantos* demonstrate the particular evolution in his thinking that I am referring to. The entire group of middle cantos (XXXI–LXXIII) emphasizes his political and economic ideas, very much at odds with the prevailing poetic interest in the lyric during this time. This middle group of cantos has given some trouble to critics, who seem disposed to skip over it. This is understandable, for by training and tradition (and em-barrassment over this whole period in Pound's life), literary scholars have not been prepared to deal with, or were not very comfortable about, Pound's vision of political economy, at least until quite recently.[10] None-theless, Pound himself gave those cantos prominence in his edition of the *Selected Cantos*.

Pound was very conscious of his own change from literature to economics.

---

[9] Pound, "The Individual in His Milieu" (Oct. 1935), in *Selected Prose,* 274.
[10] Emery's book *Ideas into Action* is an early exception.

> You might put the question in the following form: What drives, or what can drive a man interested almost exclusively in the arts into social theory or into a study of the "gross material aspects" videlicet economic aspects of the present? What causes the ferocity and bad manners of revolutionaries?[11]

In the same essay he confesses that his previous notion, that economic problems could be solved for the artist without regard for the common man, was mistaken, and he offers an apology.[12] Although still believing that "the effects of social evil show first in the arts,"[13] he has clearly evolved toward a more comprehensive view about the inevitability of economics: "No thoughtful man can in our time avoid trying to arrange those things in his own mind in an orderly fashion."[14] Pound wrote: "I, personally, know of no social evil that cannot be cured, or very largely cured, economically."[15] He invoked tradition to defend his shift of emphasis: "The diseased periphery of letters is now howling that literature, and poetry in especial, should keep within bounds . . . leaving untackled a great deal of the subject matter that interested such diverse writers as Propertius, Dante and Lope de Vega."[16] Pound had not changed the members of his pantheon, but clearly he was seeing them differently. As to ferocity and bad manners, Pound's writing and radio speeches show that he shared them with other revolutionaries. He also shared some of their motivating forces: compassion and a hunger for social and economic justice.

V

The gradual prominence of a statal sense in Pound's poetry begins in Cantos XXXI–XXXIII, which were published in the July–September 1931 issue of *Pagany*. Although primarily adapted from the writings of Thomas Jefferson, they include other materials, for instance, part of a speech made by Senator Smith Brookhart against the nomination of Eugene Meyer to the Federal Reserve Board:

> put into the mouths of the directors of the Federal Reserve
> banks the words they should say . . . "You have got more
> than your share, we want you to reduce, we can not let
> you have any more." (*C*, XXX, 164)

---

[11] Pound, "Murder by Capital" (July 1933), in *Selected Prose*, 228.
[12] Ibid., 230.
[13] Ibid., 229.
[14] Pound, *ABC of Economics* (1933), in *Selected Prose*, 247–8.
[15] Pound, "Murder by Capital" (July 1933), in *Selected Prose*, 229.
[16] Pound, "The Individual in His Milieu" (Oct. 1935), in *Selected Prose*, 272.

What Pound refers to here is the fact that in 1930, after pursuing an inflationary policy for several years, the board abruptly cut back the supply of money, a move that some economists believe was a principal cause of the Depression. Pound received a copy of the speech from Senator Bronson Cutting and wrote to him on 20 March 1931:

> Thanks for the Congressional Record of 28 ult. Brookhart's speech against Meyer seems to me very important. Have long thought Wilson wrecked the govt. but lacked detailed information. There is no reason the Federal Reserve Board shd. be a private instrument of the executive. . . . That effectively bitches the Jeffersonian system. Destroys balance between execut. judic. and legislature.

Pound's politics were beginning to creep into his poetry.

Cantos XXXI–XXXIII are arranged to show the multifaceted mind (*polumetis*) of Thomas Jefferson, but they are also arranged thematically to show how revolutions succeed but then fall into decline. Pound employs examples from American, French, and Russian prerevolutionary and postrevolutionary history to illustrate his theme, but he also uses Jefferson to take a few swipes, by implication, at contemporary Europe: "English papers . . . their lies" (*C*, XXXI, 154), and "the cannibals of Europe are eating one another again" (*C*, XXXII, 159). One isolated phrase occurs in Canto XXXIII that may indicate that Pound was reevaluating his position: "Litterae nihil sanantes" (*C*, XXXIII, 161) ("Literature curing nothing"). Pound typically puts his more private feelings into a foreign language (this has been noted especially in the Pisan Cantos), so the phrase deserves close attention. Perhaps literature could cure, or at least diagnose. Perhaps it could not.

Pound had previously used the technique of extended quotation found in the Jefferson Cantos. It first appears in Cantos VIII–XI, the Malatesta Cantos, which concern the life of Sigismundo Malatesta, another man whom Pound called "*polumetis*" (*C*, IX, 36). There too he relies extensively on primary historical documents, "canto as cento" as noted by William Chace.[17] The tie between Malatesta and Jefferson is further emphasized by the opening of Canto XXXI: "Tempus loquendi, / Tempus tacendi" (*C*, XXXI, 153). "A time to speak, a time to keep silent," Malatesta's personal motto,[18] is inscribed on the tomb of Isotta degli Atti, his mistress and third wife. Pound also relies on this technique in Cantos XXIV–XXVI. He will employ it most extensively in the later thirties, in his Chinese and Adams Cantos. Apart from its obvious value in conveying the flavor of the life and times of a historical personage, the technique of montage acts as a projective device for Pound's psyche.

---

[17] Chace, 50.
[18] Terrell, 120.

Through his choice of passages to include, he both consciously and unconsciously reveals his concerns of the moment, without having to articulate them fully to himself. What these Jefferson Cantos show is the extent to which Pound's mind had started to become preoccupied with political and economic topics.

Beginning in Cantos XXXI through XXXIII, and growing clearer in the remaining cantos of that group of "Eleven New Cantos" published in 1934, a new theme emerges. Lloyd G. Reynolds defines it as a realization that "the progress of culture depends on the health or sickness of the economy, which in turn depends largely on the monetary system."[19] This new awareness of the relation between economics and culture derives from the work of Leo Frobenius, as we saw. Pound in Cantos XXXI–XXXIII, though, has not as yet fully arrived at this theme, nor will it be completely realized until the next group, "The Fifth Decad of Cantos," is published in 1937. There is also in these middle cantos a growing statal sense, an admiration for those just rulers and statesmen who have exemplified, as Jefferson and John Adams did, an understanding of how a fair economic system is a component of a well-ordered state. These ideas dominate Pound's poetry of the thirties. In fact, this statal sense is one key difference between early and middle cantos.

VI

Although Pound did not ignore politics during this period, he was not yet obsessed by it. There are occasional references to political and economic subjects in his correspondence of 1930 and 1931. Certainly the First World War was still on his mind when he wrote in April of 1930 to the editor of the *Hound and Horn* about the "scandal of the Mertons."[20] According to Pound, the war was prolonged unnecessarily because "traders on both sides were selling 'necessities' to the neutrals with the knowledge or intentional ignorance that these necessities would help the other side go on fighting" (ddp). Scandals and revelations concerning war profiteers were common then, and this letter shows that Pound shared in the general outrage. In the same letter he goes on to say: "THE SANE METHOD OF STUDYING HISTORY consists (or wd. if it were ever practiced, consist) in learning what certain great protagonists intended, and to what degree they failed in forcing their program on the masses" (ddp). This thinking is characteristic of Pound's literary criticism: His vision of art, as espoused in "How to Read,"

---

[19] Reynolds, 394.

[20] "The Australian firm of Merton was caught, in 1914, cheerfully selling lead to Germany at half the price it was selling to England," Pound wrote in "Jews and the War: 1940," in *Il Meridiano di Roma,* 24 Mar. 1940.

depends upon "the masters" and "the inventors" who shape
for others. By transferring his canons of judgment from art t
Pound was able to move confidently into an entirely new fie
But Pound was not yet ready to concede that the artist shou
involved in politics. In another letter to the editor of the *Houn*
attacking Nicholas Butler, chairman of the Executive Comm
Carnegie Endowment for Peace,[21] as well as the press, war profiteers,
copyright laws, article 211, passports, and the Eighteenth Amendment,
he stated:

> There are points, a very limited number, at which the government, or
> rather the misgovernment, of a country becomes the affair of an author.
> . . . So long as laws are made with even mediocre sense, a writer shd.
> stick to his composition as hermetically as an inventing chemist sticks
> to his laboratory. (ddp)

I would like to stress here that these topics, on which Pound wrote fairly
frequently during this period, did not represent as yet a commitment to
politics on Pound's part. Instead, Pound was responding to certain actions
by governments or bureaucracies that impinged upon his sensibility or
freedom as an artist. Pound himself insisted that his campaign about these
matters was "civic not political,"[22] and I think that we should accept his
distinction. I take *civic* to mean an area of concern where a political action
has an impact on an individual's life and livelihood (e.g., the concern a
merchant would have for parking regulations around his store), rather
than a wider concern for the system of government as a whole, taken in
a more abstract and disinterested sense. Pound's civic sense foreshadowed
a broader political interest to come.

Pound had begun correspondence with several members of both the
Senate and the House of Representatives. Asked for the names of the
literate members of the Senate, Senator Cutting responded to Pound's
request on 9 December 1930: "Borah and Norris and LaFollette and
Hiram Johnson and Tydings and Wheeler and Walsh of Montana and I
suppose Dwight Morrow and not much else. But don't say that I said
so." Pound's correspondence with several of these men was to give him
the illusion of having influence in the political affairs of the United States,

---

[21] Andrew Carnegie's peace efforts were an occasional target of the *New Age*. Referring
to the massacre at Homestead that he instigated and the opening of the Palace of Peace
in the Netherlands, Orage wrote: "Last week this building at the Hague was opened
with some pomp and circumstance and Mr. Carnegie, the Homestead butcher, was
decorated. . . . if the Carnegie type wants international peace, it can secure it. We may
feel the grim irony, but there can be little doubt of the power of international finance
to prevent war if it is so minded" (4 Sept. 1913, 531).
[22] Stock, 282.

an illusion that was shattered when he visited Washington, D.C., in 1939.

H. L. Mencken was a frequent correspondent and was not shy about speaking up. On 13 January 1931, in a response to an article that Pound sent him, he was both acerbic and telling in his criticism:

> If I printed this it would disgrace you. There is not an idea in it that has not been hashed together so carelessly that it is simply devoid of effect. You are talking of an imaginary United States. Come back and take a look, and you will do the thing all over, and in an entirely different way. . . .
>
> The show over here is the best in the world. A hundred million morons are trying to erect a civilization – and failing appallingly. But is it dull to look at them? Then it is dull to see a hanging. I put in a month at Los Angeles, the worst large city in the world. I came away delighted.

Mencken's point was well taken. To an increasing degree, Pound was addressing an imaginary United States, one that he had left behind twenty-three years earlier. He had missed the growth of the United States as a world power, he had missed its participation in the war, and he had missed the cosmopolitan and prosperous twenties. America had changed a great deal while Pound remained in Europe.

VII

Rapallo was proving a congenial place to work, and his activities in 1931 were primarily literary. His articles for *L'Indice* appeared as frequently as twice a month and must have kept him busy. A letter to A. Hyatt Mayor in October of 1931 told of work on Cantos XXXVI–XL and boasted of the success of *L'Indice*. In its second year, its circulation increased to 12,000 and 13,000, "AND the readers appear to think about what one writes for them." It was a productive time for Pound.

Yet as 1931 progressed, there was a growing realization that the economic depression would not be a transitory phenomenon and that it was having worldwide repercussions. There is the beginning of a shift to the political and economic in Pound's work as 1931 drew to a close. In a long letter to Senator Cutting of 9 October he recommended shortening the work week and maintaining the same weekly wage through government subsidy. He was reading Marx's *Capital*, which had just appeared in an Italian translation, and he commented to Cutting: "I wonder really whether anyone in America has taken the trouble to detach Marx's tenth chapter from the rest of his sometimes indefinite writing." Pound's continuing study of economics was beginning to assume more relevance to contemporary events.

Pound's edition of Guido Cavalcanti's *Rime* appeared in January of 1932. It had originally been scheduled for publication by a British firm in the late twenties, but the firm failed. Pound remained bitter over the failure for many years. As he wrote to T. S. Eliot on 6 April 1935: "God knows the bloody britons have robbed me. And god knows I was induced to spend a lot of money on that Cavalcanti; thru yr/ good will and thru being double crossed by Dela Mare." Thus he had one more grudge against the British. He did manage to rescue the fifty-six pages printed by the British publisher, and the edition was completed by the Marsano publishing company of Genoa – "an edition pieced together among the ruins" (tr) he called it.

Pound was proud of his accomplishment of seeing the Cavalcanti into print. His graduate training at the University of Pennsylvania had been in Romance philology. In 1932 he submitted the work to that university in lieu of a doctoral thesis, but they declined to award the Ph.D. because he had not fulfilled all of the requirements.[23] The most unusual feature of the edition was its photographic plates, which reproduced sample pages from many manuscripts. As he wrote to H. B. Lathrop on 16 December 1931: "The edtn. ought to serve as a START for a new method of handling international texts."[24]

The critical reception of Pound's edition was mixed, ranging from approbation to scorn. Etienne Gilson, the distinguished French medievalist, called it a "magnificent edition," and wrote: "I fully realize what a claim he [the editor] has on the gratitude of his readers."[25] Gilson could not determine who the editor was from the book: The edition lists only the initials "E. P." Mario Praz had better information about what was going on in Italian publishing circles. In another contemporary review, he was less enthusiastic:

> It seems to me that it was Bertram [*sic*] Russell who said one time to illustrate certain extraordinary combinations of the universe, that if 12 monkeys proceeded for centuries to strike at random as many typewriters, one fine day a sonnet from Shakespeare would emerge. In the case of *Cavalcanti* by Ezra Pound this seems the method employed, even if the result is not as satisfying.[26]

The review is so excessively negative that one suspects that Praz was striking at Pound for the excessive and brash didacticism that he employed to introduce Italians to modernist literature in the literary pages of *L'Indice*.

---

[23] Ibid., 300.
[24] Pound, *Selected Letters*, 237.
[25] *Criterion*, Oct. 1932.
[26] Reprinted in Mario Praz, *Cronache letterarie anglosassoni*, 4 vols. (Rome, 1950–66), 1:175ff.

Pound's ideas underwent a transition during the First World War, and he became increasingly concerned during the twenties about social and political issues, but his own activity during this time was predominantly literary, not political, in nature. "How to Read" marks another transition, in that Pound felt impelled to seek a social justification for art, but Pound's activities in 1930 and 1931 follow patterns that are familiar from his London and Paris days. He was a loyal follower of Douglas, but he had not yet discovered Gesell, whose ideas would provide a practical mechanism with which to implement Social Credit's basic program. The Depression had begun, but it had not yet reached its worst point, and its effects were still moderate in Europe. Pound had been accepted by the Italian intellectual community, but for his literary, not his political or economic, interests. We can conclude that Pound was ready for a radical shift in his activity, the shift from poet to pamphleteer, but that the shift had not yet occurred. Pound in 1930 and 1931 was still very much the man of letters, the writer and critic who was on the threshold of change, but for whom change had not yet come.

4

The Turn to Fascism

I

In the early thirties Pound was eager to engage with anyone interested in discussing economic issues, and although he still continued to do articles on contemporary literature, his new direction was apparent as he took to chiding writers in reviews for their ignorance of contemporary economics. One of Pound's new correspondents was Monsignor Pietro Pisani, titular archbishop of Costanza of Scizia and assistant to the Papal Throne. Pound was interested in canonical doctrine about economics and sent Pisani books, pamphlets, and clippings. Pisani evinced the polite curiosity of a high church official, but he did answer Pound's questions about medieval church economic doctrines. Pound also sent him a copy of his *Rime* of Cavalcanti, and he was delighted when Pisani in turn presented it to the pope. In Italy, at least, he was recognized for his work.

Pound continued his correspondence with American politicians. Senator Bronson Cutting wrote to Pound on 23 January 1932 to report on the failure of the copyright bill, which the senator had supported. When Pound responded on 11 February, his interest in the bill was perfunctory: "*Yes.* I had observed from rept/ of Copyrt/ Com/ that the extent of the proposed act was already somewhat in excess of the four words applied to the matter in the King James version." His real interest was revealed in the rest of the letter. There he spoke of the imbecility of the dole and the pressing need to reduce the work day to four hours and implement public works programs, citing favorably as evidence that the work day in Moscow was reported to be five and a half hours and that fascism was "*arranging* that people be kept employed. . . . May be paternalism but very intelligent use of it." Pound was beginning to think that the world's problems had progressed far beyond literary transgressions of "thou shalt not steal" or the idiocy of the passport regulations. In a March letter he warned Cutting about "going down with that rotten boat . . . the successive shitpails/ Harding, Coolidge and Hoover," adding that "not even the infinite and bootlicking patience of the American citoyen CAN be expected to reinstate" the Republican party.

Of course, Hoover lost badly to Roosevelt in November. H. L. Mencken was delighted and wrote on 26 November: "For some reason or other the fellow is unbearably offensive to me. . . . Roosevelt is a weak sister, but he'll be better than Hoover. I look for a circus during the next year or two." The American economic situation was growing rapidly worse. Mencken wrote a month later: "The United States begins the new year in the depths of despair. I have never seen anything more astounding or amusing. Even the Rotarians begin to admit there can be such things as bad times." Pound's attitude toward Roosevelt was guardedly optimistic. During Roosevelt's first months in office, Pound wrote: "Early in March the President published a vol. admitting about half of what I had written."[1] The half he did not admit to knowing was the Douglas "clog" principle: "The discrepancy between distributed power to purchase needed goods produced and producible is cumulative. Under the present system 'every industry creates a mass of prices faster than it creates the power to buy.' "[2] But Pound had words of praise and hope for the new president:

> Until we get clear recognition of these points from the President, any one is perfectly free to argue that his present policy is just one more inflationary wheeze and that the old wire danglers have sold dollars short, laid in stocks of foreign currency, etc.
>
> At any rate he has introduced a new terminology and several new concepts into the circle of scoundrels and cannon feeders, pimps assembled in London and calling itself an Economic Conference.[3]

From his comment on the "old wire danglers," we can see that Pound was already starting to subscribe to a conspiracy theory of economics, that people were manipulating the economy for their own profit. His comment about selling dollars short was to prove prophetic, though, when Roosevelt later devalued the dollar, a move Pound complained about vociferously. But at the beginning, he was willing to give the new president a chance.

II

By this time, Pound had begun serious work on economics, starting his *ABC of Economics* in February of 1933. And, further evidence

---

[1] *New Democracy*, 25 Aug. 1933. Roosevelt's book was entitled *On Our Way*.

[2] *New Democracy*, 25 Aug. 1933.

[3] Ibid. I have refrained from marking Pound's text with the conventional *sic* here and throughout this book because it would become hopelessly distracting for the reader, as will be seen.

of the perspicacity of Italians (or at least of his growing connections in Italy), he was invited to give a series of ten lectures on economics at the Luigi Bocconi University, "an economics and commercial university in Milan."[4] The *ABC* was published by Faber & Faber in April; its dust jacket notes that "Mr. Ezra Pound was asked to deliver ten lectures in an Italian university – on economics, not on the mummified muses."[5] That blurb certainly sounds like it was written by Pound, so we may take it as indicating his new attitude.

Pound's increasing celebrity in Italy was both reflected and enhanced by his meeting with Mussolini on 30 January 1933. When the audience was granted, news of it was printed on the front page of the Rapallo newspaper, *Il Mare*, ("Pound da Mussolini") and it certainly gave him further status in the town. The meeting had a decisive effect upon Pound. By most contemporary accounts, Benito Mussolini was an immensely charming man, but his effect on Pound goes beyond charm. He was overwhelmed by the Italian dictator, as his subsequent references show. In Canto XLI:

> "MA QVESTO,"
>   said the Boss, "è divertente."
>   catching the point before the aesthetes had got
>   there;
>   Having drained off the muck by Vada
> From the marshes, by Circeo, where no one else wd. have
>   drained it.
> Waited 2000 years, ate grain from the marshes:
> Water supply for ten million, another one million "*vani*"
> that is rooms for people to live in.
>   XI of our era. (*C*, XLI, 202)

Pound stresses Mussolini's quick grasp of the essentials of a situation, in this case the *Cantos*. The occasion of the above remark was Pound's visit to the Palazzo Venezia in Rome, which was granted to Pound after many previous requests for an audience had been denied. Pound sent ahead to *il Duce* a copy of his first thirty cantos, and Mussolini was looking at them when Pound was ushered into his presence. It is easy to speculate on Pound's excitement about this momentous occasion and about the opportunity he believed it might give him to have some influence on the Italian head of state. But for a busy politician it was merely one of perhaps a dozen appointments that afternoon, and an aide probably told Mussolini who Pound was and what was to be accomplished from the visit before handing him the copy of the *Cantos*, all just before Pound entered.

[4] Stock, 308.
[5] Ibid., 309.

What is the meaning of Mussolini's remark, "*Ma questo è divertente*"? It can be literally translated as "But this is amusing," but it also comes close to a more routine remark, as when the Italians say, "*Ti sei divertito?*" meaning "Did you have a nice time?" Is this, then, the point of the *Cantos,* that they are "amusing"? One begins to distrust Pound's perception here, since he seems eager to belittle his own work to illustrate the quickness and essential correctness of Mussolini's judgment. There is another explanation for the comment, told by Pound to William McNaughton at St. Elizabeths years later. It seems that when Pound entered the reception hall, Mussolini was with a pretty young lady, who was teaching him English. When he came across a passage in the *Cantos* in which one of Pound's characters was speaking in a dialect, he asked what it was about. Pound explained, and Mussolini laughed and called it *divertente,* evidently the correct response, at least for a dictator, as sanctioned by Pound himself.[6]

Our doubts about Pound's reaction to Mussolini are not assuaged by his further account of the meeting in *Jefferson and/or Mussolini.* "THE SECRET OF THE DUCE is possibly the capacity to pick out the element of immediate and major importance in any tangle; or, in the case of a man, to go straight to the centre, for the fellow's major interest. 'Why do you want to put your ideas in order?' "[7] Mussolini's question came after Pound, explaining his work in economics, had mentioned that he wished to put his ideas in order. Mussolini's reply must strike us as pedestrian at best, but for Pound it is yet another indication of the man's astonishing capacity. Pound's response to Mussolini's inquiry was "for my poem," but his willingness to diminish his own activity by omitting his response shows Pound's great need for belief.

Interior decorating offers further evidence: "The term 'gerarchia' [hierarchy] is perhaps the beginning of a critical sense, *vide* the four tiles and the dozen or so bits of insuperable pottery, pale blue on pale brownish ground, in the ante-room of the Palazzo Venezia."[8] This perception is in keeping with Pound's view of the "totalitarian" in culture, a term, it should be stressed, that he used in a special way, following Frobenius. All culture, in this view, is of a piece, and a culture with a just economic order will also excel in its art. A wise ruler will have, it follows, exquisite taste, and capacity for governance can be determined by considering the waiting room.

---

[6] "It was his rendition of a dialect Canto excerpt, from XVI by one account or from XXXV by another, that Mussolini had once pronounced 'divertente,' " according to Kenner, in *The Pound Era,* 540.

[7] Pound, *Jefferson and/or Mussolini,* 66.

[8] Ibid., 85.

Even more serious doubts about Pound's judgment occur in the next passage of Canto XLI, after the assessment of the *Cantos* as amusing:

> Story told by the mezzo-yit:
> That they were to have a consortium
> and one of the potbellies says:
>> "will come in for 12 million"
> And another: "three millyum for my cut";
> And another: "we will take eight";
> And the Boss said: "but what will you
>> DO with that money?"
> "But! but! signore, you do not ask a man
> what he will *do* with his money.
> That is a personal matter."
> And the Boss said: "but what will you do?
> You won't really need all that money
> because you are all for the *confine*." (*C*, XLI, 202)

The *confino* was the fascist punishment for political dissidents and consisted of exile to a remote village or island. "Mezzo-yit" means half-Jew and is certainly derogatory. Terrell believes that the storyteller shares Pound's view of these businessmen,[9] and I think that he is correct, since he has related the story with such relish. Pound retells it, with Mussolini's sadism intact, with obvious gusto, and although the point of the story may be that swift justice saved the state millions, it nevertheless confirms us in our view that Pound's judgment is distorted. He seems to enjoy the dictator's toying with his victims: The whole point of the story is that Mussolini knows in advance that he will send them into confinement in a remote rural village. Pound's vicarious pleasure in Mussolini's sudden and arbitrary exercise of power is disturbing.

The reasons for Pound's exaggerated esteem of Mussolini are not easy to see. Fredric Jameson calls it manifest hero worship,[10] and it certainly is at least that. As I mentioned, Mussolini was an enormously charismatic man, and at this time (and up until Italy's entry into the Second World War) there was overwhelming popular support for him in Italy. Pound himself goes on to portray this devotion in Canto XLI: "'Noi ci facciam sgannar per Mussolini' / said the commandante della piazza" (*C*, XLI, 202), which Pound suggests means something like "we'd get scragged for Mussolini."[11]

I can almost see the need for Pound to believe that other people were "on the job," to use one of his favorite phrases, so that he could relax

---

[9] Terrell, 167.
[10] Jameson, 120.
[11] Pound, *Jefferson and/or Mussolini*, 27.

his efforts for the arts and for economic justice. This wish shows up in his letters from time to time in these years in another recurring phrase, "papa can't do everything." Pound was nearing fifty and perhaps felt his energy, prodigious as it was, beginning to flag. For whatever reason, and I do not wish to attempt a psychoanalytic interpretation here, though I suspect that a plausible one could be constructed, the figure of Mussolini is highly cathected[12] in Pound's psyche.[13]

Another factor in Pound's support of fascism arising from his visit to Mussolini was the illusion of effect that it gave to Pound. He could believe that he was not just another man of letters, remote from the circles of power, motivated by *ressentiment,* but a man working in the new medium, halfway between thought and action, that Lenin invented. Pound could believe, since he was consulted by the head of state, that he had influence. When he traveled to the United States in 1939, his attempt to see President Roosevelt failed; he saw instead Secretary of Agriculture (later Vice-President) Henry Wallace. But in Italy he could go to advise Mussolini; he could write to him about economic matters. His work was appearing less frequently in English and American journals, but in Italy he wrote with authority.

Devoting more and more of his time to political and economic causes, instead of to his art, Pound needed to be convinced of the success of his efforts; he had to sustain the illusion of having an effect. He repeatedly sought further interviews with Mussolini, though to no avail. Ironically, *il Duce* finally showed some interest in pursuing Pound's economic ideas in May of 1943, only a few months before his arrest and ouster by the Italian government. But his invitation to meet with Pound was sent to Pound's hotel in Rome after he had left for Rapallo, and soon it was too late.[14]

III

Around this time, Pound began to write articles about economics. He reviewed two books by Irving Fisher, a professor at Yale, for the *New English Weekly,* a journal founded by Orage after his return to

---

[12] I use this term in the precise sense in which it is employed in Freudian psychology, to indicate the concentration of psychic energy upon a given object, a process associated with primary narcissism. See Leland E. Hinsie and Robert Jean Campbell, *Psychiatric Dictionary,* 4th ed. (New York: Oxford University Press, 1970), 113–14.

[13] Some time after I wrote this, I had occasion once again to talk with Dr. Jerome Kavka, who was doing his residency in psychoanalysis at St. Elizabeths when Pound first was incarcerated there and who examined Pound. Dr. Kavka agreed that Mussolini was unusually important to Pound and noted that Pound was greatly traumatized by his death.

[14] Zapponi, 56.

England in 1932.[15] Pound was very enthusiastic about the first, *Stamp Scrip*, which recommended a way out of the world depression through an experiment that had first been conducted in the Austrian village of Woergl. A stamp equal to 1 percent of the value of the note had to be attached to all paper currency at the beginning of each month for it to retain its face value. The effect of this was to speed up the circulation of currency, because an unused note would either decline in value or be subject to a monthly tax. This Gesellist experiment worked until it was forbidden by the central bank.[16] Pound was less enthusiastic though still impressed by Fisher's other book, *Inflation?*. He was clearly encouraged by the fact that Fisher, "an authority to the point of being consulted by the President of my highly questionable country,"[17] apparently thought along the same lines he did.

There is evidence in the correspondence from this time of a growing rift between Pound and Douglas. Orage attempted to mediate between the two, admitting to Pound, in a letter of 15 February 1932: "The *weaknesses* of the Credit propaganda, which are indeed serious, are not due to the theory; but to the personnel and pitch of the exponents." But Pound, too, came under some criticism from Orage, who wrote, apparently about a draft of *The ABC of Economics*, on 3 July 1932:

> I think your style of writing is definitely – not intentionally of course – calculated to give the reader the impression that you are condescending to be explicit and explanatory as to bloody fools &, in the process, giving yourself damned real trouble other than that of spitting it out & getting it off your chest. And I think that its publication in any form, serial, pamphlet or book, would only result in a "curiosity" of literature which posterity on account of your poetry would read with delight but which your contemporaries would simply snort at.

Orage's criticism about Pound's economic writings remains accurate. Pound's prose is obscure and frequently refers rather than explains, although the difficulties clear up when his articles are read as a group. As to posterity's delight with his economic writings, that is another matter, though I do not believe that they are to be dismissed entirely.

Douglas wrote to Pound on 9 January 1933 about his pamphlet *The ABC of Economics*: "I have sent on your M.S. to Faber & Faber more or less without comment because I think that its appeal is more in its readability than its meticulous accuracy on technical points." Douglas, I believe, was simply trying to assert his own area of expertise here and

---

[15] Orage's return to political and economic journalism, and Pound's turn to them, coincide perfectly. Pound was to contribute almost two hundred items to the *New English Weekly* during the thirties.

[16] *New English Weekly*, 26 Oct. 1933.

[17] Ibid., 16 Nov. 1933.

did not actually have any technical objections to the work. Pound had written it "in ignorance of Gesell,"[18] an economic writer whom he was to discover shortly thereafter, and who would decisively influence his views.

Douglas was not happy with Pound's new interest in stamp scrip and Gesell but nonetheless wished to keep him within the fold. He wrote to him on 4 July 1933: "The real trouble about the Woergl scheme is what has happened to the Woergl scheme, which is another way of saying that the problem of reforming the financial system is not how to reform the financial system but how to strangle the bankers." Douglas had come to the same conclusion as Pound: that economic reform depended on political reform and the exercise of political power.

Aside from bankers, two other groups also drew Pound's ire: the press and munitions manufacturers. Sir Zenos Metevsky (Sir Basil Zaharoff), the notorious international arms merchant, shows up again in Canto XXXVIII, making profits on both sides of any conflict. In his first appearance in Canto XVIII, Pound wrote: "They ain't heard his name yet" (C, XVIII, 83). This time, however, he is known, and his activities are tied to the arms trade in general and to payoffs to the press in particular. During this period Pound was reading such books as *Mercanti di Cannoni*, *The Bloody Traffic*, and *L'Abominable Venalité de la Presse*, which provided him with many of his specifics about weapons manufacturers. Pound wrote about arms merchants and the press in an article, "Orientation and News Sense," where he also states: "Two countries [Italy and Russia] and *only* two have made any attempt to face modern reality,"[19] his admiration for Lenin competing with his admiration for Mussolini. "Correlating guns with profits," he wrote to Wyndham Lewis on 18 September 1933, was the first step in understanding the causes of war.

Pound and Douglas also disagreed about the value of Italian fascism. Pound wrote to him on 13 October 1933:

> I have been in this country for some time and I have seen with me own eyes. . . .
> I have also seen simple material phenomenon/ improved actual conditions/
> As to "where the money and ideas" etc. The MONEY, this from you!!! Ain't you heard of the printing press.

The remedy for depression and deflation was, simply speaking, for the government to issue money. Whether the money it issued should be borrowed or just printed and whether it should be put into circulation through social welfare or public works (though never through the pur-

---

[18] Pound, "The Individual in His Milieu" (Oct. 1935), in *Selected Prose*, 277.
[19] *New English Weekly*, 5 Jan. 1933.

chase of weapons) were secondary matters. Pound concluded: "The efficient value of an idea depends not only on its validity but on WHO
has it." Thus the need for a political program. His work on economics
and his meeting with Mussolini were beginning to coalesce.

Pound's concern with economic, political, and social issues was to
occupy him almost entirely for the next ten years. Although I think that
it is understandable, and probably appropriate, that in response to a
worldwide economic and political crisis a man of Pound's ability might
turn away from an exclusive concern with poetry, it is worth mentioning
the direction his poetry was taking when his change of interest occurred.
He had composed two operas, *Le Testament de François Villon* and *Cavalcanti* (the latter in the summer of 1932), and had begun to explore
seriously the relation of poetry to music. Certainly Olga Rudge had some
influence on this new direction, as undoubtedly did his friend George
Antheil and the musical activity that had its beginning in the lively
Parisian concert world. In a letter of advice to T. C. Wilson on 30 October
1933, Pound wrote:

> I had to write my Villon and Cavalcanti operas to get STARTED; and
> God knows the circumvolvent unconsciousness of the WHOLE gor-
> damn question is peasoup thick.
>   Have you ever studied solfege? If not, go set in the nearest jazz hell
> and LOOK at the *printed music* while they are playin' the tangos. . . .
> Learn musical notation. . . .
>   The music tip is very serious, but you'll need at least a year's work,
> and damned hard work, (Buy a metronome) before you can publish
> anything. Probably five years. A new movement can't be seriously
> tackled in five weeks. And keep it under your hat, for the present.

Pound was increasingly serious about this musical direction his work
was taking. In November of 1933, he arranged with the mayor of Rapallo
for the use of a hall for concerts; his involvement with this concert series
was to last for several years. One can only speculate about what influence
a close involvement with music might have had on Pound's poetry had
he felt free to pursue it. As it was, the political and economic crises of
the decade intervened, and there is scant further mention of the "new
movement" he foresaw in poetry, something one regrets.

IV

Pound wrote his *Jefferson and/or Mussolini* in February of 1933,
the month after his audience with *il Duce*. Subtitled *L'Idea Statale, Fascism
as I Have Seen It,* the book was not published until April of 1935. Although it was clearly meant to appeal to an American market, Pound
claimed that forty publishers turned it down. Its author was identified

with the phrase "Ezra Pound, Volitionist Economics," almost as though Pound was the spokesperson for an economic school or movement. In a foreword observing that over two years had passed between manuscript and publication, Pound carefully noted that it was "printed as a record of what I saw in February 1933."[20]

Since *Jefferson and/or Mussolini* is Pound's only book about his political theories, and since it concentrates on Italian fascism, it bears detailed examination. Although some of his views were to develop further in later years, particularly those involving economics and Confucius, the book is Pound's first major public apologia for Italian fascism and his first attempt at a coherent political philosophy. As we shall see, despite the book's disjointed and confused appearance, it does present a coherent political doctrine. I shall first attempt to systematize Pound's principal arguments, and I will then proceed to an account of some of the problems, fallacies, or misconceptions implied in some of those arguments. Whatever reservations we may have about some of the book's premises, it does mark a decisive turn to fascism in Pound's thought, and it must be considered carefully.

Not surprisingly, the principal focus of the book is on Benito Mussolini, not on fascism. Although Jefferson gets equal billing in the title, it quickly becomes clear that his name is added to provoke the American reader into considering the merits of fascism. Jefferson's America is discussed in the book, but Mussolini receives the most attention. *Il Duce* is introduced as a man who commands intense feelings of loyalty and devotion among the Italian people: "NOI CI FACCIAM SCANNAR PER MUSSOLINI," Pound quotes one of them as saying, a phrase he later repeats in the *Cantos*, "We'd get scragged for Mussolini." Whether one can believe this or not, apparently Pound does, and he seems half-envious, half-awed when he adds almost immediately: "This kind of devotion . . . doesn't come to a man like myself for analyzing a movement with an historical perspective" (26–7).

Pound's own psychological involvement with the figure of Mussolini becomes increasingly visible as the book proceeds, and it is certainly a component of Pound's high regard for him. Mussolini is an "artifex," with a "passion for construction" (34). "Take him as anything save the artist and you will get muddled with contradictions," he adds (34). The Mussolini who emerges is an idealized individual, a mixture of artist, editor, and leader, a Pound, Orage, and Lenin combined. "MUSSOLINI DEBUNKER," Pound adulates. "The Duce sits in Rome calling five hundred bluffs (or thereabouts) every morning" (35). The stature and

---

[20] Pound, *Jefferson and/or Mussolini*, iv. All further references in this chapter to pages from this text will be given in parentheses following the quotation.

omniscience of this godlike figure grow later in the book: "And even here is the hand or eye or ear of the Duce, the Debunker par excellence, for the deputies and the ministers know that there is an EDITORIAL eye and ear – precisely – an editor, who will see through their bunkum" (74). Pound's enthusiasm and praise for Mussolini are so fulsome that again one begins to believe that *il Duce* fulfilled some psychological need for Pound, if only the need for him to believe that someone else "was on the job": "By taking more responsibility than any other man (save possibly Lenin) has dared to assume in our time Mussolini has succeeded in imparting here and there a little of this sense to others" (37). This assessment of Mussolini was not entirely mistaken. Denis Mack Smith, in a biography severely critical of Mussolini, admits that his experiences as editor and journalist were essential elements in his winning power and that "he was probably the best popular journalist of his day."[21]

Pound's fascination with the man of action who could cut through numerous obstacles to achievement is not new. The early poetry and the *Cantos* celebrate men such as Bertrans de Born, Odysseus, El Cid, and Sigismundo Malatesta, morally ambiguous figures at best. Such men are seldom bound by legal codes or ethical scruples, and Mussolini is no exception. Pound relates the story of a friend of his, a distinguished jurisconsult, who is worried because "he don't from one day to another know what the law will be" (76). Pound thinks this admirable: "Mussolini may at any moment find out that some laboured and ingenious device for securing a fair amount of justice in some anterior period and other earlier states of society NO LONGER works" (77). Denis Mack Smith gives another account: "Judges like the legislature had to become subordinate to the executive – that is, to himself. Fascism, he said, had a perfect right to appoint judges who were fascists and to punish or dismiss those magistrates who failed to decide cases the way he wanted."[22]

Of course Mussolini, with press laws passed on 20 June 1925, had established control over the domestic press, and in a number of ways asserted control of the foreign press as well, so Pound, as avid a reader of newspapers as Mussolini, had few unbiased sources of information. One indication of Pound's skewed perception is that when Pound was presented with an account of a real problem, as he was by his friend the jurisconsult, he dismissed it or used it to further glorify Mussolini. He even went on to claim that there were fewer difficulties with this situation than with England's "sloppy" laws (77), which cheated men because no one could determine what they meant. Pound admires the pragmatic

[21] Mack Smith, 67.
[22] Ibid., 101.

elements of Mussolini's approach, without considering very deeply some of their dangerous implications.

There was clearly a considerable predisposition on Pound's part to believe in Mussolini and therefore in Italian fascism. The two may be considered almost identical, since a carefully cultivated myth of *mussolinismo* was the one essential dogma of his regime.[23] "*Mussolini ha sempre ragione*" ("Mussolini is always right") was a slogan that appeared everywhere throughout Italy. As Mack Smith states: "Even non-fascists were quickly caught up in this cult of the man who alone could be trusted, the benevolent ruler who was perhaps being deceived by subordinates and surrounded by inferior beings, but who would eventually put all to rights."[24] Pound too may be said to have succumbed to the dictator's cult of personality. Some of his eagerness to accept these beliefs so readily might have been due to the problems Pound encountered in England, problems of gaining acceptance, getting his work published, convincing others of the worth of Eliot and Joyce. Pound believed that in every generation there was born someone with natural taste, whose judgment and discernment in aesthetic matters was naturally right. Time and his own conviction had proved him right about his literary judgments, and he extended his view to the political sphere. Such an exceptional individual need not be hampered by law or custom: Mussolini's "authority comes as Eirugina proclaimed authority comes, 'from right reason' and from the general fascist conviction that he is more likely to be right than anyone else" (110). Certainly this is a comfortable kind of belief for an intellectual. The problem lies in the ignorance it reveals about the fundamentals of the political process, democratic or authoritarian, through which power or authority is derived. "Right reason" has very little to do with authority, even as regards the proclaimed dogmas of the church. In this regard Pound was politically naive. The pope who announced Johannes Scotus Erigena a heretic centuries after his death understood far better the real basis of authority than did the otherworldly medieval philosopher.

V

Pound had lived in Italy for over eight years at the time that he wrote *Jefferson and/or Mussolini*, and a great deal of the book is taken up with his observations of contemporary Italian society and its situation under fascism. He knew Italy very well, and his comments about the peculiarly Italian nature of fascism as a response to specific Italian prob-

[23] Ibid., 103.
[24] Ibid.

lems are well reasoned and often very perceptive. To begin, his view of the advent of fascism as a reaction to particular Italian political circumstances at the end of the First World War is, though briefly stated, one to which many scholars would subscribe today:

> The communists had NOT the sense, they simply had not the simple arithmetic and executive ability needed to run a village of five hundred. . . .
>
> As to the socialists, a liberal or something of that sort said to me: "They had the chance and *per vigliaccheria . . . per VIGLiaccheria* (because of cowardice) refused to take it." (27–8)

Pound is referring to an incident in 1920 when revolutionary Socialists seized control of a number of factories in northern Italy. The government chose not to intervene, but the Socialists were unable to pursue their advantage and the general strike failed.

Pound is also correct in stating that some of Italy's problems arose as the result of the Treaty of Versailles: "I take it the only point the Allies at large were, on arrival, agreed on, was that they should not keep their agreements with Italy" (33). The frustration of Italy's territorial ambitions by its allies on the winning side of the war, as well as disillusion with the war effort as such, played an important part in its subsequent political history.

Observations concerning the different regional characteristics of Italy and the regionally specific nature of fascism continue throughout the book. Pound takes the apparent inconsistency of Mussolini's speeches as proof of his perceptivity. The speeches of the Italian dictator differ "from town to town. For the guy knows his eggs and his Italy. The speech at Forlì was at Forlì and not at Torino" (65). Many scholars today would now agree with Pound that fascism, far from being monolithic, must be approached on a regional basis, because its practice differed in the various regions. *Il Duce's* varying speeches represented his understanding of Italian politics and, like many of the "theoretical" documents about fascism written by Mussolini and others, were fitted to the situation at hand. To Pound, Mussolini's inconsistency represented good rhetoric.

Pound had his own very particular view of modern Italian history: "Italy had a risorgimento, a shaking from lethargy, a partial unification, then a forty-year sleep, from which the next heave has been the work of one man, pre-eminently, with only here and there a notable, perhaps a very temporary, assistance" (89). Although the ultimate failure of Italy's parliamentary liberalism after the *risorgimento* is generally conceded, it can hardly be dismissed as a "forty-year sleep." And Pound had a great deal of respect for the cultural achievements of Italy. But he is not here trying to be the careful historian; instead, he is trying to exalt one man,

Benito Mussolini. This emphasis on the important role of the great individual in historic events is a significant component of Pound's political and historical thought, as it was for his literary criticism. We shall examine it in more depth later, but first we shall return to Pound's catalog of the accomplishments of his hero and his capsule history of modern Italy.

Pound states that the first act of fascism was to save Italy "from people too stupid to govern, I mean the Italian communist, the Lenin-less communist. The second act was to free it from parliamentarians" (94). All of this follows rather standard partisan accounts of the role of fascism in "rescuing" Italy. More credible are Pound's specific claims for Mussolini's tangible accomplishments: "No one denies the material and immediate effect: *grano, bonifica, restauri,* grain, swamp-drainage, restorations, new buildings, and, I am ready to add off my own bat, AN AWAKENED INTELLIGENCE in the nation and a new LANGUAGE in the debates in the Chamber" (73). Pound continues his emphasis on the power of the individual to direct events (note his phrase "the Lenin-less communist") while including some of his more recent political ideas (espoused in "How to Read" and the *ABC of Reading*), for example, that good and efficient government follows precise use of language. Although many of Pound's observations about Italian society are sound, the same cannot be said of his eighteenth-century political notions, as we shall see.

VI

One of the principal components of Pound's political ideology was his insistence that fascism as a political form was valid only for Italy. Given later events, and Pound's indictment for treason, this belief cannot be overemphasized. Pound's own extensive international experience had shown him the great differences that exist between countries. It also put him at odds with the Comintern and the notion that a single political solution is valid for all nations. Pound never advocated the adoption of fascism by other nations. In a similar vein, he did not believe that communism would be of much use in countries other than Russia. His belief that political systems must be suited to the temperament and tradition of individual nations is a sound one that is often overlooked by his critics. "Italy is not Russia, nor is America Italy, nor is Russia America, etc., and I do not 'advocate' America's trying to be either Russia or Italy, *und so weiter*" (40).

> I find no metaphor for the bathos of those denizens of developed countries who kneel and ask Russia to save 'em. . . .

> There is no use in thinking about shoving this state of things suddenly
> onto a totally different people with utterly different habits. (36–7)

Pound did believe, however, that some features or successes of foreign
systems of government could challenge other governments to show a
higher level of concern for their citizens, a kind of international standard
for political achievement not unlike the international standard that he
championed for the arts. After an extended discussion of nineteenth-
century American history, with close attention to the bank war of the
1830s, Pound closes section XXV emphatically:

> This is not to say that I "advocate" fascism in and for America, or that
> I think that fascism is possible in America without Mussolini, any more
> than I or any enlightened bolshevik thinks communism is possible in
> America without Lenin.
>   I think the American system *de jure* is probably quite good enough,
> if there were only 500 men with guts and the sense to USE it, or even
> with the capacity for answering letters or printing a paper. (98)

Note here Pound's eighteenth-century conception of politics, influenced
no doubt by his reading of America's founding fathers and his reading
of Voltaire, as well as his boyhood in Philadelphia and its unavoidable
monuments to our eighteenth-century heritage. A political movement is
composed of a group of literate men, formed into committees of correspondence, with a few of them possessing a printing press so as to pass
on their conclusions to the masses.

Pound was sympathetic to the plight of people hit hard by the tough
economic times of the thirties. The Great Depression motivated him to
pursue his economic studies with the hope of finding a way out of the
worldwide dilemma. He was not the fascist ideologue that some have
portrayed him as, but was eclectic and pragmatic in approach. To some
extent, he was a fascist propagandist simply because he lived in Italy
during this time. If he had lived in Moscow, his writings could have
taken on a different color.

Pound believed that communism, despite the fact that it evolved in
Russia, a country he considered backward compared with the West,
presented a challenge to other nations during those troubled times:
"Damn the bolsheviki as much as you like, the Russian *projects* have
served as stimuli BOTH to Italy and to America. Our democratic system
is, for the first time, on trial against systems professing greater care for
national welfare" (104). This is an accurate and succinct reading by Pound
of some of the major political trends of the thirties. It also demonstrates
that his basic concerns were economic. Pound thought that the state
should take control of a nation's credit. State control of credit was the
achievement of communism, his hope for Italy, and his wish for the

United States and other Western democracies. One of the final statements in *Jefferson and/or Mussolini* is: "As for a spread of fascism, if it could mean a transportation of the interesting element of the decade, it would not need parades, nor hysterical Hitlerian yawping" (127). For Pound, the "interesting element" was economic. And he saw, in the evolution of fascist economic policies, a hope that the principles he advocated would be put into practice.

VII

Part of *Jefferson and/or Mussolini* is devoted to a consideration of four other nations – the United States, Great Britain, France, and Russia – usually with the intent of comparing their systems of government with Italian fascism. Pound's scattered references to England and France are invariably negative in tone. Although much of his journalism later in the decade is damning of England, that country is only briefly mentioned in *Jefferson and/or Mussolini*. Because Pound's principal interests were economic, Russia under Marxism and Leninism is the nation most frequently discussed. Pound had purchased an Italian translation of *Capital* and read it closely (it is one of the most heavily marked books in his library). Although Pound was opposed to the export of ideology (in this he followed Mussolini, who stated that fascism was not for export)[25] and believed that a nation's political forms are best developed indigenously, he recognized the challenge that communism presented during the thirties and felt that challenge could not be ignored.

Pound's ideas about Russian communism developed in two directions. First, he felt that there were basic similarities between the Russian and the fascist revolutions. Second, he felt a great deal of admiration for Lenin as a man of action in the mold of his hero, Mussolini (this was not an entirely accidental comparison, for the contemporary figure most admired by Mussolini was Lenin).

> The best government is that which translates the best thought most speedily into action.
> Such translation is undoubtedly more speedy and dramatic when a nation has slipped behind and has merely to catch up with the pacemakers. Thus the leaps of Russia and Italy in many matters of detail. (91)

It should be noted here that Pound clearly states that the Italian and Russian revolution, far from setting examples for other nations to follow, were merely attempts to close the gaps between the two countries and

---

[25] Ibid., 59.

more advanced societies. Pound does give the fascist revolution an edge over Lenin's Marxist one:

> The fascist revolution is infinitely more INTERESTING than the Russian revolution because it is not a revolution according to a preconceived type. . . .
> Lenin did not have the Vatican in his front garden. He knew his Russia and dealt with the Russia he had before him. (24–5)

Both Lenin and Mussolini were Poundian heroes. Both were men who understood the specific historical situation existing in their countries, and both were decisive enough to turn that understanding to account. Both were artists of a new kind of art form that Pound envisioned, halfway between thought and political action. Their successes and the successes of their respective parties came about through their capacity for appropriate action. Pound relates admiringly: "There is Lenin's calm estimate of all other Russian parties: They are very clever, yes, they can do EVERYTHING except act" (34). But Pound idealized them further. They were not just desirous of power. Both men took full responsibility for the welfare of their people. "Power is necessary to some acts, but neither Lenin nor Mussolini show themselves as men thirsting for power. The great man is filled with a very different passion, the will toward *order*" (99). This statement represents more political naiveté on Pound's part. Mussolini was a man obsessed by power, and he was enormously skilled in gaining it. Although Lenin's intentions may have been ideologically purer, he too was a practical politician who understood well the acquisition and uses of power. Pound is overlaying an ideal medieval schema, Dante's *directio voluntatis*, on the ruthlessness of twentieth-century politics.

Pound's political eclecticism is well illustrated by his admiration of both Lenin and Mussolini, a position that few people took during the ideologically charged thirties. Lenin, according to Pound, had already "entered into world history," (104) and Mussolini was on the verge of following in his footsteps. Pound's eclecticism, in matters of both politics and economics, is the source of a great deal of the confusion about his views during this period. He insisted upon using what he considered to be the best features from differing economic and political systems. He tried to bring people bent on reform into agreement by emphasizing how their views converged rather than diverged, an activity that was puzzling or incomprehensible to many of his more doctrinaire correspondents. C. H. Douglas was just one of those who could not understand some of the fundamental points of agreement between Social Credit and Gesellite economics because of superficial details that appeared contradictory. As we shall see, Pound was more correct than not in his attempts at synthesis, but these attempts led to his alienation from several groups that insisted upon strict ideological conformity. Pound was a pragmatist, not an ideologue.

As one would expect from the book's title, Pound does devote a number of pages to the United States: to Jefferson and the founding fathers, to the corruption of the ideals of the American Revolution during the nineteenth century, and to the problems facing the country during the first year of Franklin Delano Roosevelt's presidency. The purpose of *Jefferson and/or Mussolini* was not only to present a favorable account of the Italian dictator to the English-speaking world but also to relate what Pound found to be the aspects of fascism relevant to the problems faced by the United States.

> The challenge of Mussolini to America is simply:
>   Do the driving ideas of Jefferson, Quincy Adams, Van Buren... FUNCTION actually in the America of this decade to the extent they function in Italy under the DUCE?
>   The writer's opinion is that they DON'T and that nothing but vigorous realignment will make them, and that if, or when, they are made so to function, Mussolini will have acted as stimulus, will have entered in American history, as Lenin has entered world history.
>   That don't, or don't necessarily, mean an importation of the details of mechanisms and forms more adapted to Italy or to Russia. (104)

Pound shared with Brooks Adams an essentially tragic view of American history according to which the country had lost its original purpose and heritage. Still, unlike Adams, Pound was optimistic about the possibilities of recovering the earlier and better heritage by meeting the challenges to the American system implied by fascism and communism. This task would be accomplished by borrowing what was workable in those systems and adapting it to the forms of American democracy. The workable ideas for Pound were chiefly economic, and in many respects they were adopted by Roosevelt in the thirties. At the same time Pound continued to insist that a country's government is uniquely the result of its character and history and should not be tampered with by internal or external forces.

> Why it should be supposed that a "soviet" would function where extant deliberative bodies do not is somewhat beyond me. Simply: the soviet is not the direct line for the U.S.A. Half the energy required to change a state legislature into a soviet would recharge the extant form and make it function IF there were the prerequisite skill and knowledge. (109)

To repeat, Pound explicitly rejected the Comintern position here and shows confidence in the ability of the U.S. system to adapt to changing circumstances, a stand that set him apart from many radical intellectuals of the thirties.

Pound's attitude toward FDR a year after his election was ambivalent. In his preface, written in September of 1933, Pound states that "nobody 'saw Roosevelt coming'" and expresses a cautious hope that he would have a positive impact upon the American economic situation (ix). In the same preface he invites American readers to "try to 'place' F.D.R. *in relation* to contemporary phenomena in other countries" (x). This was a worthwhile insight and in some ways prophetic. But in the body of the text, Pound wrote that "the Press howls that we should GIVE more power to Roosevelt, i.e., to a weak man, or a man generally supposed to be weak, a man who has shown NO UNDERSTANDING whatsoever, and no knowledge whatsoever of contemporary actuality" (108). This was written before the preface, so Pound's opinion of FDR obviously improved. It is worth noting how Pound expanded H. L. Mencken's offhand remark about Roosevelt being a "weak sister" into "a man generally supposed to be weak," though Mencken's view was shared by other members of the American press.

Pound changed his mind again before the book was published. In a foreword written in April of 1935 he stated that "the September Preface (1933) indicated a flutter of hope, that has grown steadily more fluttery and less hopeful" (iv). Pound's attitude toward Roosevelt remained ambivalent throughout the thirties, but he turned decisively against the president after the beginning of the Second World War. Pound admired the fact that Roosevelt recognized the economic problems and was enough of a leader to get something done about them, but he disagreed with the means FDR used to lift America out of the Depression, insofar as they relied on government borrowing. This feeling was reinforced by his American political correspondence, which was with a group of mostly Republican senators and representatives who were opposed to Roosevelt.

Pound's Jefferson, the other major figure in the book, is a hero very much in Mussolini's image. He emerges as a bold man, willing to get things done. Pound during this time had been reading the *Collected Works of John Adams,* which, along with the *Collected Works of Thomas Jefferson,* a gift from Eliot in the Paris years,[26] provided him with much of his information about the American Revolution. His historical method was, once again, the same as the aesthetic method he championed in the *ABC of Reading*: To understand a subject, you go to the works of the inventors or masters of that subject. These volumes provided Pound with many selected insights into eighteenth-century America. For example: "When a particular emergency arose he [Jefferson] showed no regard for liberties

[26] Stock, 247.

in the declaration of EMBARGO" (71). Here Pound chose to highlight Jefferson's pragmatism and disregard of law. Pound then went on to compare Jefferson's action with Mussolini's ban on the emigration of Italian workers, which, Pound maintained, was an important step toward the reconstruction of Italy. He concluded by comparing such constructive uses of authority, represented by Jefferson and Mussolini, with incorrect use, represented by the introduction of U.S. passports by Woodrow Wilson, though he does not explain how to differentiate between the two.

Pound's reading was further in evidence in his summation of Jefferson's character in Odyssean terms:

> Jefferson was *polumetis,* many-minded, and as literature wasn't his main job, this multiplicity is now recorded, item by item in his letters, one interest at a time, and the unreflective reader gets simply the sense of a leisure without perceiving the essential dynamism of the man who did *get things* DONE. (89)

Pound went on to say that Mussolini's job was to be "both Jefferson and Pat Henry, or both John Adams and Jas. Otis" (89). Pound even seemed to identify somewhat with Jefferson and defended him against detractors in a statement that might be equally applicable to Pound himself:

> Jefferson has a reputation for having made excessive statements, which might happen to any voluble man if a few of his remarks were perpetually considered apart from their context, and apart from the occasions when they were published and the contrary excesses they were designed to correct. (114)

Pound, at the time, had not yet made his most excessive statements about politics, but he was on his way. Perhaps he knew himself well enough to see the path he was on.

VIII

Pound's political views and his understanding of the political process were very much influenced by his reading of Jefferson and Adams and his knowledge of the American Revolution. His political philosophy, as has been noted, is close to an eighteenth-century ideal and praxis. Political movements, in this view, come into being through the understanding, will, and direction of individual men. These men work in conjunction with others of like nature, with whom they are in communication so as to present their views to a wider public and orchestrate the changes that follow. For Pound, with the lessons of the Russian and fascist revolutions close at hand, these changes can take place either in a dictatorship, where the dictator "organizes the power" (108), or in a democracy, where "a sufficiently active segment of the public" is "persuaded to combine and compel its elected delegates to act decently in an even moderately intelligent manner" (104).

Here we have Pound's political program in a nutshell: the methods he would rely on for the rest of the decade and on into the war years. His is certainly a vision of the political process that would appeal to a member of the clerisy. It begins with cooperation, consensus, and communication among a small group of intelligent men. These men, who presumably know one another, form what can be described as committees of correspondence, writing to each other to air their ideas and reach agreement. This view can explain the thousands of letters that Pound wrote during this period, his frequent admonitions to his correspondents to get in touch with each other, and his frequent inclusion of addresses in his letters. It also explains his incessant letters to "elected delegates" and his correspondence with men in positions of influence: senators and representatives in the United States, ministers and party officials in Italy. Finally, his attempt to disseminate the conclusions and views of his "nucleus" through journalism may be seen as corresponding to the small-press pamphleteering of the American Revolution, updated during the Second World War to include radio.

Pound's eighteenth-century political vision is inhabited by a moral perspective located somewhere between Confucius and Dante. When a political system breaks down, its failure is precisely attributable to individual failure of virtue:

> When men of understanding are too lazy to impart the results of their understanding, and when the nucleus of the national mind hasn't the moral force to translate knowledge into action I don't believe it matters a damn what legal forms or what administrative forms there are in a government. The nation will get the staggers. (95)

Thus individual virtue predetermines the success or failure of the political system. This is a Confucian notion: For there to be order in the state there must first be order in the family, and for order in the family there first must be order in the individual. But failure of virtue for Pound most often means failure of the will, understood in a very specific sense: "The problem of democracy is whether its alleged system, its *de jure* system, can still be handled by men of good will; whether real issues as distinct from red herrings CAN be forced into the legislature (House and Senate)" (103). Pound's "will" is the medieval *directio voluntatis,* the direction of the will, the phrase that "brings us ultimately to Confucius and Dante" (16). *Directio voluntatis* as Pound uses it, is emphatically not the "will to power." Although recognizing that power is necessary for some political actions, the will that Pound admires is a "will toward order" (99), similar, as he sees it, to the passion of an artist for constructive effort. Pound's view is founded upon intentionality (note the apposition after his name on the title page: "Volitionist Economics"). The ideal government is made up of men who possess Confucian sincerity, the Dantean *ben d'inteletto,* and the *directio voluntatis.* No matter what the *de jure* system, it needs a *"de facto* government composed of sincere men willing the national good" (95).

Pound was sensitive to the charges leveled at fascist Italy by critics abroad and was quick to respond to them in *Jefferson and/or Mussolini.* He took up the issues of censorship of the press and curtailment of individual liberty. As to the first, he was quick to draw comparisons between Italy and England:

> Now what about prejudice. Censorship of the Press!. . . .
> As the Duce has pithily remarked: "Where the press is '*free*' it merely serves special interests". . . .
> Honest thought, I mean serious sober thought intended to be of public utility, is, in England, merely excluded from all the Press. (41)

Of course this echoes the view that Pound absorbed from the *New Age.* Pound went on to say that he read about the lack of freedom of the Italian press in foreign newspapers, particularly the Paris edition of the *Chicago Tribune,* and presumably these papers and his correspondents were his sources for other criticism of the fascist regime that he answered in the book. To some degree, *Jefferson and/or Mussolini* can be seen as an attempt to answer or dispel some of these stories about Italy. Unfortunately, Pound began to make some dubious distinctions:

> A great deal of yawp about a free Press proves on examination to be a mere howl for irresponsibility. . . .
> If you were talking about the liberty of a *responsible* Press that is a very different kettle of onions, and is something very near to the state of the Press in Italy at the moment. (41–4).

Pound is begging the question. Following a remark by Mussolini that Pound used for a time on his personal stationery, "liberty is a duty, not a right," he is claiming that in the Western democracies freedom of the press is freedom to be irresponsible and thus somehow it is not real freedom, whereas the Italian press is really free because it is somehow really responsible. This is irascibility, not argument. Although not well presented by Pound and tending to show how lightly he took some of the substantive ideas of Jefferson, this issue still arises today, representing as it does a real tension between the media's demand for complete freedom of information and the government's concern for effective use of power (effective, of course, as perceived by the people in power).

As for personal liberty, Pound makes some interesting points about the changing necessity for state intervention in the modern age:

> Not only do frontiers need watching but man in a mechanical age, you me 'n' th' other fellow, need help against Kreugers and Hatrys. The demarcation between public and private affairs shifts with the change in the base of production. A thousand peasants each growing food on his own fields can exist without trust laws. (45)

This observation is still valid. But there are disturbing notes in Pound's defense of personal liberty in Italy. He speaks of an incident when he was seated at an outdoor cafe. A group of black-shirted fascists went by and Pound did not stand up. He reports that "nobody hit me with a club and I didn't see any oil bottles" (50–1). The reader is not convinced by his testimony to freedom in Italy, unless of course Pound is speaking only of his own personal freedom.

He later offers further evidence from his own experience: "As personal testimony to PERSONAL feeling, I feel freer here than I ever did in London or Paris. I am willing to admit my capacity for illusion, but right or wrong, that is my feeling" (74). When, before or since, has Pound ever been willing to admit his capacity for illusion? Or hedged so much? Later, too, he seems to avoid the problem of personal liberty in fascist Italy by sidestepping the issue: "It has become utterly impossible to show that the personal resilience of the individual is less, or the scope of individual action, his fields of initiative, is any more limited, under Mussolini than under our pretendedly republican system" (104).[27] But what Pound has done here is to change the meaning of the word *freedom* from the more traditional sense of lack of limits to the different idea of possibility for action, a subtle change, but one with serious consequences. Pound has not addressed the crucial question of what happened to opponents of Mussolini's regime. He knew of the institution of the *confino*, internal political exile whereby opponents of the fascist regime were banished to remote and tiny villages within Italy, a fairly mild and humane measure for a totalitarian regime. But it is not clear what else he might have known about. The press was controlled, but he must have heard rumors about harsher treatment given to enemies of the regime. I do not believe that Pound was lying here or deliberately concealing facts. Knowing the Italian people and their essential tolerance, perhaps he just could not believe that worse things were happening. But he is refusing to meet the accusations and is attempting to skirt their impli-

---

[27] Pound had earlier expressed a similar attitude toward the rule of an enlightened despot in his article "Regional XIV" for *New Age*: "I have the feeling that my personal liberties would have been safer under an enlightened pontiff – say Nicholas V or Leo X – than in the reign of President Wilson" (23 Oct. 1919, 432).

cations. Having seen what good the fascists were doing, he is willing to overlook what evil transpired. This is pragmatism taken to extremes.

Although the style of *Jefferson and/or Mussolini* is often disjointed and confusing, typical of Pound, the work did present a coherent political philosophy. Pound had a vision of the well-ordered state and of the steps that were needed to achieve it. But there were problems with Pound's vision that went beyond his advocacy of Mussolini and Italian fascism. Many people admired Mussolini at the time the book was written, among them Winston Churchill.[28] Pound's book contains many valuable and interesting insights about the nature of the modern state, about American history, and about Italian society, but it is still fundamentally flawed as a political treatise for this century. The eighteenth-century rationalist character of Pound's political thought is at the root of the problem.

The problem is adumbrated in the book's epigram. "NOTHING IS WITHOUT EFFICIENT CAUSE" Pound writes in bold capitals (v). This belief was the foundation of many of his glaring misjudgments over the next twelve years. To begin with, social problems are far too complex to be analyzed in the simple mechanical terms of cause and effect adduced by Pound's epigram. The distinction between "efficient" and "sufficient" cause becomes blurred, and almost no human action can be described as being due to a sufficient cause. Societal interactions are not molecular interactions and are most frequently the product of numerous, vague, and sometimes unspecifiable forces. One is fortunate to identify necessary causes; contributing causes are beyond analysis. Pound's eighteenth-century notion of cause gets in his way here; the world of history is not a mechanical windup watch whose actions can be precisely observed and charted; in the human realm, Vico supplants Descartes and Newton.

If, as Pound asserts, nothing happens without an ascertainable efficient cause, then in the world of history there must be people who set things in motion, whose actions cause events. Taking this view, one works backward from cause to volition or intention, and from there it is only a short step back in the causal chain to evil. Pound recognizes that there is some difficulty in getting things to happen in the world, so he acknowledges that owing to the complexity of political action, frequently a number of people must work together to achieve something. Following his model, this effort must be intentional, hence his drift toward belief in conspiracies. Pound's faith in efficient cause deludes him. On the surface it is plausible enough, seemingly self-evident and incontrovertible. But if economic and political events are seen as the result of proximate causes, instead of as the result of forces only half understood, and if these events are going badly, then one works backward from caused

---

[28] See, e.g., Diggins, Chap. 4, "Mussolini as American Hero."

to cause to agent, and from there (a concession to complexity) to conspiracy.

Pound's logic betrays him, though he is consistent in its application. Thus his insistence in *Jefferson and/or Mussolini* on the primacy of ethics and his focus on *directio voluntatis,* the direction of the will. If events can be controlled by intelligent individuals who have discerned the mechanisms of efficient cause, then such individuals will act for good or evil depending upon their individual virtue. Pound had a highly developed sense of individual moral responsibility, but (as Eliot maintained) an exaggeratedly simple sense of individual depravity. If Pound was deficient in his conception of evil, it was not of the possibilities of individual evil but of the inherent nature of evil, or, as we might say today, of the systemic nature of evil, where things do not go well, or they do not go as planned, despite the best of intentions, because of our inability to grasp the complexity of the many factors involved.

So Pound, the Confucian, the Dantean, and the rational man, needed to understand the economic and social turbulence of the thirties and the crime of World War I in terms of the success or failure of individual virtue. Eventually this would lead him in search of the imaginary international malefactors who deliberately caused social collapse for personal profit. But in *Jefferson and/or Mussolini,* it merely led to his insistence on "the will to order" (not "the will to power"), on "sincere men willing the national good," and on "500 men with guts and sense" leading the way back to a just society.

This idea also led him to the personal conviction that one man could change and direct the course of history, a notion that was present in his poetry of the time (for example, in the figure of Leopold of Tuscany in Cantos XLII–XLIV) as well as in *Jefferson and/or Mussolini*: "Lafayette and Co. kept running down to Tom's lodgings to find out how they ought to behave, and how one should have a French revolution. The royal bed or whatever they called it was toppled over and T.J. went back to the United States" (14). This is Pound's version of the French Revolution: conversation among friends not too dissimilar from Eliot or Hemingway dropping in on Pound in London or Paris, a literary revolution. Similar is Pound's repeated insistence that fascism was not possible without Mussolini, nor communism without Lenin. The individual is superior to the ideology and actually creates it: "I offer the hypothesis that: when a single mind is sufficiently ahead of the mass a one-party system is bound to occur as an actuality whatever the details of form in administration" (125). Again, this recalls the "inventors" and "masters" of "How to Read." It is not difficult to see the relation between this political idea of Pound and his ideas about activity and progress in the arts, although it is difficult to reconcile his view with our understanding of Jeffersonian democracy. The resolution for Pound is that Jefferson was a virtuous man who dominated his time through the force of his intellect and personality.

IX

Another difficulty with *Jefferson and/or Mussolini* is Pound's claim that political actions should be judged by aesthetic criteria: Pound insists that no estimate of Mussolini is valid unless it treats him as an artist. "When Mussolini has expressed any satisfaction it has been with the definite act performed, the artwork in the civic sense" (100). Thus Pound allowed himself to dismiss any apparent contradictions in Mussolini's political philosophy or actions with the excuse that he was an artist and not bound by ordinary rules of consistency. This excuse was doubly convenient, since apart from resolving inconsistencies, it also tended to help Pound convince himself that his political perceptions were correct. Who possibly was in a better position to judge the work of a fellow artist than Pound, one of the preeminent critics of this century? Thus, by a neat shift of ground, Pound became a political authority. This shift of ground allowed him to occupy two worlds of differing values; it also eased Pound's identification with his hero, Mussolini.

The book's mixing of aesthetic and political spheres continues as Pound concludes that Mussolini has exquisite taste, both in poetry and pottery, and that men of taste, such as himself, know politics. What Pound did not realize was that most successful politicians are ciphers, allowing their constituents to project onto them their own images and aspirations. The statements are vague; the promises vary from region to region. What is presented is the decisive, charismatic individual. Mussolini was particularly accomplished in this regard, and Pound was taken in. Walter Benjamin observed that fascism was the aestheticization of politics; Pound's case confirms Benjamin's view of the mixture of the two realms.[29]

As we have seen, this unification of the artistic and social realms was further justified by the work of the German anthropologist Leo Frobenius. Frobenius's concept of *paideuma* provided Pound with the basis he needed for validating his judgments in both fields.

> Anyone who has seen the furniture at Schonbrunn ought to understand the flop of the Austrian Empire, and anyone who saw it before the flop ought to have known that the flop was coming.
>
> Frobenius has outstripped other archaeologists and explorers
> (a) because he doesn't believe that things exist without a cause;

[29] Benjamin, 241–2.

(b) as a corollary, because he considered that the *forms* of pottery, etc., had causes. (83)

Pound's idea about efficient cause was beginning to permeate his thought. The notion that there is some important relation between art and culture was, however, not entirely new to Pound, though Frobenius gave the idea new force for him. As he states earlier in the book: "I am a flat-chested highbrow. I can 'cure' the whole trouble by criticism of style. Oh, can I? Yes. I have been saying so for some time" (17). The trouble here is not entirely with Frobenius or his concept of *paideuma,* the idea that cultures form unified wholes and that the state of a culture can be read from its artifacts. The trouble lies in Pound's use of the idea as the ground for his instantaneous diagnoses of culture, made without looking closely. In this respect *paideuma* surpasses even the "ideogrammic method" in its ability to justify hasty judgment and carelessness. Of course, Pound could overlook the implications of *paideuma* when convenient; at best he could come up with only a weak apology for fascist art: "It would be difficult to defend the contemporary public muniments in ANY country" (106).

Also disturbing is Pound's fascination with the new art form "halfway between writing and action"[30] that he said had been invented by Lenin. Mussolini was an artist in this new form. And Pound revised his previous thinking to approach Filippo Tommaso Marinetti and Gabriele D'Annunzio with a new respect, even a certain amount of envy:

> Any smart schoolboy can make fun of some detail or other in Marinetti's campaigns, but . . . it [is] much more difficult to match the mass record of Marinetti's life, even if you limit it to his campaigning for public education in aesthetics and omit the political gestures, which any good writer might envy. You must judge the whole man by the mass of the man's results.
>
> As with d'Annunzio, anyone can repeat jokes about hairwash but until the dilettante writer has held up the combined rascals of Europe, he had best confine his criticism of Gabriele to questions of stylistic embroidery. (107)

Pound refers here to D'Annunzio's September 1919 raid on Fiume.[31] Neither Marinetti's nor D'Annunzio's work had been a part of the Pound canon, and he battled futurism in London in an earlier period. But his presence in Italy, where these two writers were lionized by the Italian

---

[30] Pound, "Bureaucracy the Flail of Jehovah" (1928), in *Selected Prose,* 217.
[31] Pound had earlier expressed cautious approval of D'Annunzio in his "Revolt of Intelligence" in the *New Age:* "If Sig. d'Annunzio were only a less mixed type, if he only stood more clearly for literary integrity, if he were not part histrion" (13 Nov. 1919, 21). But now Pound was looking for the new mixed type and the new art form, and finding them in D'Annunzio.

government, combined with his new longing for an aesthetics of action, caused him to take a position he would not previously have considered.

Pound's admiration for D'Annunzio and Marinetti derived largely from his belief that they had progressed beyond mere intellectualism or aestheticism to a life of action, one in which they could put their ideas into effect. Pound envied them for that, and he began to espouse some dangerous notions in his personal impatience for activity. This interest in politics is not unusual for a writer: One need only consider Yeats, who actually had some political effect, for an example. But it led Pound to some questionable conclusions. "Let us deny that *real* intelligence exists until it comes into action" (18). "The Anglo-Saxon is particularly inept at understanding the Latin clarity of 'Qui veut la fin veut les moyens.' Who wills the end wills the means" (34). Pound is all too eager, in his impatience, to discard the caution and fairness of the Anglo-Saxon common-law tradition in order to embrace the excess and injustice of an authoritarian government. These observations show Pound at his most careless. His impatience to correct economic problems and his untoward regard for Mussolini led him to place the dictator above the law, with considerable flippancy, as we saw earlier in the story of the distressed lawyer who did not know from one moment to the next what the law was. Although he backtracked a little from the extremity of that position by going on to criticize English laws that in the time of Lloyd George, Pound claimed, could not be understood, his authoritarian sympathies are clear. The means do not matter; what counts is the purity of the intention and the desirability of the result: "A GOOD government is one that operates according to the best that is known and thought. And the best government is that which translates the best thought most speedily into action" (91). He expands on this:

> To translate knowledge into action I don't believe it matters a damn what legal forms or what administrative forms there are in a government. . . .
> . . . any means are the right means which will remagnetize the will and the knowledge. (95)

Pound was completely oblivious to the dangers of this statement and to the potential of such statements to cause human suffering. Nor is there any evidence to suggest that Pound was merely being rhetorically extreme here, in an attempt to shock his audience out of lethargy and into some kind of awareness. He apparently believed in what he was advocating; the best one can say is that he did not think it through.

Belief was an important component of Pound's commitment to Italian fascism; what was known as *fede fascista,* fascist faith, is mentioned frequently in the text and in Pound's correspondence during the war. "Any

thorough judgment of MUSSOLINI will be in a measure an act of faith,
it will depend upon what you *believe* the man means, what you believe
that he wants to accomplish" (33). And, "if you don't believe that
Mussolini is driven by a vast and deep 'concern' or will for the welfare
of Italy . . . then you will have a great deal of trouble about the un-
Jeffersonian details of the surface" (34). Of course, the "details" included
a loss of civil liberties, such as the right to opposition parties, that Pound
readily dismissed. He wrote that "as an act or declaration of faith, I do
NOT BELIEVE that any constructive effort has been hamstrung in this
country since the Marcia su Roma [the March on Rome, when the fascists
seized power in 1922]" (74). This reliance upon declarations of faith gives
pause. Pound apparently was aware that at times he had to suspend his
judgment; evidently he was quite willing to do so.

Like any believer, Pound was troubled by moments of doubt. The
most pronounced of these occurs at the end of the book. It is prepared
for by a remark of Orage: "Orage's admission [was] that Italy was better
run or more efficiently run than any other country, but he followed this
by a claim that it was just being neatly tied up in a bag for delivery to
the international sonzov" (93). Orage's criticism, that Mussolini was just
an instrument of international capitalism, was a fairly common one at
that time, voiced frequently by communists, for example, in the columns
of *New Masses*. That this possibility worried Pound we can see from the
close of *Jefferson and/or Mussolini*:

> Towards which I assert again my own firm belief that the Duce will
> stand not with despots and the lovers of power but with the lovers of
> ORDER
> *to kalon*
> POSTSCRIPT OR VALEDICTION, on going to press after two years
> of writing. These things being so, is it to be supposed that Mussolini
> has regenerated Italy, merely for the sake of reinfecting her with the
> black death of the capitalist monetary system? (128)

Neither order nor *to kalon,* the beautiful, is really the issue here, but
economics. No other statement could show so clearly just to what extent
Pound's belief in fascism was based on his belief that Mussolini would
implement the economic scheme Pound envisioned.

5

The Discovery of Gesell

I

Although Pound came to C. H. Douglas and Social Credit through Orage and the *New Age,* he discovered the work of Silvio Gesell on his own. This discovery represents an advance in the maturity of Pound's economic thought. His understanding of Gesell represents his best claim to genuine credentials as an economist. Although Douglas may be dismissed as unimportant in the history of economics, Gesell, though he may ultimately be relegated to the footnotes, cannot. Gesell provided Pound with an education in economics, and Pound's advocacy of Gesell, in face of opposition from Douglas and Orage, and his attempt at melding the two positions signal his coming of age as an economic theorist.

How plausible were Pound's theories of economics? Because much of Pound's support for Mussolini's regime was predicated upon the view that fascism would provide the opportunity to put into practice his ideas of economic justice, the answer to this question will give us an inkling of the degree of sympathy we will finally feel about Pound's enthusiasm for Italian fascism. It will also give us a basis for addressing further questions: Was Pound deluded by what he saw happening in Italy and were his hopes for those economic reforms unjustified? Did Pound lose his way as a poet by turning to the subjects of politics and economics and including these concerns so prominently in the middle cantos?

Another question offers insight into the first. After fifteen years as an active supporter of C. H. Douglas's Social Credit movement, why did Pound so suddenly and ardently embrace the theories of Silvio Gesell and attempt to unify the ideas of the two men? Did Pound perceive a flaw in the Douglas scheme? Although he was later to call Social Credit only "the doorway through which I came to economic curiosity,"[1] Pound

---

[1] Pound, "A Visiting Card" (1942), translated by John Drummond, in *Selected Prose,* 312.

122

(CROSS OUT PREVIOUS ROUTING
CODES.   USE OCLC CODE TO
ROUTE BOOK)

MINITEX - PALS
DIRECT BORROWING SERVICE

USE THIS BOOKMARK ONLY WITH
MATERIALS REQUESTED BY DIRECT
BORROWING. THESE ARE THE ONLY
DESTINATIONS WHERE DIRECT BOR-
ROWING BOOKS CAN BE SENT OR
RECEIVED.

OCLC CODE	LIBRARY
MNB	Bemidji State University
MBE	Bethany Lutheran College
MNF	College of St. Benedict
MNS	College of St. Scholastica
TRC	Concordia College - Moorhead
MNG	Gustavus Adolfus College
MNR	J. J. Hill Reference Library
MNM	Mankato State University
MLR	Minn. Legislative Ref. Lib.
TRM	Moorhead State University
TRN	North Dakota State University
RCC	Rochester Community College
MNV	Southwest State University
MST	St. Cloud State University
MNJ	St. John's University
MNY	St. Mary's College
MNO	St. Olaf College
MCR	University of MN - Crookston
MNU	University of MN - Twin Cities
MNI	Winona State University

had not given up on trying to merge the two groups supporting Douglas and Gesell when he wrote to Douglas on 29 September 1935:

> AS POLITICAL measure; considering same aims and same criterion re/ what money and credit system shd. DO, I think we shd/ promise the various Gesellite and Gesellizant groups. . . .
> That Social Credit party promises to HEAR what the Gesellite groups have to say, and that IF in given case the Gesellite MACHINERY FOR CANCELLATION be found more suitable . . . we wd. use it.

This reasoning is in line with the various underconsumption theories, all of which "attributed all the major fluctuations in the economy to one single defect, the lack of sufficient purchasing power."[2] All that was needed, according to these theories, was a device to correct this problem. Marxists, on the other hand, believed that the periodic cycles of boom and bust were symptomatic of a much deeper flaw in the capitalist system itself. Pound's suggestion to Douglas was a sensible one, and the fact that Douglas was not at all receptive probably bespeaks pride or stubbornness.

Pound did recognize a key defect in the Social Credit program, one that has been pointed out by Finlay much more recently. Pound wrote to Odon Por in August or September of 1935: "early formulation of A plus B must have been poor. I mean the expression POOR. as so many have NOT understood it as implying RATE OF FLOW." His correspondence with Por, a Hungarian-born economist who had influential contacts within the fascist government, was a rich one during this period, and it will be considered in more detail in the next chapter. Por wrote to the Social Credit Secretariat in London and sent Pound a copy of his letter of 25 March 1935:

> The corporate system now definitely at work is heading straight towards S.C. or something near to it. Not consciously yet. For instance, self-sufficiency and "the abolition of artificially created scarcity" (in Mussolini's words) are immediate aims. Finance is well under the control of the state.

Earle Davis has contended that Social Credit was not being implemented in fascist Italy and that Pound was deluded on this point. He has also correctly hypothesized that Por had an important influence on Pound's perception of "the intent and execution of Mussolini's program."[3] Indeed, Pound's correspondence with Por (which started in 1934) gave Pound good reason to think that the reforms that he advocated were being implemented by Mussolini's regime. On 15 March Por had written

---

[2] Nicholls, 53.
[3] Earle Davis, 157.

to Pound directly: "In the March number of Civiltà Fascista I am out for self-sufficiency or ec. nationalism cum S.C., . . . insisting on militant autarchy." *Civiltà Fascista* was an official journal of the regime, so Pound had reason to hope for the future of Social Credit in Italy.

Pound's ideas about economics derived fundamentally from ethics: "You can not make a good economics out of a bad ethics."[4] Along with Thomas Jefferson, he believed that "the earth belongs to the living," a motto he borrowed to use as the epigram to *Social Credit: An Impact,* published in 1935. He called this motto Jefferson's "main contention," the root from which another idea, also dear to Pound, sprang: "A nation had no right to contract debts that could not reasonably be paid within the lifetime of the parties contracting."[5] These ideas relate to other Jeffersonian ideals: rejection of hereditary privilege and the conviction that "the best place for keeping money is in the pockets of the people," slightly emended by Pound to "the best place for a nation's reserve of credit is in as many individual pockets as possible."[6] We can gather from this that Pound was sympathetic to the living needs of unemployed workers and gave those needs priority over the mortiferous privilege enjoyed by accumulated capital. Whatever we may finally decide about the correctness of Pound's economic theories, his moral sense and human sympathy were not lacking.

In our decidedly post-Keynesian age, Pound's writings on economics seem at times, even to the untutored among us, quaint, naive, or a bit obvious. It is clear to us now that in a period of severe economic depression it is vital to ensure that money is put into circulation. But it is important to realize that much of what Pound was advocating was quite radical for the thirties. As Lloyd G. Reynolds has remarked, "It was Pound's fate to publish just a little too early."[7] Keynes himself did not become a Keynesian until the appearance in 1936 of *The General Theory,* a book that was revolutionary in its later impact. Mainstream academic economists before Keynes believed that the cause for the Great Depression was simply that the cost of labor had somehow gotten stuck at too high a level and that it would eventually come down. Even when massive unemployment continued, these economists would not lose faith in Say's law and the supply and demand curve. Keynes's proposed solution of government fiscal intervention through deficit spending, even coming from the most respected economist of the age, found little favor from professors of economics.

Pound lacked formal training in economics, probably a decided ad-

[4] Pound, "The Individual in His Milieu" (1935), in *Selected Prose,* 282.
[5] Pound, *Jefferson and/or Mussolini,* 115.
[6] Ibid., 80–1.
[7] Reynolds, 398.

vantage during that time. Of course he was criticized by professional economists for his radical outlook, but he was also forced to grapple with problems unhampered by preconceptions. This freedom led him, as we shall see, to some important insights. As he said sympathetically of Silvio Gesell, an economist whom Keynes also admired: "Gesell was right in thanking his destiny that he had begun his study of money unclogged by university training."[8]

Pound's method of economic study merits comment before we proceed to consideration of its content. Not surprisingly, it parallels his method of literary study: a combination of establishing valid contemporary principles and definitions and then going back into history to find similar, corroborating insights or examples. This historical dimension of Pound's work puts him at a far remove from most economists nowadays, who tend to work at microeconomic levels and neglect the history of their discipline; it also makes the task of assessing Pound's thought more difficult, since there are few reliable studies of past figures whose work was outside mainstream economics. He wrote about this tendency: "The history of money is yet to be written. . . . Vast mines of anecdote lie still unexploited."[9]

Pound clearly enunciated his basic program in 1935:

> We need in economics:
> 1. Simplification of terminology;
> 2. Articulation of terminology ("distinguish the root from the branch")
> We need:
> 3. Less intolerance towards converging movements;
> 4. To hammer on root ideas;[10]

The first two points are typical for Pound and follow from his interest in Confucius (the quotation is from the *Ta Hio*) and Dante. The fourth point expresses Pound's confidence that there are a few hidden, elementary principles in economics that, if understood, will give the necessary base on which to build a correct economic system, and that similar problems (and solutions) arise under a wide variety of cultural circumstances. The third point was a chief Poundian concern during the thirties. Pound believed that it was not enough to understand economics but that understanding had to be translated into governmental policy. During the thirties many different groups advocated economic reform. Pound saw similarities in the superficially diverse proposals, yet the groups frequently quarreled with each other and among themselves. Such dissent was particularly true of Social Credit. Not only were there competing

[8] Pound, "The Individual in His Milieu" (1935), in *Selected Prose*, 273.
[9] Ibid., 272–3.
[10] Pound, *Social Credit*, 13.

factions within the movement, but Douglas, Pound believed, often showed a remarkable lack of tolerance for other, similar ideas. Real reform could only be accomplished by a unified political effort. An earlier version of his program, showing this drive toward convergence, had appeared in his *ABC of Economics* in 1933: "The aim of this brochure is to express the fundamentals of economics so simply and clearly that even people of different economic schools and factions will be able to understand each other when they discuss them."[11] To clarify, to define, and to unite for action, then, were the motives behind so much of his activity in economics during the thirties.

II

Pound discovered Silvio Gesell in 1934. A monetary "heretic," Gesell was a disciple of Pierre Joseph Proudhon. Gesell's principal work is *The Natural Economic Order,* the first four parts of which appeared in 1906 (the fifth and final part appeared in 1911). The second edition of this work, in one volume, appeared in 1916, the third edition in 1919, the fourth in 1920, the fifth in 1922, the sixth in 1924, and the seventh in 1929, attesting to its popularity and to the troubled times in which it appeared. Gesell was an early advocate of the quantity theory of money, a view that was later championed by Irving Fisher in the United States and John Maynard Keynes in England, and is now accepted. At the time Pound became interested in him, however, his views were not widely credited. One critic commented that "his intellectual equipment for the task he had set himself was mediocre" and noted "the most glaring absurdities and inconsistencies in the argument as a whole."[12]

Pound's eclectic approach to economics has been noted. He wrote:

> All questions of how measures can be taken, how enforced, are questions of politics. ECONOMICS is concerned with determining WHAT financial measures, what methods or regulations of trade, etc., must be taken.... *There may even be several economic solutions to any problem.* Gasoline and coal both serve as fuel.[13]

Pound was not an ideologue. He was an economic pragmatist, who was searching to unite diverse economic factions where he felt they had broad

---

[11] Pound, *The ABC of Economics* (1933), in *Selected Prose,* 233.

[12] Myers, 68–9.

[13] Pound, *ABC of Economics* (1933), in *Selected Prose,* 247. This work, "written in ignorance of Gesell," as Pound later stated, anticipates Gesell's thought in another way. In it Pound wrote: "A small amount of 'money' changing hands rapidly will do the work of a lot moving slowly, etc." (254). Even a critic of Gesell, such as Myers, admits that "his chief contribution to monetary theory was his emphasis upon the importance of the velocity of circulation of money" (68).

interests in common. This approach was not welcome to Major Douglas, who demanded regimentation, not intuition, from his supporters. What caused Pound to shift from being a confirmed Douglasite to one who advocated a symbiosis of the Gesell and Douglas positions?

Pound's support for Social Credit derived from his meeting with Douglas through Orage, but it continued because Social Credit accounted for an easily observable phenomenon – the decrease in purchasing power – by a superficially simple theory. His disillusion may have come through a combination of his difficulty with C. H. Douglas and his realization that the deeper one got into Social Credit theory, the more obscure it became. Further, Social Credit lacked a practical mechanism to put its ideas into effect. Gesell offered such a mechanism, which was tried in practice in the Austrian village of Woergl. It was probably the Woergl experiment and Irving Fisher's account of it that led Pound to Gesell.

In 1932, a Gesell supporter was elected mayor of the town of Woergl, near Salzburg. Burgermeister Michael Unterguggenberger decided to use the opportunity given by his new office to put Gesell's idea of stamp scrip into effect. Fifteen hundred workers out of the town's population of forty-three hundred were employed for public works projects. Their salaries were paid with village scrip, whose notes needed to be stamped at the rate of 1 percent of their face amount each month to maintain their value. The plan was put into operation on 1 August 1932 and ended a year later after a successful lawsuit against the village was brought by the Austrian National Bank for infringing on the bank's monopoly for issuing currency. The plan seemed to work, because several nearby villages were preparing to follow Woergl's example.[14]

Pound apparently wrote to Douglas about this experiment, because Douglas replied on 4 July 1933, in a letter we have already quoted:

> The real trouble about the Woergl scheme is what has happened to the Woergl scheme, which is another way of saying that the problem of reforming the financial system is not how to reform the financial system, but how to strangle the bankers. Any sermons on this text will be appreciated.

This letter shows up in Canto XLI: "Said C.H. 'To strangle the bankers ...?'/ And Woergl in our time?" (C, XLI, 205). Douglas's view of his relation to Pound displayed in this letter, that of prophet to priest, is worth noting. Pound, who was "not a disciple by nature,"[15] probably found Douglas's lack of receptivity annoying. Pound continued with his efforts, however. In January of 1934 he wrote to Giovanni Scheiwiller, looking for an Italian or French edition of Gesell's *The Natural Economic*

[14] Myers, 149–51.
[15] Reynolds, 392.

Order – apparently he did not trust his German and did not yet know of the English edition. Pound persisted in corresponding with Douglas about Gesell, as we see from another of Douglas's letters, of 3 September 1934: "Gesell's practical proposals seem to me merely a continuous and heavy tax. Any validity that they have rests on the assumption the plant of civilization does not belong to the consumer."[16] This shows that Douglas had not read or considered Gesell very carefully, since Gesell is emphatic that the money generated for the public treasury from his scheme will be offset by "a proportional reduction of taxation."[17] Pound's reply came, apparently, by way of a letter to the editor of the *Morning Post,* dated 27 September: "While Douglasites, with a laudable ambition to eliminate taxation altogether, object that Gesell's stamp is an oppression, more moderate economists cannot fail to consider this form of tax in comparison with the brutal and murderous income tax current in England." Pound's enthusiasm for Gesell continued to grow. On 3 October, Orage wrote to him, warning: "It just won't do. We've got enough to contend with without hanging Gesell round our necks." But Pound had decided that the two movements should converge, and he was trying to use his influence to make that happen.

He wrote again to the editor of the *Morning Post,* on 6 December 1934: "Dr. Fack, the Texas editor and publisher [of Gesell] has recently called off his attack on Major Douglas, recognizing that . . . they have a common cause in educating the public." In a conciliatory letter to Douglas on 26 December Pound admitted:

> Gesell OMITS one fundamental dissociation, which yr/ aged friend EZ makes in his kindergarten primer. I haven't yet found Gesell distinguishing between permanent (or quasi), durable and perishable goods. The minute one does that one has to consider proportion between fixed and diminishing money.

I think Pound had not fully understood Gesell on this point, because there is at least an implicit distinction between those kinds of goods made in Gesell's book, though the implications are not drawn out. Pound later hinted at what he meant by this remark to Douglas. He wrote that "a just proportion between a fixed and a diminishing money would equate the value of all goods to the value of available money."[18] Around this

---

[16] The beliefs that the plant of civilization belongs to the consumer and that the means of production should be in the hands of the worker strike me as similar, Social Credit's cultural heritage approaching Marxism.

[17] Gesell, 221. Further references to this volume in this chapter will be indicated by page numbers in parentheses.

[18] Pound, "The Individual in His Milieu" (1935), in *Selected Prose,* 277.

time Pound wrote to Eliot, recommending Gesell and offering to summarize his work for the *Criterion*.

What Pound saw in Gesell at first was that stamp scrip was an easily understandable mechanism to put Social Credit into action. He wrote:

> The problem that faces us (as Douglasites) is no longer that of understanding the problem or its solution, it is a problem of educating the public. In that campaign Gesell seems to me boundlessly useful. . . . He did not however, provide, as Douglas does provide, and uniquely, a means of getting the purchasing power into the places where it is MOST needed.[19]

Gesell's stamp scrip actually could accomplish the Social Credit goals, in a fashion more comprehensible to the layperson. That was Pound's initial reason for his enthusiasm for Gesell. In fact, in 1933, before he had read Gesell, he was advocating stamp scrip in his correspondence, probably out of enthusiasm for the Woergl experiment but also because it was simple and easy to grasp. He wrote to Virginia Price in February of 1935: "Study of Gesell is very pleasant and OUGHT to lead to Douglas, as Gesell does NOT answer all the questions though I personally believe Gesellism cd. be used in perfecting or simplifying Douglasite mechanism (i.e. as added gadget, NOT as substitute)." Although that was the reason for his initial attraction to Gesell, Pound found much more when he turned to a serious consideration of what Gesell had to say.

III

Gesell's most fundamental belief was that the economic order should be founded on untrammeled self-interest and competition and that the old order had allowed "thousands of years of unnatural selection – selection vitiated by money and privilege" (xi). Thus he was a Social Darwinist, but one who felt that competition in a capitalist society was not free but rather had become distorted by the monetary system that was in effect. His aim was to restore free competition through reform of the economic system so that "right evolution, eugenesis," (xi) would become possible. "Purposeful constructive reform must be directed towards suppressing all privileges which could falsify the result of competition," he wrote (xiii–xiv). Pound, a firm believer in the superior individual, would not have disagreed.

Gesell was an avowed disciple of Proudhon (1809–65), an economic thinker and anarchist who, although espousing Marx's labor theory of value, believed that the most direct way to implement social reform was through monetary reform. Proudhon did not successfully specify the

[19] Pound, *Social Credit*, 14.

way in which monetary reform was to be accomplished and was considered a monetary crank by economists until his reputation (like that of Gesell) was rehabilitated by John Maynard Keynes.[20] Spiegel notes that "both Proudhon and Keynes attacked financial capital while accepting private industrial enterprise, and in their theoretical argument both integrated monetary theory into the general body of economic principles."[21] Proudhon's disciple, Bakunin, took the anarchist movement of his acknowledged mentor in the direction of terror and violence, which has led to its being considered a forerunner of fascism.

Gesell also acknowledged a debt to the "Manchester school of economists," as modified by "subsequent Darwinian additions to their doctrine." Although the name of that group was originally a derogatory one, given by Disraeli, the group attained national influence in 1839, and the name "Manchester School" later became applied to laissez-faire economists in general.[22] Gesell held that they erred in believing that the starting point for competition was truly free. "It was assumed, sometimes from dishonest motives, that the conditions of competition in the existing order (including the privileges attached to the private ownership of land and money) were already sufficiently free" (xiv). Gesell wished to clear the ground for free competition through the elimination of the privileged position of capital:

> The Manchester economists, through ignorance of monetary theory, adopted without criticism the traditional monetary system which simply breaks down when the development foretold by the Manchester economists sets in. They did not know that money makes interest the condition of its services, that commercial crises, the deficit in the budget of the earning classes and unemployment are simply the effects of the traditional form of money. The Manchester ideals and the gold standard are incompatible. (xvi)

Linking the monetary system and the periodic business crises that plagued the industrial nations was a deep insight into the nature of the economic cycle that, although not fully developed, marks Gesell as being an original economic thinker well in advance of his time.

This mention of the gold standard should remind us that Gesell's work stands very much in the context of the nineteenth-century debate concerning the nature of money, as his occasional references to the bimetallists also makes clear. This debate today is almost forgotten. The United States effectively went off the gold standard in 1933,[23] and despite oc-

---

[20] Spiegel, 450–1.
[21] Ibid., 771.
[22] Ibid., 360.
[23] Friedman and Schwartz, 471. From the international standpoint, the United States went off the gold standard in 1971.

casional suggestions that it be revived, most today would consider the question settled. It is thus easy to forget just how passionately the gold question was argued and just how disastrous England's return to the gold standard under Chancellor of the Exchequer Winston Churchill was considered to be.[24]

Essentially the debate centered on the question of whether money got its value from precious metal or from the state. Those advocating the gold standard, the monometallists, believed that the source of monetary value derived from its backing in gold; they also supported the right of free coinage, the right of possessors of gold to bring in their bullion to a mint and have it made into coins. Those favoring the state definition of money advocated bimetallism, the use of a silver standard as well as the gold one; their arguments gained particular prominence in the last decade of the nineteenth century. Gesell absorbed these arguments and took them further to advance a quantity theory of money. A figure later read and admired by Pound, Alexander del Mar, was a polemicist on the state side of this debate, indicating where Pound stood. Another key concept in this evolving debate was whether "money was considered primarily 'neutral' instead of as an active instrument affecting the level of output and the distribution of income."[25] Gesell, Pound, and Keynes clearly favored the use of money as an instrument of public policy, which now seems correct. Reading Gesell was an education for Pound, a summary of the chief points in favor of the state position.

Despite these stands, neither Gesell nor Douglas nor Pound favored state control of economic life apart from the reforms they proposed. Gesell went so far as to say that if the reforms he advocated were not enacted, the only remaining choice would be communism (xvi–xvii), a false dichotomy as Keynes would show. In fact, Gesell believed that "defects in our system of land tenure and in our form of money . . . produced Capitalism, and Capitalism produced, for its own protection, the State as we know it – a hybrid between Communism and the Natural Economic Order" (xxiii). This view may not be as far-fetched as it seems at first. Ferdinand Braudel has made a similar point, and Guy Davenport, following his reading of Braudel, comments:

> The state came into being as a tax collector for the interest on loans involving the capitalist and the state (an armaments manufacturer, for instance). The business of the state became that of taxes, and the business of the capitalist was to see that the state consumed more than it could ever pay for.[26]

[24] See, e.g., Keynes, *Economic Consequences of Mr. Churchill.*
[25] Spiegel, 589.
[26] Davenport, viii.

Although this connection went beyond Pound's interest in the economic problems of his time, it corresponds to his belief that a mutually beneficial relation between arms manufacturers and capitalists leads to periodic war.

IV

Gesell acknowledges his debt to Proudhon early in the book and often. He believed that only Proudhon had found a solution to the general problem of all socialism, "the abolition of unearned income, of so-called surplus-value, also called interest and economic rent. The method generally proposed for this aim is Communism" (1). Gesell believed that communism presented no danger to industrial capitalism. He wrote, "it is positively an advantage . . . to capital to have Marx and Christ discussed as widely as possible, for Marx can never damage Capital. But beware of Proudhon" (4).

Gesell begins his book with a thorough critique of Marx, which is the source of Pound's frequent contention that Marx never understood the nature of money.[27] According to Gesell, Marx misconceives capital as real wealth instead of "an economic state, a condition of the market" (4). Since for Marx, surplus value came from "the abuse of power conferred by ownership," the remedy would be "the political supremacy of the dispossessed" (5). For Proudhon, however, "surplus value is subject to the law of demand and supply," and "the remedy is the removal of obstacles preventing us from the full development of our productive capacity" (5). The primary obstacle is the nature of money. If its supremacy were altered by a change in its nature, there would be no way to prevent workers from continually increasing production "without hindrance, disturbance, or interruption, [and] capital would soon be choked with an over-supply of capital (not to be confused with an over-production of goods)" (4).

By exposing the arbitrary nature of money as an expedient wholly under the control of the state, not as a value inherent in a rare commodity, Proudhon (and Gesell) opened the way whereby the state could be expected, in times of crisis, to accelerate the productive capacity of the nation through the creation of capital at an expanded rate. This expansion is what actually occurred in Great Britain during the First World War. By leveling the field, Proudhon (and Gesell) would achieve the social

---

[27] Arthur Kitson had made the same point in his article "The Root of All Evil" in the *New Age*, perhaps following a reading of Gesell: "Karl Marx, who understood a good many things, did not understand the science of money. . . . Among the many reformers of the past century, one name stands pre-eminent. . . . P.J. Proudhon" (27 Feb. 1913, 400).

goals sought by Marx, though by simpler means. Thus, whereas Marx would advocate tactics of strikes and crises, Proudhon would urge that strikes and crises were the most powerful tools of capital, "whereas nothing is more fatal to it than hard work" (5).

Proudhon's central insight was that money, owing to the superior competitive advantage it held over labor and goods, can block production when it is not extracting its usual tribute: "As soon as capital ceases to yield the traditional interest, money strikes and brings work to a standstill" (7). Having discovered this, Gesell continues, Proudhon decided to raise goods and labor to the level of money, to level the field. To put this "into practice, he founded exchange banks. As everyone knows, they failed" (8). Gesell acknowledges his debt to Proudhon, recognizing that Proudhon discovered the true nature of capital "fifty years earlier" (7). His own contribution, he claimed, was to discover a method to put Proudhon's idea into practice.

It was impossible to alter the nature of goods, as Proudhon tried, so Gesell proposed altering the nature of money to bring the two sides into a more equal competitive balance. Proudhon did not recognize that money was both a medium of exchange and a store of value (or medium of saving), an insight that Pound borrows from Gesell; had he made that distinction, he might have anticipated Gesell's proposal. Gesell's solution is as follows: To make money, which is both a commodity and a medium of exchange, descend to an equal level with goods, we must subject it "to the loss to which goods are liable through the necessity of storage. ... Money and goods are then perfect equivalents; Proudhon's problem is solved and the fetters are burst that have prevented humanity from developing its full power" (9). In other words, Gesell proposed to make money subject to decay.

The rest of *The Natural Economic Order* is devoted to working out the logic of his proposal. Gesell possessed a first-rate mind, and though some of the proposals, such as the one to make available "free-land" for settlement, strike us now as hopelessly outdated (Pound, too, thought Gesell's free-land proposal unworkable), his thorough analysis is impressive. Much of his book remains suggestive and valuable as a historical document that can give us a good grasp of the origins of the concept of money that we now accept as given. Gesell was an idealist, and he wrote with much greater clarity and thoughtfulness than Douglas, qualities that undoubtedly attracted Pound. Because Gesell was not by training an economist, he approached the subject without jargon or preconceptions. By force of intellect alone, he rethought the field of economics, in response to the economic crisis of the late 1880s. Keynes rightly called him "an unduly neglected prophet... whose work contains flashes of deep insight."[28] He provided Pound with an original and basic education in economics and an understanding of the true nature of money.

There is an occasional flair for the poetic in his writing, unusual in economics, that is also pleasing: "The term 'measure of value' sometimes applied to money in antiquated writings on economics is misleading. No quality of a canary bird, a pill or an apple can be measured by a piece of money" (12). Pound certainly would have agreed with that, and he would have liked Gesell's view that although the workers should have the right to "the whole proceeds of labor," such proceeds should be "apportioned by competition," not leveled as was advocated by the communists (13). Following this view, no proceeds from labor are given to the capitalists in the form of interest or rent, but a superior person who works hard is rewarded for both effort and ability. Workers "must stop the leaks in their wage-fund; they must protect it from parasites. . . . The whole of the product of labor, with no deduction for rent and interest, must go into the wage-fund and be distributed to the last crumb among its creators" (52). Despite the occurrence of the word *parasites,* recalling the rhetoric of revolution, Gesell had a plan to put his reform into effect that was nonviolent and recognized previous property rights: "Present landowners will receive full compensation, in the form of State-bonds, for the loss of their rents" (55). Although at first glance this might seem to merely transfer the privileges of property owners to bondholders, it should be noted that Gesell had an involved plan to introduce his monetary reform simultaneously with the nationalization of land, in such a way that the changes in the monetary system that he advocated would have invalidated those privileges.

Gesell was also "a moralist and thence an economist," as Pound wrote about A. R. Orage. Gesell would have agreed with Jefferson that the "earth belongs to the living":

> 1. Competition among men can be carried on fairly and in accordance with its high function only if all special private or public rights over land are abolished.
> 2. All men without exception must have an equal right to the earth. . . . No private individual, no State, no society must retain any kind of privilege over the land. (55)

Gesell was vehement, as was Pound later, about the disastrous effect of the gold standard and the propensity of the moneyed classes to engage in conspiracy:

> We must here recall that our present currency laws offer no guarantee whatever that currency policy may not any day be directed, at the

[28] Keynes, *The General Theory,* 353.

bidding of the creditor class, towards a general fall of prices such as occurred in 1873 when silver was demonetized. . . . at the expense of the debtor class. (70)

The idea that money was more than a neutral medium of exchange and could be manipulated for the good of a class, and thus perhaps also for the good of a society, is a key one for Gesell and Pound.

V

Much of Gesell's study of the nature of money depends on the bimetallist debate of the nineteenth century. He draws upon that literature to provide the underpinnings for his proposal and, in doing so, helps Pound to his central insight about money and to a recollection of the impassioned debate from his youth that provoked William Jennings Bryan's memorable rallying cry.[29] But Gesell first sets out what he be-lieves are the reasons for the neglect of serious consideration of the question of money. He criticizes university professors of economics, in a way that must have caused Pound to nod in agreement: "The exclusion of criticism of the existing order from university teaching prevents uni-versity professors from penetrating far into the nature of money," and "the pedantic obscurity with which monetary theory has been treated by scientists has caused the public to despise a subject which is never-theless of vast importance to human development" (98). Pound, of course, with his scorn for the "beaneries," as he termed universities and his attempt to educate the public on the ABCs of both reading and economics would have found Gesell's views especially congenial here.

The demonetization of silver provided Gesell with the evidence he needed to pursue his claim:

> The inscription made the thaler and its material one and the same con-ception; the demonetization of silver proved the existence of two con-ceptions of the thaler. The withdrawal of the right of free coinage of silver made the thaler transparent, so that through the silver we saw its inner nature. We had believed that a thaler was merely silver, but now we were forced to recognize that it had also been money. (101)

Since it was the inscription, not the metal, that made the coin money, then the metal itself, any metal, was not important. Gesell writes: "'The Reichsbank promises to pay the holder. . . . . .' should be changed to 'This is 100 Marks'" (103). It is the law, not the metal nor the promise

---

[29] "You shall not crucify mankind upon a cross of gold" (1894). Pound's first published poem was a limerick about Bryan in the *Jenkintown Times–Chronicle* of 7 Nov. 1896, just after his defeat. It begins: "There was a young man from the West / He did what he could for what he thought best." It is cited in Carpenter, 36.

to redeem a paper note in metal, that is important. Although this conception of the nature of money is by now familiar and comfortable to us, it must be realized that when Gesell, and Pound, were writing, it was by no means obvious. By the time that Pound wrote his three-part article on economics, for the prestigious academic journal *Rassegna Monetaria*, he had clearly absorbed the lessons that Gesell had to teach: "Even in the exchange of a disk of precious metal for goods, that which determines in the first place the quality of money is the die of the State."[30]

The fundamental error then prevailing was that most theorists on money started from the idea that it had value. Marx in particular fell into that misconception according to Gesell:

> "Value" is a chimera, a mere product of the imagination.
> Marx, whose economic system is founded upon a theory of value, uses almost the same words: "Value is a phantom" – which does not, however, prevent him from attempting to conjure up this phantom in three bulky volumes. "Abstract from the worked-up substances all material properties," says Marx, "and only one property remains, namely value." (109)

Gesell notes that " 'products of labor' not 'substances' were Marx's words, but the expression is misleading. What remains after this abstraction is not a property but simply the history of that object – the knowledge that a human being has worked upon it. . . . Marx mistook the origin and history of products for their properties" (109). There is no such thing, he argues, as property separated from its substance. Thus Marx begins his work with an illusion. Instead, money is a commodity, pure and simple, according to Gesell. Pound, who was fully aware of the importance of Marx, adopted Gesell's critique in his own writings. Keynes also believed that the answer to Marxism was to be found in Gesell.[31] Gesell notes that there is no talk of "value" in the business world, except in terms of probable price in the future. There are only prices, determined by the laws of supply and demand.

Since a theory of price will apply equally to price and value, a theory of value become superfluous. The real nature of money, for Gesell, lies in its existence as an independent commodity among commodities, whose price is determined afresh every time something is purchased with it. The illusion of value and the mistaken notion that conversion to gold makes a paper note valuable were to Gesell the greatest obstacles to economic progress. Pound went back to Aristotle to find the basis of this distinction, and the subsequent confusion it caused:

[30] Pound, "Toward an Orthological Economy," *Rassegna Monetaria* 5–6 (May–June 1937): 391. Pound's article appeared in three parts, in three consecutive issues: May–June, July–August, and September–October.
[31] Keynes, *The General Theory*, 355.

Aristotle has left us a word of uncertain and complex meaning: χρεία. Usefulness, desirability. . . . Aristotle "was right" but he meant to say that the value of a monetary unit "is worth what you can get for it." . . . Let's begin, for example, with the term "money." Aristotle defines it badly, or rather he does not define it, but speaks of it without really defining it. And humanity has remained for twenty centuries in this state of half darkness.[32] (tr)

The First World War gave evidence for Gesell's contention that there was a better way to administer the currency. His elegiac tone in speaking of the war would have suggested to Pound that Gesell's memories of it were as sad as his own. Of the ersatz materials necessitated by the war and the blockade, Gesell observes: "The substitute products of the war were dear and bitter. Only the substitute for gold, paper-money, failed to make us sigh for peace" (115). Although the First World War gave many further proofs of his theory (his book was originally published in 1911), Gesell adds in a later edition that he had "no wish to gain anything from the war, not even material for proving a theory" (135).

VI

After separating money from the gold standard, and from a hypostatized theory of value, Gesell proceeds to establish the necessary basis for money. Since money's first use is as a medium of exchange, it is important, according to Gesell, that "the holder should be indifferent to the money-material" (123). Otherwise, its free circulation would be impaired. The issue of money should be in the hands of the state and protected by law; it would be a "manufactured product" (128) protected by state monopoly. In a final swipe at those who believe that money need be backed by a precious metal, Gesell points out that when that was the case, the state could destroy metallic money without breach of law (as it did when it demonetized silver), but "paper-money can only fall with the State itself" (133).

If the state would alone issue and guarantee a paper currency, what would give security to its value? In an answer that would have been pleasing to Pound, who believed that only education, not law, could free men from error, Gesell said: "The only real security would be the monetary education of a sufficient number of men who, in the event of legislation affecting monetary standard [sic], would form a bodyguard, so to speak, to protect the mark from bunglers and swindlers" (136–7).

---

[32] Pound, "Toward an Orthological Economy," *Rassegna Monetaria* 5–6 (May–June 1937): 390.

He reemphasized that point again when he stated: "The security of money can only be attained by a sound conception of currency policy shared by the people and their rulers" (143). This is somewhat idealistic, but it is precisely in keeping with Pound's attempts during the thirties to educate his readers about currency issues, even in the *Cantos*. Gesell is less hopeful in the later edition, when he points out that despite the postwar experiences of inflation, deflation, and stabilization, there was still no mention of a monetary standard in the constitution of the German Republic (136).

Should a paper currency be introduced, people would need the state to offer protection from radical inflation and deflation. The "self-evident conclusion" that Gesell reaches about this question is that "independently of time and place money should always obtain the price it obtains to-day." He makes a few suggestions about how this could be put into effect. Essentially, "the demand for this paper-money would be exactly as large as the supply of wares awaiting sale, which in turn would depend upon the production of wares" (127). To measure and prevent inflation or deflation, variations in the "value" of money would be gauged in comparison with the average price of a group of commodities, a suggestion that one runs into occasionally today, to stabilize the value of the dollar, but which does not consider, as Gesell did, that a moderate rate of inflation could at times have beneficial effects for a society.[33]

Having laid the foundation for the proposal in the minds of his readers (and after reading Gesell's thorough analysis of the nature of money, the reader is quite prepared to agree with him and to agree with Pound's statement in echo of Gesell that Marx did not understand the nature of money), Gesell needs only a few more steps before his "radical" solution will seem plausible. The first step is to reemphasize the commodity nature of money.

> The offer of money was and is correctly called the demand for commodities. Where the stock of commodities is large, the demand for money is large. Similarly it can be said that where the quantity of money is large there is necessarily more demand for commodities than where the quantity of money is small. (The limitations of this statement will soon appear.)
>
> Is there any demand for commodities other than that which the supply of money represents? (158)

To adjust demand for commodities, when such are plentiful, one then need only increase in some manner the quantity of money. Gesell notes

---

[33] Pound remembered this when he wrote to Jorian E. F. Jenks of the British Union of Fascists on 14 March 1940: "IF I were in charge of the system proper money shd/ (and wd/) be measured by a price index (i.e. a list of essential goods/ of certain grade, beef/ wool/petrol. . . . eggs of a certain weight/ In short the most basic index/ of say 20 commodities in most general use."

that money is useful solely insofar as it circulates and that although the old form of money is under some compulsion to circulate, the new form that he proposes will be under "absolute" compulsion to circulate (167). Because of this "technical improvement in money," it will circulate faster. Pound saw this as the central point in Gesell:

> Gesell concentrated on the concept of *circulation,* and planned the means in order that they wouldn't stagnate. Blood circulates in the veins....
>
> I don't say that Gesell's system (*Schwundgeld*) is indispensable, but I declare that a man who doesn't understand the *reason* for it will never be a true economist. Gesell has calculated or found a rough means to make a proportion of the power to buy spoil or be consumed *pari passu* with the consumption of food, the wearing out of clothes, and the burning of coal and gas.[34] (tr)

This emphasis on the velocity of money is recognized, as we mentioned, even by his critics, as an important contribution to economics.[35] (Keynes felt that Gesell's emphasis on demand was one of his key contributions.)[36] Gesell's own formulation of his key idea is as follows: "Demand, then, is determined by the amount of the stock of money and the velocity of circulation of money. Demand increases in exact proportion to the increase of the stock of money and of the velocity of its circulation" (170). Two problems occur with the old system of money that cause hardship and unfairness. The first is that gold is a stable material, not given to decay. Commodities are perishable and must be disposed of in time. This gives an unfair advantage, according to Gesell, to holders of money over holders of goods. Pound's version of this was: "Gesell starts from another fundamental perception, that is of the relative duration of different kinds of goods"[37] (tr). The second problem is that when the supply of money becomes insufficient, prices fall, and when prices fall, more money is withdrawn from circulation (taking advantage of the more stable nature of gold), causing commerce to become impossible. Not only that, but an actual fall in prices is not even necessary for the withdrawal of money from circulation. It is enough that people merely believe that prices will fall for it to happen. These dual problems cause a breakdown in modern economies (178–80).

Gesell shared the belief that because of the technical accomplishments of modern industrial society, we have greatly improved our production of goods and should be enjoying an age of plenty. An increase in the

---

[34] Pound, "Toward an Orthological Economy," *Rassegna Monetaria* 9–10 (Sept.–Oct. 1937): 1103.

[35] Myers, 68.

[36] Ibid., 69.

[37] Pound, "Toward an Orthological Economy," *Rassegna Monetaria* 9–10 (Sept.–Oct. 1937): 1102.

supply of goods did lead to an increased demand for money. But, "because we have not balanced this greater demand for money with a greater supply of money, the prices of wares have fallen" (181). In a society with an inelastic supply of currency, tied to the gold stock, and with increased industrial and scientific uses for gold, gold would have to be discovered in unusual quantities to avoid periodic and severe economic crises (Gesell posits a need for a 5 percent annual increase of gold for currency uses, a version of the constant monetary growth later advocated by Milton Friedman) (190). Pound recognized this idea from another economist he had been reading: "David Douglas Hume had already seen that prosperity was not dependent on the quantity of money in a given Nation but on the fact that this quantity was growing (we specify that the growth must be slow and constant)"[38] (tr). To prevent commercial crises, prices must be prevented from ever falling. This could be accomplished by:

> 1. The separation of money from gold and the production of money in accordance with the needs of the market.
> 2. A form of paper-money so contrived that it will be offered in all possible circumstances in exchange for wares. (190)

When money is in short supply, there is a demand for credit, which, under Gesell's system, always represents an "evasion of the demand for money" (165). Capitalism, in this view, is the system "in which the demand for loan-money and real capital exceeds the supply and therefore gives rise to interest" (190).[39]

Gesell recognized that his proposal would require two types of currency, one for circulation and one for saving, a distinction that Pound also adopted in his writings:

> [All of Gesell's doctrine] derives from a correct definition of money. Money isn't valid if it is a title to something that isn't deliverable. And to balance the power to acquire with the goods (and services) available, it is necessary that these titles disappear with consumption; or that a method is found to maintain the total of available money in an *efficient* relation with the total available goods and services.[40] (tr)

He expanded: "Gesell, seeing that gold lasted and goods did not, wanted money that would adapt itself almost automatically to the disappearance of goods. These are ethical actions"[41] (tr). Recognizing the necessity of two types of currency, Gesell then introduces his plan to put money and

[38] Pound, "Toward an Orthological Economy," *Rassegna Monetaria* 5–6 (May–June 1937): 393.
[39] Keynes also admired Gesell's monetary theory of interest.
[40] Pound, "Toward an Orthological Economy," *Rassegna Monetaria* 9–10 (Sept.–Oct. 1937): 1102–3.
[41] Ibid., 1106.

wares (demand and supply) on an equal footing. He calls his new type of money "Free-Money," a phrase not meant to be precise but rather suggestive: free because it is no longer dependent upon gold and is free to all on an equal basis. Gesell explains:

> 1. Free-Money is issued in 1-5-10-20-50-100 and 1000 dollar notes (bills) and in perforated sheets of stamps resembling postage stamps, value 1-5-10-20 and 50 cents. . . .
> 2. Free-Money loses one thousandth of its face value weekly or about 5% annually, at the expense of the holder. The holder has to keep the notes at their face value by attaching to them the small change stamps [for most notes weekly]. (216)

This is the essence of stamp scrip, the reform that was tried in Woergl. Pound greatly admired this new conception of money, although he quibbled with the method for its implementation: "I don't insist on the revenue stamps. I could live well enough without the pleasure of adopting a second variety of postage stamp"[42] (tr). A "Currency Office" would regulate the amount of money in circulation according to the "needs of the market in such a manner that the general level of prices remains stable" (217). This resembles the function of the Federal Reserve Board, although Pound did not see that. A separate currency mechanism for import and export, involving gold and an international monetary agreement where possible, would be provided and regulated by the Currency Office. Since the currency in circulation would decrease at an annual rate of 5.2 percent, it would have to be replaced as needed, which would provide revenue for the office and for the state and a concomitant reduction in taxes (218). Pound saw this as providing the sanest method of revenue for government:

> The State, or whoever furnishes a measure for exchange, works. Inasmuch as this measure is stable or varies systematically, in a way clear to all, the State or the issuer of money deserves compensation. This is the ethical foundation for the revenue stamps of Avigliano [an Italian economist] and Gesell or for *demurrage charges*.[43] (tr)

Because this ethical method of raising income was available to the state, the fact of a state having to borrow money seemed even more outrageous to Pound. Apparently ignorant (or forgetful) of the fact that Italy, too, borrowed to finance its social programs, Pound attacked some familiar targets:

---

[42] Ibid.
[43] Pound, "Toward an Orthological Economy," *Rassegna Monetaria* 7–8 (July–Aug. 1937): 710.

The State has absolutely no need to pay "rent" for its credit, that is, to borrow it from big, professional usurers as they do in almost every country unaware and too tied to harmful preconceptions, for example, in my most disgraceful homeland, the United States, in France, . . . in England.[44] (tr)

This is the basis for his complaint against Roosevelt.

Among the benefits that Gesell listed for his Free-Money system are the removal of the economic causes of war and the facilitation of international trade through a currency agreement based on common interests (219). Like other economic reformers of that era, including Pound (and Hobson before him), Gesell saw trade conflicts between nations and the aggressive seeking of markets through colonization and dumping as principal causes of war. By removing the gold standard and making the power of money equal to that of goods and labor, he believed that a major cause of international friction would be removed.

Pound saw the advantages of the Gesell system as "at least" the following: (1) The "pseudo-democratic countries" would be freed from domination by "the bankers and the usurers." (2) The monthly addition of a stamp equal in value to 1 percent of the value of the note would provide the state with a significant income, without the expenses of collection, "that would be automatic and almost free of bureaucratic interference." (3) "Instead of piling up 'astronomical' debts with National Bonds, like Roosevelt, every state debt . . . would cancel itself in 100 months." (4) "Treasury notes could continue to be held privately, as a means of saving for those who wished to provide for old age and family, but they would be considered a State dividend for a worthy class of citizens, not an inescapable necessity for a government that wishes to use its credit."[45] This last remedy was obviously not clearly thought through by Pound; as a solution it would seem at the very least vulnerable to Gresham's law, that bad money drives out good, and would require careful implementation. But Gesell is valuable to Pound as much for the education and analysis he provides as for any specific cure he proposes.

VII

Gesell's *The Natural Economic Order* does not rise or fall on the merit of its proposal for stamp scrip or even for free land. Its value is based on its excellent and thorough analysis of the monetary system. Some form of stamp scrip would have probably worked in the thirties to solve the principal problems of the Depression, although there were

[44] Pound, "Toward an Orthological Economy," *Rassegna Monetaria* 5–6 (May–June 1937): 395.
[45] Ibid.

administrative hurdles to be cleared before it could have been put into practice. Interestingly enough, after so carefully laying the ground for his radical reform, he first disposes of a "simple reform" that seems more workable and attractive: that of a government-managed supply of paper money. According to Myers, Gesell in later years seemed to have realized that the reform he desired could have been accomplished this way.[46]

The simple reform that he found inadequate consisted in allowing the state to issue or withdraw paper money according to its estimate of demand determined by the general level of prices. "The quantity of money in circulation is to be increased when prices fall and to be decreased when prices rise" (193). Gesell notes that such reforms were successful in Argentina and other countries and called attention to the possibility of a paper currency. The currency could not be redeemed in gold but only by use. But he believed that such a scheme had one serious defect: "In every other respect this paper-money is . . . indistinguishable from ordinary paper-money; it may be used or misused for saving or as a reserve for speculation. Demand is left in possession of all the privileges it possesses over supply" (193–4). The problem with this idea, what he called the "crude quantity theory of money," was that the amount of money in circulation would not necessarily correspond to the total stock of money available. As a consequence of this, "the price of money is independent of the stock," and economic prosperity once again depends upon confidence or its lack (205). The simple reform would allow money to maintain its traditional advantages over goods and labor, and thus he rejected it ("we must make money worse as a commodity if we wish to make it better as a medium of exchange" [213]). This "simple reform" is in effect in most countries today; Gesell's work, in part, made it possible.

In the remaining pages of the book, Gesell presents the advantages of his plan from the viewpoint of fictional characters representing various professions: shopkeeper, bank clerk, exporter, manufacturer. The "Disciple of Proudhon" offers Gesell thanks:

> With the introduction of Free-Money, our whole program has been fulfilled. The goal towards which we had been groping has been reached. What we had hoped to attain by means of complicated vaguely-conceived institutions such as exchange-banks and cooperative societies, namely a perfect exchange of goods, has been realized in the very simplest and easiest way through Free-Money. (261)

Pound, at least, raises ghosts for more serious purposes than self-congratulation. A character called "the Theorist on Economic Crises" appears to comment on the "new theory, one of the best in my collec-

---

[46] Myers, 64.

tion," the theory of underconsumption, and notes that it sounded "plausible" but was meant to appeal only to the proletariat (272–3).

The remainder of the work contains additional material that is of some interest to us. Gesell acknowledges what Pound would have recognized as Douglas's idea of the cultural heritage: "James Watt in his grave does more work to-day than all the horses alive. It is not labor, but the result of labor, the product, that matters" (282). And, echoing Pound's volitionist economics, he states: "A conscious action must be substituted for a dead mass of gold, since the monetary standard cannot be conceived as a substance, but only as an action, as an administrative measure" (288). (Or perhaps an intention, or volition, as in "Volitionist Economics.")

It is easy to imagine how excited Pound must have been in discovering the work of Gesell, and how much it would have confirmed and furthered his own thinking. Although Pound never came close to the breadth and profundity of Gesell's economic writings, they did help him achieve some clarity in his own writing about the subject. His respect for the man is evident: "Two men have ended the Marxist era. Douglas in conceiving the cultural heritage as the greatest and chief fountain of value. Gesell in seeing that 'Marx never questioned money. He just took it for granted.' "[47] Of course, the mechanism of stamp scrip allowed Pound a way to explain monetary reform to his audience and urge them to put it into effect. Its simplicity and justice impressed him: "Gesell questioned the privilege of money over and above all other products of human ingenuity. . . . He, thereupon, devised a tax on money, which requires no bureaucracy to levy it, and which falls with utter impartial justice on every hoarder or delayer of money."[48] Chace has noted, correctly, that "Pound is as eager to recommend a specific remedy as he is to find a specific cause,"[49] and this tendency is evident here, although in this case Pound was probably more justified than usual in his ameliorist enthusiasm. In any event, once read, Gesell was immediately elevated to the Pound pantheon. His monetary invention, Pound said, needed to be assessed in comparison with "the only other two systems in our time worth serious attention."[50] The other two were, of course, Social Credit and Italian fascism. At another point he slightly expanded the list to reflect other directions of his economic self-education: "There are four live currents in the economic thought of today: 1) Douglasism; 2) Gesellism; 3) canonist economics that derives its origin from Saint Ambrogio and that evolves with Saint Antonino [of Florence] 4) the corporate

[47] Pound, *Social Credit*, 13.
[48] Pound, "The Individual in His Milieu" (1935), in *Selected Prose*, 275.
[49] Chace, 8.
[50] Pound, "The Individual in His Milieu" (1935), in *Selected Prose*, 276.

economy, with its politics of land reclamation, the battle for wheat, grain pools, [and] family dividends"[51] (tr).

Still, Pound was apparently frustrated by his attempts to bring the two groups' work to each other's attention:

> Between Douglas and Gesell there is a contest of justice with justice, neither, of a right, excluding the other's justice.
>
> Take it at the surface and wrangle over detail and you will get nowhere, or merely into a tangle. Carry it down to its root *in justice* and you will find no needful contradiction. . . .
>
> So long as Douglasites refuse to consider (if they any of them really do so refuse) the unjust privileges of money above any other product, so long as the Gesellites refuse to consider the cultural heritage (the increment of association, and the possibilities inherent in a right proportion in the issue of fixed money and Schwundgeld, monnaie fondante, stamp scrip) for just so long will both groups sabotage each other and delay economic light. . . .
>
> No Douglasite can improve on Gesell's criteria for money.
>
> No Gesellite will get deeper than Douglas's fountain of values. . . .
>
> Neither side shows adequate readiness to define their lines of agreement with the other.[52]

He later complained that free and open economic discussion did not exist in either Gesellite or Douglasite publications. "They quarrel among themselves," he wrote[53] (tr). Pound was consistent in his attempts to apply the economic program that he had outlined previously: to simplify and define economic terminology, to stress root ideas, and to promote mutual tolerance among movements that aimed at similar goals and shared a common mistrust of basic elements in mainstream economics and their resulting failures. He had set ambitious goals for himself. He wished to see the best elements of the thought of Douglas and Gesell combined with a view toward putting them into action; he believed that his native land and his two adopted lands of Britain and Italy probably offered the most promising climates for these ideas.

Whatever our final judgment will be about his activities during this period, several points should be made here. First, Pound had a basically sound intuition about both the economic causes of the crisis of his time and the direction that society should take to remedy that crisis. Second, he chose to act upon his perception with a program that demonstrated a self-understanding both about his skills and about how he could best contribute to economic reform. Third, he was consistent in the imple-

---

[51] Pound, "Toward an Orthological Economy," *Rassegna Monetaria* 5–6 (May–June 1937): 392.

[52] Pound, "The Individual in His Milieu" (1935), in *Selected Prose*, 275–6.

[53] Ibid., 397.

mentation of the program he set for himself. With that in mind, and with our consideration of the climate of economic opinion of his time and the writings of C. H. Douglas and Silvio Gesell now complete, we can turn to consideration of Pound's economic synthesis, his own understanding of the problems, and how he perceived these ideas as being put into action in Italy and neglected in Great Britain and the United States.

VIII

Pound's economic thought tends to arrange itself in a series of dichotomies, not only of problem and solution, but also of evil versus ethical action, goods versus their monetary representations, fixed money versus stamp scrip, unconscious versus volitional economics, distributive scarcity versus productive plenty, usury versus the abundance of nature (or the increment of association), ignorance (and the possibility of crime) versus education (and the unmasking of error), the gold standard versus paper (statal) money, avarice versus the just price, bad banks (the Bank of England) versus good banks (the Monte dei Paschi), and so on. These dissociations were to enable him to articulate clearly his own thinking on economic matters. Regrettably, dichotomized thinking can become automatic, separated from observation and complexity, and tend to ever sharper polarities. That symbolic process would lead Pound into trouble during the Second World War, as it became more exaggerated and obsessive.

Economics has become the public policy science of our century, and much of Pound's work of the thirties anticipates or reflects this gradually developing state of affairs, as Pound moves easily from one realm to the other, drawing implications from economics to urge a course of action in politics. A good part of this intertwining of the two realms lies in his awareness, mentioned earlier, that economics could no longer be considered a neutral and descriptive science but had become inextricably bound up with politics and had to be a conscious instrument of policy and intervention. "In politics the problem of our time is to find the border between public and private affairs," Pound wrote; "in economics: to find a means whereby the common-carrier may be in some way kept in circulation."[54]

Pound did not reject other solutions to the economic problems of his time; in fact, he probably welcomed any discussion of economics. One remedy he especially desired was the shortening of the working day to four or five hours. He recognized that this "would so aid the general

[54] Pound, *The ABC of Economics* (1933), in *Selected Prose,* 240.

distribution in all civilized countries that they could carry on without other change for a considerable period."[55] He even introduced monetary reform into that proposal: "By simple extensions of credit (paper credit) it would probably be possible to leave the nominal pay exactly where it is, but it requires an almost transcendent comprehension of credit to understand this."[56] But even the shortening of the working day would not enable governments "perpetually to dodge the problem of a fair and/ or adequate distribution of credit slips. Called the problem of money or of the fiduciary system."[57] This observation was written before Pound discovered Gesell, and so lacks completeness, but even in *The ABC of Economics* Pound saw the need for a controlled inflation: "The financial executive would have one main function. . . . to determine, and so far as possible to keep steady, the rate of increase in the printed certificates of value."[58] Under this earlier system of Douglasite certificates, Pound anticipated that the best step toward a national dividend "could (?should) be made by this direct payment in newly conceived money for work publicly needed."[59] The only difference between this recommendation and the Roosevelt program of public-works spending was that under Pound's plan, the government would not need to borrow the money but could simply issue it.

Pound's criticism of Marx follows Gesell and Douglas: "I have already cited both Tour du Pin and Marx as IGNORING money, as being unconscious of the problem IN MONEY."[60] That argument, as we have seen, derives from Gesell. He later used Douglas as well: "Marx saw that 'value arises from labor' but he didn't see that an enormous amount of work had *ALREADY* been accomplished by our ancestors, inventors of mechanical processes. Douglas demolished Marxism with that perception"[61] (tr). One should not take this dismissal as evidence that Pound took Marx lightly – far from it. He had acquired the Italian edition of *Capital* in the early thirties and his markings and annotations show that he studied it with unusual care. These markings give us some idea of his dialogue with Marx. Apart from the exasperated "neglect of style" annotation in Part 1, Chapter 1, we soon see that Pound fundamentally disagrees with Marx's notion of money. In section 4 of that same chapter, Marx writes that

[55] Ibid., 249.
[56] Ibid., 244.
[57] Ibid., 249.
[58] Ibid., 261.
[59] Ibid., 263.
[60] Pound, "History and Ignorance" (1935), in *Selected Prose*, 268.
[61] Pound, "Toward an Orthological Economy," *Rassegna Monetaria* 9–10 (Sept.–Oct. 1937): 1106.

it was the analysis of the prices of commodities that alone led to the determination of the magnitude of value, and it was the common expression of all commodities in money that alone led to the establishment of their characters as values. It is, however, just this ultimate money-form of the world of commodities that actually conceals, instead of disclosing, the social character of private labour, and the social relations between the individual producers.[62]

At this point, Pound writes emphatically "*no*" and substitutes the word "banking" in Italian for the word "commodities," changing the phrase to "this ultimate money-form of the world of banking." Pound did not agree with the commodity theory of money advocated by Marx, who found an intrinsic value in money (gold). In Part 1, Chapter 2, Marx writes:

We have seen that the money-form is but the reflex, thrown upon one single commodity, of the value relations between all the rest. That money is a commodity is therefore a new discovery only for those who, when they analyze it, start from its fully developed shape. The act of exchange gives to the commodity converted into money, not its value, but its specific value-form. By confounding these two distinct things some writers have been led to hold that the value of gold and silver is imaginary. The fact that money can, in certain functions, be replaced by mere symbols of itself, gave rise to that other mistaken notion, that it is itself a mere symbol. Nevertheless under this error lurked a presentiment that the money-form of an object is not an inseparable part of that object, but is simply the form under which certain social relations manifest themselves. In this sense every commodity is a symbol, since, in so far as it is value, it is only the material envelope of the human labor spent upon it.[63]

Pound of course disagrees with this analysis, and in his marginal notes replaces "in certain functions" with "all," correcting the faulty phrase, in his view, to "money can, in *all* functions, be replaced by mere symbols of itself." Thus for Pound, money does not have intrinsic value based on the "labour-time required for its production." Instead, money has only price.[64] Money does not serve as "a universal measure of value," as Marx states at the beginning of Chapter 3, but it is a "universal measure of prices," the words Pound substitutes in the margin.[65]

Money for Pound was "a fiction, an artificial creation of human in-

[62] Marx, 75–6. Pound's markings are in the Italian edition, now at the Humanities Research Center at the University of Texas at Austin.
[63] Ibid., 90.
[64] Ibid., 91.
[65] Ibid., 94.

genuity."[66] For Marx, and for Ricardo, the value of money depended on how much it cost to produce gold, which was the true money. Not surprisingly, the British Marxist critic Peter Nicholls faults Pound's economics because it does not conform to Marx's understanding of money: "The conception of money as a fiction, a simple sign, is thus dismissed by Marx as a mystification of the capitalist exchange-process . . . money is no mere symbol but 'the form under which certain social relations manifest themselves' (Capital I, p. 94)."[67] This is too orthodox, dismissing Pound's argument by reference to a canonical text. Nicholls is correct as far as he goes, but instead of calling attention to the fundamentally differing ideas about money, nominal versus real, that separate Pound from Marx, he simply states the Pound was in error. Pound respected Marx, but only as providing the occasion for dialogue. Pound counters:

> [Gesell] saw (to his eternal glory) that Marx did not question money.
>   Douglas saw the limitation of Marx's value theory. He saw that if value arises from work, a vast deal of that work has already been done by men who can no longer eat its fruit, namely by the dead, by Edison, Carleton, and ten thousand others.[68]

All in all I find Pound more convincing here than Nicholls or Marx. And in contemporary understanding, the quantity theory of money has overcome the commodity theory, held by Marx, Ricardo, and the classical economists.

Pound, however, has much in common with Marx. Pound admired Marx the social crusader: "Parenthetically, the errors of Marxist materialism are much clearer in its results than in the pages of Marx where his noble indignation clouds the mind of the reader, for example, in Chapter X of *Das Kapital* where Marx is a pure historian when he protests against the excessive length of the working day"[69] (tr). In his cultural and social writings, Pound came to share with Marx the view that the economic level was the fundamental level of analysis of any society. The health, the art, the degree of justice of any culture were determined by whether or not it had a just economic system. In that sense, Pound can be considered a Marxist. Further, as Nicholls points out, even after his break with Michael Gold and the *New Masses,* Pound engaged in "a continuing dialogue with the American Left."[70] As we might expect from his self-proclaimed program to bring together converging movements,

---

[66] Surette, *A Light from Eleusis,* 90.
[67] Nicholls, 143.
[68] Pound, "The Individual in His Milieu" (1935), in *Selected Prose,* 278.
[69] Pound, "Toward an Orthological Economy," *Rassegna Monetaria* 9–10 (Sept.–Oct. 1937): 1104.
[70] Nicholls, 79.

"his contributions amounted to an attempt to transcend party divisions and to construct an economic and cultural programme accessible to conservatives and radicals alike."[71] In a period of political orthodoxy, such an attempt has as little chance of succeeding with dogmatic Marxists as it did with dogmatic Douglasites.

Essentially, money for Pound should be wholly an instrument of the will, the will to collective betterment of a people. It does not, therefore, represent anything except the putting into effect of a social program: "You can issue sound money to express the will of the people, which amounts to saying you can issue it against services wanted. You cannot issue sound money against land, or against anything undeliverable." Money, for Pound, is a type of social contract. It is "a form of agreement; it implies an agreed order." The problem that existed in the thirties was, simply, "inadequate monetization,"[72] a problem based on an outdated and superstitious concept of what money was. Surette is quite emphatic and correct in stating that the view of money that Pound held, that increased productivity in a society must be matched by an increased volume of money in circulation, the quantity theory of money, "has prevailed among economists."[73] As Pound said concisely, "The function of money or of a currency and credit system is to get the goods TO the consumer, that is to the whole people.[74]

The principal problem with these monetary proposals for reform advocated by Pound lies in the danger of uncontrolled inflation. Both Earle Davis and Leon Surette have pointed this out; Surette calls inflation "the Achilles' heel of Social Credit monetary theory."[75] He is wrong to claim that Pound never faces the problem, because Pound acknowledges it frequently. Pound does not, however, give precise details about how the government would determine how much money to put into circulation.

The need to put more money into circulation was recognized in various countries during the thirties. Pound realized that more precision was necessary to make this remedy into a fully articulated program:

> Inflation was said to be "understood" in Germany after the war. There are now almost universal cries for inflation (German, U.S.A., and elsewhere).
>
> There are very few demands for *control* of inflation.

---

[71] Ibid.
[72] Pound, *Social Credit*, 10, 7, 13.
[73] Surette, *A Light from Eleusis*, 88.
[74] Pound, prologue to *Social Credit*.
[75] Surette, *A Light from Eleusis*, 167.

> Inflation is perhaps the ambiguous or camouflaging homonym for a dozen or more manoeuvres.[76]

He complained in the same essay that all of the schemes suggested thus far had left out the question of control of inflation.[77] Pound insisted that inflation and a steady increase in the volume of money in circulation were not necessarily the same thing and that prosperity lay in following the latter course of action (following Hume, as we have said). He believed that it was "perfectly easy to increase the volume of money in circulation without debasing its value,"[78] as long as the flow of money was an adequate representation of desired goods and services available. "When prices are fixed by government the value of a unit of money does not decline until you print it against more goods than people want or against more services than they want."[79] His favorite example of this was taken from Orage: "Would you call it inflation to print tickets for every seat in a theatre, regardless of the fact that the house had hitherto been always two thirds empty *simply because* no tickets had been printed for the greater number of seats?"[80] Pound's argument about inflation, however, seems more designed to put people's minds at ease than resolve the dangers should the schemes he advocated be put into effect. He probably believed that the details concerning control of inflation would be solved once the monetary system had been changed and that they were therefore less important to his task.

Pound, then, was in the camp of those who in the thirties advocated monetary proposals dependent upon a radically new conception of money as a way out of the world's economic difficulties. It is therefore not surprising that he was shortly to discover the work of the third major proponent of such a solution, Frederick Soddy, whose 100 percent reserve scheme was advocated by a group of economists at the University of Chicago and by Professor Irving Fisher of Yale. Soddy was a professor of chemistry at Oxford and the Nobel laureate in his field in 1921 for his work in radioactivity, but in the midtwenties, influenced by Ruskin, Kitson, and Gesell, his work turned to economics.[81] Pound quotes him approvingly in *Guide to Kulchur.*[82]

Having thus covered the theoretical bases for Pound's ideas about economics and having seen that they were on the whole sound, despite

---

[76] Pound, *ABC of Economics* (1933), in *Selected Prose,* 250.
[77] Ibid., 237.
[78] Ibid., 263.
[79] Pound, *Social Credit,* 17.
[80] Ibid.
[81] Myers, 71–105.
[82] Orage also thought highly of him, as shown in his "Notes of the Week" column for the *New Age*: "Professor Soddy's admirable letters to the 'Times' independently confirm the financial analysis published in these columns" (3 June 1920, 67).

their at times eccentric formulation, we are now ready to consider in some detail his activities on their behalf, chiefly through correspondence and journalism, in both Italy and the United States from the midthirties to the midforties.

Part II. Pound's Worlds at War

6

The Wizard in General Practice

I

Starting in 1933 and continuing to 1939, Pound's attention was increasingly absorbed by his musical activities in Rapallo. He had been a music critic, writing under the name of William Atheling, for the *New Age* in columns appearing from 1917 to 1921. He was a composer as well. Now he was to take up a new role, that of impresario. His musical activities began when Olga Rudge and Gerhart Munch rented the local cinema house in June of 1933 to present a series of Mozart violin sonatas, "Mozart Week" as it was advertised. With Pound's services as publicist and organizer, these concerts expanded to become the first regular music season (winter 1933–4) in Rapallo, launched in October of 1933.[1] This series was a remarkable effort by Pound, evidence of the high degree of musical culture that could be achieved in a small town. The authorities in Rapallo, eager for another tourist activity, readily gave him permission to use the town hall.[2] Undoubtedly this provided him with further evidence for the superiority of the fascist system: Local institutions were responsive to local initiatives.

With his "Eleven New Cantos" in preparation, it is not surprising that his political and economic correspondence for 1934 is rather sparse. Orage wrote twice to Pound, on 22 and 26 August, urging him to return fully to literature and the *Cantos*, where he could really have an effect. Eliot raised some question about the comprehensibility of the *Cantos*, playfully advising in a letter of 5 June: "What about a Mother's Day Canto. There's a good Idea. You come to me to teach you some Sales Sense." Pound wrote to Senator Borah on 2 June: "Cantos XXXI/XLI are due for publication in N.Y. . . . they summarize some of the country's glory/ and

---

[1] Schafer, 331–9.
[2] Stock, 316.

IF intelligible should assist the reform of the party [Republican]." He repeated a similar observation to Eliot on 16 February 1935: "Aint it enuff that I write a nice practical XI Cantos to instrukk the reader in hist/ and econ/. . . . Whereas as a kneelection doggymint, thet buk OUGHT to be gittin' circulated."

His letters to U.S. politicians, particularly Republican senators, continued, commenting on occasional economic and political issues, as well as on the upcoming presidential campaign. He was particularly upset at the 1934 devaluation of the U.S. dollar; he seemed not to realize that it represented the issuing of debt-free money. Tellingly enough, his complaint was not expressed in terms of the desirability (or lack thereof) of the depreciation of the dollar as an economic policy but rather in terms of how it affected the Pound household. On 23 March 1934, he wrote to Senator Bronson Cutting: "The present idiotic administration is already robbing my pore and 74 year aged father of 40% of his pension." In a similar reversion in his personal crusades of the twenties, Pound in 1935 was telling any Italian who would listen that Italy should eliminate the import duty on coffee, ostensibly for the good of the tourist trade. The Italian government had put strict import controls, long overdue, into effect in 1934 in response to trade restrictions that had been in effect for several years in other European countries.[3] This action was a necessary step to halt the erosion of Italian gold reserves, but for Pound the resulting higher price of coffee was another nuisance.

Odon Por first wrote to Pound toward the beginning of April 1934. He introduced himself as "an old New Age–Orage man . . . trying to propagate Social Credit here." He wanted to know from Pound what Mussolini thought about Social Credit, offering the opinion in a letter of 24 April that he saw "a very strong tendency to reach back to Guild Socialism, encouraged by the Duce." The Pound–Por correspondence would develop into the richest one of this period, and it serves to explain a number of Pound's positions, as we shall see.

Pound saw himself as an apologist for Mussolini and fascist Italy, and he was particularly angered at the prejudice against Italian fascism abroad. In early April 1934, he complained to Ubaldo degli Uberti that "no one has heard of the left wing of the fascist party, for ten years fascism was supposed to be reaction in the pay of the bankers." Although this reference to left-wing fascism may strike us as puzzling today, it is an accurate reflection of the diversity within the Fascist party itself and of the roots of many of its programs in Mussolini's early advocacy of Syndicalism and Socialism. Pound was reacting to the frequent charge leveled during the period by the American Communist party that Mus-

[3] Welk, 172.

solini was merely a club used by capitalists to beat down the proletariat. Reflecting his *New Age* background, Pound would continue to espouse a version of Italian fascism that emphasized its socialist roots. He wrote to Sir Oswald Mosley on 29 July:

> You *could* have an international significance IF you will look forward, instead of playing round with the theatrical side of fascism. There is a vast amount of UNORGANIZED velleity toward monetary reform. The only fascism that CAN work in Eng/ or France or America is fascismo di sinistra [left-wing fascism].

This letter reemphasizes the importance for Pound of fascism as a means for monetary reform.

Although Pound crusaded for a better understanding of Italy, he seemed to be arguing at cross-purposes and was not making much of an impact on his correspondents. Douglas wrote to him on 29 May voicing another commonly heard complaint: "What I should like to hear from you is a statement as to the increasing or otherwise freedom of the Italian subject of all classes to get up and crow upon his own dunghill, no matter whether his views are official or otherwise." Pound's response on 2 June seems lame, avoiding the question:

> Castor oil was a specific (as alternative for shooting oirish martyrs). . . . The chief argument FOR fascism, I mean what got me PRO/ was the extreme idiocy of *all* bejob all ALL the antis. . . . The boss knows what I think. He don't tell me to shut up or moderate my views.

A further indication of just what Pound was willing to overlook about the erosion of liberty in fascist Italy is seen in a letter of 10 May 1935 to the police authorities in Rapallo, asking permission for John and Elsie Drummond to be on his terrace on the day Mussolini was to come through Rapallo in a parade. He wrote that he had personally known them for years and would take full responsibility for their conduct. Apparently this kind of restriction did not bother him.

Despite its sparseness in political and economic matters, the 1934 correspondence is fairly typical. There were a moderate number of letters to U.S. politicians, urging the usual ideas (Borah complained on 3 January that it was not fair "to give us so much 'hell' at so great a distance," inviting Pound to come back to the United States). His ambivalence about Roosevelt continued: FDR was "a hen with his head cut off" and "the great artist of the carom shot," but "honest" and ahead of him on economics. And there was consistent praise for Mussolini and the details of fascist economic reforms. Still, the relative paucity of the political and economic correspondence during 1934 testifies to Pound's temporarily suspended interest in those themes. The world seemed to be recovering from the economic depression, there were no major political crises, and his poetry was going along well.

Alfred Richard Orage died on 6 November 1934, shortly after giving a radio speech on economics, which Pound heard. Coincidentally, Pound was approached around this time by the Ministry of Press and Propaganda to give a radio talk for the Italian Broadcasting Company (EIAR). Pound was enthusiastic about the talk, because it gave him the opportunity to make new contacts within the Italian government. He wrote to Galeazzo Ciano, then undersecretary for Press and Propaganda, informing him of Orage's death and adding ominously: "I'm still not sure his death was by natural causes." Pound wrote again to Ciano on 23 November 1934: "I am greatly honored by the invitation to speak to America, and will be in Rome... unless I drop dead on the railway platform running." Pound gave the talk on 11 January 1935. The speech was about "the economic triumph of fascism" according to William Bird, who wrote about hearing it to Pound in a letter of 2 May 1935. Apparently Italian officials had difficulty understanding what he was talking about since he had trouble getting another invitation to speak.

Pound's renewed interest in the arts was also reflected in a personal letter to Olga Rudge of 4 January 1935:

> Oh well, he [Pound] figgered if they git this econ. stuff *fixed* there iz a lot fer him to do apart from *parnassus*.
>   There is a Arnaut and two oprys and 20 years woik on chinkese, and a nuther *decent* book on Gaudier. . . .
>   Yaas, yass, we can go on wiffout Mr. Roosevelt to purrvide us wiff occupation.

(In their correspondence, Olga and Ezra frequently referred to themselves as "she" and "he.") Interesting here is his perception that poetry was to provide him with diversion during periods when more important political and economic matters were not at hand. Along the same lines, in a letter dated 10–13 June, Pound wrote to Por: "Looks like a *morte saison,* but no reason why progress shd/nt prog/ QUIETLY despite the Negus and the white man's burden. I suppose I'll have to take to culture or something for a few months." Mention of the Negus and the white man's burden referred to the increasing talk about war between Italy and Ethiopia: a war that Mussolini had been planning for over ten years and that finally broke out in October. Pound's indifference to the coming war in Africa indicates just how "natural" racist and colonial attitudes were during that period. As judged within the context of his time, Pound was not a racist. He contributed a letter and an article about Frobenius to Nancy Cunard's ground-breaking book, *The Negro Anthology;* Frobenius's importance in publicizing the importance and vitality of African culture was later more widely recognized.

Pound's attitude to Roosevelt remained ambivalent during this period, alternating between harsh criticism and hopeful optimism as he reacted to various reports from his correspondents and the press. Part of this ambivalence was undoubtedly due to the difficulty of finding a coherent approach behind FDR's many programs and statements. On 6 February 1935, Pound wrote to Congressman George Holden Tinkham of Boston:

> Roosevelt is a wonder, the way he has taken up EVERY damn wheeze that has been tried or proposed in England and found idiotic/ every economic fad is amazing. Whether the country is lucky to have 'em tried once and for all and done with, I don't know.

Two days later, citing an unnamed source, Pound wrote to Por: "Roosevelt is reported to KNOW that Social Credit is what is needed, 'Give me a congress that will accept it and I will do my part.' " To what extent this was based on fact, and to what extent on Pound's need to believe, is not clear. Evidently, however, Pound stood by the hope that Roosevelt would pursue an intelligent economic course.[4]

One of Pound's most sensible correspondents during this period was the Sicilian journalist and translator Lina Caico. Caico continually wrote gentle letters, giving Pound an alternative view of Mussolini's regime. On 30 January 1935, she wrote:

> I shall believe in Italian economics when the load of taxes will lessen – We can't move we can't breathe without being taxed. Poor people can't keep a dog, because if it isn't a cane di caccia [hunting dog] or a cane di guardia [guard dog] then it is a cane di lusso [literally, a luxury dog] 150 lire a year. I know a bookbinder who by stinting and contriving had made himself a lovely little shop. He had to take away all that woodwork and wrought iron because it was lusso, enormously taxed.

Caico was a modest individual, who seemed very pleased to be writing to such a well-known literary figure and occasionally worried that her letters bothered Pound. On 25 February he had to reassure her.

> You are certainly not a seccatura [annoyance]/ but a comfort/ only problem is TIME. Were we not as a Japanese friend said "at the crisis point of the world we must be saved by SOMETHING" meaning to E.P. sane economics, I would take pleasure in discussion of style, licherchoor, etc.

---

[4] That hope was kept alive by Irving Fisher, who had written to Pound on 23 October 1933: "I think the President is quite clear-headed on the subject of reflation. . . . I think Mr. Roosevelt is quite willing to try stamp scrip, or was, but most of the Congressmen were not willing to vote for it when it was brought before them."

As is evidenced also by the cantos he was writing in the thirties, Pound considered his primary duty to be social involvement. Despite her shyness, Caico was always very frank in her views. To emphasize her point about the high Italian taxes, she wrote to Pound on 3 September changing his own words used to criticize Great Britain and endorse Gesell into a critique of the high taxes in Italy:

> "The brutal and murderous income tax current, *in Italy,* and the devastating tax on inheritance to which *we Italians* must submit as well as the host of suffocating tributes paid by us semiconsciously on all our consumption and dealings" – How beautifully you put it.
>   One penny on eight shillings which you really possess; but that would be Paradise.

Pound, however, as a resident foreigner, did not pay many Italian taxes, and he ignored her point.

II

He was greatly influenced in his views, though, by Odon Por. Their correspondence had increased in frequency as the two men found they shared many interests. Por had lived in Italy since 1903, except for a time spent as special correspondent for *Avanti* in London in 1912, where he also helped to edit the *Syndicalist,* the first syndicalist paper in England. In addition, he also wrote for the *English Review* and the *New Age.* Por defined himself in an early letter (28 March 1935) to Pound as "Syndicalist. Guild Socialist. NOT fascist. Free lance." He wrote a number of books, including one of the first serious books on fascism in 1923. He was very interested in Douglas's ideas and had come out of retirement in 1933 because the corporate system being set up in Italy reminded him of the guild system and attracted his interest, and also, perhaps, because of financial need.

Por was the director of the Rome office of the Milan-based Institute for the Study of International Politics and was making an uncertain living through that and his journalism. When he and Pound first started corresponding, he was writing an article a month on the New Economics for the important journal *Civiltà Fascista,* edited by the Italian philosopher Giovanni Gentile. Por was in frequent financial trouble during this period, and Pound loaned him money on several occasions.

Por's influence on Pound's economic thinking was considerable. In fact, much of Pound's faith that Mussolini's political system would lead to the adoption of Social Credit and Gesellite policies can be attributed to his correspondence with the Hungarian economist. For example, on 22 March Por wrote:

The corporate system now definitely at work is heading straight towards S.C. or something near to it. Not consciously yet. For instance, self-sufficiency and "the abolition of artificially created scarcity" (in Mussolini's words) are immediate aims. Finance is well under the control of the state. It has no more that occult power that it still has in other countries, except Russia. The big banks are virtually nationalized. A self-sufficient economic system run by Guilds must reform its monetary system.

I am doing some groundbreaking. That's all. . . . the It. corporate system seems to be the very system in which S.C. can be inserted (must be inserted, otherwise it will frustrate itself).

The phrase "occult power" contains that hint of conspiracy which we have seen in the *New Age* and which frequently devolves into anti-Semitism. Por apparently seemed to approve of the Russian Revolution and its economic results. Because Pound needed to have faith that Mussolini was putting economic reforms into effect, it is easy to see why he would have been very influenced by Por. He also admired Por's lucid prose style, writing to the economist that he had "at times, one of the best styles of any man writing on econ/. . . . Most of the bastids can't WRITE fer nuts" (4 February–14 April 1935).

Pound's attention was attracted by two American demagogues of this period, the Reverend Charles Coughlin, whose Radio League of the Little Flower reached a wide audience, and the governor of Louisiana, Huey Long. On 13 April he wrote a letter to Long that is so grotesque and out of touch with its reader that it is embarrassing to read. What follows is the entire text, with approximately the original spacing:

> KINGFISH; You iz' goin' ter
> need a CABINET
> DIFFERENT
> from the present one. You iz goin to need a sekkertary of
> the treasury whose name is NOT Morgenthau/stein, or
> Richberg/ovitch
> or Mordecai Ezekiel OR Perkins.
> You is going to need a Sekkertary of the Treasury,
> THATS ME.
> I'm a tellin you 'cause no one else will.
> LET THE NATION USE ITS OWN CREDIT
> instead of paying tax FOR IT
> to a gang of sonsofbitches that DONT own it.
> an my regards to ole Bronson Cutting.

Except, perhaps, for the last line, where he mentions his acquaintance with the U.S. senator, it is difficult to imagine just what Pound thought he was accomplishing by writing this letter. Perhaps he wanted to impress

Long with his audacity. Although his letters to intimates such as Olga Rudge or T. S. Eliot contain many playful passages and much hokey language, and although his letters to regular correspondents contain unconventional spelling and grammar, Pound is usually much more controlled when writing to public figures, at least at first. The figure of Huey Long may have invited this kind of grotesquerie, but his letter had no apparent sarcastic intent: It is quite serious. It shows just how much Pound was beginning to lose touch with both his language and his native land.

Pound was also impressed by the Reverend Charles Coughlin, a Catholic priest in Michigan whose weekly radio broadcasts contained social commentary mixed with a dollop of Catholic doctrine. Pound wrote to Coughlin on 18 February 1935 explaining his economic program. He wrote again on 30 May praising Coughlin's book *Lectures on Social Justice.* Coughlin never engaged in a serious correspondence with Pound and just returned routine letters of acknowledgment, but that did not stop Pound from believing he had found a new ally. Pound wrote to Por on 18 August expressing hope about three of the prominent social reformers in the United States: "don't underestimate Huey Long. further along than Townsend [author of the Townsend Plan, an unrealistic proposal for government-funded retirement] or Coughlin, tho Coughlin will be going social credit before many months, or I miss my guess." Pretending to be "in the know" or to possess inside information, Pound was able to use his network of correspondents and his U.S. citizenship to pass himself off as an expert on America in his dealings with Italians.

Pound highlighted Social Credit more than Gesell in letters of this time for several reasons. First of all, Por's own background and interest were in Social Credit, so that was the natural direction for their correspondence to take. Second, Pound was urging Douglas to make Social Credit more active as a political force, and Douglas seemed to be responding to his advice. Pound had used his connections in Washington to help arrange for a reception given by Senator Bronson Cutting in 1934 for Douglas, at which a dozen or so senators and representatives interested in credit reform were present. From several letters we learn that Douglas did not make a favorable impression on the guests. Third, and probably most important, a Social Credit party had recently won an election in Alberta, so Pound undoubtedly saw more promise in the movement's possibilities. In fact, after the electoral victory, Douglas traveled to Alberta as an adviser, apparently with unsatisfactory results.

Pound's enthusiasm continued, for on 2 September 1935, he wrote to Douglas proposing that he be sent as a Social Credit delegate to the Dominion Parliament in Quebec. He listed as his qualifications "la don de la parole," twenty-five years' European experience, possible syndication in the U.S. press, and political connections. "All spider webs," he admitted. He was looking for expenses for the voyage across the Atlantic and a dollar a day for hotel. His request to Douglas and, perhaps, his letter to Huey Long seem to indicate that he was casting about for a position in politics, or at least considering the possibility.

Pound's belief in the power of individuals to influence events was unabated. He wrote to Father Coughlin on 29 August: "For God's sake get to a radio and help our Canadian Brethren. After the Alberta sweep the Dominion election COULD be swung." Pound had a naive faith that a person to whom he had sent a few letters, and who had probably expressed a polite curiosity about his activities, was wholeheartedly supporting his cause. Like many political newcomers, Pound could not tell the difference between a politician who was being accommodating and one who was making a commitment. For example, Crate Larkin mailed Pound a copy of the following letter (obviously a form letter) that Coughlin had sent to Glad Zoeller on 25 November 1935:

> I am highly pleased to learn that you are interested in the money question.
>
> Of course newspapers do not print this story because newspapers, as a rule, depend chiefly upon their advertisers for a living; the advertisers, in turn, depend upon the bankers for their financing.
>
> You can rest assured that the series of depressions which have marked the history of America, especially since the Civil War, will be multiplied in the future in their frequency unless we restore to Congress the right to coin and regulate the value of money.

This letter would have convinced Pound that the priest was a man after Pound's own heart, and it was the kind of evidence that, for Pound, would have marked Coughlin as being on his side, despite the vagueness of the last sentence as a political recommendation.

Odon Por, apart from keeping up Pound's faith, was useful to him in more specific ways. He gave Pound some help in making editorial contacts, writing to him on 14 June: "The editor of *Civiltà Fascista* asks you to write him an article on anything except economics. Of course your economics may ooze in." This is interesting because it shows a typical attitude taken by editors to Pound's writings at this time, even in Italy: anything but economics. Despite Pound's boast that only in fascist Italy would a poet be invited to speak on economics, the Italians were occasionally leery of what he would say. In response, Pound suggested a translation of Canto XXXVIII. Pound also tried to enlist Por's aid and Roman connections in helping him secure another interview with Mussolini, apparently on the strength of the recent appearance of his book *Jefferson and/or Mussolini*.

Pound's Italian correspondents frequently berated him for his elliptical style. Lina Caico wrote to him about his volitionist economics questionnaire complaining that the questions represented eight chapter titles for a book not written.[5] Carlo Izzo, who was working in Venice to translate Pound's poetry into Italian, wrote that *Jefferson and/or Mussolini* would be helped by explanatory footnotes, especially for an Italian audience unfamiliar with the Jeffersonian references. An Italian edition of the book was projected at the time. In his response, attempting to explain the book to Izzo, Pound wrote in late August or early September of 1935: "It is intended to break down absurd and bestial false representation of Italy. Ten years idiotic calumny in Eng. and U.S. press. BUT it is also MY de Monarchia or anti Macchiavel."

III

The likelihood of Italian military intervention in Abyssinia was increasingly evident, and Pound took up his accustomed role as apologist for the Italian regime. He apparently accepted official fascist propaganda about the need for war to defend Italian settlers in the colonies of Eritrea and Somalia. Pound wrote to the editor of the *Morning Post* on 11 August 1935: "Could the Foreign Secretary or any other loyal Briton tell me to *what extent* inhabitants of Italian Africa should be slaughtered at whim by Abyssinians *without* receiving protection from their own government?" He went on to say that while he regretted

---

[5] In August of 1934 Pound compiled a "volitionist questionnaire" about economics and was circulating it to a number of his correspondents:

> WHICH of the following statements do you agree with?
> 1. It is an outrage that the state should run into debt to individuals by the act and in the act of creating real wealth.
> 2. Several nations recognize the necessity of distributing purchasing power. They do actually distribute it. The question is whether it should be distributed as favour to corporations; as reward for not having a job; or impartially and per capita.
> 3. A country CAN have one currency for internal use, and another good for both home and foreign use.
> 4. If money is regarded as certificate of work done, taxes are no longer necessary.
> 5. It is possible to concentrate all taxation onto the actual paper money of a country (or onto one sort of its money).
> 6. You can issue valid paper money against any commodity UP TO the amount of that commodity that the people WANT.
> 7. Some of the commonest failures of clarity among economists are due to using one word to signify two or more different concepts: such as, DEMAND, meaning also responsible.
> 8. It is an outrage that the owner of one commodity can not exchange it with someone possessing another, without being impeded or taxed by a third party holding a monopoly over some third substance or controlling some convention, regardless of what it be called.

any unpleasantness that is likely to distract the public mind from such subjects as Social Credit, Gesell, the Gran Consiglio and the organisation of the Corporate State and the chances of a National Dividend, I still draw meagre comfort from the pedagogical aspect of your own palukas weeping over the disaster to Italian finance imminent or inherent in warfare, while our French allies, and in particular the "Economique et Financiere" Agency are taking the diametrical opposite line and assuring us that "war will decrease unemployment."

Here he departs somewhat from his original reason for getting into the study of economics in the first place, which was to avoid the causes of war. Instead, Pound invokes the possibility that war might even help the Italian economy (it did not). Perhaps because he is quoting someone else he does not notice the inconsistency. Pound, as I have stated, was not a systematic thinker. At least, the shift does not appear to trouble him.

Pound supported Italy's intervention in Abyssinia, or at least he considered it so inevitable that he seemed to convince himself of its necessity on economic grounds. He wrote to Douglas on 29 August: "Abyssinia the ONLY place Italy cd. oblige the gun buzzards by having a war AND doing herself any good. much happier place fer a war than say the aussstrian border. IF the pacifists working for the gun buzzards let it stay local." Apparently Pound is not troubled by the fact that he is taking both sides of the argument here. His approximate reasoning seems to be as follows: There is a group of powerful conspirators who force wars for their own profit. We have worked for twenty years to oppose that group. Italy might as well give in and find a war to her profit. Again, logical consistency is not Pound's strong point. Pound had a marked tendency to find evidence convenient to his conclusions, and his fascist faith and his unconscious assumption of the superiority of European culture led him to rationalize the Italian involvement in Ethiopia.

The reference to the Austrian border is to well-publicized Italian troop movements in 1934 that were aimed at preventing the Anschluss Hitler desired; Mussolini had publicly threatened war with Germany should Austria's independence be threatened. One disastrous result of Italy's war with Abyssinia was to allow Hitler to occupy the Rhineland in 1936 and to force Italy away from its anti-Nazi alliance with Britain and France (the so-called Stresa Front), toward an alliance with Germany.

Pound apparently recovered his economic perspective enough to excuse Italy's growing conflict in East Africa, turning his initial study of economics as a means of avoiding war into a means of justifying its inevitability. He wrote to Por on 21 September 1935: "Present capitalist monetary system LEADS to war as only instrument of consumption compatible with usury." He also informed Por that he was going to buy the 5 percent bond offered by the Italian government to finance the war in Abyssinia. When the war officially began in October, Pound was eloquent in advocacy of the Italian position. In his correspondence with William Borah, a member of the Senate Foreign Relations Committee, Pound defended the Italian action in convincing detail. Responding to Pound on 30 October, Borah expressed some sympathy with his view that the opposition to the Abyssinian war in the League of Nations was a result of "orders from London." In a long, effective, and coherent letter to Borah of late November (Pound could be perfectly clear when he wanted), Pound pointed out the barbarism of the Abyssinians, the number of Englishmen who were against the League of Nations sanctions, and the harm the sanctions were doing to the world economy. He went on:

> What is NOW wrong with the picture is the definition of Italy's activity in Abyssinia as war. I thought it was, and was sorry Italy had started, but the evidence which that cub Eden KEPT out of court, or out of consideration at Geneva, plus what I have had viva voce from Rocke PLUS the way Italy has gone ahead, road building, etc. educate one.

In the same letter Pound expressed approval for Roosevelt's declaration of neutrality. Pound wrote to Cordell Hull on 19 October 1935: "If Italy wasn't driven into Abyssinia, and if Mussolini hasn't stopped MORE wars than all the British liars put together, I will eat my hat and breeches. . . . The crass fiction that this is an affair between Abyssinia and Italy deceives no one." Pound was seriously deluded about Italian culpability for this war.

Pound's activities during the war in Abyssinia foreshadow his activities during the Second World War. To begin, England's response in mobilizing the League of Nations sanctions against Italy aroused his anger so much that it marked a permanent change in his view of that country. He wrote to T. S. Eliot in late November, echoing a view expressed in the *New Age:* "League of NATIONS. never anything but league of bank pimps. Nothing but WAR makes debt fast enough to satisfy the city [the London banking industry]."[6] Again, Pound did not notice the inconsistency in his views here. Even with the kind of propaganda that was being spread by the Italian press, he certainly must have been aware that Italy was responsible to some degree for starting the war. The missing steps in his reasoning may have been that the League sanctions only prolonged the war without changing its inevitable result, though these arguments are not specifically mentioned. In the same letter he calls

---

[6] Orage had written in "Notes of the Week" for the *New Age*: "A League of Nations such as is now being advocated would plainly result in an International financiers' paradise" (18 July 1918, 180).

Geneva, the site of the League, "the hole of hell and root lair of usury," again echoing a *New Age* view.

Pound's condemnation of England and the League increased in fury and irrationality as the war continued. He even reached the point where he blamed England for the entire war. In a letter of 9 January 1936, to Senator J. P. Pope, he wrote:

> England with an almost invisible wire slip noose around Italy's neck for years, pretends that Italy is aggressor. The Geneva shop front ought to be correlated with the geneva gold report of 1930. . . .
>
> Seems quite probably that England wants Italy to do the thankless work of settling Abyssinia, and then to grab the results.

Although Pound's constant effort was to trace the economic causes of war and human misery, his habit of mind in studying these causes can only be described as tending to the paranoid, used here not in the clinical sense but in what I wish to call a semantic sense. Pound finds meanings and connections where there are none, or where they would have to be clearly explained for others. His elliptical habit of style prevents him from explaining the connections he saw, and the result is a fragmentary and disjointed syntax. This is not to say that his conclusions are all incorrect. Pound had very good instincts and his intuitions often proved to be true. Nevertheless, the communication between poet and reader frequently breaks down, in a kind of semantic schizophrenia (again, my phrase), and neither Pound's anger nor his energy is enough to restore it. Such verbal manifestations would indicate psychotic levels of paranoia and schizophrenia only when the individual's ability for "reality testing" (the phrase used in psychiatry) breaks down, and there is no evidence of such a breakdown in Pound at this time. Paranoids have enemies too.

During the last months of 1935, Por tried to get Pound another spot on Italian radio. In a letter of 21 December Por advised Pound to write directly to Galeazzo Ciano, who had become minister for Press and Propaganda in June, "offering your services on the Radio. . . . Do not tell in the letter that you have spoken about this before to some of the functionaries at this Ministry – because they may suppress your letters. Mention to him your Am. connections." Ciano had volunteered for duty in Abyssinia, however, and was no longer with the ministry. On 30 December Por wrote again: "I think that you might be called here next week to arrange everything – broadcasting."

Around the same time Pound wrote to Por: "British Ital Bulletin offered to pay me and of course I can NOT accept money for writing Ital propaganda/ and they officially possibly cant afford to offer me a proper SALARY." He did, however, suggest that they might provide two rooms for him in Rome so that his trips there would not be so expensive. In late December, Pound started the first of about thirty articles for the *British–Italian Bulletin,* a supplement to *Italia Nostra,* an Italian newspaper published in Great Britain. These articles on various pro-Italian subjects continued on approximately a weekly basis throughout most of 1936. They probably led to the request from Luigi Villari of the Ministry of Foreign Affairs, on 13 March 1936, for permission to include something by Pound in "an anthology of British and American writers who have published articles in favour of Italy in the present dispute." Pound's connections to the Italian government were increasing.

His views on the Abyssinian war, though perhaps not well reasoned or informed, seem nevertheless sincere, and they were undoubtedly partly the product of the racist and colonialist bias so much a part of European and American thinking of that time that it was almost unconscious. He wrote to Por on 4 April 1936:

> Italy needs colonies to EMPLOY her sons. SHIT!! The function of modern engineering is to create unemployment. . . . she damn well needs Abyssinia to INSURE economic independence/ That is to control enough materie prime [raw materials] to tell the buggarin bank in Westminster/ Eden/ Cranbourne/ etc. to go bloody damn well to hell.

Pound was apparently proud of Italy's defiance of England and the League of Nations, as he mentions that act as among his reasons for admiring the fascist government in one of the radio speeches later on: "Along about the time Tony tin-toes Eden was tellin' Italy where to get off at, and she did NOT GIT. There came a day when Italy sat up sassy and defied fifty-two so-called nations, England among 'em."[7] When the Abyssinian war was over, he wrote to Ubaldo degli Uberti on 7 May: "A vurry neat little war and a vurry nicely timed finish." Pound was against war, but by that he meant war in Europe. A colonial war was a different matter. Although such views may trouble us fifty years later, they were so much a part of Western thinking at the time that it is almost anachronistic to find them disturbing now, except as they still persist.

IV

Although his occasions for self-reflection are rare, Pound was not without some insight into his own character. On 5 April in a letter to Archbishop Pisani, he acknowledges that he was seldom moved, except "by the habitual IRA, nel senso medioaevale [RAGE, in the medieval sense]." Pound represents John Adams as conforming to his own character. He changes Adams's original statement, "In short, I never shall

---

[7] Pound, *Ezra Pound Speaking,* 102. Broadcast of 20 April 1942.

shine till some animating occasion calls forth my powers. I find that the mind must be agitated with some passion, either love, fear, hope, &c., before she will do her best,"[8] to the Adams Cantos' "must be (IRA must be) aroused ere the mind be / at its best" *(C, LXIII, 353)*. Pound was furious from perception: from the frustration born of his confidence that he clearly saw the economic misconceptions at the root of the problems of his time and of his inability to persuade anyone to put his solutions into effect.

Pound was much impressed by a speech made by Roosevelt in Atlanta on 28 November 1935, for he mentions the speech favorably to several of his correspondents in early 1936. He wrote to Por on 2 January: "Mr. Roosevelt made an ASTUTE speech at Altanta. . . . After three years soc/ credit HAMMERING he AT LAST admits america lives on a third rate diet because the peePULL aint got PURR/chasing power to git more and better grub." In a letter on the same day, he also praised the speech to Senator Borah, adding: "BUT he offers false dilemma/ the dirty old clothes of England/ DOLE based on pity (or fear the starved will git nasty) AND public works on fascist model."

Odon Por had been promoting Pound in Rome, using his contacts in the Italian capital, and Pound was invited by the Ministry of Press and Propaganda to come to Rome to discuss doing some broadcasts. In a letter of 3 January, Por urged Pound to seek a regular position with them, but at the same time he cautioned: "Limit yourself when in contact with his people . . . to what you want to say on the radio – do not talk about money & so on. It confounds them – they don't understand anything & the whole thing has this reaction: they think you are a crank and try to avoid you." Pound's problems with audience understanding were not limited to English speakers. Italians too were put off by his economic theories.

Pound, who had many idealistic traits, was not tempted by the possibility of a regular position per se without the understanding that he would be free to speak about what he wanted. He wrote back to Por on 4 January: "What do I want to talk about on the RADIO? unless it IS money?? . . . I don't WANT to say ANYTHING on the radio." Because of the Atlanta speech and because of his connections with several Republican senators, Pound's mind was back on the United States, and he told Por that it might be better for him to go back there, to talk to Borah and possibly Roosevelt ("the great white melon-eater"), especially if he could get a discount on a ticket. He was aware that the presidential campaign had already started, and he was hopeful that Borah, who enjoyed a reputation as Capitol Hill's most eloquent speaker, would get

---

[8] Sanders, 124.

the Republican nomination. Again, Pound probably hoped to be able to talk himself into some official position in Washington.

In a second letter to Por on the same day, Pound clarified his agenda:

> SECOND fytte. . . .
> Now in ORDER of importance things worth doing (apart from production of immortal art, which can be as well done on Thursday as Tuesday) IZ AZ follows. 1. Stave off pan European war. . . . 2. Get sane economics started SOMEWHERE.
> I shd/ like (and how) to get the issue into the NEXT presidential election.
> I should LIKE for a number of reasons to see the Capo del Governo [head of state].
> I don't care a hoot about talking over the radio UNLESS it conduces to one or all of the above activities.

Pound continued to take a rather casual attitude toward his art, subordinating it to his economic and political interests. He sent a copy of one of his articles for the *British–Italian Bulletin* along with the letter, so Por could show samples of his work to those in charge. At the same time, he asked Por to look into getting his journalist's card renewed (it entitled him to a 70 percent reduction on railway tickets). The above letter demonstrates clearly that Pound initially was interested in broadcasting for Italian radio as a means for spreading his economic views. The Italian ministry apparently was not interested in having Pound ride that hobbyhorse and reacted coolly. At first, Por informed Pound that his broadcasts would be put off until March, because the January and February dates were all taken up. Then on 21 March Por wrote again: "Mascia says: (Yesterday) Ministry of Stampa [the press] – that he can't put you on the wireless – because you said strange things before. . . . Never mind. It is impossible to be understood everywhere by everybody." Pound wrote back immediately to explain: "All I said before wuz cause they stuck a title on me, and I hadda xxxplain it." We can see that it was not easy for Pound to gain access to a forum for his ideas, not even in Italy. In a letter of 13 May, Por commented on the problem thus: "The Foreign Office is afraid of you – so is the Ministero Stampa."[9]

For Pound, more evidence that Mussolini was leading the country in the correct economic direction came when the Italian government took major steps toward banking reform in a decree issued on 12 March 1936. A supervisory office was established and given authority over all banks in the country. The Bank of Italy was made into a public institution, and its private shareholders were bought out; it was transformed into a national bank whose business was confined to other banks, akin to the

---

[9] There is some indication that Pound delivered another radio talk on 20 December 1936.

U.S. Federal Reserve. New shares for it were issued, but their ownership was confined to banks and insurance companies. At the same time, the Banca Commerciale Italiana, the Credito Italiano, and the Banca di Roma, the three largest private banks, were transformed into publicly held institutions through the issuing of stock.[10]

Pound learned of this reform early, and he wrote to Por on 4 March. The letter is an indication of how dependent he was on Por's opinion about economic matters in Italy. The reform seemed like excellent news, but he wanted to check with Por:

> How much *have* we got with this nice new Bank reform? Nationalization of credit? social credit sindical credit/ no democracy, waaal, no tears/ I am, nacerly, keeping up FRONT, it must be an advance. I don't see how the damn international kikes are to get past it. . . .
>
> Shd/ I yell HOORAYAAAAAY fer the Noo Bank act or keep quiet? I mean, does it call for LOUD commendations? . . .
>
> At any rate if you are sittin up, and have analyzed the bank act, you might tell ME a little MORE. HAVE I got to read ALL of it, as well as whats in the whypers? Or shd/ I go into a funk hole and occupy myself with moozik and poesy until its time for the next heave?

It is remarkable just how willing Pound was to be led by Por on this issue, indicating a certain lack of confidence when it came to understanding the import of economic legislation, as well as his need to believe. We can see how Pound could have considered the bank reform an answer to one of his repeated demands that a nation's credit be placed in its own, not private, hands. At any rate, he did not wait for Por's go-ahead but wrote to Douglas on the same day:

> In estimating the Italian bank reform. . . .
>
> At least it means that the NATION uses the nations credit/ not at mercy of mere gang of foreign jews. . . .
>
> I don't at first sight see anything in the decree that wd/n't be necessary "ennabling" act toward anything you wd want to recommend.
>
> It is nationalization of credit, nationalization at top over species of syndicalization of structure.
>
> The govt. controlls the quantity of credit to be issued.
>
> Ought to mean end of bank state inside the official state.

Por sent him the text of the bank law with a letter on 23 March, commenting, "Here we are – the sovereignty of the State extended over the financial system," and indicating that it represented a revision of the corporate system toward the left. Responding, Pound made the characteristic comment that the law was all right as long as it was run by Mussolini, but that it would not work in England or France, a remark

[10] Welk, 218.

very much in line with his belief in the necessity of the individual. Still, it is easy to see how he would have been convinced that the reform he had advocated for so long was finally being put into practice in fascist Italy. In an April letter to Por, he even anticipates a return to his old profession: "1937!!! do you expect ME to be still an economist by 1937? . . . I xxxpekk to be ritin muzik and poesy by 1937. hell thazz anno XV and then some. econ/ shd/ by then be handed over to Larkin's trained staff of accountants." His view of his own economic activity was that it was a temporary measure for desperate times, and he contemplated the resumption of his artistic work after economic good sense was put into practice. It was poetry, then, to which he was really devoted.

Meanwhile, though, Pound had found a way to unite his two concerns: He announced the completion of his cantos about Siena and the bank of the Monte dei Paschi (Cantos XLII–XLIV) to Por in a letter of 7 September (he had Cantos XLII–LI ready by November):

> I have worked in Siena Tuscanyi Lorraine Hapsburg. 1765 to 1792. P Leopoldo and Ferd. III FURER along, more enlightened than any modern state. Free trade error corrected in controll at frontier. Nap. ended state debt. taxes halved. etc. etc. I have just done THREE CANTOS of shout about that and Monte dei Paschi so EZ SEZ and he KNOWZ.

Pound had not given up on his economic or poetic activity but had redefined one in terms of the other. As he wrote to John Drummond on 16 June: "Without study of econ/ motivations NO *histoire morale contemporaine* can be written" (ddp). His good friend Manlio Dazzi, who had helped Pound with his edition of Cavalcanti and was helping him read through the difficult Latin of Claudio Salmasius's book *De Modo Usurarum,* recognized the change. He wrote to him on 26 May: "I see you always immersed in the economic question. On your part it is an act of generosity towards the world because for the material well being of future generations, you give up so much of your poetic activity."

Pound's conception of the relation between art and political concerns had certainly changed. He wrote to Ronald Duncan on 25 October: "A man who is too stubborn or silly to learn economics IN OUR time has NO moral value whatsod/never" (ddp). Among his correspondents, there was only one clearly dissenting voice about the new direction Pound's work had taken. H. L. Mencken wrote to him on 28 November:

> You made your great mistake when you abandoned the poetry business, and set up shop as a wizard in general practice. . . . Thus a competent poet was spoiled to make a tin-horn politician.
>   Your acquaintance with actual politics and especially with American politics, seems to be pathetically meagre.

Mencken's first statement is amusing. His second statement is quite accurate. Pound had a deficient sense of practical politics. Although this did not prevent him from successfully treating political topics in his poetry, he lacked discernment about the meaning of contemporary political events.

V

To what extent was Pound correct in his view that the Social Credit and Gesellite positions he advocated were coming into action in Italy? Earle Davis has said that Pound was taking Mussolini's statements of his intentions for facts and was deceived, since Mussolini did nothing to reform the monetary system in Italy. "Even though the picture is a mixed one," Davis concludes "the facts do not bear out the major contentions advanced by Pound."[11] Because of the impact of his later involvement with Hitler, it is difficult today to arrive at a balanced assessment of Mussolini's economic achievements. Fortunately, that task was rather admirably accomplished by an economist, William G. Welk, whose *Fascist Economic Policy: An Analysis of Italy's Economic Experiment* appeared in 1938. Since many of Davis's conclusions are based upon Welk, we will consider Welk's book and its analysis briefly.

Welk notes that a key difference between Italian fascism and New Deal democracy lay in the role of labor. Under fascism, all labor disputes were settled by arbitration; strikes and lockouts were prohibited. In the United States during the thirties, workers had the right to strike, although it was difficult to employ that right effectively as a weapon, given the massive unemployment of the time. Although unions were encouraged in Italy, and confederations of workers' and employers' groups formed the basis for representation in the fascist government from 1934 onward, the interests of all groups were subordinated to the national interest, and disputes were settled in Italian labor courts. Welk characterizes these courts as fair and sympathetic but acknowledges the charge that the fascist syndical system was "a tool used by the capitalist class and a dictatorial political regime . . . to keep the mass of Italian workers in subjection." Nevertheless, he notes factors that compensated Italian workers for their loss of freedom, including a new and constructive attitude toward the problems of labor, Mussolini's socialist origins and sympathy for the workers, and the presence of a leftist branch of the Fascist party.[12]

The first four years of fascism (1923–6) saw "a period of continuous industrial growth and prosperity," though "much of it was the result of

[11] Earle Davis, 152–3, 169.
[12] Welk, 76–85, 150–2.

an overexpansion of credit and speculative activity."[13] The government reacted to inflation and expansion just as any other Western industrial nation would have, through a policy of consolidation and contraction, leading to the growth of unemployment in the years 1926 to 1928.[14] When the worldwide depression struck, Italy suffered too, but the effects were alleviated by prompt government intervention, "due, in many instances, to the prompt personal action of the head of government."[15] Government programs included financial help to troubled industries and an expanded program of public works that encompassed land reclamation, the development of hydroelectric power, electrification of the railroads, and the construction of highways and public buildings. Social programs were instituted that assisted the unemployed, including unemployment insurance, strict government control of internal migration, the shortening of the work week to forty hours, and special grants to distressed areas. In a speech in Milan on 6 October 1934, Mussolini stated that:

> the economic objective of the Fascist regime is greater social justice for the Italian people. What do I mean by social justice? I mean the guarantee of work, a fair wage, a decorous home, I mean the possibility of evolution and betterment. . . . If modern science has solved the problem of multiplying wealth, science, spurred on by the state, must now solve the other great problem, that of the distribution of wealth, so that the illogical, paradoxical, and cruel phenomenon of want in the midst of plenty shall not be repeated.[16]

Clearly, Pound found those remarks, and the social programs that resulted, very much in keeping with his idea of the responsibility of the government to resolve economic problems, and he enthusiastically and frequently referred to that speech. Of course, there is little difference between the program and the one instituted by Roosevelt, except that the fascist one went into effect more easily and more quickly, since many of the mechanisms for state intervention in the national economy were already in place. Pound, quite naturally, was impressed by the one program he saw up close.

How were these programs paid for? Essentially, the same way they were paid for in the United States. Public debt in Italy rose "from about one-half billion lire in 1930–31 to over three billion and a half in 1933–34."[17] Taxes were very high and put an increasing burden on Italian taxpayers. The only action taken by the Italian government that resem-

[13] Ibid., 161, 162.
[14] Ibid., 163, 164, and 165.
[15] Ibid., 167.
[16] Ibid., 120.
[17] Ibid., 171.

bled the remedies proposed by Social Credit was the devaluation of the lira on 15 October 1936, which reduced its gold backing by about 40 percent. This was not an Italian initiative but was in response to similar measures taken by other gold bloc countries.[18] When Roosevelt acted in a similar fashion to depreciate the gold dollar by 40 percent on 31 January 1934, Pound complained at length even though such an action could be construed as creating debt-free money in good Social Credit fashion.

Thus, although Pound was largely correct in his theoretical understanding of economics, he was wrong in thinking that Italian economic policy was different in any essential respect from that of other Western nations of the time. He appreciated the real economic achievements of Mussolini's regime while remaining unaware of similar achievements by Roosevelt's New Deal. Later, in one of the radio broadcasts, he listed his reasons for admiring the fascist government:

> drainin' a powerful amount of swamp land which OTHER Italian governments had been lookin' at since the time of Tiberius Caesar and signally failed to get DRY. . . . the increase of grain yielded in Italy. . . . national health bein' improved. . . . increase in living quarters for the NOT-rich sectors of the nation's community . . . the question of water supply. . . . the question of electric power. . . . the Italian railway runnin' by electricity.[19]

These are, in fact, substantial accomplishments. But Pound's belief that the reforms he hoped for were about to be put into effect in Italy was just that, a belief, an act of fascist faith, though one that was supported by his extensive correspondence with Odon Por.

VI

The Spanish Civil War began around this time, and in June Mussolini appointed Galeazzo Ciano, his son-in-law, as the new foreign minister, with instructions to arrange Italy's involvement.[20] With his view of England, Pound was quick to lay the blame. In a letter to Por of 23 October, he wrote:

> Excellent analysis of Spain suggests England wants fighting prolonged so that Spain will be dependent on London, not Italy and Germany. usual wash of lies re/ Italy and promised naval bases BUT. POINT IZ. UNLESS New Economic ideas go into Spain FROM HERE London WILL controll Spain after the shindy.

[18] Ibid., 177–8.
[19] Pound, *Ezra Pound Speaking*, 101–2. Broadcast of 20 April 1942.
[20] Mack Smith, 206.

Although he had given up completely on England, where he had lived for so long, and had turned toward Italy, his new home, he still maintained a considerable feeling of loyalty to his native country. In response to a question about the possibility that he would change his citizenship, Pound wrote to M. D. Zabel on 6 November: "H. J. at the end; and Eliot in the mature prudence decided the citizenship was not worth having. I have never come to that and I don't expect to; but whether this is attributable to qualities of HEAD, I shd. be loath to say" (ddp). Despite the example of two other famous expatriates, Henry James and T. S. Eliot, Pound never considered himself as anything other than a loyal American.

Pound's position on the Spanish Civil War was not yet clear. He wrote to Por on 14 November:

> There is a great deal of FEELING over Spain/ anti-fascist. Young and foolish men quite sincerely enraged over killing of Lorca/ evidently a damn good poet. The play of making Picasso director of Prado; also enormous card with intelligentzia. I hear Franco has revoked the donation of land to peasants. that also foolish UNLESS he sets up something like Italian colonno laws/ QUICK/

Apparently, Pound in 1936 had neutral feelings about the conflict although in a December letter to T. C. Wilson he stated: "NO European nation will stand for RUSSIA in Barcelona, it dont matter what kind of ribbon the Slav puts in his hair" (ddp).

At the beginning of 1937 Pound was busy reviewing the galleys for "The Fifth Decad of Cantos." He wrote to Tinkham on 27 February that he was taking notes on John Adams and the Chinese emperors, apparently working on both at the same time. His affection for the older man was genuine, though he sometimes ridiculed his views, including Tinkham's conviction that there would be a European war in 1939. He wrote to his Japanese correspondent, Katue Kitasono, on 11 March: "Uncle George is crossing the Pacific next summer and I hope you will be able to meet him. He IS the America I was born in, and that may have disappeared entirely by now." Pound had not been back to the States in over twenty-five years.

Pound's latent anti-Semitism, although hard to define, was manifesting itself more frequently at this time. It was an American anti-Semitism, common to his generation and to the United States before the Holocaust, the kind that had resulted in exclusion from country clubs, from certain kinds of business firms, from certain suburbs, but never in pogroms. Mencken's letter to Pound of 24 January 1937 is fairly typical of this attitude: "New York has now become almost wholly Jewish. I am not sure that it is a change for the worse, but nevertheless it is somewhat startling. The principal holiday of the year in the town is Yom Kippur. Virtually all offices are closed, and the streets are almost deserted." Pound would not have noticed any Italian anti-Semitism. Mussolini's racial laws had not yet been passed, and the Jewish population in Italy was small. Further, Italians are tolerant by nature and have been suspicious of governments of any kind for more than a millennium. When the racial laws went into effect, they were often ignored, and even when the German army took over by establishing the puppet government of Salò in 1943, their efforts to deport the Jews to camps were largely frustrated by active resistance from the Italian people, fascist and nonfascist alike. Of the 40,000 Jews in Italy, fewer than 20 percent were exported to the death camps, a tragically high figure but smaller than that in all but two or three other European countries.[21]

Lina Caico had warned Pound about the plight of the Jews in Germany. In a letter of 14 March she wrote, in support of a request that Pound help her assist a German–Jewish pianist in Berlin: "They may only have intercourse, trade, etc. among themselves, and as only few have remained, and the poorest, this means they cannot work or do anything." Pound's reply of 15 or 16 March reveals his growing anti-Semitism:

> I know ALL about jews/ Let her try Rothschild and some of the bastards who are murdering 10 million anglo-saxons in England. I know there are jews and jews/ BUT until they will accept the responsibility for governing at least Palestine and defend at least ten acres of ground against savages AS all other races have done/ and until they accept the fact that all other races have suffered/ and until they at least participate in study of and on usury system NO I am not having any more.
>
> I have for 25 years known almost EXCLUSIVELY musicians crushed out by the damn system WHICH the jews NEVER attack. New York is ganz verjudet. Let her go to N York or palestine where they have the "greatest" orchestra in the woild; vide Toscanini, 83 jews and one wop/ Jews are always longing to leave. I rescued one here and he flourished.
>
> They are the GREAT destroyers of value/ the obliterators of all demarcations/ the shifters of boundary stones.
>
> Occasionally a good one has to suffer for the sins of the race.

---

[21] A three-day symposium on the Jews in Italy sponsored by Brooklyn College's Humanities Institute and the Italian Foreign Ministry was reported in the *New York Times*, 14 Dec. 1986, 24: " 'Italy was one of the sparks which illuminated human goodness, compassion ar.d tolerance,' said Paul Bookbinder, an associate professor of history at the University of Massachusetts. 'The record of the Italians,' he said, 'compared well with that of the Danes, Finns and Bulgarians who actively resisted Nazi efforts to systematically deport and murder Jews.' " Further discussions of this important subject are found in Zuccotti, *The Italians and the Holocaust*; de Felice, *Storia degli Ebrei Italiani sotto il Fascismo*; Michaelis, *Mussolini and the Jews*.

Although such writing is shocking now, we must bear in mind that it was written before the horror of the Holocaust, which changed decisively the way that anti-Semitism of any degree can be viewed. Again, we must avoid the inclination to think anachronistically when we review these parts of Pound's writing, as much as we avoid those critics who continue to insist that Pound was not anti-Semitic. He was anti-Semitic; he was also pro-Zionist.

Caico's response on 17 March was gentle: "Really, you're getting economics on the brain! I don't deal with races but with individuals." Pound would not calm down, though. He responded to her almost immediately, with his characteristic rage:

> GET down to USURY/ the cause WHY western man vomits out the jew periodically/ the JEW won't take responsibility for civic order he WONT organize a state/ he is a god damned Iriquois Indian/ necessary defense against parasites/ JEW parasite on principle// IF you are content to be sheep all right/ but MAN declining to be GOY to jewish shearer will defend himself.

Pound wrote to James Taylor Dunn on 18 March about the same problem, in a calmer mood, almost as if apologizing for the above:

> Even in Eng/ and Italy people are being forced into anti-semitism by Jewish folly. I mean people who never thought of it before and who ON PRINCIPLE are opposed to race prejudice and race discrimination. . . .
> All that line of talk distracts from the MAIN issue. If the Jews wd. take any sort of part in econ/ reform as distinct from communist obscurantism and financial obscurantism there wd. be no need of any anti-semitic stuff at all. . . . It is hard as hell to do justice. A minority race can NOT fight in the open. Not if it has any sense at all. The small jew suffers for the sins of the big gombeen man. The fight ought NOT to have been fought on the lines of race prejudice. Only way to avoid that is by spread and acceleration of economic light.

This ambivalence in his private correspondence between anti-Semitism and dislike for racial prejudice is very characteristic. Caico was right. Pound did have "economics on the brain." The problem later becomes, especially in the radio speeches, that the economic concerns and arguments fade, while the strident anti-Semitism gains steadily in prominence. Pound never knew of or condoned any of the horrors that were being committed upon European Jews during these years, but his remarks both public and private served to encourage those who knew, condoned, and acted.

VII

Pound still had correspondents, such as J. W. G. Dunn, to whom he wrote almost exclusively about small magazines, his work on Vivaldi and Cavalcanti, and his literary work in general, and very little about politics or economics. Pound was trying to get a library of the music of Jenkins, Dowland, and Vivaldi published by the photographic method used in his edition of Cavalcanti or by the new method of microphotography. He was in correspondence with a group of poets in Japan, the VOU group,[22] that he was boosting and praising. And he had been offered a lecture tour on poetry and literature in the United States for the winter of 1937 or the fall of 1938 that he was seriously considering. Still, despite these ongoing concerns, Pound had redefined the place of literature and the arts. As he wrote on 18 November:

> My Dear Christ Highest Douglass. . . .
>   You might tear off the following questionnaire and answer it yes or NO.
>   There are two ways of spreading an idea,
>   1. party organization
>   2. permeation of
>   a. amorphous public
>   b. organized groups.
>   When not in controll of a billionaire bunkers and shitters press LITERATURE and the arts are the best means of communicating with a large public/ I dont mean that the work of art or letters makes IMMEDIATE contact with the multitude, BUT it infiltrates/ Yeats and D'Annunzio have had effects. The masterwork or the best of its time is like orders from the STAFF, from the high command.
>   Yr/ god damned muddling britons dont like to admit this/ even if Shelley did tell 'em so.

Pound has gone from the rather pristine notion that great writers carry responsibility for the clarity of the language, which is the medium of public discourse, an idea presented in the *ABC of Reading,* to a very literal reading of Shelley's dictum that poets are the unacknowledged legislators of the world. And it is interesting that the examples he chooses, Yeats and D'Annunzio, are two poets who had clearly articulated, public, political roles in their native lands. I take this as further evidence that Pound at least entertained the idea of a political role for himself at this time and that he had tired of being "merely" a poet. In a time of world crisis, he wanted a more active part.

---

[22] "The word VOU has no meaning as the word DADA. only a sign. One day I found myself arranging whimsically these three characters on the table of a cafe. That's all" (Katue Kitasono to Pound, 16 Mar. 1938).

Intellectually, Pound's new position finds expression in his 1938 book, *Guide to Kulchur* (written in 1937). It is a work of astonishing range and ambition. Permeated throughout with economics, it represents Pound's attempt to "put his thoughts in order" (or, at least, in motion), and it is a bravura performance. Since Pound's key economic ideas have been discussed in separate chapters, we will only touch on other of the book's leading concerns.

The most notable quality, apart from its crankiness, that *Guide to Kulchur* possesses is the seeming effortlessness of the writing. Pound ranges over 2,500 years of human culture without appearing ever to stop to catch his breath. In fact, the book serves as an excellent example of Pound's own definition of culture: "what is left after a man has forgotten all he has set out to learn."[23] The distance between this book and the *ABC of Reading* shows just how far Pound had traveled in his thinking in four years. To begin, it contains very little on literature. It asserts that the two historical principles, the two causes of human history, "were economic and moral" and that "at whichever end we begin we will, if clear headed and thorough, work out to the other." That is the book's intent, one that it achieves. In short, *Guide to Kulchur* is Pound's attempt to do what he states that Confucius did: to "live in a responsible world ... [and to] think for the whole social order." Asserting that "rapacity is the main force in our time in the occident," Pound examines culture to distinguish carefully between a predatory, "*grab-at-once* state of mind"[24] and one based on larger, statal concerns of economic justice. Considering Pound's other work at this time, there is a surprising lack of contemporary references, appropriate, perhaps, to the long perspective he wishes to take. Or perhaps Eliot, and Faber & Faber, had insisted on that.

Confucius ("Kung") fares very well in the book; Aristotle less well. Each is judged on the basis his ethical system provides for a well-run state. The Catholic church is treated largely with respect, it lapses for only a few centuries, whereas Protestantism and Judaism are judged harshly. There is some overt anti-Semitism, along with the statement that "Race prejudice is a red herring. The tool of the man defeated intellectually, and of the cheap politician. No one will deny that the jews have racial characteristics, better and worse ones."[25] Reflecting his interests at the time, there is a large amount about music. Fascist Italy is praised, but not uncritically. England is condemned. The nineteenth century is depicted as the vilest in human history. Pound ranges over

---

[23] Pound, *Guide to Kulchur*, 195.
[24] Ibid., 31, 29, 15–16, 41.
[25] Ibid., 242–3.

the entire cultural history of the West, with apparent comfort and certitude.

Pound was aware of his ambition. As he said of the book in a letter to J. D. Ibbotson of 27 February 1937: "Have just agreed to do a universal history of all human Kulchur or whatever, in approx 70,000 words. where angels etc//." Among many other things, it is a Poundian history of economic thought, a revisionist history, naturally, notable from our point of view for its evidence of how thoroughly Pound had assimilated his economic readings. All told the book is remarkable as an attempt to define the necessary components of a just and well-ordered state, and it is worth careful study. As it relates to Italian fascism, it contains a clearly articulated principle: "No biography of a public man or of a ruler or prime minister can henceforth be accepted as valid unless it contains a clear statement of his finances, of his public acts in relation to public financing."[26]

VIII

Pound's cultural interests were undoubtedly given a boost by his work on *Guide to Kulchur*, the proofs of which he corrected in early 1938. His study of the de Maillac *Histoire Generale de la Chine* and his correspondence with the Japanese VOU group of poets led to an increasingly active concern with oriental culture, a concern that would grow continually over the next several years, continuing well past the end of the war. He wrote to Tinkham on 12 January about the use of microphotography for oriental studies: "English, as only possible medium or middle ground between STATES of mind represented by inflected language and ideogram, where one word can be all parts of speech." He wanted Tinkham to help him secure an invitation from Harvard or Yale to lecture on Confucius or Mencius. Nor were the favors one-sided, as Pound during this period alludes to various possibilities that would promote a Tinkham run for the presidency in 1940. On 2 March 1938, Pound wrote to Por: "The perfect state should move like a dance," appending two ideograms to that statement.

That he was thinking of returning to the United States in some capacity is also shown by his correspondence with Dr. Joseph Brewer, of Olivet College. They discussed the possibility of Pound's teaching there, either in May–June or in September–October. Pound wrote to Brewer on 6 May: "The trouble with July is that it wd. cancel my sea-bathing which ... keeps me fit for work." He also corresponded frequently with Ibbotson during this time, about various ideas for the reform of college

---

[26] Ibid., 116.

curricula, about Vivaldi, Purcell, and others, and about the prospect of a decent library of the unpublished great composers. In *Kulchur* he suggested doing a microphotographic edition of such composers as Boccherini.

The results of his work on the Chinese and Adams Cantos started to show up in his letters. He wrote to Mencken on 19 February: "Not one American in 900 has any idea of what the Founders INTENDED the U.S. government to be" (ddp). On 2 June he wrote to Kitasono:

> I am in the middle of de Maillac's *Histoire Generale de la Chine*. . . .
>
> I have found mention of the "Ti-san" – sort of notes left by Emperor Tai-Tsong; Tang A.D. 648, for his son. I am trying to think out the "100 best books" for proper Ideogrammic library. . . .
>
> The first government note (state ticket not bank note) that I can find record of is of Kao tsong 650/ but the form already developed, so I suppose Tai tsong knew the system. Sane economics, very interesting. . . .
>
> Tai tsong very respectable emperor. (ddp)

Economics appeared everywhere. Pound's attention had partly shifted to the East.

IX

Although Germany had never been one of Pound's chief interests, his study of Frobenius and the new possibility of an alliance between Italy and Germany undoubtedly drew his attention. He wrote on 13 May 1938 to Claude Bowers, the U.S. ambassador to Spain and author of *The Tragic Era:* "Badoglio [Mussolini's chief military adviser], Hitler both sound on money" (ddp). Pound was considering going up in July for a month at Frobenius's institute in Frankfurt, and his attention was drawn to the economic programs of Germany under Hjalmar Schact, president of the Reichsbank, mostly through the coverage they were getting in the Italian fascist press. When the threatened subjugation of Czechoslovakia by the Nazis brought Europe to the brink of war, Pound wrote to Laurence Binyon on 29 September:

> I hope yr/ country isn't going to war to keep up the price of gold; i.e., help the Rothschild and squander another five million anglo-saxon lives. At any rate, I have worked 20 years to prevent it and refer the lot of you to Canto 45 and a few others (mine). . . .
>
> War against Germany wd/ be war AGAINST a clean concept of money. Hence the press vilification of the authoritarian states. Pax vobis. (ddp)

Along similar lines he wrote to Douglas on 14 September: "Fack [Gesell supporter and editor from Texas] the rabid Gesellite now recognizes Mus

and Hit/ probably doing the JOB of freeing us from internat/ capital."
He seemed to be simply including Hitler in his favorable comments from
time to time, perhaps in conformity with the new, positive view of Hitler
taken in the Italian press, though his interest in Germany remained minor.

His interest in Italy, and the reputation of Italy abroad, however, was
still keen. When Por complained in a letter of 8 September: "*American
opinion* re Italy is getting *dangerous*. Some serious action ought to be taken
to appease it," Pound exploded:

> For five years or at least since 1933 I have been TRYING to get it into
> the head of yr/ bloomink gerarchs [officials] that AMERICAN opinion
> MIGHT become dangerous, and that some steps toward keeping that
> jew ridden and finance cankers country OUGHT to be taken. WD/ the
> goofs LISTEN to papa?? They would NOT. . . .
> At present my line is that "three million nice young ang/ saxons
> ought NOT to die in order to make the Skoda gun works [in Czechoslo-
> vakia] safe for international finance.

In fact, Pound was finally starting to get some attention from official
fascist circles about his ideas. He published a three-part series on his
economic ideas in the reputable academic journal *Rassegna Monetaria,* and
his friend Ubaldo degli Uberti had found an avenue of approach to
Cornelio di Marzio, the editor of the equally prestigious journal of ideas
Il Meridiano di Roma. In a letter of late September or early October of
1938, Pound carefully coached degli Uberti about what to say to di
Marzio. The letter shows that Pound was fully aware of the problems
he was having in getting into print, and it gives a brief summary of his
program:

> There IS a resistance to my ideas because they shock the ignorant; and
> the ignorant *start* resisting the moment they see my name. I mean once
> they have been jolted. . . .
> Point being that I have always been far ahead of public opinion, in
> fact so far ahead it has been nearly impossible to get printed.
> My economic course/ Douglas, reform of credit control, Mussolini's
> Italy, and Its RELATION to other economic ideas. Drive for *mutual*
> comprehension of Fascist, Douglasites, Gesellites, and the few catholics
> who know what the canonist doctrine is.

This statement is revealing, for it shows that Pound, who had always
been a member of the artistic avant-garde, now considered himself also
to be a member of the economic avant-garde, as, in truth, he was. He
had already published one article in *Il Meridiano*. It was to become his
most important outlet for the next few years. By the beginning of 1939,
Pound was corresponding with di Marzio, offering advice about economics and the effective presentation of Italian economic ideas for use

in foreign propaganda. Ubaldo degli Uberti, in a letter of 5 February 1939, informed Pound that di Marzio had invited Pound to contribute to his review. Pound was so happy with this news that he offered to split his fees 50–50 with degli Uberti. The latter declined, though he said that if Pound insisted, a 25–75 split was more than generous. Pound contributed two more articles to *Il Meridiano* before the Second World War, but since most of his writing for them came after the war broke out, we will reserve consideration of it until the next chapter.

Pound was supportive of Senator Borah's isolationist stance and wrote to him on 13 January:

> BRAVO BORAH,
>
> My Dear Senator,
>
> KEEP AT IT. What every decent man in Europe wants is a sane Europe and NO WAR west of the Vistula.
>
>   It is damned hard to get this simple statement into print in America. . . .
>
>   Indubitably the drive for war last year was from gunbuzzards/ Rothschild implied. . . .
>
>   Here's to the next president and may he not be a democrat. . . .
>
>   As to ambassadord/ Bill Bullett is capable of seeing with jew colouring, and I wdn't trust Kennedy with a six pence.

There were very few return letters from Borah. "No war west of the Vistula" was to be Pound's oft-repeated slogan during the next few months. The river runs from the Carpathian Mountains through Warsaw to the Baltic Sea near Danzig, roughly bisecting contemporary Poland. Pound's view here is apparently the same as the one he took toward the Abyssinian war: War, due to the economic circumstances involved, was probably inevitable, but it should be confined to a distant area in Eastern Europe, away from those countries dear to him. That these views were, in part, racially motivated becomes clear in a letter from Pound to George Tinkham of 20 January: "Considering the extent whereto the Nation has been bitched by dumping swill into it, since 1866, not only swill of Europe, but the slop of descendants of tartars, so low in the human scale that even a conversion to Judaism meant a cultural advance." Apparently he felt it a lesser evil if Germany and the Soviet Union were to fight over Poland.

Pound enlarged on his views in a letter (in Italian) to Gerhart Hauptmann on 15 January. The German Nobel Prize laureate spent a few months each year in Rapallo, where Pound had long known him.

> Europe and the world needs to understand the formula: no war west of the Vistula. . . .
>
>   Two great nations have lost the game of international finance. This

fact is of course not understood in America, and news of it is suppressed and falsified. In France and in England the battle is more difficult because the most dangerous enemies are inside. Germany and Italy were victims of FOREIGN financial power, from Basel, London, and France creditors and lenders were oppressing them. It seems to me that Germany and Italy little understand the difficulties of reformers and the internal attempts in England, frequently expressed in ideologies alien to the dominant form of thinking in Italy and Germany.

We have need of a greater comprehension. Europe has need of a system of coexistence. (tr)

This letter must be seen in the context of its time as a call for peace, completely at odds with the bellicose statements toward France that Mussolini was then making. Although Mussolini had been hailed as a peacemaker throughout Europe for his role at the Munich Conference (between Hitler, Neville Chamberlain, prime minister of Great Britain, Edouard Daladier, premier of France, and Mussolini), his part there was simply to persuade the democracies to give Hitler what he wanted. The Nazis had twice offered Italy a formal alliance, in May and September of 1938, but Mussolini had not accepted their offer, probably feeling that he needed time to prepare the Italian people for this new shift.[27] Perhaps after he returned from Munich, Mussolini realized that despite his hero's welcome, only Germany had benefited from the settlement. At any rate, by the end of 1938 he was making public demands that France cede to Italy Tunis, Corsica, and Nice. Chamberlain visited Rome in January of 1939 to try to repair the Stresa Front, but by that time it was clear that Italy would side with Germany. Denis Mack Smith notes that "by the beginning of 1939 there was something increasingly frenzied and irrational about Mussolini. The threat of using force was again made explicitly and in public."[28] It would be interesting to speculate about the degree to which Pound responded to this change in his hero and reacted in sympathy.

Pound was rapidly finishing the Chinese and the Adams Cantos at this time. He wrote to Olga Rudge on 21 February: "Waaal, he'z done clean typeskrip of 52/3/4 and of wot he sent her, but two iz gotter be humanized. Too condensed as they set." Two days later he reported to Ronald Duncan: "Am swatting at Canto 56." On 6 March he reported further progress to Henry S. Swabey and suggested a blurb for an edition of his collected poems:

I am retyping Cantos 52/71 and it needs ALL (bldy well ALL) papa's intelligence. . . .

---

[27] Mack Smith, 223–4.
[28] Ibid., 226–7.

> nobody else gits continental headlines "Il Poeta Economista" [the
> Poet–Economist]. . . .
>   E. P. with Por one of first to compare and correlate the DIFFERENT
> contemporary programmes: Corp. state, Doug, Gesell.

Pound was apparently proud of the recognition his work on economics
had received through the *Rassegna Monetaria*.

He wrote to Agnes Bedford in April: "I have pushed off Cantos 52/
71 to Faber and started again on Vivaldi." When he received them at
Faber, Eliot had some problems with Canto LII, which provides the
transition to the world of the Chinese Cantos. He suggested omitting
the name of Rothschild from the latest group of cantos so as to avoid
libel or substituting the name of Bleistein as the metrical equivalent.[29]
The line read: "Rothschild's sin drawing vengeance, poor yitts paying
for Rothschild / paying for a few big jews' vendetta on goyim" *(C*, LII,
257), and it was followed a few lines later by a description of a member
of the Rothschild family on the beach at Rapallo. Pound wrote back on
18 July:

> I fail, blast you, to see the use in spelling leprosy and syphilis "chicken
> pox"/ if the Pubrs/ wish to be responsible let 'em use a blank, i.E., a
> line of TEN dots. . . .
>   Lot of good antiYittism brewing, but the place so wholly poisoned
> with the Talmud that the airyhens don't know which end is what.//
>   I recommend you to study the Talmud in yr/ search fer the root of
> eviln and cert. for heresy.

In the same anti-Semitic vein, to which Eliot was at least partially sympathetic,[30] he wrote back on 5 August in response to Eliot's request for
a title for the work to date: "But fer the narsty near eastern flabour,
might call it Septuagint. Hower time we had a European faith/ deloused
of ALL palistinian jewsociations. Mebber simple title SEVENTY ONE
wd. be a good one."

X

With the international situation rapidly deteriorating, Pound was
seriously considering a trip to the United States. He was undoubtedly
encouraged in this plan by a letter from Mencken of 6 March:

> The New Deal is going downhill rapidly. The country is in far worse
> condition than it was before its salvation was undertaken, and the boobs
> are beginning to be restive. If a suitable demagogue can be unearthed,

---

[29] This remark clarifies Eliot's intent in his own poem "Burbank with a Baedeker: Bleistein
      with a Cigar."
[30] Ackroyd, 303–4.

it will be easy to beat Roosevelt next year. Unfortunately, no really
promising candidate is yet in sight.

Pound had developed fairly promising connections with a number of
major figures in the Republican party through his correspondence. He
probably felt that an early trip to the United States would enable him
not only to place his ideas before his influential friends but perhaps also
to play a role in the forthcoming campaign. Again, I think it likely that
he had some kind of government post in the back of his mind, perhaps
in either the State Department or the Department of the Treasury, should
some of his correspondents achieve power. Although this would offer
further evidence of his political naiveté, Pound was a very energetic and
persuasive, even domineering, speaker in face-to-face meetings, and he
was probably counting on this ability to secure more influence.

Pound mentioned his possible trip to several correspondents. Wyndham Lewis, who had written him on 20 February to say that his portrait
was ready and that there was some possibility that it would be bought
by the Tate Gallery, advised:

> As to whether it's worth your while to expend a fourth class fare to
> the U.S.A. – how can I say? It depends on what you want to get there.
> If you go with a fascist cockade you will get *nothing*, that is quite certain.
> On the other hand you would have a great deal of fuss. If you refrain
> from ramming Mussolini down his throat, you might establish useful
> connections with some publisher and an editor or two.

Good and perceptive advice, but Pound would have been reluctant to
relinquish a celebrity role in his native country after so many years'
absence. An undoubted part of his stature was his ability to manipulate
the press, and he had early on discovered that bad press was better than
no press at all. He responded to Lewis the same month:

> And as fer Murka/ I have something much more unpleasant/ something
> that will rile 'em a lot more than Littoria or hacken Kreuz/ I.E. and
> namely the *CONSTITUTION* of the U.S. which they have never read.
> ... Of course if they thought I was coming to America to STAY that
> wd/ rile 'em still WUSS.

The last sentence shows that the thought of a permanent return to the
United States had already occurred to him. Pound wrote on 27 March
to Katue Kitasono to give a slightly embellished account of his trip: "I
have been out of that country for 28 years and don't know what I can
effect. I should like my trip to result in better triple understanding (Japan/
America/ Italy). But I am not on a mission or anything save my own
affairs." During January Pound had been discussing with Kitasono the
possibility of becoming a correspondent for the *Japan Times*, primarily

for the purposes of continuing to remain eligible for a journalist's card. There was also some talk about Pound becoming a visiting professor at either Tokyo or Kyoto Imperial University.

Without question the rapidly worsening situation in Europe prompted Pound to look seriously into a return to his native land. Mussolini's public statements showed that he was trying to provoke war with France, and in such an eventuality Rapallo would be uncomfortably close to the front line. Hitler invaded Czechoslovakia, annexing more of that country than had been agreed upon in Munich. Franco's forces were finally victorious in Madrid at the end of March, to a great degree because of Italian military assistance, provided at substantial cost in lives, equipment, and "loans." And Mussolini invaded and conquered Albania in April.[31] In May of 1939 Italy and Germany signed a treaty of alliance.

Pound was worried about these developments, as his 8 April letter to Ronald Duncan shows.

> There SHOULD be no war. The only EFFECTIVE attitude is WILL against war. The only way to get anything done is by convergence. . . . *MY* position is: NO war west of the Vistula. Europe is whatever civilization we've got. . . .
>   OUR job is to keep the revolution from being idiotic. . . .
>   Suppose the real revolution in Germany and Italy shd/ flop. . . . revolutions are often betrayed. . . . who carries on?

Pound's doubts about Italy here are worth noting. In private, his *fede fascista* had started to waver. During this period, Lina Caico continued to offer him good advice about the real situation in Italy. On 9 January she had written him about his weak points: "Once you have seen the good [in fascism] you won't look at the bad. . . . And you who find lies in Genesis and in the English press, are quite content with the truth in Italian newspapers" (speaking, among other things, of the suppression of the pope's Christmas speech in the fascist press). She elaborated on these points in a letter of 25 March:

> Something else that is wrong with you is that when you have seen the value of some fact clearly it keeps you from seeing the value of subsequent events. You are beclouded by your past vision. That's your way in politics. Because you saw that something was good, you see everything perfect. And when a failing strikes you, you can't see it as a consequence of something you approved of.

Pound's trip home thus should be seen as taking place amidst doubts about his own role and the increasingly bellicose stance taken by Mussolini.

---

[31] Mack Smith, 228–30.

Pound arrived in New York on 20 April. The *New York Times* reported that he "advised America to keep out of Europe, and said that bankers and munitions interests were to blame for present turbulent conditions in Europe rather than the heads of totalitarian States."[32] Later he traveled to Washington, D.C., where he spent a couple of weeks seeing various senators, congressmen, and administration officials. He saw Henry A. Wallace, then secretary of Agriculture (later vice-president) because Roosevelt was too busy to see him.[33] Undoubtedly the fact that Mussolini had found time to see him crossed Pound's mind. The trip was not successful, and Pound's attempts to present his economic and political ideas, and to broach the idea of a position in the U.S. government, met with little enthusiasm.[34] His visit to Washington is captured in Canto LXXXIV:

> "an' doan you think he chop an' change all the time
> stubborn az a mule, sah, stubborn as a MULE,
> got th' eastern idea about money"
> > Thus Senator Bankhead
> "am sure I don't know what a man like you
> > would find to *do* here"
> > > said Senator Borah
> Thus the solons, in Washington,
> on the executive, and on the country, a.d. 1939. *(C, LXXXIV, 537)*

Stock interprets this, correctly I believe, to indicate that Pound had discussed with Borah the idea of serving in some official capacity and observes that Pound took Borah's answer as a comment on the sad state of the country in 1939. It may have been, but the reader can also interpret it as a reflection of Pound's lack of fitness for government work, since Borah's remark could easily have been the ambiguous comment of a clever politician realizing that Pound would not fit and could not be employed. This lack of success in Washington must have been disheartening, and it certainly served as proof that in Italy he could have more effect.

He returned to New York, where on 22 May he had lunch at the Restaurant Robert with H. L. Mencken, who tried to arrange a corresponding column from Pound with the editor-in-chief of the *Sunpapers*, John Owens. Mencken was unsuccessful for political reasons, as he explained in a letter of 4 October: "The *Sun* is supporting Roosevelt in a large way, and so I assume that there is no chance of your joining its foreign staff. I am sorry indeed. I nominated you in due form, and believe

---

[32] "Ezra Pound, Back, Censures Bankers," 21 Apr. 1939, 18.
[33] Norman, *Ezra Pound*, 359.
[34] Stock, 360–6.

that you'd have been a valuable acquisition." Here was another reason to dislike Roosevelt and for Pound to believe that he was not appreciated in his own country, at least in official circles.

After a conversation with Pound, a reporter for a New York newspaper wrote:

> Literature, it must be said, is now a minor theme in the Poundish symphony. It's all right as a starting point, but presently – or imme-diately – the talk turns to economics, propaganda, and to what he calls "left-wing Fascists" in Italy, his most recent home. Names of big-wigs in Fascist intellectual circles swim to the surface of his flood of words.[35]

Most of the reported conversation concerned Pound's criticism of Britain, Shaw, and the lack of freedom of radio speech in England.

His alma mater treated him well and granted him an honorary doc-torate on 12 June.[36] After his return to Italy, Pound wrote on 14 July to J. D. Ibbotson about coming to the United States again the following spring, inquiring whether it would be possible to do five lectures for Hamilton College, for five hundred dollars plus "mild" expenses. Por wrote to him on 8 August: "Your first interview – on landing – was reported in all papers here & made a good impression." War was very near. Tinkham wrote to Pound on 28 August: "If there is war, as it is the only political 'out' for Roosevelt, he will do everything to get us in. ... Already the English propaganda is thundering." The Second World War began on 1 September 1939, the year Tinkham had predicted.

[35] Edmund Gilligan, "Ezra Pound Excoriates Britons," *New York Sun,* 26 May 1939, 10.
[36] The *New York Times* in a laudatory article stated: "He would have been a professor himself if he hadn't majored as a prophet" (13 June 1939, 22).

7

The Second World War

However close Pound had come to supporting the Axis position, the outbreak of the Second World War must have been a shock to him. Despite all of the indications in the previous year that Europe was moving nearer to war, the invasion of Poland represented a failure for Pound of twenty years' effort to understand the economic causes of conflicts in order to try to prevent them. And, with his family on the Continent, he must have had some concern for their safety, no matter how distant or quiet the war might have seemed at first.

His immediate reaction was predictable. The English were at fault. He wrote to Por in September of 1939:

> Wotever Adolf has been up to, and nobody seems to be able to formulate any worse charge than that he misled the goffdddamndest liars on earth namely the British govt.
> Germany is about 90% right in this shindy, and Eng/stinking/land I.E. the yitts that run her, 100% wrong.

Pound expected that Tinkham and other isolationist Republicans in the House and Senate would manage to keep the United States out of the war.

Such a position was very much in accord with Italy's interests, as Por was aware. He wrote to Pound on 6 September with a hint of a job offer:

> For G's sake don't be so mysterious and complicated.
> I have been approached yesterday re. giving a more efficient turn to our propaganda.
> If you have some suggestion to make re. OUR popularity in Am. (and not Adolf's) we are ready to listen.
> I am underlining: don't be monomaniac – there are a thousand and

one reasons and not merely one reason for the situation the fix we are all in.

Pound was quick to take a hint. He needed money, and it would be a pleasure to get paid for writing about his political and economic beliefs, utilizing his interest in U.S. history. He responded immediately, writing to Por on 7 September:

> THAT, of course is a different line. And if I got to popularize Italy and NOT Adolph, you have got to learn and USE American history. . . .
> World peace is a good line for the U.S. it wd/ be NEARER if it were certain that governments of Eng/ France and the U.S. would never buy another ounce of gold.
> The nicer Adolph can be persuaded to behave, the more popular the Boss will be for PURRSUADING Adolph to be courteous. . . .
> Let the chews BUY a hunk of Poland from Adolph. The only sane proposal was that Rumania, Russia, and Poland shd/ provide a NATIONAL HOME for the zionist tartars.
> GET that, the vast mass of disturbers are NOT semite but descendants of tartar converts/ no more right to JeruSalem than have Choctaw injuns.

Pound is referring to the centuries-old conversion of a Russian tribe to Judaism and is here broaching what will become his characteristic attitude, a kind of anti-Semitic Zionism: prejudice against Jews combined with a recognition that they need a homeland, though not necessarily in Palestine. Apparently, Pound still hoped that a peaceful settlement could be found to the war and that Mussolini could regain the respect of Europe by reasserting his old role and acting to restrain Hitler. It was unrealistic and fanciful thinking on Pound's part, though well intentioned.

Por, although reminding Pound that he did not have the authority to act, on 9 September sounded him out on the possibility of writing a short pamphlet, signed or unsigned, to be called, if signed, "Pound, An Open Letter to Americans." The next day, Pound responded with conviction:

> I will SIGN what I write and will write whatever I know to be FACT or the right as I know and understand it. . . .
> If the perfect equilibrium has been bitched/ that is the fault of Sanctions/ England with France and Italy cd/ maintain a balance. . . .
> Unnerstan I am FOR monetary reform and for ITALY. I prefer Adolph to Monty Norman, Rothschild and Sasoon.
> War on germany is war on an honest concept of money. BUT civilization comes from the Mediterranean.

Pound did not have any great knowledge of German finance, to which he refers infrequently, though apparently he had gained new respect for it since 1935, when he remarked: "Germany under the heel of Dr. Schact (no better than William or Von Papen) has suppressed all her *Freiwirtschaft* organisations and deserves whatever she gets."[1] Pound here is expressing a certain nostalgia for the stability brought on by the Stresa Front and a regret that the League sanctions had destroyed that stability. Although this view is correct as far as it goes, it does not recognize that the crucial destabilizing action was Mussolini's African adventurism. The next day, 11 September, he sent Por the draft of a mild letter, addressed to the English, and proposed a far more scathing one, to be addressed to the United States condemning England. "America's place is OUT of this damn war," he said. Por was leading him into working for the Italian government on some propaganda projects, but Pound was eager to be led, caught up in the new project, and probably, in the new possibilities for earning income. He changed his plan to go to Venice and arranged instead to meet Por in Rome on 22 September. Por received both letters but preferred that Camillo Pellizzi, who had recently returned from his position as professor of Italian at the University of London, do the one for the English.

II

Pound's correspondence of this time with Congressman Jerry Voorhis of California blamed the war on England and urged that the United States remain neutral. He hoped the war would be confined to Eastern Europe and argued that only England wished to extend it beyond Poland. In fact, for a time it seemed that this wish for a limited war might be granted. France managed only a feeble offensive on Germany's western front around 17 September, and by the end of September, Poland was overrun. In October, things settled into what the American press named "the Phoney War," with little military action on either side.

Pound's letters of the time continue to reflect a growing anti-Semitism. He wrote to Wyndham Lewis in September: "America is damn well to keep out of the war/ BAD enough to have european aryans murdering each other for the sake of Willie Wieseman and a few buggarin kikes." He expanded on this in a further letter to Voorhis of 24 October: "It is impossible for anyone in America to judge Europe if they insist on neglecting the jewish problem. Only the jews want war. Only Russia and the jews stand to gain by European war and Russia has already had her slice." This last sentence refers to the fact that the Soviet Union invaded Poland from the east on 17 September and divided that country in an uneasy accord with Germany. On 6 October, having realized his

---

[1] Pound, "The Individual in His Milieu" (1935), in *Selected Prose*, 278.

immediate ambition, Hitler offered peace to England and France. The offer was refused.

Some restraint gave way in Pound's psyche with the onset of the Second World War, for his anti-Semitism suddenly becomes a more pronounced feature of his letters. His correspondence with the composer and pianist Gerhart Munch shows this loss of control most clearly. Munch, an anti-Semite, in his letters gave Pound ample opportunity to respond in kind. Pound resisted the temptation until the outbreak of the war, when his letters to Munch shift from cultural to political subjects and contain many anti-Semitic remarks. Pound's overt and virulent anti-Semitism, therefore, seems tied to the start of the Second World War.

During this least propitious time, Pound was settling into the task of writing the final, *paradiso* section of the *Cantos*. He wrote on 24 October to Eliot: "Now about writin more cantos/ It will take TIME. If you wuz to find me a nice TEXT of Scotty the Oirishman (index name Scotus ERIGENA, nut Dunce kotus) I might get through another FOUR canters in six months or I mightnt." A further letter to Eliot of 18 January 1940 confirms this, with Pound stating "29 canters to write," showing that the intent was to write an even one hundred, as did Dante. The resumption of fighting was to interrupt his plans, although Mary de Rachewiltz has said in conversation that her father's notebooks show that some parts of the Pisan Cantos were written during the wartime period.

H. L. Mencken was firmly of the belief that Roosevelt would do everything in his power to get the United States into the war, despite his statements about staying neutral, and Mencken's views influenced Pound. Pound's correspondence with him during this time included a piece of light propagandistic verse directed against England, entitled "Barrak Room bullud":

> Oh its 'Tommy this' and 'Tommy that' an
>   'Tommy where yer ole tin hat'
> And tommy this an tommy that
>   and Tommy shoot the coons
> and lay down your bleeding bolliks★
>   fer the Rothschilds and Sasoons
>
> Oh we've lent our gold to Poland
>   or our paper to buy guns
> and now to git the interest
>   we must sacrifice our sons
>
> And yet in my opinion
>   There is ope fer Hengland yet
> if they'd lay off shooting german lads
>   and shoot★ this cabinet

Pound offered the following suggestions to make the poem printable and "to avoid charge of inciting of justifiable violence": that at the first asterisk "lights and livers" be substituted for "bleeding bolliks," and at the second asterisk "sack" be substituted for "shoot." He sent the poem with a letter of 27 October, adding: "Strictly anonymous or recd. by our palace mejum from Mr. Ruddybloody Kippling, deceased/ several verses omitted due to the excentricities of the ouiji board." Despite the humor of the poem, it reflected Pound's view that the war was caused by international finance, that it was a "loan capital war." Whose loan capital it was, he was not quite certain, at times blaming the English, at other times speculating that it was really the American moneylenders, working against England (as he wrote in a letter to Katue Kitasono on 28 October 1939). It should be noted that by this time even the English were starting to subscribe to Pound's view of Neville Chamberlain's lack of effectiveness.

In letters to both Mencken and Tinkham during this period, Pound seemed seriously interested in finding some job back in the United States. He complained to Mencken on 31 October that "my bloody country OUGHT to start supporting me SOON. The shitten govt. of England is stealing 35% of my royalties to spend on poison gas and masks." And when Tinkham complained that his Boston office was absorbing a great deal of his time because of the collapse of his private secretary of 32 years' experience, Pound seriously suggested, on 2 November, that Tinkham give him the job. Pound was undoubtedly considering repatriation.

At the same time, Pound was promoting projects for himself in Italy. He and Por were discussing the possibility of an Italian and American magazine of thirty-two pages an issue, with subjects to be split evenly between the two countries, presumably in an effort to increase good will. Pound was to have served as editor, and he contemplated inviting George Santayana, who lived in Italy, to contribute. In a letter of 14 December, Por informed Pound that the estimate for the magazine was sent to Alessandro Pavolini, the Italian minister of Popular Culture and director of Italian propaganda. Although apparently nothing came of it, Pound's interest in this kind of project, which he envisioned as rediscovering the words of the American founding fathers and presenting the real history of his country, was to continue with more success during the Salò period in the latter part of the war, as we shall see in the following chapter.

Ubaldo degli Uberti located a copy of Johannes Scotus Erigena for Pound, so he began work on his paradiso section of the Cantos. On 2 January 1940, Pound wrote to degli Uberti about anti-Semitism: "ME trying to put over a dangerous idea WITH TACT and so it wont be noticed reminds me rather of an elephant trying to climb a tree. However

I am not out for pogrom; I want to get semitism at its damn'd ROOT."
It is worth noting that Pound did not think of himself as anti-Semitic
and resented it when William Carlos Williams told people that he was.
Although Pound does not elaborate on what he means by root (it seems
to be some mixture of Old Testament religion, Protestantism, and
Taoism), the remark about pogroms seems clear enough. Unfortunately,
Pound's own anti-Semitism was being reinforced by items he was reading
in Italian newspapers. On 2 November 1939, he wrote to Tinkham:
"There is a steady flow of quotation from Swedish and Dutch papers
showing that Europe is gradually awakening to the non European nature
of yitts." And again, to Tinkham, on 7 November, Pound wrote: "I see
quotes from Scandinavian papers etc. the idea of the jew hoping the
european white man will exterminate himself seems fairly well diffused."

Questions of Jews and race seemed to obsess him during this time;
these subjects are mentioned frequently in his letters. On 18 January he
wrote to Douglas McPherson of Philadelphia, who was contemplating
a new magazine.

> Just to keep down fanaticism you might note that the Italian present
> regulations leave place for ANY jew who is loyal to Italy. Apart from
> the fact that only full blooded jew or 50% racial *professing* jews are
> debarred from key positions.
>
> By RACE I do not mean what's printed on a passport. The melting
> pot has been tried and FAILED. Some blends are O.K. but the others
> rot in three generations even when the mulatto happens to be good.
> . . . We want our Italians Italian; french french; ang/sax ang/sax; Dutch
> dutch. That is enough for any man, with a very occasional hybrid. . . .
>
> I think as an editorial position we shd/ say: It is not antisemitic to
> warn working jews that they and NOT the big jewish financiers will
> pay for international finance's promotion of war. Usocracy is NOT
> our ideal of what government should be.

The rejection of the melting pot was a fairly common idea for a man of
Pound's generation and background in the United States: The notion
that somehow the old colonial stock had been supplanted, or the nation
had been weakened, by the waves of immigrants arriving in the late
nineteenth and early twentieth centuries was shared by many whose
family fortunes had declined.[2] Again, we see a typical ambivalence in
Pound's thought, between his hatred for an imagined group, the usocracy, which he believed was made up primarily of Jews, and his sympathy
for the average Jew, who was being victimized, along with everyone
else, in the war caused by the usocracy. He wrote in January to Mencken
along the same lines: "Don't be anti-semite/ warn the poor hebes that

---

[2] Wilhelm gives an account of Pound's sense of his family's decline in fortune (155–9).

the kahal is gittin 'em in bad ALL over Europe and Asia." Apparently he was either aware of the growing anti-Semitism in Europe or, again, just registered what the Italian press was reporting.

The mail between the United States and Italy was being occasionally held up by the British navy, so communication with his native land became increasingly difficult for Pound. Mencken wrote Pound on 5 February that American and Italian ships were being forced into Gibraltar, and mail pouches seized: "Some of the letters are afterward remailed by the English, but not all. The American State Department has protested formally . . . but only formally. Both Roosevelt and Hull are so violently Anglomaniacal that they are not likely to put up any effective resistance." Mencken was of German descent and had suffered during the anti-German scare during the First World War, so he was particularly sensitive to the attempts by Roosevelt to involve the United States in another European war. Mencken was not the only one to believe that Roosevelt was seeking war: There was an active group of opponents to FDR's foreign policy in the Congress, and Pound had corresponded with many of them. George Tinkham had sent Pound a copy of his press release of 29 January 1940. It was entitled: "The United States Is Treading the Road to War, Declares Congressman George Holden Tinkham of Massachusetts in Press Statement Denouncing the Roosevelt–Hull Foreign Policy," and it outlined in some detail the alleged foreign policy mistakes and provocations of the United States. Tinkham charged that the United States was "proceeding toward tragic involvement in the present war step by step, as it did in the last war; first, arms; then, credits; and finally, men." Pound still was somewhat ambivalent about Roosevelt, though, and wrote to Mencken in February that FDR was not so bad but that he needed to get rid of the "sec/ of the Treasury. There is the real govt. and I suspect Frankie has forgotten all about there being any such department."

III

Pound continued to write for the prestigious *Il Meridiano di Roma*, and in a letter to di Marzio of 14 March he made suggestions about possible topics, asking di Marzio to state clearly and frankly what further work Pound could do. He made a point of saying that he had a reserve of ready articles because the English and American presses were closed to him. On 18 March he wrote again to di Marzio, offering to do a weekly column for *Il Meridiano*, selecting the best items from the Italian press for highlighting and comparison (duplicating the column "Press Cuttings" from the old *New Age*). Pound was an avid reader of Italian newspapers, reading daily *Popolo d'Italia, Giornale di Genova, Regime Fas-*

cista, Gazetta Popolare, Corriere Mercantile, and *Corriere della Sera.* In fact, a lot of Pound's correspondence during this period involves attempts, direct or indirect, to promote work for himself. These attempts were more difficult since some of his traditional channels were cut off. But as some became blocked, others opened. On 15 March Katue Kitasono wrote to Pound stating that the *Japan Times* was willing to designate him as Italian correspondent. When this went through, he wrote to di Marzio on 11 April stating: "I am finally promoted by the Supreme Parnassus to journalistic dignity." Actually, the official accreditation was useful in fascist Italy, where, as I have mentioned, journalists were entitled to substantial discounts on rail transportation.

Pound's articles in the period between 1939 and 1943 for *Il Meridiano di Roma* are almost exclusively on political and economic topics; scarcely a handful treat his cultural concerns. *Il Meridiano*'s publishing Pound's work on those topics demonstrates that he had achieved a certain status in Italy as a political and economic commentator, though there were occasional references, even within the pages of the journal, to the difficulty that some readers had in understanding him, both because of the content of his articles and because of his imperfect mastery of Italian.

The editor of *Il Meridiano* was Cornelio di Marzio, who held the prestigious and influential post of secretary-general of the Confederation of Professionals and Artists in 1935–6 and again in 1939–43. Di Marzio was not a traditional fascist bureaucrat, as Philip V. Cannistraro notes:

> He gave his official support to many of the most promising and avant-garde writers, artists, and intellectuals of the period, frequently protecting them from the harsh censorship policies of the regime and often providing outlets for their work when the more intransigent *gerarchi* (leaders) opposed them. He worked closely with Antonio Bragaglia's Teatro degli Independenti, sponsored exhibits of modern and Jewish artists at the Confederation's Galleria di Roma, and... published an outspoken newspaper called *Il Meridiano di Roma,* which was eventually suppressed by the regime.[3]

Il Meridiano provided Pound with the kind of journalistic outlet he needed, and di Marzio's activities would have given him further proof of the intellectual and artistic freedom available in fascist Italy.

Although a few of the articles bear disturbing titles, such as "Jews and the War," "The Jew: Pathology Incarnate," and "Anglo-Israel," the anti-Semitism of Pound's writings for *Il Meridiano* is mild and only occasional. Many of the articles contain restatements of the already familiar economic ideas, but at times new insights surface as Pound revisits old concerns. To some extent we can say that, like Orage, Pound conducted his own

[3] Cannistraro, 170–1.

economic education in public, in the pages of the various journals for which he wrote, so as we read these works, as Pound reviews the components of his economic system, different emphases appear and different connections are made.

The most striking of these new insights is Pound's new articulation of the tie between Social Credit and Italian fascism. He repeats his previous idea that "any important monetary-economic mechanism would be absorbed and set in motion more quickly by Fascism than by any other existing system"[4] (tr). However, he had noticed a deeper, theoretical connection between the two movements: "Where Mussolini talks of the State, Douglas speaks of the 'increment of association,' and the more the Scottish engineer clarifies his verbal manifestation, the nearer he comes to the Mussolinian ideal"[5] (tr).

Pound connects the two movements more closely, and more to his own satisfaction, by adding an idea to Douglas: "Douglas derives values . . . from the cultural heritage, that is, the total accumulation of mechanical inventions, *and for that matter, customs and the habit of acting in an orderly manner, etc.* Which accords best with the statal idea?" (emphasis added)[6] (tr). Pound has expanded Douglas's idea of the cultural heritage beyond the accumulation of useful inventions and has subsumed it under the fascist notion of the state. He wrote that "credit is a collective product, that is, statal. It depends on civic order. . . . Money . . . is a symbol of *collaboration* inside a civil system"[7] (tr). Thus in an additional way credit is social, based on the order established by the state, which is another form of the cultural heritage. In this way Pound finds a further link between the ideas of Douglas and Mussolini. The symbol of fascism is the fasces, the bundle of individual rods that, when grouped together, form a unity that surpasses individual identity. This bundle, the collective state, was another cultural product, to which everyone had a right. "Credit is a social product, and every citizen (even the unemployed, even the aged and children) contributes to its formation. He contributes by his attitude, civic habits, and conduct. Every individual citizen has the right to participate in the gains of the State"[8] (tr). Thus, according to Pound, all citizens have the right to participate in the economic well-being of the state, not through alms given by the charitable or through aid given in fear of social disturbance, but fundamentally, as members and citizens of that state. This is a humane and worthy vision of an ideal social order.

[4] Pound, "Concerning an Economic System," *Il Meridiano di Roma* 5, no. 48 (1 Dec. 1940).
[5] Pound, "Why Certain Fogs Still Exist," *Il Meridiano di Roma* 5, no. 29 (21 July 1940).
[6] Pound, "Concerning an Economic System," *Il Meridiano di Roma* 5, no. 48 (1 Dec. 1940).
[7] Pound, "Promissory Note," *Il Meridiano di Roma* 7, no. 31 (2 Aug. 1942).
[8] Pound, "Social Credit," *Il Meridiano di Roma* 7, no. 39 (27 Sept. 1942).

IV

Cantos LII–LXXI were published in London in January of 1940. Because these cantos have largely been ignored by critics, excerpted as they are from Chinese history and the *Works* of John Adams, it is worth mentioning briefly what Pound himself thought of them. In a letter of 28 October 1939 to Katue Kitasono, Pound wrote:

> My Cantos 52/71 are in the press. . . . Creator of the United States and of something not unlike a dynasty in America. The fall of which meant the END of decent civilization in the U.S. or at any rate a great and pestilent sickness in American government. And I wd prefer to write about history for the moment, including current history.

And on 23 March 1940, Pound wrote to Tinkham:

> I dunno if it is LEGAL for congressmen to read poetry. . . . and I dont in the least care whether you consider it as poetry or as telegraphic notes, but I am sending you Cantos 52/71. . . .
>   If you can stand the choppy delivery (and damn it IF one is getting the gist of 12 folios onto 100 pages, one has to cut something,) I am free to doubt if there is a quicker way of Meetin Mr. J. Adams. 62/71. The Chinese Cantos 52/61 at least show it didn't all start last tuesday morning.

Clearly, Pound was aware of the problems the reader would have with those cantos but felt that the didactic points were worth making. In a letter to Pellizzi of 4 May, he stated that these last cantos were "SIM-PLER," and in a further letter of 7 May, he suggested that a bilingual translation be made of them because "the brevity of statement is such that I think they can not be wholly ruined by a translator. The substance wd have to remain."

The phoney war continued until the spring. In fact, things seemed so quiet that T. S. Eliot planned to visit Rapallo in the spring of 1940. But the six-month lull ended suddenly with the conquest of Denmark and Norway in April. Mencken wrote to Pound on 15 April:

> By the time these lines reach you, Roosevelt may be in the war. He is lathering to go, and the invasion of Norway has furnished him with his long awaited excuse. . . .
>   There is not much chance of monetary reform in the face of the war. I agree with you thoroughly that the present system is insane, but I am not convinced that any of the new ones are much better. The totalitarians, to be sure, achieve a great deal more at much less expense, but I have some doubt that they make life more comfortable for the average man.

Pound could not see the wisdom of this observation, that during a war
monetary reform (as opposed to monetary collapse) would be difficult
to achieve because there would be far more pressing matters to attend
to. Instead, for the next few years he would continue to hammer upon
the necessity of sane economics, although in a retrospective sense, as
explaining the causes of the war, as much as in a prospective sense,
advocating reform.

Pound completely lost confidence in Roosevelt during this time, the
result principally of the president's actions to support Britain in the
second half of 1940 and also of Pound's correspondence with Tinkham
and Mencken. Another reason for Pound's changing attitude was Roosevelt's devaluation of the dollar and the decision taken six years earlier,
in January of 1934, to buy gold at a fixed price. The price set for gold
led to its overvaluation at first and was, in effect, a decision to support
the price of a commodity.[9] Apart from his personal interest, since it was
a move that diminished the effective worth of his father's pension, as
we have mentioned, Pound became obsessed with this action and wanted
to know from whom the Roosevelt government had bought its gold at
the higher prices, and in order to enrich whom. Tinkham helped Pound
get the answers to his questions about gold purchases and on 14 May
forwarded a letter from the director of the Mint on gold acquisition "for
the fiscal years 1932–1939 inclusive," but apparently Pound was not
satisfied by the explanation, for he continued to raise the issue. As noted
previously, this was the only action taken by Roosevelt that could be
considered in accord with Social Credit principles.

The sudden collapse of France in May and June of 1940, the entry of
Italy into the war on 10 June, his growing anti-Semitism, and his new
suspicion about the FDR gold policy all blurred in Pound's mind, pro-
ducing a kind of pseudo-insight into causation as evidenced in the following letter of 18 June to the isolationist Democrat from Montana,
Senator Burton K. Wheeler:

> I have read a regulation that only those foreigners are to be admitted
> to the U.S. who are deemed to be useful etc/. The dirtiest jews from
> Paris, Blum?? Mandel, certainly the pimp Reynaud have gone or are
> going to the U.S. Some sense of history ought to be aroused. These
> pimps for Lazard, Rothschild, Beir, Sieff etc/ are all part of a pox.
> England rotted since 1694; France since Necker took in his Swiss syphi-
> lis. Every country where these swine have been allowed to set up a rule
> within a rule, has been rotted. France has gone under. England's last
> Poland. The forces that put that utterly utter Morgenthau into the
> treasury will do the same to the U.S. unless stopped. . . . Four years

[9] Friedman and Schwartz, 472.

more of rot/ 4 years more of gold buying at 15 dollars too much per ounce (HELL! he has already put ten Billions of the people's money into the pockets of the gold swine, and 4 billions of it excess profits.)

Part of this tirade is due to Pound's reading, in April, of the *Protocols of the Ancient Elders of Zion,* a notorious anti-Semitic document purporting to show how the cycles of war and peace, inflation and deflation, and prosperity and depression are controlled and manipulated by a small group of Jews acting in conscious conspiracy. Pound knew of the dubious provenance of this book but nevertheless started to wonder. He wrote to Por on 11 April:

> By the way; have you ever read the Protocols; or have you as I was, [been] putt off by rumour that they were fake/ DAMN dull, hideously written, but complete code, and absolute condensation of history of the U.S.A. for the past 50 years. as Henry Ford and Sidenham said/ "show an amazing knowledge." Drum/ has dug up source, in a pamphlet against Napoleon II [III] pubd/ in the 1860's. The russian text a mere summary of the high spots.

Pound's own copy of the *Protocols* is unmarked, showing that he did not have a very high regard for the book. In fact, he was suspicious of it though he mentioned it in several letters. He wrote to the Reverend Henry S. Swabey, an Anglican clergyman: "You better, all of you, read the protocols, not as the emanation of any sect, but as a very brief and clear description of process." Pound did feel that there was some deliberate attempt to conceal economic truth and that the result would be that ordinary Jews would suffer for economic manipulations performed by a few very wealthy ones. He wrote to Por on 11 July: "No use mere caccia al ebrainini [going after the little jews]. He must chase the ebreiAZZI/, the big buggars. Protocols provide for superficial antisemitism as part of plan to confuse the issues. Besides the swiss swine (dynasties) in the Bank of Frogs are NOT yidds." Part of Pound's conviction resulted from his very selective reading. He did not have access to a good library but relied entirely on his own large but unbalanced collection. As he read, he was looking for historical incident, analysis, or evidence to back up his own economic theories. Conspiracy theories by their very nature cannot be verified in any ordinary sense nor can they be "falsified"; that is, there is no evidence or testing procedure available to show that they are not true. For example, an argument that a person was dead and could not possibly have been involved might be met by the counterargument that he was only apparently dead: "And Metevsky died and was buried, *i.e.* officially, / And sat in the Yeiner Kafé watching the funeral" *(C,* XVIII, 81). Since, for the believer, there exists only evidence, no matter how scattered or improbable, indicating that a conspiracy theory

is true, Pound found traces in history to back up his beliefs. His mistake
was not in his insight into economics but in his insistence in ascribing
agency to every economic and historical occurrence. As he wrote to
Senator Wheeler on 19 July:

> I trust you will get due credit for what you have done to keep young
> America from being slaughtered for Lazard, Hambre and Rothschild.
> I take it the danger is not wholly eliminated, but that if Germany moves
> fast enough it may be postponed for 15 years. . . .
>
> The great evil is Morgenthau, or the force that keeps it in office.
> WHEN is the public going to be TOLD efficiently that the U.S. was
> sold up the river in 1863 by traitors and the agents of Rothschild and
> their gang??? This is the cardinal fact of U.S. history. . . .
>
> To keep war fever from rising again/ what about a little NEWS about
> German land laws, Bauernfahig, etc. U.S. error after Jackson opened
> up the land to settlers, was in NOT preventing it from being bought
> up and turned into latifundia [large estates].

We have the characteristic themes here: an economic reading of American
history (to which there is more sympathy today than there was in Pound's
time); a view that economic history repeats itself or, even more radically,
that a conspiracy repeats itself, achieving a continuing existence over
time; a conviction that he has seen to the root of things (the "cardinal
fact of U.S. history"); and a tendency to see history through the lens of
current policies of the fascist regime, in this case Mussolini's action in
breaking the power of the rich landowners in Italy and similar German
laws that he read about in the Italian newspapers (his knowledge of
Germany remained very sparse throughout this period). There are insights to be had from Pound here, but there is also a semantic paranoia
at work: a tendency to read more meaning into some events than they
can ordinarily bear, a kind of interpretative overload.

Pound's friends recognized problems of scattered references and frequent obscurity in his articles, and they offered helpful suggestions. Por
wrote to him on 21 July: "If you allow a suggestion: the sometimes
obscure passages – which so irritate your benevolent readers – should be
cleared in notes." Pound's reply, on 23 July, is revealing: "[What] I
NEVER seem able to get into YOUR damnblock IS that I have NO
bloody means of knowing WHAT the hell you or other readers consider
OBscure. It all looks simple to me." The problem here may have been
complicated by Pound's arrogance, but I think it is primarily a rhetorical
split from his readers, a semantic schizophrenia. Imagism taken too far
or, rather, imagism coupled with the ideogrammic method carries this
danger of losing contact with its audience. Redundancy is necessary for
communication, but apparently Pound could not see this, and his situation in these years is one of increased isolation from his intended au-

dience. The Italian authorities had similar problems with Pound. On 9 August, Por advised Pound: "Your letters arrive a little late because they are all read by the censors. Write more clearly, otherwise the censors are obligated to study them too closely." There was no reaction from Pound to this news that his mail was being intercepted by the Italian authorities.

V

Although Pound continued to hope for peace, it became clear during the summer of 1940 that Britain was not going to ask for terms and the war would continue. The war caused a serious disruption of communication: American newspapers arrived in Rapallo by way of Japan, and Pound was unable to cash American checks. His father's pension checks were arriving only sporadically from the United States, and Pound's royalty checks from England were not arriving at all. Dorothy's small annual income was also cut off by the war. Thus Pound, who contributed to the support of Olga, Mary, and Dorothy, and felt responsible for his parents, was in increasing financial difficulties. There are various indications of this in the correspondence, mild at first. He wrote to Por on 28 July: "I shall do an article or rather several for Meridiano – one on question of paying authors living wage. @ any rate WHEN they are recognized as useful to the state – failure on that line wd. mean self confessed flop of the system." He also was trying to hunt up work. Again to Por, on 7 August, he wrote: "De F/ [De Feo] asked me who cd/ translate yr/ Pol/ Econ/ Soc/ [*Italy's Policy of Social Economics*] and I sez EZ can."

Pound's financial difficulties, his sense of being cut off both from his royalty payments and from outlets for his writing in England and the United States, his apparent uncertainty about whether he could make a living in Italy, all of these factors, when combined with a sense of conspiracy, served to feed his growing anti-Semitism and caused him to come to some increasingly far-fetched conclusions. He wrote to Por on 2 September: "I wish you wd/ nab the jew yachts full of emeralds lyin orf the Irish coast/ if they haven't yet sailed to the hesperides. also stop all the yitts going to the U.S. and founding pub/ houses to drown out everything save yiddery." There is something half comic in this image of yachts full of emeralds anchored off the Emerald Isle, with its veiled allusion to the nymphs who guarded the golden apples of Hera, causing us to wonder just how seriously Pound took these stories. Nor is it clear just what Por was supposed to do to "nab" the yachts. Soon, however, all trace of humor would be gone from such attacks.

In late summer or early fall of 1940, Pound decided to leave Italy with his family and return to the United States. Serious preparations were made for the move. The Pounds turned over their most prized and valuable possessions, including the Gaudier-Brzeska sculptures and drawings, the Dolmetsch clavichord, and Pound's own library, to the degli Uberti family for safekeeping. By 23 October, the artworks and treasured mementos were transferred to Rome, and the bulk of Pound's own library was stored at young Riccardo degli Uberti's studio in Genoa.[10] Ubaldo's son, though assuring Pound that his property would be in good hands, nevertheless urged him, in a letter of 4 October 1940, to stay in Italy:

> I can understand that you may think that by your pen and by your speech you may influence your fellow citizens toward a greater understanding of the European situation. But from here you have already done and may continue to do all that is possible – Over there you cannot do any more. (tr)

Riccardo degli Uberti went on to assure Pound that in the unlikely event the United States should enter the war, Pound would have nothing to fear from the Italian government. He also warned of the risk of Pound's falling into the hands of the English during the voyage home.

As of 5 September 1939, American consulates in Italy had begun to advise inquiring citizens that they should return to the United States as soon as possible.[11] This primarily passive attitude was strengthened in the spring of 1940, when Secretary of State Cordell Hull sent a telegram to William Phillips, U.S. ambassador to Italy, on 15 May: "We agree that in light of your conversation with Ciano today the time has come when you should strongly urge all Americans to leave Italy at the earliest possible opportunity."[12] Financial assistance was made available in the form of loans to those Americans who would otherwise be unable to pay their own way, and the government sent several ships to Europe to help evacuate citizens who wished to return home. Nevertheless, the difficulties faced in securing reliable transportation were very great. American sailings from the Mediterranean and from Genoa to the United States were soon halted, and the only alternative was to arrange rail transportation through invaded France and the Iberian Peninsula to the Atlantic coast of Portugal. From there the sea crossing was hazardous, not to mention expensive: $300 per person or $1,800 for the entire Pound party, an enormous sum in those days. The only other alternative was the newly inaugurated Pan American Clipper service, which Pound tried

---

[10] This account of Pound's attempt at repatriation is adapted from my article "The Repatriation of Pound, 1939–1942," 447–57, which should be consulted for more detail.

[11] National Archives, Suitland, Maryland, U.S. State Department Record Group 84, file number 300, Rome.

[12] Ibid.

to book. As he wrote to George Tinkham on 7 November: "I packed up at the beginning of October to come home, but in Rome found NO clipper places till Dec. 15." As can be clearly seen, Pound did make a serious attempt to return to the United States in the fall of 1940 but was thwarted by the difficulties in arranging safe passage.

Pound's financial problems continued to plague him, and he wrote to Por on 31 October inquiring if it were possible to do a paid series of lectures. Por responded with concern on 6 November:

> Write me a letter in which you tell me *clearly* how your finances stand, why they won't cash your American checks, and how much the payments that you had in the past received regularly are piling up (or were piling up). Pellizzi wants to do a report on it to someone who could help you.

Pound responded on 9 November with characteristic reticence and some pride: "It is not a question of the possibility of making my income in the future approach that which I received in the past. It is a question of making it suffice for the modest needs of a writer." In December, Por helped out by sending Pound a check to pay back part of the money Pound had lent him.

VI

Pound was at this time trying to find more work for himself and sought a meeting with Alessandro Pavolini, minister of Popular Culture and director of fascist propaganda, though he was continually put off. His correspondence with Luigi Villari, who had recently transferred to the Ministry of Popular Culture, shows his increasing interest in Italian propaganda. Not surprisingly, this increased interest occurred at the time when Pound was in some financial trouble. Expatriate intellectuals commonly involve themselves in the peace or wartime propaganda efforts of their adopted country. After all, just how else could Pound support his family? Further, it is also common for the outsider in a society to demonstrate hyperconformity and for an immigrant to profess a superpatriotism. I mean here neither to excuse Pound's actions nor to question their sincerity, just to point out that they should not surprise us too much. Pound admired Mussolini and Italian fascism and believed in many of its doctrines while questioning or criticizing others. As the war dragged on and with information from other countries cut off, the points of coincidence between his beliefs and the announced policies of the fascist regime increased.

Pound became a student of propaganda, hoping to promote a job for himself in Italy so he could support his family for the war's duration. He wrote to Villari on 2 December:

> IF a propaganda dept. dont KNOW what is being HEARD and said and repeated in another country how the . . . . .etc/ can it PUT any idea whatsodamnever INTO that country? . . . .
>
> By the way, VERY good stuff in english from Germany yesterday/ taking up motif they have used well before. i;e; Housing project. Barnes cd/ get busy on that line. Better FACTS, INFORMATION re/ advantages of german and italian system than attacks on Winston, which will be discounted OR exceeded by people in eng.

Apart from acting as unofficial admonisher of the Italian propaganda service, Pound repeated his desire to act as a kind of executive clipping service, a collector and summarizer of important news items from the American and European press. He offered these services to make Italian propaganda more effective at keeping the United States out of the war. As was typical for Pound, his initial approach was low key, making use of his correspondence network. He wrote to Ubaldo degli Uberti on 2 December:

> I want to be able to earn my living honestly in postwar Italy, without recourse to foreign sources. BUT it is not the moment to haggle nor to await stipends etc. nor to annoy ministers etc/ etc/. In the meantime, I can DIGEST as much as you wish of foreign newspapers, or better magazines, in English or French.
>
> The problem IS that neither I nor those responsible for propaganda receive enough of those magazines.

This kind of work would have been attractive to Pound since, with the help of Olga Rudge, he engaged in it anyway on a daily basis, skimming newspapers and magazines to find articles on topics that interested him or that demonstrated the correctness of his views.

Pound's eagerness for propaganda work continued in early 1941. He wrote to Pellizzi on 11 January revealing another important motive for his activity: "I will BUST i.e. EXPLODE if some use isn't made of me. Megaphone to shout out this or that to deaf americans." Pellizzi tried to help Pound by phoning both Ungaro and Paresce of the Italian foreign radio, trying to persuade them to give Pound a spot on Italian radio. He promised Pound on 16 January that he would hear from them.

Pound's obsession with economics continued unabated, but he had started to recognize the difficulty of reform. On 26 January 1941, he wrote to Giacomo Barnes:

> The state never needs to borrow. certainly never needs to pay rent on its own purchasing power (pay PRIVATE individuals for use of its own credit).

> BUT under some circumstances even a state may find it OPPOR-
> TUNE not to rush too fast, or hurl itself too suddenly against ingrained
> habits of thought of the majority of the citizens.

One of those circumstances assuredly must have been the condition of war, where the state frequently intervenes to effectively devalue the currency, or when confidence is eroded. Even Pound would probably have recognized that a radical change in the nature of the Italian currency during wartime would have produced panic and confusion among the populace. He seems to have adopted a more practical approach because in the same letter he cautions Barnes about throwing out the old system before the new one is in place. The war had started to grind down even Pound's idealism.

Por came through again when on 30 January he wrote to Pound offering him, on behalf of the Fascist Confederation of Industrial Workers, 2,500 lire to translate Por's new book, *Politica Economico-Sociale in Italia Anno XVII–XVIII,* which had been published the previous year, and apologizing for the small amount of money available.[13] Pound responded with alacrity, writing Por on 2 February: "We're at war and it isn't the time to bargain and argue over figures." The support for his work from the fascist union gave him a sudden insight, which he communicated to Por on 5 February: "We have lost 10 years not addressing ourselves to the Trade Unions instead wanting to speak to the bourgeoisie and petty intellectuals." Working with his usual speed, Pound finished a first draft of the Por book on 15 February.

VII

Pound finally succeeded in his effort to get on Italian radio. According to Leonard Doob, he had been writing for the EIAR since late 1940 and began recording for them in January of 1941.[14] He received an offer dated 18 January 1941 from the Ministry of Popular Culture to collaborate in their transmissions to North America and Great Britain, offering compensation of 400 lire, presumably for each speech. Pound would travel to Rome and stay there for seven to ten days each month, recording speeches that were played at 4 a.m. to reach New York at 10 p.m. There were a minimum of two per week to America; at times, if suitable, they were rebroadcast to England and Australia. In a letter to

---

[13] To give some idea of the value of these figures, Pound's rent in 1940 was 500 lire a month.

[14] Pound, *Ezra Pound Speaking,* xi. In a letter of 4 May 1940 to the minister of Popular Culture, Pound had outlined a lucid rhetorical scheme for radio propaganda for the United States with numbered points grouped under the headings "scope" and "methods."

Ungaro of 6 February Pound discussed some of the problems of attracting an audience for his broadcasts and asked Ungaro's advice about whether he should "compose scripts with calm and detail/ or let the anger boil?" In this letter, as in others, he shows both an awareness of the special problems of the new medium, short-wave radio, and also of his own emotions: "Returning here I drafted a half-dozen little speeches/ right now I 'boiled'/ in short such a rage as to be almost indecipherable." Here, as elsewhere, Pound, although normally quite reticent about his emotional life, is perfectly aware of his tendency to rage. Such self-awareness is not usually associated with the insane, and I think it provides further evidence of Pound's sanity during this time. As we will see, rage came to predominate in his radio broadcasts.[15]

Pound's mind was on the new problems posed by radio. He was very conscious of the need for advertising and occasionally composed notices (program notes) himself. He sent one to Ungaro on 6 February:

> Today at 4:15 p.m. (EST), Ezra Pound, the expatriate American poet who lives in Italy and loves it, discusses on the Italian short-wave radio "The Limitations of Human Understanding." Democratically speaking, he's a stinker, but academically he is a fine example of an American gone totalitarian.

This ad has a "teaser" effect of arousing curiosity, while at the same time making use of a deliberately deceptive title and a colloquial expression to gain audience interest. Clearly, Pound was confident enough of his views that he wished a large audience for his speeches. On 15 February he wrote to Pellizzi, and the letter offers further insight into his concerns of that time:

> I was a bit stupified that last evening chez vous. Mind wrapped in triple problem/
> 1. How to get my goddddddam compatriots to unhook radio receiver AT ALL.
> 2. How to appeal to their god damn prejudices sufficiently to KEEP 'em listening.
> 3. How to slip over something that wd/ be equivalent to killing Morgenthau and the god damn kike agents and leading Jewsfeldt to gawd or an honest life.

The third point contains unabashed and unsublimated anger frankly expressed; it was probably due to his conviction that Roosevelt was being

---

[15] Flory's view, that "we are faced with a simple alternative. Either his rhetoric in the radio broadcasts . . . [was] the consequence of genuine delusion, or he was, in his normal state, full of anger, hatred, and destructive feelings" (*The American Ezra Pound*, 163), oversimplifies the matter. A gentle, kind, and generous individual, Pound would usually repress overt expression of rage and hostility.

led into the war on the side of England and was caused by Pound's hearing of Roosevelt's various actions taken during this time to aid the English. On 11 March, the American Lend-Lease Act was passed.

In his attempt to gain an audience, he composed a note that was to be sent to a number of his friends and correspondents in the United States. Pound supplied a list of names and addresses to Villari, and a typist prepared the individual letters. Pound insisted, however, that no other propaganda be sent to the people on the list. Perhaps he was embarrassed about it, or perhaps he did not want to be considered by his friends as merely a propagandist for the Italians. The note reads in part as follows:

> SANITY for the U.S.A. consists of collaborating, and getting ready to collaborate with the NEW EUROPE. . . .
>
> P/S/ I have made 8 transmissions from Roma radio/ and shall make more if permitted. This is the only way of communicating with my friends in the U.S. without loss of 5 or 8 weeks. Post useless in most cases as British steal it at Bahamas etc/ When transmitting I am on ____ wave lengths and at ____ Rome time/ equivalent to ____ N. York and S. Francisco ____.

Pound apparently felt a need to justify to his friends both his position and the fact that he was broadcasting for the Italians. Also, it seems that he was feeling increasingly isolated and out of touch. The international community in Rapallo had diminished drastically in number. One consequence of this was that the Amici del Tigullio were no longer putting on their concert series, since it had depended on the foreign subscribers to break even.

Just how far out of touch Pound was at this time is shown by a 25 March letter to Katue Kitasono, in which he revealed his plan for peace between Japan and the United States:

> Note for you and VOU club/ that I sent yesterday to United Press a statement of plan for Pacific Peace// We shd/ give you Guam, but INSIST on getting "Kumasaka" and "Kagekiyo" [two Noh plays] in return. i.e. INSIST on having 300 Noh plays done properly AND recorded on sound film so as to be available to EDUCATE such amerikn stewdents as are capable of being cultur'd.

It is not clear just how seriously Pound took his proposal to exchange U.S. territory for films. It can be considered idealistic, naive, or simply out of bounds. Perhaps he was trying to charm his Japanese friends by impressing them with just how highly he valued their Noh theater. Exactly how grave the world situation had become apparently had not yet registered on Pound.

He continued to travel to Rome to record speeches for Italian radio, but his function extended also to giving general advice about Italian propaganda and the kinds of arguments that they could use for maximum effect in the United States and various other countries where the Italian broadcasts were sent. He wrote with a kind of pride to Ungaro on 26 April 1941: "Oh yuss. I see by a Chicago rag that I am 'charged with fascism' and that critics have been trying to defend me, but that the label must stick . . . waaal; waaaal; waaaal." Pound still had hopes that the war would end before the United States was brought into it. He wrote to Ungaro on 11 April: "In fact Americans should NOW start thinking how Danes, French and even the remaining kikes in Europe will be fed, when the war is ended, and bank paper will NOT float across the atlantic." He wrote again to Ungaro on 28 April:

> Also useful *if possible* to make CONCRETE and specific proposals of the treatment that would be offered to these populations "if" the Axis wins./
> We people of the Axis have no intention of exploiting nations with taxes of interest on debt.

Again, Pound's view is naive. He did not know what was really taking place.

But Pound was very agitated, as another letter to Ungaro of the same day, written at 5 a.m., shows. Coming up with ideas and approaches for Italian propaganda dominated his thinking; he starts that letter: "I get up from bed to send you two ideas." He frequently listened to the broadcasts as well but only those sent on the medium wavelengths since he did not own a short-wave set, and he offered critiques and encouragement. He was being paid 350 lire ($18) for the broadcasts that he recorded or wrote and 250 lire ($13) for shorter notes that he prepared and they accepted for use. This was enough for Pound and his dependents to live on (Olga received rent of 300 lire a month for her modest, three-room house in Venice until it was sequestered) but not much more.

Pound did not read all of his speeches himself, as is clear from a 27 June letter to Ungaro:

> I like Morelli's reading of my stuff. The anonymous stuff is in some ways better than the personal/ When anonymous I can be omniscient/ when I speak in my own voice I have to be modest and stick to what I have seen first hand.
> And for England it is O.K. England is NOT strictly my affair. But for the U.S.A. it is different. All the U.S. runs on "poic'nality"/ they are MOSTLY below the level of ideas/ cant understand an idea/ all they can get is SO/ and/ SO SAID so. . . .
> bank account still frozen. but I suppose someday it will liquefy.

Pound's own checking account was frozen because of some complication for which he blamed Roosevelt. He was trying to get it liquefied again, using his fifteen plus years as a resident of Italy as a way around whatever law had blocked it. He wrote to Pellizzi on 29 June: "I expect to nibble away at my reserves waiting for the storm to pass." His financial problems were still with him, as his father's checks did not arrive, and he was responsible for feeding five other people. The galleys for the Por book were ready in May. Por wrote to Pound on 5 May, begging him to make intelligible and legible corrections when he received them. Pound had earlier complained of the difficulty of proofreading, in a letter to Por of 7 March that also sheds some light on the genesis of some of the textual errors in the *Cantos:* "This GOd buggaring job/ I NEVER prepare my own ms/ for press even in english/ and to fix it so as NO printer's errors are possible/ blood and SHIT. I cant get over more than 20 pages per day even tho I took a week's rest before starting. sic itur ad as/ ininity." At the end of June he finally finished correcting the galleys of the Por book.

Financial motives alone were not responsible for his commitment to his work. Apart from his beliefs, he was becoming a well-known figure in Italy, owing, no doubt, to his writings for the prestigious *Il Meridiano di Roma,* and this fame probably appealed to his vanity and compensated for his increased isolation. He also enjoyed the respect of his neighbors in Rapallo, who referred to him simply as "the Poet."

Pound's correspondence for the remainder of the year continues in very much the same way. He was a committed and dedicated Italian propagandist, and he used his knowledge of history and other cultures to suggest various "slants" to be used in broadcasts to different countries: For South American countries, Pound suggested references to United Fruit and the way other Yankee companies had interfered in Latin American affairs, buying governments and politicians; for Canada, Pound wanted to remind them that 54 percent of their tax money was going to support the British effort in the war; for China, he favored telling the Chinese that Mussolini and Hitler applied Confucian principles in governing; for the Americans, he wished to reveal that it was not the Axis navy but the British navy that had cut off their trade with France, Spain, Portugal, Sweden, and the rest of the world; for the English, he suggested that the Italians cast doubt on whether or not Roosevelt and the Americans would ever come to their aid. When Germany invaded Russia on 22 June 1941, Pound's earlier sympathy for the Bolshevik revolution was forgotten, and he was quick to suggest attacks on the Soviets as well, as his letter to Ungaro of 19 July shows:

I shd/ PLAY up all the sob stuff/ not elaborate it, but all possible FACTS, such as 80 thousand Lithuanians bumped off by Russians/
I should invite the U.S. SENATE (not the department of Shit [State]

presided over by Mr. Hell [Hull]), but the U.S. SENATE to send
observers and men to RECORD the proofs of bolchevik methods. . . .

American woman said yesterday: "Could be peace in Europe next
month if Roosevelt wd/ only die."

VIII

Once Russia entered the war, Pound was cut off from his correspondence with Katue Kitasono. On 16 September, he wrote to E. E.
Cummings, complaining about his isolation:

> Well now wot the hell do we think of it all/ If I aint a seein' it clear
> and whole, and hole, I wanna be told and told. I can't git any american
> news worth a pea hen/ And when I do see an american paper it is full
> of goof, and nothing about the few remainin distinguished figgers on
> the american seen. I try to tickle up old Max now and then/ wot does
> HE think of the shindy/ in fact what do you or does ANYone think
> of it?

Although Pound complains about not getting American newspapers, he
says that when he does see them, they are not worth anything. This
letter reinforces our sense of his isolation and of his occasional doubt.

Pound was by then fully engaged in working for Italian propaganda.
As the war dragged on, he had fewer and fewer options. Apart from
leaving with his family for the United States, it is hard to see what else
he might have done except continue his work for the Italian government.
Even leaving Italy was soon to be out of the question. His father, who
had been practically housebound for two years, fell and broke his hip in
November 1941. It is difficult to imagine Pound abandoning his invalid
father, with uncertain means of support, to return to the United States.
Thus, even before America entered the war, Pound was left without
attractive options. His duty to his family meant that he would have to
stay, making a living the only way he knew how.

On 7 December 1941, the Japanese attacked Pearl Harbor. On 9 December, Pound wrote to Adriano Ungaro:

> I think I had better make certain points quite clear from my side.
>
> 1. Even if America declares war on the Axis, I see no reason (from
> my point of view) why I should not continue to speak in my own
> name, so long as I say nothing that can in any way prejudice the results
> of American military or naval (or navel) action, the armed forces of the
> U.S.A. or the welfare of my native country.
>
> But contrary to a suggestion made to me yesterday, I see considerable
> reason for NOT continuing an indirect participation.
>
> I mean to say that there are certain things which I believe I have a
> right to go on saying until the congress (and senate) i;e; the authorized

legislature of the U.S. pass a definite law either prohibiting certain subjects or prohibiting the use of foreign radio as a means of making it known that one is saying them.

I believe the effect of what I can say (in accord with my own conscience and the law of the U.S. as I understand it) would have more weight in the long run if it can be proved that I am not indulging in clandestine propaganda of any kind.[16]

As the U.S. is not yet legally at war with Italy, I will continue to send you notes signed and unsigned until [no more].

This is a remarkable letter from a man in so desperate a situation. Pound had no way of returning home without abandoning his family. He had no way of earning a living as a writer without continuing to work for the Italian government. He was aware of the possibility that this work might be considered treasonable, and he explained why he rejected that argument, according to his understanding of the law. Pound made it quite clear to his Italian superiors that under no circumstances would he say anything that might bring harm to his native country, and being a man who possessed the courage of his convictions, he refused to continue only with anonymous work. A man intent on treason, or even a less honorable man, would not write such a letter or, perhaps, any letter at all.

It should be recalled that Pound's indictment for "radio treason" was the first of its kind ever issued by an American grand jury. From the letter to Ungaro, it is clear that Pound had no treasonable intent and believed that what he said over the radio was in conformity with his duty as an American citizen. From a letter to Ungaro written the very next day, we can see that Pound was already back at work, suggesting ideas for future speeches. This is not the course of someone with doubts about the rightness of his actions. Pound wrote again to Ungaro on 12 December:

Naturally, nothing but stukas and human projectiles can win this war, BUT, damn it all, nothing but propaganda can prevent its degenerating into a ten year war of inexhaustible exhaustion/ at any rate the enemy oughtn't to have absolutely free play with 180 million ang sax in Eng/ and U.S.A. The hysteria might turn into fanaticism if left to the autochthonous newspapers in "them paats."

What is not clear in this letter is who "the enemy" is. One must presume, by now, that to Pound the enemies were Jews who, as he imagined, surrounded Roosevelt and controlled newspapers and publishing houses.

[16] In this and the preceding paragraph, Pound exhibits an understanding of several points of law, including the "mere words" doctrine (discussed later) as a defense against a treason charge and the importance of not providing clandestine material.

Pound saw these individuals as distinct from the Anglo–Saxon inhabitants of the United States and England. The evidence for this comes from the radio broadcasts; the first of these broadcasts to be reprinted, one from 2 October 1941, is already decidedly anti-Semitic, as well as anti-English.[17]

Two letters to Cornelio di Marzio from this time further illuminate Pound's motives and give us a touching picture of the responsibilities he assumed for his family's welfare. On 16 December Pound wrote:

> It seems to me that my work must continue. Twenty or, more visibly, ten years of work for a New Europe.
>
> My tools are here; that is to say, my books. If there is a more fundamental task than my Chinese studies, I am at your disposal.
>
> I am now responsible for my 83-year-old father, who a month ago broke his hip; at his age I don't believe that it will heal (and with him my 82-year-old mother). The old man has not left the house for two years; he therefore cannot leave Rapallo.
>
> Olga has a small house in Venice, and she gets 300 lire a month in rent. But you already know her situation. Besides, I must also provide for a ward. (tr)

In a previous letter, Pound had described Olga as an indispensable help to him in his work and semidependent upon him for her livelihood. There was some question on the part of the Italian authorities about her status, and her house in Venice was later sequestered as the property of a resident alien. Therefore, although it was rented to a naval officer, she had difficulty in collecting any rent. Apparently di Marzio, in his role as the important secretary-general of the Confederation of Professionals and Artists, was able to help her, perhaps in gaining some work papers, for in the same letter Pound says: "I thank you for what you have done for Olga." The ward Pound refers to is his daughter, Mary. Today it seems a cold word to use, but attitudes toward illegitimacy were different then, and Pound was customarily guarded in what he told others.

Despite Pound's willingness to continue with his radio broadcasts, there was some uncertainty at the Ministry of Propaganda, and Pound was instructed to suspend his talks for a while. He objected to that and wrote to di Marzio again on 28 December:

> It seems to me that my speeches on the radio must continue IN MY OWN NAME, and with *my* voice, and NOT anonymously....
>
> But if this isn't a war between two systems of IDEAS (and not an

[17] Citations from the radio broadcasts will be taken from *Ezra Pound Speaking*. All citations of the radio broadcasts in this chapter will be from this book, but for purposes of clearer chronology, they will be referred to by speech number and date in parentheses following the text.

affair between two villages, or a question of geography), well then we're back to 1917 and there never was a REVOLUTION.

Perhaps a word from you when you see the Minister... would be more useful than a letter from me, which would fall into the hands of a secretary, and not being written in Tuscan, the perfect idiom, etc.

I can't write anonymous letters!!! and much less etc/etc/ Either one fights, or one does not fight. (tr)

Further letters from this period indicate that Pound had to struggle to continue his radio broadcasts, which had been suspended. Perhaps this struggle results from his financial difficulties, but it is not the course of a man uncertain about the rightness of his actions. He did not have an easy time securing access to Italian radio, but he persevered, using his network of correspondents and friends. The letters also demonstrate that Pound believed that he was fighting in a battle on the side of economic justice. He wrote to Por on 29 December reiterating his conviction that the war was a struggle between two conflicting economic systems: "Happy New Year. Note: this war is a war between two principles, between two orders/ I must continue my work/ and in my own name; with my own voice; not anonymously." With this comment and in the letter to di Marzio cited earlier, Pound expressed an idea that prefigures his later conception of the war as a millennial war between usurers and honest workers. In this way he was able to rationalize the fact that he was siding with Italy against his native land: The war was not a national war but a class war, a war for a higher good, against the age-old enemies, avarice and usury. We have noted the dichotomizing tendency present in Pound's thinking; this is another example of it at work.[18]

A further example of this kind of simplistic and formulaic thinking can be seen in the growing virulence of Pound's anti-Semitism during this period. I would suggest that it was impossible for Pound to recognize that he had joined in a war against the United States and that therefore he was forced to believe that the government of his country had been subverted in some way. His tendency toward anti-Semitism, which he had fought against for many years, changed, then, into full-blown racial hatred, evolving from his need to avoid a conscious realization that he had joined forces with the enemies of his native land. Similarly, his attitude toward Roosevelt, which although highly critical had always been marked by ambivalence even as late as 1940 (he favored Roosevelt over Willkie in the 1940 election), changed to one of harsh contempt. On

[18] Orage had made a similar point about the First World War in his "Notes of the Week" for the *New Age,* and Pound had echoed it in a column of his own shortly thereafter. Orage wrote: "For six months we have never ceased to emphasize the most essential feature of this war, namely, that it is a war of ideas" (11 Feb. 1915, 393).

25 December, Pound wrote to Adriano Ungaro, again urging the need for continuing his broadcasts:

> A few weeks' silence no harm. Possibly useful. Might arouse curiosity. In fact so far so good. But I have something to say in reply to Roosevelt's New Year's proposal. It has not Zweck/ no point, unless I say it. . . .
> Useless to curse Roosevelt UNLESS you KEEP ON ASKING: WHAT puts lunatics into office?

A week later Pound wrote to Ungaro: "From Roosevelt's New Year's proclamation, a sort of special Yom Kippur for Ersatz yids. It would seem that the American president has added RELIGIOUS mania to the list of his 'peculiarities.' " This allusion to religion refers to the visit by Roosevelt and Churchill to the tomb of George Washington at Mount Vernon on 1 January. The two prayed together for an Allied victory and Roosevelt proclaimed the day a national day of prayer.[19] Churchill also comes under attack for his supposed ties to a small group of wealthy Jews.[20] In a 31 December letter to Ungaro, Churchill's Ottawa speech comes under attack:

> That Buggah Churchill mustn't be allowed to get away with his FAKE "unity of the race." Blood, tears, DEBT and slavery to the Jews! is his number. You do not found a racial movement by selling your own race to another.
> M. [Mussolini] and H. [Hitler] built up on a race basis/ Churchill unifies with yidds/ The U.S. was founded as meeting place for nations/ Church; cant unite with the ten races in the U.S./ no use letting him get away with the idea that U.S. is all ang/ sax/.
> 2 ruling castes/ it has had. First ang/ sax, and now yidds. it is ONLY with arrival of the second, that Churchill has had the unity letch./// "The jewish jockey riding the british mare" that phrase shd/ be useful.

It is not clear how Pound knew of Churchill's speech, perhaps through a radio news commentator, but his source was either inaccurate or Pound jumped to erroneous conclusions, because there was no appeal to any "unity of the race" within the speech delivered before the Canadian Parliament, except of course through the symbolic statement made by his presence. Deplorably, this kind of shrill hostility gets worse during the next eighteen months, with Pound's anti-Semitism reaching its most violent and consistent form in his radio broadcasts.

[19] *New York Times*, 2 Jan. 1942.
[20] The *New Age* and Orage never expressed anything but severe criticism of Winston Churchill. In "Notes of the Week," Orage remarked: "It is very seldom that we find ourselves in even approximate agreement with Mr. Churchill" (19 Mar. 1914, 609); and again: "For Mr. Churchill . . . we ourselves have as little respect as anybody" (6 May 1915). Pound's hatred for Churchill was probably first derived from Orage.

IX

Pound's difficult personal situation is best revealed in a petition from the Ministry of Foreign Affairs to the Ministry of Finance composed by Pound and dated 15 January [1942]. In it, Pound asks for exemption for himself and for his family from the financial restrictions put into effect for foreigners:

> blocking of bank accounts; and of his safe deposit box: and exemption of his Secretary Olga Rudge; from the seizure of their goods (a tiny three-room house in Venice, Calle Querini 252, S. Gregorio)[21]
>
> Pound has done much work unpaid. Before the war/ he and his wife both brought their property to Italy when it was liquid/ note both have the medal of the first loan of the Littorioa/ done as an act of fascist faith, at time when local Italian entourage was not investing/ or that P. understood that there was a Ligurian caution being exercised. at any rate, act shows fascist faith not a thing of this year/
>
> Minuscule house in Venice contains books etc/ of little value/ Rudge considered more a colleague than a secretary/ several of his best points due to her looking up old periodicals, and remembering items/ also well deserving for her own musical research, vide Vivaldi notes publications of Accademia Chigiana di Siena/
>
> by its very nature, much of his work can NOT be paid for in money. He shd/ be freed of mental distractions (needless worries) so that he can devote all of his intelligence for present work. (tr)

The cautious, even obsequious tone of this petition is certainly not typical for Pound and gives us a glimpse of his precarious situation in Italy. The only lapse into his more usual brash style – "when local Italian entourage was not investing" – is quickly tempered and qualified, albeit ironically. The petition also shows that when Pound needed to, he could compose a careful, logical, and effective document, again, at odds with the interpretation that he was psychotic during this period. We also get an idea of the nature of Olga's work for Pound at the time; she was more of a partner than a conventional secretary. Because of financial problems they were having, Pound also tried to get Olga put on the official payroll of the Ministry of Popular Culture. Apparently, this request was not successful, for Pound made a similar request again to di Marzio on 22 December 1942:

---

[21] The Pound family bank accounts and safe-deposit boxes had been blocked on 21 December 1941 and 18 April 1942. Even with his numerous connections with government officials, he had considerable difficulty getting these restrictions lifted. In September of 1942 he was allowed 1,000 lire per month for living expenses drawn from these accounts, but he had to apply for special permission to buy a marker for his father's grave and to pay off 5,000 lire of his father's debts. The various restrictions were finally lifted in late 1942 and early 1943.

To respond to your question, Olga Rudge has been for years an autonomous colleague, and it pains me that she is, even if only pro forma, considered a dependent. She has been of great help to me, scrutinizing papers and magazines, etc. . . .

In Siena I was always angered by the fact that such a fine violinist was reduced to the role of musicologist. . . . She prepared, as you know, the first thematic catalog of the collection of Vivaldi manuscripts at Turin, etc. . . . She did not receive any notice of the confiscation of her small house in Venice (a house with only three rooms, one for each floor). She invested her tiny patrimony there. . . . She is as deserving of an exemption as I am. (tr)

Pound's father died in February, a merciful occurrence since he had been in great pain and conditions were deteriorating in Italy, with food already scarce. Mary de Rachewiltz recalls encountering a peasant woman, buying three eggs from her, and bringing them back to her mother's house above Rapallo, thrilled to be able to contribute something to their dinner:

But at home, though Mamile [Olga] was pleased with the gift, she said we must be careful, as foreigners we must not do anything illegal. And Babbo [Pound] disapproved because Italy was fighting a war and no one must indulge in black market. My rashness had brought to light my parents' insecurity.[22]

This memory gives another insight into the uncertainty of Pound's position in Italy. Although he had many friends in the fascist regime, there is always a heightened suspicion of foreigners during wartime, even of those zealous in their support of a nation's cause.

From his correspondence, the impression we get of Pound's activities during the period between the entry of the United States into the war and the invasion of Italy and the arrest of Mussolini in late 1943 is that he was almost exclusively engaged in the preparation of his radio speeches and in giving aid to Italian propaganda. He also continued to write for *Il Meridiano di Roma,* and of course he continued with his Confucian studies, but his work for Rome Radio dominated his letters from this time. We therefore turn to a consideration of those radio speeches.

X

The Pound radio speeches do not make for pleasant reading. Of the 120 speeches reprinted in the volume edited by Leonard W. Doob, 31 are clearly anti-Semitic. By this I mean they go beyond the occasional

---

[22] De Rachewiltz, 153.

name-calling, though name-calling itself can obviously indicate racial or religious prejudice, to making offensive assertions in an unambiguous manner about Jews. Despite the fact that there are relatively frequent statements in the speeches that he is not referring to "small Jews" but to "the sixty Kikes who started this war," (no. 32, 30 Apr. 1942), this distinction is lost in the mass of material that is so evidently anti-Semitic. Although Pound continued to be somewhat ambivalent about his anti-Semitism, and he made occasional attempts to avoid it, in the radio speeches it is clear that the usocracy he so hated is dominated, in his mind, by Jews.[23]

Professor Doob, who worked on propaganda and psychological warfare directed against Italy, Germany, and Japan during the Second World War, states in his introduction that Pound's broadcasts "never attained great popularity."[24] In fact, Pound's correspondence of the time indicates that he was very conscious of that problem and frequently reminded his superiors that they would need to develop a greater awareness of the audience for the broadcasts. He wrote to Ungaro on 23 February 1942:

> MUST/ MUST! MUST think of the listener's frame of mind. I am the only LISTENER in yr/ little circle. The listener is grateful for an interesting speech/ he turns on apparatus at SET hours/ if he gets something good like Rad/ Revolution of BREMEN Mirror, he hunts for it/ regrets if he can't find it/ but irregularity bewilders him/ You people haven't time to listen, and you are too busy to want to.

Pound, then, was conscious of the problems of audience, at least inasmuch as they were posed by the new medium of radio. Many of his texts, though, continued to ignore the problems that an audience might have with what he was trying to say. The other consistent feature of the radio broadcasts, along with their anti-Semitism, is their frequent incoherence. Even with an awareness of Pound's fields of reference and of his usually obscure, elliptical, and difficult style, my impression of about twenty of the speeches is that they were partly or completely incomprehensible: rambling, incoherent, garbled, disjointed, and almost impossible to follow. If these were the difficulties experienced by the reader familiar with Pound's work, one can imagine how inaccessible these speeches would have been for a listener, facing, in addition, the reception difficulties of short-wave radio.

---

[23] Flory offers a useful insight about anti-Semitism in the radio speeches: "Even when the hold that his antisemitic delusions had over him was too strong to break, his moral conscience could still act to inject caveats and responsible qualifications of irresponsible assertions; to make him veer abruptly away from dangerous subjects into irrelevancies, nostalgic reminiscences, and unidentifiable allusions; and, in general, to stir up such mental confusion that finally the only victim . . . of these broadcasts was Pound himself" (*The American Ezra Pound*, 155).

[24] *Ezra Pound Speaking*, xii.

Pound was aware of the problems his speeches caused; the speeches themselves frequently allude to this awareness. In a talk about one of his preoccupations, international loan capital, he said: "I lose my thread some times. [There is] so much that I can't count on anyone's knowing [about]. Thread, as they call it, of discourse" (no. 15, 8 Mar. 1942). In fact, Pound seems resigned to the fact that his audience will have difficulty following him: "I do not expect perfect and COMplete comprehension of these discourses on the part of all of my audience. I should be content if I get over even a small part of what I am driving at" (no. 25, 13 Apr. 1942). More than a month later he made a similar point: "Do be patient. I know the air isn't the habitual place for bedrock, but I might get one auditor in ten thousand who was willin' to follow an argument" (no. 42, 28 May 1942).

It is not entirely clear what the officials at Rome Radio thought about Pound's speeches, although we get a hint of their attitudes from some statements that Pound himself made. In his speech of 19 June 1942, he asked: "Do you follow me? Do you follow me? Or am I to be once more accused of speakin' in a rambling manner" (no. 48). He had written to Ungaro, in a letter quoted earlier, on 23 February, with a similar comment: "told I am gettin comprehensibl-er . . . which is as may be." In any event, Pound was fully aware that his speeches were difficult to follow. It may have been that the Italian authorities finally lost patience with him: There is a more than six-month unexplained gap in his speeches, between 26 July 1942 and 18 February 1943. When he resumed broadcasting, he made the same point: "I suspect I talk in a what-is-called incoherent manner: 'cause I can't (and I reckon nobody could) tell where to begin" (no. 61, 19 Feb. 1943).

Some of the problems Pound was having in gaining an audience were beyond his control and were the fault of the transmitting equipment and the staff in Rome. On 22 April 1942, he wrote to Ungaro:

> Transmission, I RECognized my own voice, and COULD with effort identify the matter "To Aberr"/ but no one not knowing the text could have understood the meaning. In between a fine clear and strong Berlin on one edge, and B.B.C. nuisance on the other/ Only resolute determination to get Rome would have led anyone to it. It comes on 29.6 on my dial, not at 31 as announced. (fbi)[25]

This was a recurring problem, as Pound complained to Ungaro again on 5 August:

[25] Those materials I obtained from the Department of Justice under the provisions of the Freedom of Information Act are marked "(fbi)." I believe that they were subsequently turned over to the Beinecke Library at Yale.

> Transmission so BAD for last three nights that I am on point of tele-
> graphing you. It must be the transmitting microphone in the ministero/
> plenty of transmissions are CLEAR/ even Bondinini's mic/ seems wob-
> bly/ effect is either whisper or rattle/ a bump bump bump, the minute
> one turns on enough current to hear. do fer Xt'z ache have the micro-
> phones looked at. (fbi)

Apart from the many technical difficulties, the staff at Rome Radio frequently neglected to announce essential information, as Pound noted to
Ungaro in October: "It is important to announce the HOURS of broadcasts. and do it in every broadcast/ I mean AT eleven P.M. SAY when
the short waves go/ and give the HOURS in Rome AND in the receiving
countries. . . . [Otherwise] all the talk goes to waste" (fbi). Pound would
not have conducted this rather futile battle if he had thought he was
committing treason, or if he were merely working for the money. He
genuinely believed that he had an important message to convey; at times
he speaks like a man who has discovered the key to essential truth. He
did seem to recognize that his audience was small. In his broadcast of
19 February 1943, he said: "I was wonderin' if anybody listened to what
I said on Rome Radio" (no. 61). Very few, I am sure, did.

More than just static prevented Pound from getting his message across
to an audience. The speeches taken as a whole do not communicate owing
to a complete failure of rhetoric on Pound's part. The persona he adopts,
a kind of cracker-barrel know-it-all affecting an imaginary American
accent, is not one that a listener would find sympathetic. The context in
which the speeches were delivered, coming from the official radio of an
enemy country, is not one that would inspire confidence in an American
audience. Pound's persuasive strategies are naive or nonexistent: He does
not present his reasoning or his arguments; he just states his conclusions.
He has no sense of audience; at times he acknowledges he is broadcasting
to an elite; at other times he seems to be attempting to appeal to a larger
audience of "real Americans," by telling a version of American history
that he believes might be of interest to a group who were descendants,
as he was, of early pioneers. However, he does not take into account the
limited receptivity to opposing views that the American people had during that war, when there was an unprecedented national unity concen-
trated on achieving victory. When all of that is added to the incoherence
and obscure references of many of the broadcasts, it is difficult to believe
that the broadcasts had any effect at all. Pound was speaking into a void,
his mouth biting empty air.

There are a few interesting points to be derived from the broadcasts,
though they are not worth the fatigue and pain of reading through the
whole volume (unlike every other work by Pound, which, although at
times difficult, always richly repays the effort involved). I therefore reject

Professor Doob's "serious jest" that these speeches can be considered as "The Poor Man's Cantos."[26] In the broadcasts, Pound is interesting those few times he speaks about art and culture. For example:

> The futurist rooms [at the Biennale of Venice] are always an affirmation of propaganda that could get along by itself without any painting whatever. I mean the main line of futurist propaganda is an idea, the painting is an adjunct. An adjunct that proves the idea has other dimensions than the merely ideologic. (no. 52, 6 July 1942)

The broadcasts are also occasionally perceptive and sometimes represent a maturing of political judgment and a deepening of economic insight. They contain some worthwhile ideas: about the limits of the power of the U.S. presidency, about American foreign policy ("We promised 'em [the Philippines] independence, and the dirt in our national makeup prevented our keepin' the promise. Our conduct as a nation to various islands, let alone to South American republics, is NOT our title to glory" [no. 26, 16 Apr. 1942]), and about broadcasting the proceedings of Congress on radio. But the pain caused by a level of mindlessness seldom found elsewhere in Pound's oeuvre makes the reading of them dismal work indeed.

Pound saw himself as preserving and advocating the true values of the American founders and of the American Constitution. One of his broadcasts closes: "Ezra Pound speakin' from Europe for the American heritage" (no. 20, 26 Mar. 1942). He held a tragic view of American history, which he saw as having been in decline since 1863. The United States, he said, has had "economic political syphilis for the past 80 years" (no. 7, 3 Feb. 1942). According to Pound, the United States was in the war owing to the criminal acts of a mentally unbalanced president (no 6, 29 Jan. 1942); he was convinced that Roosevelt had acted illegally to involve us in the war, a view shared, by the way, by Tinkham and other Republican and isolationist opponents of FDR. What Pound did not understand was that this kind of dissent ceases to be appropriate when a nation is at war and, in fact, can be considered treasonable. For Pound, Americans had the right to free speech. He rationalized that since he had this right, he had also the responsibility to exercise it by whatever means were available. Since his normal journalistic outlets were unavailable to him, because of the war, and, according to him, because of a conspiracy, he had to take the only outlet left to him: "Radio is the only free speech left" (no. 50, 28 June 1942).

In addition to FDR, Pound blamed a small group of powerful Jews who, he felt, exerted a strong influence on the Roosevelt government.

---

[26] *Ezra Pound Speaking*, 437.

Pound believed that the decline of the United States occurred in part because the old American, pioneer stock had been supplanted by the new, corrupting arrival of immigrants: "My job, as I see it," he said, "is to save what's left of America" (no. 13, 2 Mar. 1942). In particular, the danger came, Pound believed, from Jewish immigrants: The danger to the United States was "NOT from Japan but from Jewry.... The danger is not that you WILL BE invaded, it is that you HAVE BEEN invaded" (no. 23, 9 Apr. 1942). Although his remarks obviously would serve to incite bigotry and hatred, Pound always stopped just short of advocating the persecution of Jews; in fact, he advocated a national home-land for the Jews. As I have said, Pound was a Zionist motivated by anti-Semitism.

It is easy to see how some of Pound's statements would have seemed treasonous to listeners in the United States. In the broadcast delivered on 24 March 1943, Pound said: "The U.S.A. will be no use to itself or to anyone else until it gets rid of the kikes AND Mr. Roosevelt. I don't mean the small kikes. I mean the LARGE kikes" (no. 66). In a similar vein on 27 April his speech included the following: "I think it might be a good thing to hang Roosevelt and a few hundred yidds IF you can do so by due legal process, NOT otherwise" (no. 80). Pound recognized the tension between his upbringing and respect for law, and his hatred and rage about what he believed were the causes of economic injustice and war. In the speech of 23 March 1942, he stated: "Brought up on American principles; no prejudice against any man for race, creed, or color" (no. 19). But in the same speech, he also said:

> The real causes of the conflict – the real forces IN conflict. Usury against peasantry, usury against farmland, usury against every man who does a day's work, physical or with his mind.... Against the crawling slime of a secret rule, a secret and IRRESPONSIBLE rule, that takes NO responsibility for the welfare of races, and nations, but eats like a cancer into the heart and soul of all nations.

This is the essence of Pound's view of the cause of all war, his "Bellum perenne" ("everlasting war") of Canto LXXXVI and "Bellum cano per-enne" ("I sing of war everlasting") of Cantos LXXXVII and LXXXVIII. Pound came to believe that the Second World War was just one more war in a long series of wars, a process that had been going on for a long time: "The WAR has been the same war. John Adams, Jefferson, Van Buren, and Jackson, and finally Abe Lincoln, V. P. Johnson, my Grand Dad. All fighting the kikified usurers" (no. 34, 9 May 1942). Jews were the enemy, on the side of the usurer: "The Kike ... [is] against all that is decent in America. Against the total American heritage. This is my war all right, I have been in it for 20 years. My Grandad was in it before me" (no. 33, 4 May 1942).

Here, the dichotomizing, simplifying tendency of Pound's thought comes into clear focus, with all of its attendant dangers. In this way, too, Pound was able to rationalize his position in Italy, working for his country's enemies. By converting the real war into an abstract, symbolic, perpetual conflict, where he was fighting on the side of his country's founders for the preservation of his country's true heritage, he could justify to himself the course of action to which he was already committed. Part of this retreat from real events was probably owing to his sense of having failed in his decades-long mission of determining the economic causes of war to prevent them. As he said on 13 July 1942: "I am in the agonized position of an observer who had worked 25 years to prevent it [the war]" (no. 55).

In fact, the battles of the real war do not receive extensive treatment in the radio speeches; this lack is strange since they completely dominated the news of the day on all sides. Pound's symbolic war, "PART of the age old struggle between the usurer and the rest of mankind" (no. 70, 25 Mar. 1943), so completely occupies his attention that the day-to-day reality of bombs and bullets hardly seems to concern him, until the last speeches, in May, June, and July of 1943, when the Allied bombings of Italy and the invasion of Sicily brought the war close to his door. The only part of the speeches that could even be considered a call to action to the American troops occurred on 27 April 1943, just two weeks before the complete Allied rout of the Axis forces in North Africa. Pound said: "I think quite simply and definitely that the American troops in N. Africa, all of 'em ought to go back to America: IF they can get there" (no. 80). Although this statement might seem treasonous, in the context of the actual battle situation in Africa it is simply ludicrous, as there was no chance left for the Axis at that time. Pound's infrequent other references to the military situation of the United States are unambiguous. In his speech of 26 February 1942, he said: "I don't want, the last thing I want is that any harm should come to Uncle Sam's Army and Navy" (no. 12). And on 19 March 1943, he said: "Obviously no one can advocate America's losing a war" (no. 68). But largely Pound seems to be quite far removed from the actuality of the day-to-day fighting, both in his speeches and in his letters from the time.

XI

Pound was indicted for treason on 26 July 1943, when the situation in Italy had deteriorated badly. The indictment read in part:

> That Ezra Pound . . . during the period beginning the 11th day of December, 1941 . . . being a citizen of the United States, and a person owing allegiance to the United States, in violation of his said duty of allegiance, knowingly, intentionally, wilfully, unlawfully, feloniously, traitorously, and treasonably did adhere to the enemies of the United States, to wit, the Kingdom of Italy . . . and the military allies of the said Kingdom of Italy . . . giving to the said enemies of the United States aid and comfort within the United States and elsewhere.[27]

Charles Norman points out that the "burden of the specifications which followed, and the statement with which each specification ends, was: 'The said defendant asserted, among other things, in substance, that citizens of the United States should not support the United States in the conduct of the said war.' "[28] This charge is simply a misreading of the speeches. Pound said many appalling things in the radio speeches, but it is difficult to find anything close to a statement urging U.S. citizens not to support the war effort. The real motive for the indictment was clarified by Attorney General Francis Biddle in a statement to the press:

> These indictments are based not only on the content of the propaganda statements – the lies and falsifications which were uttered – but also on the simple fact that these people [Pound was indicted with seven other Americans, who all broadcast from Germany] have freely elected, at a time when their country is at war, to devote their services to the cause of the enemies of the United States.

The distinction that Biddle was making is interesting. He asserts that, regardless of content, the very fact of broadcasting over enemy radio in wartime, under the auspices of that enemy, constitutes treason. I am not capable of saying whether this distinction would have been (or has been) sustained in court, but it seems to me to be very much open to question, particularly since these indictments for radio treason were the first ever made.

Pound learned of his indictment over the BBC, and he wrote to Biddle on 4 August, leaving the letter with the Swiss legation in Rome, which had been acting as the representative of American interests in Italy since the outbreak of the war. They forwarded it to the secretary of state.[29] Pound's letter deserves some close attention. It reads in part:

> I do not believe that the simple fact of speaking over the radio, wherever placed, can in itself constitute treason. I think that must depend on what is said, and on the motives for speaking.
> I obtained the concession to speak over Rome radio with the following

---

[27] Norman, *The Case of Ezra Pound*, 62–3.
[28] Ibid., 63.
[29] Ibid.

proviso. Namely that nothing should be asked of me contrary to my conscience or contrary to my duties as an American citizen. . . .

These conditions have been adhered to. . . .

I have not spoken with regard to *this* war, but in protest against a system which creates one war after another, in series and in system. I have not spoken to the troops, and have not suggested that the troops should mutiny or revolt. . . .[30]

At any rate a man's duties increase with his knowledge. A war between the U.S. and Italy is monstrous and should not have occurred. And a peace is no peace but merely a prelude to future wars. Someone must take count of these things. And having taken count must act on his knowledge; admitting that his knowledge is partial and his judgment subject to error.[31]

The first point to be made about this letter is to remark upon its cogency of presentation and lucidity of thought. This is not the letter of a man who is insane but of a man in full possession of his faculties. It may be comfortable to dismiss Pound's activities during this period as the actions of a crazy man, but it is not accurate to do so. The Pound who wrote that letter would have been fully capable of overseeing his defense, although Pound's confinement in the cage at Pisa may have brought about a physical and psychological breakdown.

Although a full consideration of Pound's trial is beyond the scope of this book, a recent article by Conrad L. Rushing deserves attention, as we attempt to draw some conclusions about Pound's activities during these middle years of his life. Entitled " 'Mere Words': the Trial of Ezra Pound," the article examines the legal issues surrounding Pound's indictment for treason, attempting to decide how Pound would have fared had his case ever come to trial.[32]

Rushing notes that his title refers to a legal shorthand for the standard defense to a treason charge under U.S. law, referring to a dictum that is frequently invoked, that an individual cannot through mere words be found guilty of treason. The example he uses to explain this comes from the period of the Vietnam War. Rushing states that protesters, though adhering to the enemy and giving them aid and comfort, were not charged with treason because it could not be shown that they had any treasonable intention. Their slogans, "Ho, ho, Ho Chih Minh" and "Hell no, we won't go," being only words, would not have been enough to convict them. According to Rushing, the crime of treason "requires the specific intent to betray."

---

[30] In fact, this is a precise account of the radio speeches, which, as I have stated, reflect almost no awareness of the actual events of the Second World War.

[31] Norman, *The Case of Ezra Pound*, 64–5.

[32] My account here is based substantially on Rushing's article.

The problem that Pound's lawyer, Julian Cornell, faced in 1945 was that it was not clear how Pound would be treated by the courts. Rushing observes that "Cornell was justified in doing what he could to make sure that the case of *U.S. v. Pound* was not the first of the American propagandists' trials."[33] It was in Pound's interest to have some of the more serious offenders tried first, particularly considering the haste with which William Joyce (called Lord Haw-Haw) was tried and executed in Great Britain, apparently in disregard of some well-established points of British law (e.g., Joyce was not a British citizen, and therefore claims of the British government to his allegiance were traditionally held to end at the border). The discouraging argument from that trial, from the viewpoint of Pound and his lawyer, was that the English court held that the content of Joyce's broadcasts was irrelevant; the fact of broadcasting on behalf of an enemy was by itself taken to be treasonous.

Two cases tried after Pound's insanity hearing bear upon the question of Pound's legal guilt. German broadcasters Robert H. Best and Douglas Chandler were named with other German broadcasters and Pound in the 1943 indictment. The Best case would have bolstered Pound's defense, because it would have provided a precedent for considering that the 7,000 pages of material seized by FBI agents at Pound's dwelling in Sant'Ambrogio were obtained illegally, in violation of Pound's constitutional rights. In Rushing's opinion, those documents, some of which showed Pound's anonymous activities for the EIAR, might have been used to prove that Pound's intent was treasonable. The other applicable case, the Chandler case, would have showed Pound's lawyer "that in the field of radio propaganda, 'mere words' was no defense."[34]

Rushing proposes in his article to determine whether a jury in 1947 or 1948 would have found Pound guilty of treason.

> In 1947 or 1948 . . . Pound and his lawyer could have returned to court and asked for a trial. . . . he had a chance for acquittal that was somewhat better than fifty-fifty. The FBI files showing his writings and particularly his role as Giovanni Del Bene would not have been allowed. . . . the seizure of those documents was unlawful under the Fourth Amendment.[35]

Even had Pound been found guilty, Rushing believes that he would have received a sentence shorter than the one he actually served at St. Elizabeths and that the chance for parole would have been very great.

Rushing's judgment about Pound's sanity is based on several considerations. After reading various accounts of the trial by Pound's critics,

[33] Rushing, 120.
[34] Ibid., 130.
[35] Ibid.

and by Cornell, he concluded that although Pound may have been paranoid and grandiose, he was not by any legal definition incompetent to
stand trial. Rushing's opinion on the sanity issue is also based on the
letter Pound wrote to Attorney General Francis Biddle shortly after the
indictment, a letter we have already considered. Rushing, too, considers
this to be "a most remarkable letter." In it, Pound

> argued very effectively three defenses . . . first, that the comments were
> protected by his First Amendment right of free speech; second, that the
> contents of the broadcasts were not treasonous; and third, even if con-
> strued as treasonous, he had no intent to betray because of (in part) the
> preamble that had been read out before each of the broadcasts.[36]

Rushing observes, correctly, that this letter "effectively spikes the de-
fensive claim made by Hemingway to MacLeish that Pound was insane
at the time he made the radio speeches."[37] As further evidence for Pound's
sanity, he notes a letter by Julian Cornell to James Laughlin that reads
in part: "I discussed with him [Pound] the possibility of pleading insanity
as a defense, and he has no objections. In fact, he told me that the idea
had already occurred to him."[38] Of course, if Pound knew enough to
concur in the incapacity defense, he was not incapacitated.

   Why, then, did Pound's lawyer not try to go back to trial? In fact,
Cornell did try to secure Pound's release from St. Elizabeths with a
petition for habeas corpus. The petition was denied and he was in the
process of appealing that decision when he was instructed by Dorothy
Pound to drop the appeal, for reasons that remain unclear. Because in
the eyes of the law Pound was a nonperson, a status that remained in
effect until his death, Dorothy legally had to make all of his decisions
for him. Whether the decision not to pursue the remaining means of
legal recourse was based on Pound's desire for complete vindication (since
he was never found guilty, he was innocent) or on Dorothy's satisfaction
with the status quo cannot be established conclusively.

   The second point to be examined concerns the validity of the charge
itself. Although I have very little sympathy for the radio speeches, it
seems that Pound's case is at least as strong as that of the attorney general.
Apparently, Pound was indicted under a blanket charge, meant to cover
the activities of eight radio broadcasters, seven of whom were broadcasting from Germany. The indictment simply does not fit the content
of the radio speeches. The Department of Justice became aware of this
problem, because a second indictment was prepared on 26 November
1945, after Pound had been arrested and brought back to the United

---

[36] Ibid., 114–15.
[37] Ibid., 115.
[38] Ibid., 120–1.

States to stand trial. The second indictment hews closer to the radio speeches. It accuses Pound:

> Of accepting employment from the Kingdom of Italy in the capacity of a radio propagandist. . . .
>
> Of counselling and aiding the Kingdom of Italy . . . and proposing and advocating . . . ideas and thoughts, as well as methods by which such ideas and thoughts could be disseminated, which the said defendant, Ezra Pound, believed suitable and useful to the Kingdom of Italy for propaganda purposes in the prosecution of said war.
>
> That the aforesaid activities . . . were intended to persuade citizens and residents of the United States to decline to support the United States in the conduct of the said war, to weaken or destroy confidence in the Government of the United States and in the integrity and loyalty of the Allies of the United States, and to further bind together and increase the morale of the subjects of the Kingdom of Italy in support of the prosecution of the said war by the Kingdom of Italy and its military allies.[39]

This continues at some length and accuses Pound of intentionally giving aid and comfort to enemies of the United States by purposefully broadcasting so as to create dissension among the United States and its allies. It also states that Pound "asserted, in substance, that the war is an economic war in which the United States and its allies are the aggressors" and that, further, the purpose of some of his speeches "was to create racial prejudice in the United States."[40] The second indictment is closer to the actuality of the speeches, but it depends for its success on proving that it was Pound's purpose in his broadcasts to harm the United States in its pursuit of the war, which simply was not the case. Pound did not intend harm to his native land. The government would have been equally hard-pressed to show that Pound's broadcasts had any effect on their audience; thus it seems that in a calm climate, Pound would have been acquitted. As Rushing has shown, however, in Washington, D.C., of the immediate postwar period, he may well have been convicted.

XII

In late 1942, Pound started to propose that an Italian publishing house bring out a series of books, in English, that Pound considered to be important. Pound renewed this request in early 1943, justifying it by claiming that the texts would be used for the education of Anglo-Saxon prisoners of war. The official response was initially lukewarm, though in the next chapter we will see how Pound's persistence finally won out.

[39] Norman, *The Case of Ezra Pound*, 77–8.
[40] Ibid., 78.

The situation in Italy deteriorated rapidly throughout the summer of 1943, as the Axis defeat in North Africa was followed closely by the invasion of Sicily. Under duress, people continue with their established routines, and Pound continued with his propaganda and periodic trips to Rome. There is little correspondence from this turbulent period, though on 7 August 1943, he wrote to Professor Nino Sammartano, general director of Cultural Exchange in the Ministry of Popular Culture:

> I don't know if we are yet at the freedom of speech that allows an obituary of the regime, or an analysis, but if you have assumed the editorship of the *Nazione* (which doesn't arrive in Rapallo) perhaps one could indicate some past errors. I would say that they are: 1. Not having educated the bureaucracy. For you the Tao is OK, but the bureaucracy has need of Confucius. . . . 2. Not having educated the intelligentsia, which has need of understanding before it can "obey" any simple command; or before it will consent to cooperate. HISTORY, necessary in understanding the occurrence of day-to-day events. (tr)

This letter is notable for several reasons. To begin, it shows Pound's consciousness of the fact that the fascist regime was collapsing (Mussolini had been arrested on 25 July, and Marshall Pietro Badoglio appointed prime minister). It also confirms Pound's later contention that he always felt comfortable speaking frankly, even critically, about the fascist regime. The letter reiterates Pound's conviction that people are changed by education, not by force of law, and it demonstrates the extent to which his attention had been captured by Confucius. Pound continued his activities fully aware that fascism was dying, the course of an idealist with confidence in his convictions. He was finding comfort, as the war situation worsened, in his historical studies. His correspondence with Sammartano also records a lively discussion between them of the meaning of certain key words in Aristotle, particularly in the *Metaphysics* and the *Nicomachean Ethics*.

There was some talk of Pound going to Berlin in August, but finally it was decided that he would stay in Italy and continue his work at Rome Radio. Olivia Rossetti Agresti wrote to him on 26 August 1943. Apart from the general sense one gets of the collapse of the regime from the letter, she wrote:

> The brutality of the Americans is really incredible. Signora V. told me her cook has a little sister who was staying in a place in the neighborhood of Albano; the child was with another in the fields the other day when they heard the airplanes arriving and the two children hid under a hedge; 37 peasants who were at work in the fields remained there, and the machines came low and machine gunned these men, who were all killed! This is murder not war.

Pound was aware of the bombardments and the effect they had. The Agresti letter is credible, but Pound in general was too willing to accept uncritically the version of things reported by the Italian press, such as the bombardments of churches and infants. He continued his work and was in Rome on 8 September when the Italians surrendered.

8

The Republic of Salò
and Left-Wing Fascism

I

Few of those who traveled north after the armistice of 3–8 September 1943 had any illusion about the final outcome of the war. German troops freed Mussolini on 12 September and aided him in setting up the Republic of Salò. During this period a number of fascist functionaries fled Rome for the north. They were motivated by many factors: opportunism, loyalty, greed, fear, but the chances of a military recovery seemed slim indeed to all but the most fanatic. Pound's friends apparently tried to dissuade him from leaving Rome, arguing that the war might come to an end very shortly,[1] but Pound had made up his mind. With an aging mother, a wife, a companion, and a daughter all living in northern Italy, it is hard to see how he could have chosen to do any differently than to travel north.

The next period of Pound's life, between the formation of the Republic of Salò on 23 September 1943 and Pound's arrest in early May of 1945, is the least documented of his adult years. Charles Norman, in his 450-page biography of Pound, devotes only one paragraph to this time. Noel Stock, in his excellent *Life of Ezra Pound*, does better, finding material to fill 9 pages of the 600-page biography. But the absence of material for those eighteen months remains a crucial problem for Pound scholarship, crucial because of the importance of this period to a final judgment about Pound's support of Italian fascism. This chapter will cast some light on Pound's activities during this difficult time.

There are several reasons for this lack of documentation. The war was going badly for the Axis, and Italy had become the latest battleground. Sicily was invaded on 10 July 1943, and mainland Italy on 3 September. Before Pound had his first letter published in the journals of the new

---

[1] Heymann, 139.

233

fascist regime, Naples had fallen to Allied troops. Wartime conditions were very bad in northern Italy. Aerial bombardments were frequent, communication was uncertain, and there were severe shortages of food and, important from our standpoint, paper. In addition, as the Allied armies advanced to victory, people were afraid to have fascist material in their homes. Much was destroyed, by individuals, fascist officials, and Allied armies. Thus this period causes major headaches for historians.

Despite these problems, two scholars, C. David Heymann and Niccolò Zapponi, have made some inroads. The virtue of their books, Zapponi's *L'Italia di Ezra Pound* and Heymann's *Ezra Pound: The Last Rower,* both published in 1976, is that they each contain thorough research from Italian and U.S. government archives. The books are limited in that neither man did research at the Pound Archive at Yale's Beinecke Library. This presents no problem with Zapponi's book, a scholarly monograph strictly limited in scope and quite useful. There is considerably more of a problem, though, with Heymann's book, which pretends to a broader treatment of its subject. Heymann was the first to obtain access to the Department of Justice material from the FBI investigation of Pound after his indictment for treason, and the material that he brings to bear from that source is useful. Regrettably, instead of limiting himself to that, he attempted to rehash Pound's entire life, under the rubric of "a political profile." Since Heymann's knowledge of the Italian sources is limited, his judgments are often misleading.

Pound made his way north from Rome, by foot, train, and automobile, after Mussolini's arrest, to visit his daughter in the Italian Tirol for a time. Stock, although without documentation, uses his knowledge of Italian geography and of the Italian train system to give us a very plausible account of Pound's return to Rapallo after his visit to his daughter. Knowing that Pound left Mary and got on the train in Bolzano, that the train back would go through Verona, Brescia, Milan, and Genoa, and that Salò is only twenty-five kilometers from Brescia, Stock correctly hypothesizes:

> After several weeks he returned to Rapallo by way of Lake Garda and Milan. . . . It is likely that he took the opportunity while passing around Lake Garda to make contact with the new Italian Republic then in the process of being formed at the small town of Salò.[2]

In any event, he was soon in touch with officials in the resurrected regime.

Pound did hear from his friend Giacomo Barnes on 4 November 1943 from Salò. Barnes had seen Alessandro Pavolini, the new secretary of the Republican Fascist party, and had heard from him that Pound was

---

[2] Stock, 402.

"safe and sound in Rapallo." Barnes told Pound that they were in the process of organizing a new English-language propaganda service with transmissions to be broadcast probably from Milan. He invited Pound to "come here for a few days toward the end of the month to help me galvanize the situation," adding, no doubt as bait, "it is necessary also to persuade people to insert a clause in the new statutes that permits only the state to issue money or its equivalent." Pound's interest in economics was no secret to his former colleagues, and they occasionally used it to manipulate him. Barnes mentioned that Nino Sammartano, a friend of Pound, had become the Inspector of Radio. Pound was quickly reengaged in his old activities, not only because of pressure from his colleagues and the necessity of earning a living, but more importantly because it seemed to him that the Republic of Salò was taking an important new turn in the direction of a progressive economic policy. In his first speech after his restoration to power, Mussolini had made a point that appealed to Pound, that one of the fundamental new directions of the Republic of Salò would be to annihilate the parasitic plutocracies and make labor, finally, "the subject of the economy and the unbreakable basis of the State."[3] That certainly seems vague enough, but the turn of fascism to the left combined with other, similar statements by officials of the new regime probably gave Pound hope that his long-dreamed economic reforms would soon be put into practice.

II

This new direction was confirmed immediately at the First Congress of the Republican Fascist Party in Verona in mid-November of 1943. The congress issued a manifesto that was to become the basic theoretical document for the new fascist state. Pound's daughter identifies the points important to Pound: "*La Carta del Lavoro* was published: work as basis of money. No right *of* property but *to* property. Work no longer the object but the subject of economy."[4] She points out that Pound used the phrase in the Pisan Cantos: " 'alla' non 'della' in il Programma di Verona / the old hand as stylist still holding its cunning" (*C*, LXXVIII, 478). The distinction must have been important because Pound repeats it in the Rock Drill Cantos (*C*, LXXXVI, 564). The "old hand" is Mussolini. The Italians perhaps had lost faith, but Pound had not.

Without question, the eighteen points of the Verona Program were attractive to Pound. The eighth point, dedicated to foreign affairs, called for elimination of "centuries-old British intrigues" from the European

[3] Salvatorelli and Mira, 1069.
[4] De Rachewiltz, 195–6.

continent, abolition of capitalism, and struggle against worldwide plutocracies. The final ten points (9–18) also would have attracted Pound.
They represented a conscious effort on the part of the new fascist party
to appeal to the proletariat, until then hostile to the party (though not
always to fascism). They emphasized that the basis of the republic was
labor, that private property, the result of labor and savings, was guaranteed, but that it must not become "the disintegrator of the moral and
physical personality" through the exploitation of the labor of others. It
also called for the nationalization of any part of the economy of interest
to the public welfare. Showing the dominant role of the Germans in the
Republic of Salò, it declared that Italian Jews were to be considered
foreigners and, for the duration of the war, enemies.[5]

Pound wrote to Goffredo Pistoni on 13 November 1943, defining his
political position: "I would say that I am a 'left-wing fascist,' or that I
support the continuity of the revolution of 1776, seeing points of agreement between our U.S. constitution and the most effective parts of
fascism" (tr). Pistoni was associated with the Milanese journal *Il Fascio*,
and Pound was undoubtedly trying to place some of his writing with
them. On the basis of his reading of all ten volumes of the works of
John Adams, Pound considered himself an expert on constitutions. He
wrote to Gilberto Bernabei, offering advice for the new republic:

> I believe that MODERATION is indicated; that is for the constitution.
> . . . Freedom of discussion (demarcation between freedom of discussion
> of doctrine, publication of historical facts, and personal defamation).
> Habeas corpus. Then the doctrine that money is subject to state control.
> YOU CANNOT strangle credit. It grows like grass whenever one man
> has faith in another. (tr)

Freedom of the press, habeas corpus, liberty as defined in "The Rights
of Man" (freedom to do whatever does not harm another), state control
of credit, these were Pound's recommended amendments to the Verona
Program, showing, finally, what he meant by Jeffersonian fascism and
what he envisioned his ideal republic to be.

Pound wrote to Sammartano in December with specific suggestions
for radio propaganda: "the E.I.A.R. tells me that the short waves won't
be in service for 'several months' / therefore the only possibility for
transmission to the U.S.A. will be with the strictest German collaboration." He added, "It seems to me useless to speak to England during
the Christmas season" (tr), apparently in reference to a proposal that he
do so. Pound's position with the ministry had not yet been entirely
regularized. He expressed dismay that a speech he had written that had
already been approved by Sammartano had been recalled to Salò for the

[5] Salvatorelli and Mira, 1074–5.

approval of the minister, and there were questions about whether or not he would be reimbursed for some out-of-pocket hotel expenses incurred.

In addition to his work for the EIAR, Pound started casting around for writing assignments, sending a column to Pettinato and Zappa of *La Stampa* in hopes they could use it. He wrote to them from the Prefettura in Milan, where he had "slept two nights in a kind of corridor," adding wryly that he hoped "to change hotels soon" (tr). The difficulties of travel in the new republic are reflected in a suggestion he made in a memo of 4 December 1943 to Fernando Mezzasoma, the minister of Popular Culture, for a proposed bus service from "Spezia to Salò by way of Genova, Tortona, Piacenza, and Cremona, aimed to give almost a new backbone to the Republic." In the memo Pound complained that Liguria was cut off from the rest of the republic and that it took three trains to get from Rapallo to Milan. The new bus route would improve communications and "give the impression that this new government actually exists" (fbi)(tr).

The aforementioned article had been sent to Concetto Pettinato from Brescia on 10 December 1943. It concerns economics, and no doubt to give it a boost Pound mentions "I spent a full half-hour with the Minister of Finance this morning" (tr). He recommends that they respond to Rapallo because he was uncertain about where he would be staying in Milan.

Pound had apparently found a job for his daughter with the radio office in Salò, for on 29 December 1943, Sammartano wrote that Mary Rudge had not yet come to Salò to take up service, asking Pound to invite her to come. Her account of this verifies the situation:

> Perhaps because he wanted me a bit more within reach, but mainly because culturally life might have been more interesting, Babbo looked around for an interpreting job for me at Salò. But somehow I could work up no enthusiasm for this plan and did not budge. I shared his faith in the Republic – primarily as luminous *idea* – though basically I had the Tyrolean mistrust of Italians. And my instinct for self-preservation has always been strong.[6]

Pound's motives for finding his daughter this job are not clear – perhaps he thought it was time for her to move out of the peasant village of Gais – but he apparently had some faith in the durability of the new republic. In the same letter Sammartano apologized for the bureaucratic mix-up about the hotel bill and told of his new promotion: "Tomorrow I transfer to Venice to assume the general directorship of the Office of Cultural Exchange; I hope you will give me the opportunity to greet you in Venice and avail myself of your collaboration" (tr).

[6] De Rachewiltz, 198.

Newspapers were scarce at that time, although a few did come out with some degree of regularity. Catching sight of a newspaper from Chiavari, Pound saw an article about Italian partisan activities, written by Vito Spiotta. The article was antipartisan and profascist and described actions by students, mostly propagandistic, opposing the presence of Germans in Italy. Pound wrote to Mezzasoma, on 3 January 1944, enclosing the clipping:

> The acts recounted in this newspaper clipping were done because of ignorance....
>
> It seems almost impossible to make certain people understand that ignorance was cultivated by the silence of the newspapers, which you have not yet aroused from their dirty habits.
>
> The fathers are as ignorant as the sons; the attempts of Pavolini when he was Minister of Popular Culture were always botched, etc. (fbi) (tr)

The points made here are typical of Pound. Wrong action results from ignorance, not evil. When ignorance is corrected by education, right action will ensue. The continuation of ignorance is the fault of bad newspapers and bad books. When these are improved, people's actions will follow. There may also be a subtext here, since Pound was not entirely successful in his attempts to find newspapers to carry his work, owing to his unorthodox Italian.

Pound had a tendency to adopt the rhetoric of "the betrayal of July 25–September 8" to his own purposes. The new fascist government was anxious to discredit the previous government, which had arrested Mussolini and negotiated an armistice with the Allies. Thus the newspapers of the Republic of Salò carried a great deal on the betrayal, defeatism, cowardice, and profiteering of officials of the previous government. In a letter to Mezzasoma of 11 January 1944, Pound complains of how his efforts too were undermined:

> Manuscripts by Fogazzorro destroyed. If the distinguished condemned Bottai had not sabotaged my proposal regarding the microphotograph machine, we would have saved what was intellectually important in the libraries of Italy.
>
> Someday when you have some spare time I will compile a list of my proposals that were sabotaged during the past fifteen years. (fbi) (tr)

These themes recur in Pound's letters of this period, to the point that it seems that Pound believed them himself, which is disturbing.

III

His campaign to find journalistic outlets continued, and on 4 January 1944, he wrote to Gaetano Cabella, the editor of *Il Popolo di*

Alessandria, one of the most important newspapers of the new republic. In the letter he stated that he was "looking for an editor intelligent enough to understand 1. antisemitism and the Jewish monetary system and 2. military valor and intellectual cowardice" (tr). Cabella found Pound's letter very cryptic but wrote back on 8 January that they awaited his treatment of the above arguments. When he responded on 13 January, Pound softened his position somewhat:

> It is useless to go in for anti-semitism while leaving on its feet the Jewish monetary system which is their strongest instrument of usury.
> My style is rough. I will attempt an article, but I don't know if you wish to correct it, or if you prefer that I find a disciple of the Academy of Crusca here. (tr)

The Accademia della Crusca is the Italian equivalent of the French Academy and his referring to it indicated a point on which he was sensitive: his unconventional Italian prose style.

Almost defensively, Pound was critical of the Italian press, and in particular of those writers who did not, according to him, understand economics. In a letter to Mezzasoma he summed up the problems with Italian journalism, problems that stemmed, he believed, from intellectual cowardice and that were tied to the political and economic misfortunes of his adopted country. Pound outlined three stages Italian journalism had passed through since the arrest of Mussolini on 25 July. "First: All the old maids who had swallowed the Academy of the Crusca emerged and jumped on the press to write very beautiful articles in a language to whose elegance I cannot aspire. (Among those were the dogs and the profiteers.)" (fbi) (tr). Pound specifically equates those writers having a correct, if overly refined, prose style with the Italians who betrayed the fascist ideal and supported the government of Marshall Badoglio. He places the end of this phase on 8 September 1943, when Badoglio publicly announced the armistice between the Italian government and the Allies. The second phase, after Mussolini's rescue by German soldiers, occurred in the first uncertain weeks ("about two months") of the new republic:

> The dogs (second platoon) were afraid to sign. Every line of material had some value. Empty press, scarcity of ideas and concepts, the eighteen points were made to stand out, as a historic document, a document of the history of THOUGHT.
> Third phase: Every half-witted fool jumps on the Republican press, which is now very much in style; and with a few exceptions writes for it without any adequate preparation, without knowledge of the subjects he is treating; consequently there is dullness, stupidity, and bad writing. (fbi) (tr)

He also attacked specific individuals, including Ermanno Amicucci, editor of the magisterial Milanese newspaper, *Corriere della Sera*. Mezzasoma had recommended Pound to Amicucci, but the latter thought Pound's Italian was incomprehensible and unusable.[7] Pound was more successful with *Il Popolo di Alessandria*. On 19 January, Cabella wrote to him, requesting, for reasons of space, "brief articles, both lively and polemical, on the subjects in which we have seen you are so well versed" (tr). Pound responded on 21 January, calling for a Republican fascist newspaper equal in every dimension to the Catholic *Crociata Italiana*, for propaganda purposes. He also included his typical complaints about vested interests in the business and publishing fields, complaints very similar to those he had made against the English more than twenty years before. So in this atmosphere of hysteria and denunciation Pound began his work for *Il Popolo di Alessandria*, for which he would write over forty articles over the next year. *Il Popolo di Alessandria* was one of the major newspapers of the new republic; it had a circulation of 135,000 and appeared twice a week. Pound was paid for his contributions.

On 13 January 1944, the Council of Ministers issued a decree that further developed the eighteen points of the Verona Program. These "provisions of the 13th" enthused Pound greatly. In them he saw, correctly, a movement toward the economic reforms he had been advocating for over a decade. He wrote to Mezzasoma on 15 January: "The provisions of the 13th appear to me to signify: the die is cast. Opposition will come from the mercantile industrialists, usurers, etc." (tr). The provisions that probably gladdened him the most were those pertaining to the nationalization of industries indispensable to the political and economic independence of the state. The private capital represented by those industries was to be transformed into credit, betokened by government certificates issued by the state. Here, Pound could well believe, were his dreams come alive: Social Credit realized.

In the same letter to Mezzasoma he envisioned a "propagandistic upswing" and he identified himself more closely than at any time previously with the efforts of the new fascist regime. He told Mezzasoma:

> It is obvious after the 13th that I am not an extremist, that is, I am no more leftist than the government itself. The opposition is now at the right and it is exactly among the spineless bourgeoisie in whom an educative force would arouse latent energies. They are spineless because of their ignorance of history. (fbi) (tr)

After the provisions of the 13th, Pound became furiously involved in the propagandistic efforts of the new republic, with an energy and en-

---

[7] Heymann, 144.

thusiasm that were to last till the end of the war. It is useful to look briefly at this document.

To begin, the provisions of the 13th gave a great deal of control to the workers in the various industries, both those nationalized and those remaining private. The administration of the state industries was to be given to a council of management elected by workers; for private industries, management would be composed of equal numbers of workers and shareholders. Other provisions also tended to expand the rights and privileges of the working class. All of this is logical, given the need of the new government to expand its base of support. It also fit in with the left-wing fascism announced by the Verona congress.[8]

From a purely political viewpoint, the new program attempted to save some aspects of the old-style fascism (the primacy of the party and the state) while incorporating new elements of personal liberty (habeas corpus after seven days, the right to criticize) and the demands made by the Nazi allies (Anglophobia and anti-Semitism). Although, owing to the war, many of these programs, especially the nationalization of industry, were never realized, the very fact of their enunciation was sufficient to renew Pound's faith.[9]

Further letters from this period show just how involved Pound was in the new propaganda efforts. He wrote on 22 January to Politi: "Slogans/ god damn it/ why NOT. Bolsheviks arrive at Bari, ship full of propaganda already printed" (tr). To Cabella on 29 January he wrote: "I hope to see in bold letters two of these. A NATION THAT DOES NOT WANT TO GO INTO DEBT ENRAGES USURERS. There is the whole reason for the war." In the same letter he stated: "The revolution will not happen until there is a monetary revolution. But perhaps it is not the moment to insist on this point before military recovery" (tr).

Pound pressed for the republication of his articles from *Il Meridiano di Roma* in book form to further his goals of educating those yet uncommitted to the new republic. In a letter to Cabella of 30 January he wrote: "EDUCATE ONE MUST/ EDUCARE *necesse est*," and he included a copy of the first manifesto he had helped prepare, signed by five writers of the Gulf of Tigullio and scheduled for printing the next day. "Workers, peasants, writers," he continued, "three groups in need of education. I WOULD LIKE an edition of 50 or 70 of my articles (reprint) sabotaged up to now" (tr). The manifesto was published in *Il Popolo di Alessandria* on 27 February 1944.

Pound was in the habit of sharing his proposals with quite a number

---

[8] Salvatorelli and Mira, 1075–6.
[9] Ibid.

of people. Around the same time he sent a similar letter to Giacchino Nicoletti at Salò, pressing for the edition but also including some general observations: "Style will be new when the material is new. Futurismo failed to a large extent because the newness was willed and did not come from inner necessity, but something shifting" (tr). This thinking coincided with Pound's general "totalitarian" view and his belief in a *paideuma,* the structural identity of all cultural forms. But here, instead of assigning primacy to artistic forms in the creation or anticipation of cultural trends, he seemed to be shifting his view, to an "inner necessity" of "material."

Pound finally received a positive answer to his publishing proposals from Sammartano, who had moved to Venice. In a letter of 31 January, Sammartano clarified his plans for several books. The first, about which he was most enthusiastic, would "demonstrate how Roosevelt is a scoundrel, based on historical facts" (tr). The other books were to be Volpe on Italian fascism, a reprint, presumably, of the article in the *Enciclopedia Italiana,* an Italian translation and update of *Jefferson and/or Mussolini,* and the collection of the *Meridiano* articles (*Orientamenti*). The first book planned was later entitled *Roosevelt, America, and the Causes of the Present War.* Casting about for other material, Sammartano asked about a book on English propaganda during the First World War by Churchill that Dr. Gilberto Bernabei, head of the Cabinet of the Ministry of Popular Culture, said that he had seen at Pound's house. When Pound explained that the book was by Ponsonby, the matter was dropped.

Pound, energized, started to press for the founding of a new magazine or a new newspaper for the republic, to be printed weekly in Rapallo. As he wrote to Mezzasoma on 31 January 1944, his idea was to mobilize "those who are not suitable for military service" (tr) but who had literary ability so that they could serve the new state (fbi). He stressed the need for the intelligentsia to have a central clearinghouse for debate and information, though he clarified to Mezzasoma on 27 February that he did not intend for it to be "an organ of the party" (tr). He elaborated: "Action arises from conviction and how can you convince liberals without words? Propaganda should aim for the creation of a state of mind which is conducive to action" (fbi) (tr). But the presence of the war is felt in these endeavors. Paper and the material means to make it were lacking. On 11 March Mezzasoma wrote to Pound finally giving him a definite "no" to the possibility of a weekly paper in Rapallo "due to the absolute necessity of reducing the use of paper to the minimum" (fbi) (tr). And apparently some kind of review was already in the works, prepared by Giacchino Nicoletti at Salò.

None of this discouraged Pound, who immediately shifted course. In a letter to Mezzasoma on 14 March he provided a new group of proposals:

> Please forget the idea that I want a daily or weekly newspaper in Rapallo.
> I want to achieve certain useful aims. And it seems to me we are on
> the right road. . . .
>   1. Another field of action: the street corner orator.
>   2. For the radio: due attention to slogans. . . . Let us ask the liberals,
> "Why are the usurers all liberals?"
>   A NATION that does not want to get into debt angers the usurers.
> (fbi) (tr)

This tendency to write and think in short slogans is a disturbingly common element of Pound's work in this period.

Equally disturbing is the undeniable fact that Pound's anti-Semitism,
however latent or restrained it had been for most of his life, is very
pronounced in his writing during the last eighteen months of the war.
In a letter to Mezzasoma of 7 February he rails against Jewish writers:

> For the love of God, it is simple madness to continue consolidating the
> power, the fame of a Jewish half turd who calls himself "Pertinax" (the
> same for that other turd Lippmann, JEW) by citing them by name.
>   And it isn't necessary, one can easily cite the newspaper where these
> dregs put forward their lies and nonsense.
>   Citing these scoundrels you give them importance. They don't exist
> but in the practice of "echo," creating "international journalists" or
> rather Jews of world fame. Among them there is not a line of real
> creation. (fbi) (tr)

Although there are not many such passages in Pound's letters, his anti-
Semitism reached a new level of virulence in this period.

The worst example of Pound's anti-Semitism comes from the pages
of Il Popolo di Alessandria and should put to rest any uncertainty scholars
have had about it. It is difficult to explain away this article, entitled "Race
or Illness," printed on 12 March 1944 and carrying the signature
"Ez. P.":

> It is time to make an analysis. Hebrewism isn't race, it's illness. When
> a nation dies, Jews multiply like bacilli in carrion. Like an illness, there
> can be severe cases and lesser cases. The same Jews suffer from it in
> differing intensities, almost measles or smallpox. When aryans or half-
> aryans like Roosevelt and Churchill or Eden are stricken, they are real
> lepers. Analysis of blood can demonstrate the results. A clinical eye aids
> us without need of a microscope. The infection can be induced con-
> sciously, for example, that letter from the rabbis of Constantinople to
> the Jews of Spain (already a number of centuries ago): "Enter the Church
> to poison it, make yourselves priests!"
>   The practice in South America today: a family of Jews arrives. One
> brother becomes a banker, another a priest, and the others divide up
> between theaters, brothels, and the press: Organisms infected with this
> bacillus tend toward coalition. (tr)

Although there can be no doubt about the anti-Semitic effect of this passage, one must exercise some caution in drawing conclusions. To begin with, aside from the radio speeches, the actual incidence of anti-Semitic passages in Pound is infrequent. Further, there is an illogic to it, as in the above passage. Although the metaphor of the Jew as disease is common in anti-Semitic writing, Pound takes it to an odd conclusion when he states that "the same Jews suffer from it in differing intensities" and that "aryans or half-aryans" can be "stricken." Here he has departed from his metaphor and even from his racism, as he has done before (what is an "aryo-kike"?). These departures seem to signal that Pound was ill at ease with his prejudice, which reaches the extremity seen above, with its implied call for violence toward Jews, only rarely during the period of the Republic of Salò. In any case, a full assessment of Pound's anti-Semitism is beyond the scope of this work and awaits a careful, detailed, and historical treatment.[10]

A new possibility for a propagandistic outlet arose for Pound. In a February letter to Sammartano, in addition to the contents for the proposed edition of *Orientamenti,* he speaks of the possibility of a trip to Berlin. With the Italian short-wave radio transmitters still not functioning, he saw the trip as a way of making some useful contacts among the German intellectuals. Although protesting that he did not like the cold, he still felt that the possibility of a stimulating intellectual exchange between the two countries was sufficiently important to promote the trip, saying "I should have visited Berlin three years ago" (tr). Apparently plans for the trip came to nothing, and one must imagine that was all for the best.

IV

On 16 February 1944, Pound sent Sammartano his work "on the causes of war, Roosevelt, incidence of this war in the process of world usury." He cautioned that it was not meant to be a scholarly work, an odd sort of warning considering its extreme nature, but that it was a book for those "that don't have time to read voluminous books in a moment like this" (tr). He expressed the hope that it would be published quickly. Sammartano responded on 23 February, praising the book and asking for others along the same line. He said that he found it to be "of great propagandistic effectiveness" (tr) and notified Pound that the print-

---

[10] Casillo's *A Genealogy of Demons* deals with anti-Semitism in the abstract and as a psychological symptom in Pound's structural unconscious but does not approach the topic of Pound's anti-Semitism historically. Flory's *The American Ezra Pound* also considers Pound from a psychological perspective, but it does contain useful material on American anti-Semitism of the period of Pound's boyhood.

ing press was already in operation. Pound, in the above letter, had made the further point that the first criterion of propaganda was "to seize and retain the interest of the reader" (tr), undoubtedly a valid point, but one that had little to do with the book itself (beyond its title), which was a further chronicle of Pound's reading in economics and history. His motive for writing it, though, remained the same as before: to educate the reader. As he wrote in an article for *Il Popolo di Alessandria* entitled "Etica" (printed 12 March): "Lack of honesty is the product of ignorance. . . . Against assassins, force; against mercantilists, a bit of culture" (tr).

L'America, Roosevelt, e le Cause della Guerra Presente was printed on 23 March 1944. Roosevelt figures hardly at all in its thirty-two pages. He is mentioned only twice, the first time on page 24, briefly, and the second time on the penultimate page. The Second World War is hardly mentioned. In fact, twentieth-century events have little place in the work. The book, actually more of a pamphlet, represents Pound's version of American history, beginning early in the eighteenth century but primarily focused on the nineteenth century. The emphasis is exclusively economic, attempting to illustrate his principal thesis: that "this war is not caused by a caprice of Mussolini or Hitler. This war is a part of a millennial war between usurers and peasants, between usocracy and whoever does an honest day's work with his hands or with his brains"[11] (tr). The economic details are familiar, but they are presented with a clarity not often seen in Pound's work of this period. The fundamental idea is that only the state has the right to issue credit and that this right was usurped by private citizens, "usurers," in modern history when the Bank of England, a private company, was formed in 1694. Everything follows from that central drama, though previous writers on the subject of economics and usury, from Aristotle on, are occasionally cited.

According to Pound, the Quakers of Pennsylvania (from whom he was descended) issued paper money in the first half of the eighteenth century for the public benefit. The money was lent to farmers for improvements, and a reasonable rate of interest was charged. This arrangement, a just one, brought prosperity to the colonies. Fearing infringement on its monetary monopoly and potential competition, the Bank of England, by manipulating the English government, forced the suppression of the Pennsylvania paper money in 1750. And, "after some other vexations" (tr), the colonies declared their independence (8).

The American Revolution, according to Pound, freed the United States from the international usocracy until the assassination of Lincoln, which he hints was a conspiracy by the usocracy because of Lincoln's opposition

---

[11] Pound, *L'America, Roosevelt e le Cause della Guerra Presente*, 3. Subsequent citations in this chapter will be given by page number in parentheses.

to their control of American finance. The Italian fascistic revolution continued the struggle of the American Revolution, and that was the cause of the Second World War, one of a series of wars fought for the same principles (4). International usurers, in Pound's view, create wars for their own profit, to get nations into debt, and are continually trying to stamp out any threat to their economic monopoly and any move toward economic justice. They control the newspapers and the press, which in turn maintain the ignorance of the people about economic subjects. "The Count of Vergennes had cause to say to John Adams: 'newspapers rule the world' " (20) (tr).

The conspiracy against economic knowledge is furthered in the universities. All the textbooks written for them during the nineteenth century, "the century of usury, . . . were written to maintain the domination of usury" (tr) according to Pound (21). In an uncharacteristic passage (focusing attention on himself), Pound describes the great patience required to discover these "relevant and revealing" facts about economic history in "unexamined pamphlets" where one hundred pages yield "three revealing lines" (21) (tr).

Despite constant talk of usurers and usocracy, there is very little overt anti-Semitism in this work. Of Hamilton, Jefferson's opponent and the bankers' friend, Pound says that his race "was never determined with certainty" (tr) though his abilities resembled those of Disraeli (12). At one point he speaks of the United States as "Jewish-dominated" (15) (tr), and at another he speaks of London and Washington "united in their hebrewization" (24) (tr), but those are the only specifically anti-Semitic remarks in the entire text.

The central point of the booklet is that the "first serious attempt" to fight against the domination of society by the usocracy, "after that of Lincoln, began with the fascist revolution and was asserted with the formation of the Rome–Berlin Axis" (20–1) (tr). "From the moment that Mussolini guessed the connections between the usurers in New York and their tools in Moscow, he was condemned by the international usocracy" (24) (tr). Pound had clearly changed his views on the Russian Revolution, at least for propaganda purposes, and was now maintaining that it was false and in part betrayed (24).

As can be expected, Pound gives a list of recommended books for those readers whose curiosity has been aroused, although that is partly to shore up his authority, since several of the titles would be nearly impossible to find under the best conditions. These books are familiar with three exceptions, *Das Bankgeschäft* by Georg Obst (no date given) and *De Modo Usurarum* (1639) and *De Foenore Trapezitico* (1640) by Claudius Salmasius, whose work Pound had discovered. Pound had not lost his scholarly bent, but he was attributing the rarity of these dry and obscure texts to conspiracy rather than to more plausible causes. Pound describes his own efforts as regards "the historic process and the momentary problem in particular" over "the past ten years" as being directed toward a correlation between fascist economics, medieval Catholic canonical economic doctrine, and the proposals of Douglas's Social Credit and Gesell's "Natural Order" (27) (tr). And he reemphasizes his earlier call for a clear and precise economic terminology.

Pound closes the booklet by repeating the reason for it: "to show this war as part of a series of wars provoked by the same continuing agency: worldwide *usocracy* or the congregation of high finance" (tr). That was the force at work. Roosevelt, according to Pound, was not fully conscious of his role but was acting as an exponent of a force far more extensive, the usocracy (31–2).

L'America, Roosevelt, e le Cause della Guerra Presente is a booklet that is clearly propagandistic in its intent, containing the simplicity and rhetorical design necessary for a strong impact. Yet one has the uncomfortable feeling that the simplicity and design are very close to Pound's own thinking, that he had become the perfect propagandist and believed in the truth of his slogans. He does seem to hedge at times. It is not clear whether he really believed that the Russian Revolution was false or that Lincoln was the victim of a usurocratic conspiracy. And there is an artfulness in the arrangement of the text, beyond the stylistic ease of conviction. The value of the booklet is that, for once, all his beliefs and fears were out there, in one text.

There is a clarity to a printed text that is not present in the process of its writing. Looking at the published version of one's work, an unwelcome objectivity is gained, where doubts begin to arise, even as the text continues to profess belief. I believe that seeing the printed version of *L'America, Roosevelt, e le Cause della Guerra Presente* may have had such an effect on Pound. He could not renounce a twenty-year commitment or even, particularly since the war was going badly for the Axis, give up what had become his only source of livelihood. But I sense some hesitancy at this time. Pound started to pull back. I believe he started to doubt that he had found the economic answer, or perhaps more accurately, that an economic answer was adequate for the problems war-ravaged Italy was facing.[12] And though he continued to function as a propagandist for the regime, another subject began to dominate his correspondence of this period, as completely as economics had domin-

---

[12] It is difficult to prove this impression, and I do not wish to suggest that Pound began to act insincerely. Perhaps the bombing, lack of adequate food, other wartime privations, and his age were having an effect. Casillo also finds Pound less confident "in his moral and ethical distinctions" (244) but places this decline in confidence somewhat earlier, around the time of "A Visiting Card" (1943).

ated it before. That subject, not a new one for Pound, was Confucian philosophy.

V

Sammartano wrote to Pound on 17 February 1944 saying that he had received both the collection of articles from *Il Meridiano* and the volume *Studio Integrale* by Confucius, which Pound had prepared along with Alberto Luchini early in 1942. The book had a bilingual text, Chinese and Italian, and Sammartano promised to reprint the Italian text immediately. He added that an edition of the *Meridiano* articles was highly probable.

Pound responded at once, trying to talk Sammartano out of dropping the Chinese text. He argued that one of the purposes of the new edition was to try to gain prestige for the new Italian republic in the Orient. Further:

> The profound thought of the original is so completely connected with the medium of expression that it is impossible to separate it. That is, one can read the Italian text, BUT I intend this book as a base for an entire healthy culture. As the only source not filthied and bastardized and poisoned by the jewish scum. (tr)

This last line is so jarring that it points to another possible cause of Pound's occasionally virulent anti-Semitism of this period, an attempt to please his superiors. Just what Pound meant by saying that the book would be a "base for an entire healthy culture" was not yet clear to Sammartano, though it would soon be made clear. Pound admitted that an edition only in Italian might be useful if it were pocket size, though he said that it would not have the international and scholarly scope that he desired. The next day, writing again, he decided that it would be best to go along with a pocket edition, "removing all of the scholarly apparatus."

Evidently Sammartano was continuing to suggest that Pound come to Venice, either permanently or for an extended stay, to help more directly with the publishing work, because Pound wrote to him with a counterproposal on 20 February. It was simply a question of logistics, he said. If Olga Rudge's house in Venice, which had been sequestered when the United States entered the war, was made available and restored to good condition, then a move would be considered, especially in view of the fact that a considerable number of his books and files were there.

A new enterprise for Pound at this time was propaganda aimed at prisoners of war. Concerning his proposal, he wrote to Sammartano on 20 February:

For the prisoners I continue to believe that the most suitable material is material printed abroad before the war.

This does not "stink of propaganda"/ No one can say that B. Adams wrote in favor of fascist Italy in 1903 or in 1897.

The same in a lesser way for any book or article or booklet printed abroad before the war, even if polemical. (tr)

Pound broadened this suggestion into a series of books to be translated into Italian for internal propaganda. The books he had in mind, however, could not have conceivably fit into the war effort of the republic. In a letter to Luigi Berti of 26 February, he asked if he could translate *Apes of God* by Wyndham Lewis. "Among the ruins they promise me that they will have some books printed" (tr). In a fragment of the same date he spoke of *Eimi, Apes of God,* and *Ulysses* as forming a trilogy and suggested inclusion in the series of Hardy's *Under the Greenwood Tree* because a translation by his daughter, Mary, existed.

A constant feature of Pound's correspondence from this period was his attempt to get from the ministry news and addresses of his friends. He had lost contact with many of them during the tumultuous summer of 1943 and was trying to gather writers and translators to help with the propaganda for the new republic. He wrote to Berti, asking the whereabouts of Pellizzi and wrote to Sammartano on 26 February: "Linati must be at Rebbio, but I don't know if he would be disposed to work. I don't know if Izzo would be disposed to work. He has a Jewish in-law, very capable as a translator but... Liverzani is also an excellent translator" (tr). Pound was completely taken with this idea for a series of books to be translated into Italian, and with characteristic energy he started to assemble his translating staff. This was a familiar process for him, going back to at least the early thirties, of bringing important books into Italian; only here the scope of the books had broadened to include political and economic subjects as well as literary ones.

In a second letter to Sammartano of the same date, Pound suggests another book for inclusion, without batting an eye:

For instructing our propagandists an edition (500–1000 copies) of Stalin's *The Bases of Leninism*/ with all of the material, cover, etc., as published in the 100,000-copy edition. . . . this shows how one DOES propaganda. And it is also a magnificent slashing criticism of the Roosevelt–Churchillian scum. . . .

It is necessary to make clear whether or not we are doing PROPAGANDA with immediate goals. Things to be done within three weeks; or the other activity, that is, the true and profound cultural exchange indicated by your TITLE [General Director of Cultural Exchange].

I think for the latter these would be indicated:

Cruet: *La Vie du Droit*

> Zielinski: *La Sibille* if not the book by Scarfoglio
> written as a supplement to *La Sibille*. (tr)

Pound's sympathies were clearly with the latter definition of Sammartano's job: that propaganda should be true cultural exchange. Still, to suggest to the fascist government that it reprint a book on Leninism by one of the Allied leaders during the height of the war took an unusual degree of idealism.

Pound continued, unsuccessfully, to try to make contact with Mussolini. In a letter to Mezzasoma of 1 March 1944, in which he asked to be presented to *il Duce,* he emphasized his problems in communicating important knowledge concerning foreign affairs to the dictator. He speaks especially of the impossibility of communicating the results of his 1939 trip to the United States "to anyone to whom they could have been of service." He continued: "My duty, as I see it, is to stop certain things from being believed or done because of ignorance of historic facts, among which are the existence of movements and the disassociation of the meaning of words and various terminologies" (fbi) (tr). It is not difficult to understand how such an argument for an interview with Mussolini would be considered less than urgent by his secretaries. It is more difficult to see just what there was about these reasons, true though they might have been, that Pound thought might be convincing enough for Mussolini to give him time.

Pound had not neglected his project for a cultural turn to the Chinese, as he makes clear in a letter to Mezzasoma of 15 March:

> At last I can see the manner in which to carry out a fundamental plan for Chinese studies with two aims. First: instruction in philosophy. Second: commerce with the Chinese as a manner of understanding what the Nipponese are and on what they base their culture. (fbi) (tr)

Although it certainly seems strange that the fascist government of the Republic of Salò, in the middle of losing the war, was about to embark on the publication of an entire series on ancient Chinese history and culture, such was indeed the case. Pound could be very persuasive, and he was in correspondence with many of the top officials of the Republic of Salò. He succeeded in convincing the government that despite the serious paper shortage, the threat of famine, and the other exigencies of the war, a series made up of various Chinese classics would be of value. Pound's devotion to this idea forms a remarkable part of his activity during the last year of the war, and the rest of the letter to Mezzasoma deserves reproduction in its entirety.

1. My bilingual edition of STUDIO INTEGRALE of CONFUCIUS is already done. Sammartano is printing a popular version with only the Italian text.

2. So as not to lose years we are going forward, not beginning anew each time but using studies already in existence and the best translations in French, English, and Latin with notes I could add.

L'Asse che non vacilla (Invariabilité dans le Milieu) to be translated from the French of Pauthier by Soldato. Work already begun yesterday.

3. Speeches by Confucius. Soldato will continue with this and with the

4. Book of Mencius (from Pauthier's translations).

5. Shu King 2235–719 B.C. That is, documents collected by Confucius, translated by Gorn Old. Necessary in order to understand on what Confucius based his deductions.

6. Odes, Anthology of ancient poetry collected by Confucius with the Latin translation of Lacharme, notes of J. Mohl 1752; published in 1830. I'm looking for an edition of "Spring and Autumn." An IDEO-GRAMMIC CHINESE–ITALIAN DICTIONARY to be based on what exists, but certainly to include Morrison with additions and notes by Karlgren. The plan to be submitted when we can see the possibilities.

You may say to me: But this is Chinese, not Japanese. Yes, but for contact with Italy we must know that the Roman empire did exist. Japanese culture is based on Chinese culture. At a certain moment Japan continues. For a more lively part of Japanese literature it is necessary to see the Noh (almost sacred dramas) in the only transportable manner, that is, by sound film; just as I saw "AWOI Na UYE" in Washington. To begin with Kagekiyo and Kumasaka.

I do not need a palace (like the Institute of Oriental Studies) but I would need a printing press and a zincograph. (fbi) (tr)

This enthusiasm and the breathless sense of energy unleashed and work under way remind us most of Pound's throwing himself into his column for *L'Indice*. The scope and ambition of the program are commendable, but the whole enterprise seems odd under the circumstances. It is clear that Pound is following his own program at least as much as a program for Italian propaganda. His drive to educate people and to inform them about important texts is very much in character. But it is not clear just how much Pound was in touch with the reality of the ongoing war. This program may have been a desire on his part to retreat from the reality of war, into the more pleasant garden of his Confucian studies. Pound's scholarly pursuits tend to underscore the impression I receive from the infrequent documents of this period: that Pound was beginning to have some doubts about the course he had chosen, or perhaps that he was beginning to doubt that any proposals for economic reform that he supported or any insights into the evils chronicled in economic history would make much of a difference in a world so bloodied by war. The letter was received by the ministry on 19 March and a note was attached describing the proposal in a neutral tone and adding that Pound wanted Mussolini apprised of the program.

He was clearly worked up about the importance of this project for he wrote a second letter to Mezzasoma on the same day, a clear indication in the Pound correspondence of a high degree of excitement about some idea.

> The importance of Confucian culture is this: Greece did not have the civic sense for the construction of an empire. The Odyssey is almost without an ethical sense. Greco–Roman philosophy reaches us either in fragments or is too diffuse. All was undermined by Judaism during the Middle Ages, etc. Having a solid base, systematic but succinct, China has rebuilt its empire on different occasions.
>
> Only Sunday I finally saw a possible way of presenting this culture, and without losing thirty years. (fbi) (tr)

For whatever reason, it is clear that Pound had decided that his own activity should be directed toward achieving a long-range benefit rather than to more immediate propagandistic purposes. But the approval of the ministry for his Chinese project was still in doubt. Understandably, their initial reaction was not entirely enthusiastic.

VI

Despite Pound's increasing interest in pursuing his Confucian studies, his more customary propagandistic activities continued. In March of 1944, he sent Sammartano a manuscript called *La Storia di un Reato* (The history of a crime) by Arthur Kitson, whose writings as an occasional contributor to the *New Age* we considered in Chapter 1. This was a summary, translated into Italian, of two books by Kitson, *Industrial Depression* (London, 1905) and *The Bankers' Conspiracy* (London, 1933). The latter had started as a criticism of the first report of the Cunliffe commission, which recommended the return to the gold standard eventually adopted by the British government in the early twenties. It was printed in 1933, apparently at the request of some of Kitson's friends. *Industrial Depression* treats the repeal of the Sherman Silver Purchasing Act by the American Congress in 1893, considering it the result of a conspiracy by the central banks and the cause of a major depression.

La Storia di un Reato is a twenty-four page summary of parts of those two books, with comments that bring it up to date and relate it to the Second World War. It purports to explain the war as a result of a bankers' conspiracy to profit by a return to the gold standard, by preventing national governments from issuing their own paper currency, and by encouraging war to create indebtedness. This plot by the "usocracy" (referred to once as the "*giudeocrazia,*" the "jewocracy") is seen as the fundamental cause of war and suffering. There is some evidence that the summary was overseen by Pound (both a reference to Confucius and his typical economic concerns) but that the actual translation was done by Olga Rudge. The prose style does not seem Poundian; furthermore, in Mary de Rachewiltz's copy of the pamphlet, Pound wrote "Trad. da O.R. Ciao E.P.," which undoubtedly means "tradotto da Olga Rudge" ("translated by Olga Rudge"). The book saw print on 12 May 1944 and formed the second volume of the Library of Political Culture, of which Pound's *L'America, Roosevelt, e le Cause della Guerra Presente* was the first.

With the same letter to Sammartano, Pound sent a copy of his *Oro e Lavoro* (Gold and work). He described it, however, as being unsuited for publication by the ministry, saying: "It must be READ by economists and journalists, but it is too personal, and further, too CONDENSED for a larger circulation at this time" (tr). The copy he sent had been printed in Rapallo, presumably in a limited edition.

The principal concerns of *Oro e Lavoro* are familiar, treated in other Pound works of the period. But the work begins differently, with a section entitled "The Way of Utopia." According to Mary de Rachewiltz (in conversation), *Oro e Lavoro* was conceived on Pound's walk out of Rome, north to perhaps what he imagined might be the ideal Republic of Salò. In the initial section, Pound describes an imaginary visit to the Republic of Utopia, where the inhabitants are cheerful because of their laws and "the teaching they received from their earliest school days."[13] That instruction taught people to define words and because of that to define economic terms. Their prosperity hinged upon the adoption of a Gesellite mechanism for circulating currency. Pound's tone turns from wistful to violent when he adds that because of that "they do not lick the boots of the bloated financiers or syphilitics of the market-place."[14]

Pound then continues on his accustomed course, explaining how the usocracy create wars to drive nations into debt and that once debt has been created in a nation, the usocracy use their control of the currency to deflate money, increasing "debts when money is cheap in order to demand repayment when money is dear."[15] And he takes us through, once again, the familiar historical examples. If there is any change here at all, it lies in the section on Utopia and in one sentence that is easy to pass over heedlessly. There Pound states: "One cannot hope to prevail against bad faith by making known the facts, but one might against

[13] Pound, "Gold and Work" (1944), in *Selected Prose*, 336.
[14] Ibid., 337.
[15] Ibid., 343.

ignorance."[16] Whereas before Pound had always seemed to believe that education would cure the ills of society, he is now apparently admitting to the possibility of evil that exists in spite of knowledge. And he focuses a bit less on the mechanism than on the cause: "No! it is not money that is the root of the evil. The root is greed, the lust for monopoly. *'CAPTANS ANNONAM MALEDICTUS IN PLEBE SIT!'* thundered St. Ambrose – 'Hoggers of harvest, cursed among the people!' "[17] Pound in a foreword written much later, on 4 July 1972, to Cookson's edition of his selected prose, made a similar point: "re USURY: I was out of focus, taking a symptom for a cause. The cause is AVARICE."[18] Pound critics have taken these words to be recantation, but we can see that he had the same realization much earlier; in fact, it also shows up in his correspondence of the thirties. In any event, Pound's thought seems to be shifting.

Pound continued to come up with new propaganda ideas. On 4 March he wrote to Gaetano Cabella, the editor of *Il Popolo di Alessandria,* proposing that a manifesto, similar to the one he had drawn up for the writers of the Gulf of Tigullio, be prepared. It would be for the purposes of foreign propaganda, and it would be signed by ten authors who were "very well known" (tr). What benefit this might have been is hard to imagine, but Pound was keeping busy. The days when artists' manifestos could be of any use were clearly over, at least for a while.

In a letter to Pound of 23 March, Sammartano informed him that the minister had approved the edition of Pound's articles from *Il Meridiano.* Pound was not given complete freedom in the choice of articles for inclusion, however. He was told that the collection would start with a first volume containing only articles of a political, economic, and social nature. The publication of other articles would be put off, and a second volume was hoped for soon. In addition, Pound was advised that "the minister believed it opportune to postpone for now the publication of *Studio Integrale* by Confucius" (tr).

Unfazed, Pound wrote back on 29 March, urging the utility of an edition of two Noh dramas: "KAGEKIYO where the impact reaches Homeric proportions in the memories of the old warrior. KUMASAKA where the sense of honor and punctilio is at its maximum splendor" (tr). He continued to urge, in the same letter, that the most important project was the second book of Confucius, *L'Asse Che Non Vacilla* (The unwobbling pivot) in the Italian version of Soldato, based on Pauthier, with Pound's notes. He adds: "An ideogrammic dictionary is necessary because for a long time I have planned a comparison between classical

[16] Ibid., 341.
[17] Ibid., 347.
[18] Pound, *Selected Prose,* 3.

philosophical terminology (Greek), and Chinese and medieval (already begun in my paleographic edition of Guido Cavalcanti)" (tr). Pound must have been very gratified when he received a letter from Mezzasoma a few days later. Dated 31 March, the letter states in part that arrangements had been made to examine the possibility of a translation of the *Odes* from the Latin text of Lacharme. These Confucian projects were important for Pound, and it certainly appeared that he had begun to make headway.

Pound was at the height of his activity and persuasiveness at this time. On 16 April, he wrote to Sammartano to continue to press for his Confucian series:

> Thinking toward an immediate edition of the TESTAMENT of Confucius, I reduced the new material to a minimum, which seems to me would avoid the danger that a complete edition of the *C'iung Yung* might incur, namely to distract the reader from the need for IMMEDIATE action toward metaphysical reflection. (tr)

It is necessary to understand just how important a part these Confucian studies were of Pound's work for the Republic of Salò, if only to avoid the superficial judgment by some that Pound was acting only as a servile propagandist for the fascist state during this time. In fact, as always, he was an instigator. Pound's persistence was rewarded. In a letter of 18 April, Sammartano notified him that the minister (Mezzasoma) had approved publication of the *Odes*. In the same letter, he also inquired for a more precise definition of Pound's suggestion for a second series of books, which would include a book by Brooks Adams.

Pound felt completely free in his correspondence of this period to offer criticism and advice concerning the internal affairs of the new regime. He saw his role indeed as "unofficial admonitor to the Duce and the Salò Republic," as Heymann nicely puts it.[19] In a letter to Cabella of 20 April 1944, referring to the political trials then going on, Pound urged that justice be tempered with a consideration of how people suffered under the corrupt administrators of the previous regime:

> The only distinction that I would like to see would be among men who resisted the usurers, and who were in pain, suffered, who were among the first who wanted a clean administration, who had Volpi etc. on their backs etc/ these, even if they have wavered during the first 14 of the 45 days, I would examine/ and I would judge with the "conditional." (tr)

Pound felt free to criticize, particularly problems in the "old" (before the arrest and resurgence of Mussolini) fascist regime. In a draft of an

[19] Heymann, 144.

article entitled "That Which Italy Possesses and Doesn't Possess" written two weeks earlier and found on the verso of a copy of a letter to Cabella dated 6 April, Pound wrote:

> The enemy proclaims that Italy doesn't know how to govern itself. Eh be' [so what]. It is time to look ourselves well in the face. It is time to recognize weaknesses; for example: the administration in Dalmatia wasn't perfect. From a single village in the Tirol I take the example of the Neapolitan who was sent there. He sold the schoolhouse; he sold the forest of the municipality where the peasants used to gather the leaves for compost; therefore, fertilizer derived from compost and dung was lacking. (tr)

Pound takes a story he undoubtedly heard during his visit in the Tirol with his daughter, but he makes no allowance for the typically anti-Italian attitude of the Tirolese; in fact, the story seems exaggerated. It is doubtful if Cabella ever published this article.

Even Mussolini was not immune from Pound's criticism. In a letter to Sammartano of 5 April, Pound wrote about a book by Beraud, *Ce Que J'ai Vu à Rome*. Beraud's point, with which Pound agreed, concerned the concentration of ministerial portfolios in the hands of *il Duce:* "The problem is NOT that he is the only one to have power, but that he is the only one INFORMED" (tr). Power, Pound said, must be centralized. But information must be spread to the maximum. Again, Pound's political naiveté shows through here, since he seems oblivious to the fact that in any political structure, information forms one basis of power.

Undoubtedly Pound's activities during this period were primarily propagandistic, though his views on propaganda and the views of Italian officials did not always coincide. Except for his Confucian material, Pound was not publishing any new work, another sign, I believe, that he was beginning to doubt some of his earlier conclusions. He was almost exclusively engaged in reprinting old writings, both his and others', some of which were written well before 1940. With these reprints he hoped to define his sense of the historical process so as to clarify his positions. His work was directed as much to readers of the postwar period as it was to the soldiers and citizens of wartime Italy. Few then had any illusions about the war's outcome, with the Axis pressed back on every front and Italy suffering constant aerial bombardment.

Perhaps some of this lack of new activity was due to the exigencies of war: the hunger, the hardships, the economic necessity for providing for a family by the only trade he knew. Or perhaps part of this stillness was caused by his increasing escape into the tranquil, well-ordered garden of Confucian philosophy, with its millennial perspective on the problems of war and government. Pound seems to have had growing doubts about the adequacy of his economic views. In the letter to Cabella of 20 April, cited earlier, he wrote: "HELL! for the first 15 years of study, the monetary economy seemed simple/ but after 20 years it begins to seem complicated. Perhaps I'm growing old" (tr). He was then fifty-eight years old.

VII

Pound's project for the edition of the *Odes* ran into some problems as apparently the officials at the Ministry of Popular Culture had misunderstood his wishes. He wrote to Sammartano on 22 April that he wanted a bilingual text printed in Chinese and Latin. How he reasonably expected such a book to be printed by a regime facing bombings and shortages is not clear. In the same letter he states that he and the ministry officials could clear up the confusion at their next meeting. He also announced that the translation of *Jefferson and/or Mussolini*, begun in early April, was almost ready and inquired if the proposed second series of books was to be only in Italian or in English also. Around this time Sammartano requested that Pound do an economic history of the United States and further notified him that he had consulted a Professor Soiti Nogami of the Japanese Embassy about Pound's proposal for an Italian edition of the two Noh plays. He asked Pound to forward the texts for consideration.

Pound launched himself into his new project, the second series of English-language books, with characteristic enthusiasm. In a "Service Note" of 29 April, he clarifies that the immediate purpose of his publishing proposal was to educate American and English prisoners by means of material that no one could call Axis propaganda since the books were by American and English authors and written before the war. The list included Brooks Adams's *The Law of Civilization and Decay* and *The New Empire;* Arthur Kitson's *The Bankers' Conspiracy;* Wyndham Lewis's *The Apes of God;* E. E. Cummings's *Eimi;* Christopher Hollis's *The Two Nations;* Montgomery Butchart's *Money;* Willis Overholser's *History of Money in the U.S.A.;* Pound's *Jefferson and/or Mussolini* and *LXXI Cantos* ("because they contain history in a much more condensed form than prose, especially cantos LII/LXXI, the economic history of China, 52/61, the Life of John Adams 62/71" [tr]); W. E. Woodward's *A New History of the United States;* Martin Van Buren's *Autobiography;* Claude Bowers's *The Tragic Era, Jefferson and Hamilton,* and *Jefferson in Power;* and others. This, then, was Pound's ideal list, to give what he considered a necessary historical background for his views. His suggestions are clearly idealistic, but the fact that he felt comfortable in making them and had serious hopes that they would be adopted gives some credence to his later claims that he was not passively following orders from the Italian government but was engaged in pursuing his own intellectual program. His hopes, however, were quickly cut short by Sammartano, who in a letter of 3 May stated "for the moment the publication of volumes in a language other than Italian can't be foreseen" (tr).

Pound evidently continued to be involved in Italian radio propaganda, at that time controlled by the Germans. According to Heymann, Pound and Giacomo Barnes wrote two or three items a week and sent them to Milan, an arrangement that lasted until April 1945. Heymann quotes a certain Tamburini, general director of Milan Radio, who stated that Pound was involved "in particular with a program called 'Jerry's Front Calling'" and "was receiving a monthly check from the Italian Ministry of Popular Culture."[20] I have run across no evidence to contradict this claim, and it appears plausible. In a letter of 12 May 1944, Giorgio Almirante suggested that Pound consider moving to Milan, the center of radio propaganda, so as to help strengthen the broadcasts to North America (fbi). Pound responded on 16 May with a counterproposal. Instead of moving to Milan, which he said would interrupt his work on two manuscripts for Sammartano, he suggested an arrangement similar to that which he had used before in Rome, namely, that he would travel to Milan in a truck for two or three weeks at a time and then return to Rapallo. He said: "The only value which my voice would have would be conviction, and that comes from within. That is I must believe not only in what I say, but also in the opportunity of saying it at the proper moment." He had additional concerns about his health. He complained that he needed "a certain amount of rest which to you may seem abnormal"[21] and that it was "a question of porter service since I can no longer pick up heavy suitcases." Despite these concerns, he stated that "as soon as I am convinced that I must go before the microphone I will find the means, at least I will try to find the means to get there" (fbi) (tr).

On 13 May 1944, he wrote to Cabella on a familiar theme, bemoaning the lack of an intellectual center for the republic. He cited a few interesting articles he had recently read but maintained that the lack of a good biweekly was handicapping the intellectual life of the country. The first important step, Pound said, was "to have the writers TOGETHER/ FIRST/ then to put out the magazine." He offered to start a series of

---

[20] Heymann, 150.

[21] It is possible that Pound was suffering from early symptoms of the depression that would cripple him in later years, though this is just conjecture. There were severe food shortages in Italy at this time, and Pound and his dependents suffered the effects of a near famine with the majority of Italians. A petition circulated on his behalf after the war indicated that he enjoyed no special privileges as a result of his connections to fascist officialdom.

installments on "Why Sir Oswald Mosley went to prison" (tr) (Mosley
was the leader of the British fascists). On the verso of the carbon of the
letter he started a draft of the first article:

> Debts of India to the city of London, interest paid in cotton cloth at a
> good price: ruin of Manchester! (note: the cotton mills in England)
>   Debts of South America to the city of London, interest paid in canned
> and frozen meat: ruin of cattle raising in England. Mosley, speech at
> Lewisham 1938.

Pound had always left gaps in his text, requiring the reader to make a
special effort to fill them. These gaps grew especially pronounced during
this period, leading one to believe that he had completely lost touch with
his audience. In a letter to Mezzasoma of 27 February 1944, we see another
example of this: "Many do not know that the importation from Egypt
of wheat at a good market price ruined Italian agriculture of the old
Roman Empire. Thus they are anti-fascists and at least indifferent to
autarchy" (fbi) (tr). Pound is referring to how the failure of an industry
to achieve independence from ruinous foreign competition (autarchy)
can contribute to the collapse of a nation's economy.

Pound had written about founding newspapers or a journal before.
For example, in a letter to Mezzasoma dated 6 March, he suggested that
each different locality have its own newspaper, and he had complained
about the usual subjects: the paucity of good Italian writers, the need for
control and responsibility on the part of the press, and the need for
effective propaganda. He seemed unaware of how difficult this project
would have been. But apparently he was having some success with his
publishing program, unlikely as that might seem. On 15 May, Sammartano wrote to Pound that the typescript of the *Testamento di Confucio*
had been sent to the Vallecchi Publishing Company in Florence, adding
that Pound's additions had been received and were also sent to Vallecchi.
The manuscript would be lost when Florence fell to the advancing Allied
armies on 22 August. On 23 May, Sammartano wrote again to say that
he had been informed by the director of the Barbera Publishing Company
that the book of Brooks Adams (which one was not stated, though
perhaps it is *The Law of Civilization and Decay*) had been translated into
Italian and would be published as soon as possible.

The Pounds had been moved out of their apartment at the Albergo
Rapallo; for reasons of defense all foreigners were forbidden to live on
the coast. They moved their possessions up the steep hill to Olga Rudge's
house, where they remained for the duration of the war. Pound wrote
to Sammartano on 28 May advising him of the move and his new address:
Casa 60, Sant'Ambrogio Rapallo. He added that he hoped to send his
"Introduction to the Economic Nature of the United States," which

Sammartano had requested, "by this post" (tr). On 5 June, Sammartano wrote to him to say that the minister had approved its publication. Continuing work on his series, Pound had also written to Ubaldo degli Uberti, who, along with A. Pais, was editor of *Marina Repubblicana* (literally, "Republican Navy," a newspaper for sailors of the Republic of Salò published by the Naval Ministry). Degli Uberti's new office was at the Ministry of the Armed Forces, Under-Secretary of State for the Navy, and his title was director of Press Liaison. Pound wrote to ask about the translation of Overholser's *History of Money in the U.S.A.* that degli Uberti had done earlier. Ub², as Pound liked to call him, promised that he would try to find a copy of the typescript and send it on.

Pound's publishing campaign had probably reached its zenith when he received the following letter, dated 22 June, from Sammartano:

> The booklet by Stalin on Leninism has also arrived; it is a very important work and should be known by all political, journalistic, etc., directors.
> My idea would be to publish it in a limited edition to distribute to select people, but naturally I must listen to what the Minister thinks. (tr)

One can imagine what the minister might have thought, and said, to Sammartano! That the fascist government of the Republic of Salò would even consider this project, for whatever reason, is certainly a tribute to Pound's powers of persuasion. It also backs up his repeated claim that he never felt anything but complete intellectual freedom in fascist Italy (and that the new republic had left-wing tendencies, at least on paper).

Pound continued to press for his series of English-language books "for the instruction of everyone, Italians, English, and American prisoners of war and whomever," as he wrote to Sammartano on 29 June. During this time he was working to translate a manuscript on economics by J. P. Angold, a young British poet and economist who had been killed on active service with the Royal Air Force in 1943.[22] He said that "it greatly interested him" and told Sammartano that "it would serve to balance, or as a counterweight to Stalin" (tr). In July Sammartano sent Pound's newly translated *Jefferson and/or Mussolini* to Salò for ministerial approval.

Pound's concerns at that time were not limited to publishing and propaganda. A letter to Mezzasoma on 14 September deserves review:

> My dear Minister:
>   You will have to excuse me if I write to you occasionally about matters not directly under your jurisdiction. . . . In Rapallo the main plaza has been devastated by bombs, although several of the arches

---

[22] Stock, 476.

dating back to the fourteenth century were undamaged. It now seems that "the genius" of Genoa has ordered them torn down, probably with good intentions, but. . . .

The Riviera has already lost much and we do not want the plaza at Rapallo to be among the treasures lost. These old arches resisted the bombing raid and several of them are works of art.

There is one arch in particular with a side panel that was conserved and restored with loving care by the late Luigi Monti, a friend of d'Annunzio . . . that served as a memorial to him and as a remembrance of the reawakening of ceramics (Ars Umbria).

Perhaps you can put this letter in the hands of someone who can halt the destruction. The city is so completely abandoned that I don't know who recognizes me these days.

Finally, if someone were willing, they would also do well to bring a little cement and calcimine to help the people in these mountains make cisterns so that they can go on a bit longer. The main problem in these hills is the lack of water; the evacuees (myself included) drink up what little there is left. (fbi) (tr)

Pound's concerns for art are well known. When he later read in the Italian newspapers about the destruction of Alberti's and Sigismundo's Tempio in Rimini (an exaggeration, it turned out), he reacted with some of his angriest poetry, Cantos LXXII and LXXIII. But this letter also gives us a glimpse into conditions in Rapallo at that time ("so that they can go on a bit longer" is not the phrase a man with any illusions about victory would write) and Pound's practical concern for his neighbors.

By September, the war had moved much closer to Rapallo. Pisa, Lucca, and Pistoia were all liberated by Allied and royal Italian forces. Liguria, the region around Genoa, was practically cut off from the rest of the northern Italian republic, and the postal service was functioning in an irregular manner. On 27 September, Pound sent Sammartano a second book of Confucius in translation, "26 chapters adapted to the moment."

I believe to have worked well and to have produced a work for the honor of the REPUBLIC, showing that conditions and contingencies permit a philosophical work, etc. I believe that it is better done than the first (Studio Integrale, Testamento). I am convinced that it is superior, more precise, and that truly it has penetrated the meaning of the argument. . . .

It must go into the schools. We have need of ethical instruction IN THE schools, not anti-Catholic, perhaps not even anti-clerical, but free of all polemics. (tr)

His reference to the conditions under which he was working show a clear awareness of the real military situation; his distinction "not anti-Catholic, perhaps not even anti-clerical," demonstrates a subtle understanding of modern Italian history (in Italy, since the Risorgimento, people frequently are anticlerical but still Catholic). His Confucian studies and his pride that his understanding of classical Chinese was becoming ever more precise undoubtedly provided solace for Pound during a difficult time. This impression is reinforced by a letter he wrote to the minister of Popular Culture, with a copy of the above, on the same day:

> I'll write you on other topics when I know that my letters continue to arrive.
>
> Isolation is very instructive. But Liguria must not remain too isolated because not everyone can grasp a millennial text to reinforce their morale. (tr)

The situation in the Republic of Salò was very rapidly deteriorating.

On 28 September, Pound wrote to Sammartano saying that he had sent him *L'Asse Che Non Vacilla* on the previous day. He was still working on a translation of Angold's *Economy of Tyranny* and had decided to give it the title *Il Ruolo del Finanziere* (The role of the financier). Discussing that work in a letter to degli Uberti of 16 October, Pound said that it showed that the agricultural community as a whole can never be in debt – more evidence against the usocracy.

He persevered in his cultural concerns. In a letter to Mezzasoma of 3 October, after discussing several Italian critics whom Pound found worthwhile, he turned his attention to his previous proposals to use microphotography to preserve important literary and musical materials from wartime damage.

> Among the most glorious proposals of Fascism in this field was the monumental edition of Vivaldi on the scale of imperial [i.e., of Vittorio Emanuele] expenses. I do not know if it would be apropos for the Republic, but the intellectual part could be continued. I do not know if a more modest edition would interest you nor if it is necessary to reduce further expenses.
>
> But there is publicity value in an announcement that the work continues. A skilled photographer could be found to ensure conservation. . . .
>
> I do not know if you have ever discovered the reason for the sabotage I have always met with for the past five years on the question of microphotography; this has always been enveloped in mystery. . . .
>
> In other words, a nonpolitical activity, but one which indicates the seriousness of our cultural directives. (fbi) (tr)

In the meantime, the military situation had grown even worse. His manuscript of *Orientamenti* had been sent by Sammartano to Vallecchi Publishing Company in Florence in July. On 28 September Pound wrote to him to see if it had been saved from the advancing troops. On 16 October, Pound wrote to Ubaldo degli Uberti about the manuscript and about some broader concerns:

In this moment nothing matters except for the military fact. And it is difficult to simplify my motives for wanting a national force for supernational reasons. Or rather blocks MUST persist strong enough to resist the international usocracy. In America, "States Rights" against the central bank, etc. . . .

I. Necessity of military action, without which we writers remain vain academics speaking in the void.

II. Necessity not only for Italy but for Europe and for the world, that strong organisms persist, strong enough to resist usury, usocracy without homeland and without justice, against international fraud.

3. The fight between economists delineates itself as between TWO parties, that is, those who want honest bookkeeping and those who maintain a counterfeit bookkeeping.

The rest is a technical question.

It is abundantly clear from this letter that Pound saw military defeat for Italy as a matter only of time. His concern, which will be more in evidence later on, was beginning to focus on building for the world after the war. He was not giving up his fight for economic justice, but he had started to prepare for what he would later call the millennial war.

VIII

On 20 October 1944, Pound wrote to Sammartano, enlisting the minister's help in contacting his daughter. He asked that a copy of his "Introduction to the Economic Nature of the United States" be sent to Maria Rudge at Cortina d'Ampezzo because "it seems that she remains without any news of me for a long time, and I would like her to know that I am still alive. Perhaps the mail will still work from Venice" (tr).

As mentioned before, Pound apparently continued some kind of collaboration with radio propaganda during this time, though details of it are very difficult to obtain. One of the few clues I have found is in a 27 October letter to Sammartano: "I'm sending with this a note for the radio, Ministry Office in Milan, but I don't know what they're doing. I don't listen to the short wave. 'Jerry's Front' continues, but it doesn't broadcast speeches" (tr). Unfortunately this is very cryptic. Apparently he sent some material to Sammartano for forwarding because of the poor state of mail service between Rapallo and Milan.

Conditions in Italy continued to worsen. For some reason, his new edition of Confucius could not get to press. On 2 November 1944, Pound wrote to Villari, exaggerating its value to get his work into print: "I regret that the most important thing I've done in my life has arrived at an inopportune moment, BUT" (tr). He went on to suggest the possibility of mimeographing one hundred copies. Pound also wrote to degli

Uberti on the same day: "The value of philosophy (or of a philosophy) is that it reinforces courage. Confucius is the stuff to take in the trenches." He went on to complain that the Ministry of Cultural Exchange received the manuscript of *L'Asse Che Non Vacilla* right at the moment when they suspended work. Pound's carbon copy of his letter to degli Uberti is on the reverse side of his copy of the letter to Villari, a sign of the severe paper shortage.

Pound also wrote on behalf of his edition of Confucius to Sammartano, on 11 November. He begged that at least a few hundred copies of it be printed, on any available paper, "waste paper, toilet paper, newsprint, or any other kind of paper." He said, "In this text there is a force that has nothing to do with my personality," and he added "a philosophy has value inasmuch as it leads to heroism" (tr). As Donald Gallup relates, the book was finally published (in February 1945), but because the title referred to the Italian word for Axis, most of the copies were destroyed by the Allied armies.[23]

Pound wrote to Mezzasoma on 13 November, sending some poetry and offering the possibility of a second Tigullian manifesto. But his primary concern in the letter was his plan for an edition of Vivaldi. Although there is no doubting his sincere interest in the project, the memo might be interpreted as further evidence of financial hardship, an attempt to secure work for Olga Rudge, who would naturally be expected to continue her involvement. Pound stated: "It must be done with the greatest respect for all former collaborators," and he further advised:

> INTELLECTUAL and MUSICAL interest does not require a monumental edition. For the musicologist a microphotographic edition would be sufficient. No real philologist would be happy with a summarized edition. Luciani understands this and the edition of the academy [Chigiana] had already covered the ground, that is, that a reproduction of every page of the manuscript would be an integral part of the monumental edition. (fbi) (tr)

Olga Rudge had already done extensive work on the Vivaldi edition, compiling a catalog for the Accademia Musicale Chigiana in Siena. This revelation of some of the other facets of Pound's work for the Republic of Salò helps to modify the prevailing view of his role as fascist propagandist. In fact, Pound was very adept at using the military situation to advance his enduring cultural interests and activities, often by appealing to the pride of the regime. One of the characteristic arguments that he used with fascist officials to promote publication of a work was that it would demonstrate that cultural life not only was continuing as

[23] Gallup, 74.

normal during the war but was in fact prospering under the new fascist republic.

Another letter from Pound to Mezzasoma on 18 November contains an announcement that Pound suggested for the Republican radio and a rather lengthy explanation of the reasons behind it.

> We had an armistice for the rebels and the partisans; I asked a similar measure for the refugees and those who for lack of political preparation, ignorance of history, incomprehension of the digression of the Fascist revolution in the historic process (also for weakness due to this incomprehension) have not yet joined the ranks and are waiting because they absolutely do not know what to do.
>
> Would it not be possible for the Ministry to launch an appeal through the press and through the radio more or less according to the following:
>
> "Those who have lack of history and cultural preparation, having aesthetic education but not a political economic one; in other words, all men of good will who have a small degree of culture and those who formerly opposed the errors of the regime (without being able to agree because of two or three of these errors), those who opposed the hidden treachery and the sabotage that was carried on even before the year XXI (for example, censorship not decreed by the government but that masqueraded and pretended to be official), those who have learned something of this treachery and of the chaos that followed it, are invited to bridge the gaps of their political culture." (tr)

There is a poignancy to this appeal, but it is difficult to imagine to whom Pound thought he was appealing and who would answer this kind of appeal during those terrible months, demonstrating that he was also out of touch with his Italian audience. Certainly it represents a return on Pound's part to his former faith in the good will of those who are fully educated. But the proposed announcement becomes even more difficult to understand when one sees from the context of the letter just what Pound had in mind. He explains that because defense and nourishment were the first priorities, the appeal was to be directed to people sixty years or older, invalids, or those in occupied territory. These people were to be invited to further their knowledge of economics through the study of foreign authors, whom Pound names in the letter (the usual group), and by translating and summarizing them. He continues:

> All scholars isolated in invaded territory as well as in the Republic are invited to reread the Greek and Latin classics so as to find therein the reason the enemy wants to suppress or diminish the studies of the sources of our culture and our political wisdom, which is our most precious heritage. (tr)

Although this appeal is puzzling, it contains within it a strong element of pathos. That Pound, himself approaching sixty, should issue this call for a renewed study of the classical tradition should be seen, I think, as more than a propaganda ploy and more than his usual tactic of giving his readers an assigned list of readings. I think it represents a genuine question on his part as to how the events he was witnessing had happened, how they could have been avoided, and how they could be prevented from happening again. And it represents his firmest belief and most unshakable faith: the ability of that pile of books to give the answers.

What he wanted was an appeal to "those who could do something useful for the future of Italy." He suggested reprinting sections I and III of the Tigullian manifesto from the year before, omitting II and IV. The letter, which is very long, is filled with other suggestions and other of Pound's concerns. Several impressions stand out. He had not lost his faith in the power of education; he had given up hope for averting a military defeat of Italy; and he was completely out of touch with any possible audience for his propaganda.

Another letter to Mezzasoma, sent on 28 November, contains Pound's perception of the major mistakes of the fascist regime:

> There were two errors: lack of *habeas corpus* (few cases, but enough to serve as a scandal and the fulcrum of enemy propaganda), lack of importation of real books from abroad, together with the suppression, more vaunted and publicized than was the case, of free discussion. (fbi) (tr)

It seems, then, that Pound had been disturbed by the curtailing of individual liberty that the fascist government enforced, or perhaps he had become more aware of its actuality. He added a prescription for the immediate future: "The Americans are beasts but they are not cowards. It is best to strike the ethical line: 'Americans MUST NOT be here destroying Europe/ they can't be useful this way, neither to Europe nor to themselves' " (fbi) (tr). Finally, he talked about his hopes for the future, centered on a worldwide monetary system and the kind of socialism advocated by the Republic of Salò in its Verona Program:

> We agree wholeheartedly that nationalization [of basic industries] must not be sabotaged. But for purposes of propaganda, we must also think of presenting nationalization to the nonsocialists. In nationalization I see a basis, perhaps the only basis, on which we can construct a worldwide monetary system that is honest and an accounting system that is not falsified. This is the angle I would present to the nonsocialists. For twenty years the Italians have ignored, and have abstained from helping with useful publicity, the antiusury movements in other countries. The agreement between Mosley and the Social Creditors arose from this knowledge, that is, that fascism was the only movement, the only party of action, capable of putting into effect monetary justice. (It does not

matter one damn bit what form of monetary justice; what does matter
is the DIRECTION OF THE WILL). (fbi) (tr)

Two points should be highlighted from this letter. The first is that Pound
belonged ideologically to the left wing of the fascist party, as we have
stated, and was sympathetic to those parts of the fascist agenda that called
for spending on public welfare and national control of basic industries
and economic programs. The second is that Pound believed fascism was
the political movement best capable of putting into action the monetary
reforms he envisioned as necessary to a just society. There is also regret
in the statement about opportunities missed, combined with an awareness
that the struggle would have to continue into the postwar world. Finally,
there is the characteristic Poundian naiveté: the action does not matter;
all that matters is the purity of intent. All told, this is as concise a
statement as exists for the reasons behind Pound's involvement with
fascism.

IX

Evidence of the further collapse of the situation in northern Italy
abounds in letters from this time. On 14 December 1944, Pound wrote
to Giacchino Nicoletti: "*Popolo di Alessandria* in confusion. I don't have
an outlet. Presses stopped" (tr). He then went on with a lengthy criticism
about what went wrong with the system of *ammassi*, and what to do
about it. The *ammassi* was a government program for pooling food and
other resources so they could be accounted for and rationed. It also served
to protect farmers from price fluctuation. He had made the same point
earlier in the year, in his 27 February letter to Mezzasoma:

> To make the system of *ammassi* function (after intentional sabotage), in
> order to return to the solid idea there was in enacting the *ammassi*, it is
> necessary to remember they existed to guarantee a price for the pro-
> ducers, to protect them from speculators. If we were to take a census
> knowing (and one would know perfectly) how much each person could
> produce normally, asking for the *ammassi* 80% (or some other percent)
> of the estimated production, but leaving the peasant all he produces
> over and above the estimated normal quantity (100%).
>
> He will remain happy with this and it would stimulate his production
> in his own interest and it would serve as a useful incentive for the
> *ammassi*.
>
> All of this would be controlled openly, no persecution, etc.
>
> The idea is spontaneous among various sensible people. Enforcement
> of the law comes from the consent of the people. (fbi) (tr)

The last sentence is not exactly a fascist slogan; at the end, Pound seemed
to place more emphasis on the democratic values of his native land. Pound

apparently thought of himself as somewhat of an expert on agriculture or perhaps just a good citizen trying to be helpful. The problems with the *ammassi* increased as the war brought famine; additionally, there were the cumulative effects of corruption in the accounting for goods expected and received. To Nicoletti, who was attached to the Ministry of Popular Culture in Salò, Pound made the further point that his system rewarded industry and hard work, whereas the system in force encouraged laziness and cheating.

In a letter of 22 December to Sammartano, Pound proposed a bi-monthly or monthly newsletter where "the hundred, or fifty, of the intelligentsia who work for the republic... could speak of the things that each one believed important" (tr). On the verso of this is a fragment labeled "159/ Pound anonymous 2 Dec XXIII [1944] Notes to refer also to Barnes." Two of these notes, apparently destined for use in radio propaganda, contain some of Pound's most virulent anti-Semitism.

> 3. U.S. will be left holding the baby/ when England slops out. And the U.S. betrayed. In short. I should aim/ and keep mentioning Lehman/ if not straight anti-semite; at least vs. all jews participating in plot to starve the world. They are not all in it with the same degree of present consciousness. And that form of the phrase will go farther and give appearance of loophole for the decent sheeny/ at any rate it don't excite instant pity for the beamish chewpoye. Beside the sephardim don't like the tartar yidds/ they prefer the goy as table companion/ nacherly. . . .
>
> 5. "Never bump off a chew unless he owns two million dollars." Oh well WHY NOT? Never mind why, *start* at the TOP.
>
> Merry Xmas.

This gives enough of an idea about this aspect of his radio propaganda that it is probably a blessing that very little else has been recovered from the Salò period. The conscious rhetorical intent represented by his observation that the sentence "They are not all in it with the same degree of present consciousness" would "give appearance of loophole" and not "excite instant pity" can leave little doubt as to Pound's full support for the regime's anti-Semitic propaganda, giving only a nod to his previous misgivings about harming "the small jew." These notes, with the exception of one or two words in Italian, were written by Pound in English, apparently anonymously, and for broadcast by Barnes.

Pound wrote to Mezzasoma on 26 December, evidently enclosing a rough draft of the second Tigullian manifesto with his letter. A page entitled "From the Tigullio" is filed with the letter in the Department of Justice records, and the two contain one phrase in common: "Ethics: Live in such a manner that your children and your descendants will thank you" (tr). Pound was attempting to think of slogans to boost the morale of the Italian people.

In a "service note" to Sammartano dated 30 December, Pound suggests a series of articles:

> More up to date would be the series of articles by Henry Ford published in the *Dearborn Independent*. Ford subsequently had to repudiate them under pressure, threats, etc./ the volume was reprinted in Paris in 1931. I don't know if they were ever reprinted in Italy? (tr)

He closed the note "Happy New Year April in ROME." The articles by Henry Ford were, I assume, the anti-Semitic writings, intended by Pound to serve as further support for the regime's anti-Semitic propaganda.

X

Pound's Italian Cantos, LXXII and LXXIII, begin to be mentioned at this time. He enclosed the opening of LXXII with his letter to Mezzasoma of 26 December, and they are mentioned by Ubaldo degli Uberti, to whom Pound sent part of them, under the title "Presenza." They are among the most violent of his cantos. The fact that he composed them in Italian may have been due partly to disgust with some of the actions of the Allied armies that he was reading about, such as the bombing of his beloved Tempio in Rimini, the destruction of which is mentioned in Canto LXXII, and also to the fact that these cantos were intended for publication in degli Uberti's *Marina Repubblicana*. In Canto LXXII we read: "In the beginning, God . . . Shat the great usurer Satan-Geryon, prototype of Churchill's bosses."[24] The ghost of Filippo Tommaso Marinetti appears to Pound, asking for his body so that he can continue to fight. Pound refuses, explaining that he needs his body himself to continue to fight, in his poetry, "the eternal war between light and mud"[25] (tr). In a Dantesque scene, ghosts of warriors and poets appear to Pound, urging heroism.

Canto LXXIII continues along the same line, with the ghost of Cavalcanti appearing to Pound: "I am that Guido whom you loved / for my lofty spirit / and the clarity of my intellect"[26] (tr). Again, the destruction of the Tempio is mentioned, as Guido recounts the story of a heroic Italian girl who died leading a group of Canadian soldiers onto a minefield whose holes had been dug by her brother. Twenty of the Canadians also died. The canto concludes celebrating the heroism of the girl and her sacrifice for the fatherland: "In the north the fatherland is reborn, / Oh

[24] Pound, *I Cantos*, 826.
[25] Ibid., 827.
[26] Ibid., 832.

what a girl, what girls, what boys, who wear the Black [the Fascist color]!"[27] (tr).

Considering for what a long period these cantos were suppressed, their appearance in 1985 came as an anticlimax. There is nothing either particularly shocking or particularly successful about them. They represent a competent attempt to pay homage to Dante and Cavalcanti, and they celebrate the heroism of dying to defend one's country, completely the opposite of Pound's anti-war lines in "Hugh Selwyn Mauberley." In their exhortation to heroic action, they echo a theme that repeats throughout centuries of Italian poetry, the need to reclaim the glories of the Italian past. But one learns very little from them, except how upset Pound was at the reported destruction of Alberti's (and Sigismundo's) Tempio, the first monument of Renaissance architecture.

Pound's Italian correspondents were obviously in a quandary about how to respond to these cantos. Degli Uberti complained that the cantos were too sophisticated for sailors, though he did publish them in part in *Marina Repubblicana*. Pound sent Canto LXXIII to Cabella, with two corrections added, on 9 January 1945. He also sent them to Mezzasoma, who replied in a letter of 15 January:

> I read your verses on the death of Marinetti with a great deal of interest, but as they are, they do not seem to me adaptable for publication, because a large part of the readership would not appreciate them or accord them their proper value. On the other hand, to correct them would be to spoil them completely. In any event, I wish to express to you my compliments for the lofty sentiments expressed in them. (tr)

In the same letter, Mezzasoma commented favorably on the rough draft of the Tigullian manifesto that Pound had sent on 26 December and announced the formation of the new review, to be called *New Anthology*, that Pound had pressed for in his letters.

One final point about Cantos LXXII and LXXIII deserves attention. In his essay on Henry James, published in August of 1918, Pound had this to say:

> *The Times* says: "The Americans will understand his changing his nationality", or something of that sort. The "Americans" will understand nothing whatsoever about it. They have understood nothing about it. They do not even know what they lost. They have not stopped for eight minutes to consider the meaning of his last public act. . . .
>
> America has not yet realized that never in history had one of her great men abandoned his citizenship out of shame. It was the last act – the last thing left.[28]

---

[27] Ibid., 835. Lawrence Rainey has located the source of that episode in a front-page story in *Corriere della Sera*, 1 Oct. 1944.

[28] Pound, "Henry James" (Aug. 1918), in *Literary Essays*, 295 and 297.

Pound never abandoned his American citizenship. But the act of a poet abandoning his native language in the middle of his epic must have resonance, especially considering his comments above, beyond his merely trying to get yet another piece published in the Italian press. It emphasizes the depth, and sincerity, of his emotion.

Pound's rage increasingly found an outlet in attacks against Jews, and his anti-Semitism at this time is expressed frequently. Consider these anonymous notes, sent in a letter to Cabella of 26 January 1945 for publication in *Il Popolo di Alessandria:* "DIFFERENCE. It is not for nothing that the Gospel is written in popular Greek, and NOT in the Jewish language." And:

> NOTEWORTHY SEVERITY. In the Classical Dictionary of Lempriere... we read that the Emperor Trajan *"was unusually* severe with the Jews who had barbarically assassinated two hundred thousand (200,000) of his subjects and also ate the flesh of the dead."
>
> One sees that this war between Rome and "the wicked" has already lasted quite some time. And before the so-called old bolshevism the ka'aal, that is the Jewish center had already betrayed the Hebrew nation, selling the Maccabees to the Roman Empire. This one calls "style." *Le style c'est le juif.* Or rather: the betrayal begins there. (tr)

Undoubtedly part of the motivation for this kind of writing came from his editors, who were eager to please their German bosses (though *Il Popolo di Alessandria* maintained some independence from German control).

He wrote again to Mezzasoma on 29 January 1945, renewing his suggestion for radio propaganda directed to former fascist intellectuals who had lost faith in fascism seeing the corruption of the previous (pre-Salò) regime. Pound wanted to exhort them either to come into the territory of the republic (a naive request) or to work at home preparing summaries or translations of works he would choose. He continued to have confidence in his Confucian studies. Mentioning that two quotations from Woodward and a page of his "Confucius Speaks" had just appeared in *Marina Repubblicana,* Pound closed by saying:

> I am absolutely convinced that in bringing to Italy a greater knowledge of the heroic doctrine of Confucius, I will bring you a gift of greater service than the Platonism that Gemisto brought you in the 14th century, which rendered you so great a service in stimulating the Renaissance. (fbi) (tr)

In the last months of the war, Pound repeated many of the key ideas found in his previous fifteen years' work. On 5 February 1945, he wrote again to Mezzasoma, this time about economics. In the letter he reiterated that any progress toward social justice would be like the labor of Sisyphus as long as there was tolerance for "a gray zone called MONEY or FI-NANCE where the rapport between WORK and the buying power of those who work becomes systematically falsified" (fbi) (tr). He went on to say that for fifteen years he had attempted to make intellectuals understand the convergence of Mussolini's politics with the best monetary-economic thought, which he summarized as being that no private corporation should benefit from national debt.

Things were in considerable disarray during the final months. Pound wrote to Villari on 13 February, complaining that he had not yet received copies of either *Orientamenti* or *Jefferson and/or Mussolini*. He was trying to get the Italian government to reprint Cairoli's *Il Giusto Prezzo nel Medioevale* (The just price in the Middle Ages), a work about medieval church doctrine on economics, but the officials were not responding. Villari was at the Ministry for Cultural Exchange and had written on 15 January to inform Pound that his Confucian work *L'Asse Che Non Vacilla* had been delivered to the printer. Mail was very irregular by then, and Pound did not receive the news until almost a month later.

On 15 and 16 February, Pound sent a service note and a letter to Mezzasoma, complaining that of the ninety-two books listed in the pamphlet "Il Popolo Italiano Non Ha Capitolato" (The Italian people have not surrendered), he had not seen any available. From there he launched into a list of things to be done in order to ensure better distribution of material and better publicity for books when they were printed. In the letter he amplified these points, stating that "the Jews and the bolsheviks were more intelligent in the matter of bookstores." He went on to say:

> In America the Jews not only have invaded the publications and the bookstores of the large cities but now every little county college has its bookstore and in many cases it is Jewish. Of "the left."
> I remind you of the student at Cambridge who wrote me: Two careers open to a young man of letters: bolshevism and sodomy. (fbi) (tr)

During a time when most people expected the imminent defeat of the Axis, Pound continued with his labors, again, not the activity of a man with any lack of sincerity.

A letter from Ubaldo degli Uberti got through about that time saying that Cantos LXXII and LXXIII had been published in *Marina Repubblicana* but that their distribution would be a bit sparse, owing to the difficult circumstances. Letters, when they arrived at all, were taking from two to six weeks, instead of the previous two to three days. On 4 April, Sammartano wrote to Pound that his office was soon being transferred to Milan and that ninety-nine out of every hundred items Pound submitted would be published – he no longer had to bother making proposals beforehand. This reassurance might suggest that Pound was one of the last writers submitting material to the fascist government.

The last letter I have found from the war period is dated 18 April and is from Pound to Sammartano. Pound continued the ideological fight and made this suggestion:

> It seems to me that we could adopt many books published in America by the bolsheviks (to show that Italy and Germany arrive more quickly at the *destination*. All of Marx a protest against the exploitation of the workers). . . .
>
> But all this bolshevik material must be considered in relation to a total program. We should publish it with a specific aim and scope. Taking side with the part that coincides with the present direction of the Republic.
>
> In Paris, thirteen years ago by now, when I asked Barkov: What is the difference between bolshevism and fascism? He found nothing else to say except: that's up to them. (tr)

Pound had written to Mezzasoma on 28 March: "I am still, in some senses, to the left of the Verona manifesto" (tr). This late attempt at a rapprochement with Marxism is not surprising from Pound, who had always had sympathy for Marx and Lenin, nor is it surprising for the Republic of Salò, which had attempted to reclaim some of the socialist roots of fascism. It is difficult to imagine, though, what possible effect Pound thought it would have. Presumably, as always before, he wanted to educate people about the underlying causes of war.

His idea was to be put into practice through the publication of a new series of books, consisting of the following: "1. Upton Sinclair: Letters to Judd. 2. Lenin: The Teachings of Karl Marx. 3. Lenin: Imperialism. 4. Stalin: Leninism. 5. Stalin: Response to American Union Members. 6. Karl Marx: The England That We Fight (Chapter X of Kapital)," as well as works by Kitson, Overholser, Gesell, and Douglas. He proposed to call the series "Library of Political Culture, 2nd Series, Parties of the Opposition" (tr). Certainly this was a remarkable proposal to come at that time (though there is no question about its sincerity), but, as noted, Pound may have been one of the last people to continue work for the Republic of Salò. By that time the Germans were in disorderly retreat and the Republican government had all but fallen. On the same day of this letter, Mussolini left Salò for Milan. The Allied army was approaching Bologna and the Russian army was close to Berlin. Mussolini was executed by Italian partisans on 28 April.

Kenner's account of Pound's final days of freedom is convincingly detailed. On 1 May, "Pound, formally dressed, went down from Sant'Ambrogio into the town to make his knowledge of modern Italy available."[29] The one GI whom he met did not know what he was talking about. Partisans with machine guns came to arrest Pound on 2 May. They took

> their prisoner to their HQ in Chiavari, where he was soon released as possessing no interest. He had then demanded to be taken to the Americans, and was driven to the U.S. command post in Lavagna to turn himself in.[30]

On 3 May 1945, Pound was taken into American custody.

[29] Kenner, *The Pound Era,* 470.
[30] Ibid., 471.

Selected Bibliography

Ackroyd, Peter. *T. S. Eliot: A Life.* New York: Simon and Schuster, 1984.

Aldcroft, Derek H. *From Versailles to Wall Street, 1919–1929.* Berkeley and Los Angeles: University of California Press, 1981.

Bacigalupo, Massimo. *The Formed Trace: The Later Poetry of Ezra Pound.* New York: Columbia University Press, 1980.

Bell, Ian, ed. *Ezra Pound: Tactics for Reading.* New York: Barnes and Noble, 1982.

Benjamin, Walter. "The Work of Art in the Age of Mechanical Reproduction." In *Illuminations,* edited by Hannah Arendt, 217–51. New York: Schocken Books, 1969.

Berezin, Charles. "Poetry and Politics in Ezra Pound." *Partisan Review* 48, no. 2 (1981): 262–79.

Bernstein, Eduard. *Evolutionary Socialism.* 1909. New York: Schocken Books, 1961.

Bilenchi, Romano. "Rapallo, 1941." Translated with notes and an introduction by David Anderson. *Paideuma* 8, no. 3 (Winter 1979): 430–42.

Blaug, Mark. *Economic Theory in Retrospect.* New York: Cambridge University Press, 1983.

Bromwich, David. "Comment: Without Admonition." In *Politics and Poetic Value,* edited by Robert von Hallberg, 323–30. Chicago: University of Chicago Press, 1987.

Cannistraro, Philip V., editor-in-chief. *Historical Dictionary of Fascist Italy.* Westport, Conn.: Greenwood Press, 1982.

Carpenter, Humphrey. *A Serious Character: The Life of Ezra Pound.* Boston: Houghton Mifflin, 1988.

Casillo, Robert. *The Genealogy of Demons.* Evanston, Ill.: Northwestern University Press, 1988.

Cassity, Turner. "He the Compeller." In *Politics and Poetic Value,* edited by Robert von Hallberg, 133–58. Chicago: University of Chicago Press, 1987.

Chace, William. *The Political Identities of Ezra Pound and T. S. Eliot.* Stanford, Calif.: Stanford University Press, 1973.

Chilanti, Felice. "Ezra Pound among the Seditious in the 1940's." Translated with notes and commentary by David Anderson. *Paideuma* 6, no. 2 (Fall 1977): 235–50.

Corrigan, Robert. "Literature and Politics: The Case of Ezra Pound Reconsidered." *Prospects* 2 (1976): 463–82.

Cowley, Malcolm. *Exile's Return.* New York: Penguin, 1978.

Coyle, Michael. " 'A Profounder Didacticism': Ruskin, Orage, and Pound's Reception of Social Credit." *Paideuma* 17, no. 1 (Spring 1988): 7–28.

Davenport, Guy. *Cities on Hills.* Ann Arbor, Mich.: UMI Research Press, 1983.

Davie, Donald. *Ezra Pound.* New York: Viking Press, 1975.

   Ezra Pound: Poet as Sculptor. New York: Oxford University Press, 1964.

Davis, Earle. *Vision Fugitive: Ezra Pound and Economics.* Lawrence, Kans.: University Press of Kansas, 1968.

Davis, Joseph S. *The World between the Wars, 1919–1939: An Economist's View.* Baltimore, Md.: Johns Hopkins University Press, 1975.

de Felice, Renzo. *Storia degli Ebrei Italiani sotto il Fascismo.* Turin: Giulio Einaudi, 1972.

de Rachewiltz, Mary. *Discretions.* Boston: Little, Brown and Company, 1971.

Des Pres, Terrence. *Praises and Dispraises: Poetry and Politics, the Twentieth Century.* New York: Viking, 1988.

Diggins, John P. *Mussolini and Fascism: The View from America.* Princeton, N.J.: Princeton University Press, 1972.

Douglas, C. H. *Credit Power and Democracy.* London: Cecil Palmer, 1920.

   Economic Democracy. New York: Harcourt, Brace, and Howe, 1920.

   Social Credit. Rev. ed. New York: W. W. Norton Co., 1933 (first printed 1924).

Emery, Clark. *Ideas into Action.* Coral Gables: University of Miami Press, 1958.

Epsey, John. *Ezra Pound's Mauberley.* Berkeley and Los Angeles: University of California Press, 1974.

Finlay, John L. *Social Credit: The English Origins.* Montreal: McGill–Queen's University Press, 1972.

Flory, Wendy Stallard. *The American Ezra Pound.* New Haven: Yale University Press, 1988.

   Ezra Pound and the Cantos: A Record of Struggle. New Haven: Yale University Press, 1980.

Friedman, Milton, and Schwartz, Anna Jacobson. *A Monetary History of the United States, 1867–1960.* Princeton, N.J.: Princeton University Press, 1971.

Fussell, Paul. *The Great War and Modern Memory.* New York: Oxford University Press, 1977.

Gallup, Donald. *Ezra Pound: A Bibliography.* Rev. ed. Charlottesville: University Press of Virginia, 1983.

Gay, Peter. *The Dilemma of Democratic Socialism: Eduard Bernstein's Challenge to Marx.* New York: Columbia University Press, 1952.

Gesell, Silvio. *The Natural Economic Order.* Translated by Philip Pye. Berlin: Neo-Verlag, 1929.

Goldensohn, Barry. "Pound and Antisemitism." *Yale Review* 75 (Spring 1986): 399–421.

Goldman, Francisco. "Poetry and Power in Nicaragua." *New York Times*. 29 March 1987, section 6, 50.

Gregor, A. James. *Italian Fascism and Developmental Dictatorship*. Princeton, N.J.: Princeton University Press, 1979.

   Young Mussolini and the Intellectual Origins of Fascism. Berkeley and Los Angeles: University of California Press, 1979.

Hardach, Gerd. *The First World War, 1914–1918*. Berkeley and Los Angeles: University of California Press, 1981.

Hatlen, Burton. "Ezra Pound and Fascism." In *Ezra Pound and History*, edited by Marianne Korn, 145–72. Orono, Maine: National Poetry Foundation.

Heilbroner, Robert L. *The Worldly Philosophers*. New York: Time, 1962.

Hesse, Eva. *Ezra Pound: Metodo e Follia*. Milan: Feltrinelli, 1983.

Heymann, C. David. *Ezra Pound: The Last Rower*. New York: Viking Press, 1976.

Hutchins, Patricia. *Ezra Pound's Kensington*. London, Faber & Faber, 1965.

Jameson, Fredric. *Fables of Aggression: Wyndham Lewis, the Modernist as Fascist*. Berkeley and Los Angeles: University of California Press, 1979.

Jones, Richard, ed. *Poetry and Politics*. New York: Quill, 1985.

Kayman, Martin A. *The Modernism of Ezra Pound: The Science of Poetry*. New York: St. Martin's Press, 1986.

Kenner, Hugh. *The Poetry of Ezra Pound*. Rev. ed. Lincoln, Nebr.: University of Nebraska Press, 1985.

   The Pound Era. Berkeley and Los Angeles: University of California Press, 1971.

Keynes, John Maynard. *The Economic Consequences of Mr. Churchill*. London: Hogarth Press, 1925.

   The General Theory of Employment, Interest, and Money. New York: Harvest, 1964.

Kindleberger, Charles P. *A Financial History of Western Europe*. London: George Allen & Unwin, 1984.

   The World in Depression, 1929–1939. Berkeley and Los Angeles: University of California Press, 1973.

Lauber, John. "Pound's *Cantos*: A Fascist Epic." *Journal of American Studies* 12 (1978): 3–21.

Laughlin, James. "Solving the Ezragrams: Pound at 100." *New York Times Book Review*. 11 November 1985.

Lindberg, Kathryne V. *Reading Pound Reading: Modernism after Nietzsche*. New York: Oxford University Press, 1987.

Little, Matthew. "Pound's Use of the Word *Totalitarian*." *Paideuma* 11, no. 1 (Spring and Summer 1982): 147–56.

McCraw, William. "Fascist of the Last Hour." *San Jose Studies* 12, no. 3 (Fall 1986): 46–57.

Mack Smith, Denis. *Mussolini*. New York: Alfred A. Knopf, 1982.

Mairet, Philip. *A. R. Orage*. London: J. M. Dent and Sons, 1936.

Martin, Wallace. *The New Age under Orage: Chapters in English Cultural History*. Manchester: Manchester University Press, 1967.

Marx, Karl. *Capital,* vol. 1. Translated by Samuel Moore and Edward Aveling from the third German edition. New York: International Publishers, 1967.

Michaelis, Meir. *Mussolini and the Jews.* New York: Oxford University Press, 1978.

Milward, Alan S. *War, Economy and Society, 1939–1945.* Berkeley and Los Angeles: University of California Press, 1979.

Morris, Herbert. *On Guilt and Innocence: Essays in Legal Philosophy and Moral Psychology.* Berkeley and Los Angeles: University of California Press, 1976.

Myers, Margaret G. *Monetary Proposals for Social Reform.* 1940. Reprint. New York: AMS Press, 1970.

Nicholls, Peter J. *Ezra Pound: Politics, Economics, and Writing.* London: Macmillan, 1984.

Norman, Charles. *The Case of Ezra Pound.* New York: The Bodley Press, 1948.

Ezra Pound. Rev. ed. New York: Minerva Press, 1969.

O'Brien, Conor Cruise. "Passion and Cunning: An Essay on the Politics of W. B. Yeats." In *In Excited Reverie: A Centenary Tribute to William Butler Yeats, 1865–1939,* edited by A. Norman Jeffares and K. G. W. Cross, 207–78. New York: Macmillan, 1965.

Orage, A. R. *An Alphabet of Economics.* London: T. Fisher Unwin, 1917.

Orwell, George. "Politics and the English Language." In *Shooting an Elephant,* 77–92. New York: Harcourt, Brace & World, 1950.

Parker, Andrew. "Ezra Pound and the 'Economy' of Anti-Semitism." *Boundary 2* 11, nos. 1–2 (Fall/Winter 1982/3): 103–28.

Pearlman, Daniel. "The Anti-Semitism of Ezra Pound." *Contemporary Literature* 22, no. 1 (Winter 1981): 104–15.

"Ezra Pound: America's Wandering Jew." *Paideuma* 9, no. 3 (Winter 1980): 461–80.

Perloff, Marjorie. "Fascism, Anti-Semitism, Isolationism: Contextualizing the 'Case of EP.' " *Paideuma* 16, no. 3 (Winter 1987): 7–21.

Pound, Ezra. *L'America, Roosevelt e le Cause della Guerra Presente.* Venice: Casa Editrice della Edizioni Popolari, 1944.

I Cantos. Milan: Arnaldo Mondadori, 1985.

The Cantos of Ezra Pound. New York: New Directions, 1986.

Ezra Pound Speaking: Radio Speeches of World War II. Edited by Leonard Doob. Westport, Conn.: Greenwood Press, 1978.

Guide to Kulchur. 1938. Reprint. New York: New Directions, 1970.

Jefferson and/or Mussolini. 1935. Reprint. New York: Liveright, 1970.

Literary Essays. Edited by T. S. Eliot. New York: New Directions, n.d.

Personae. New York: New Directions, 1971.

"Preface to the Memorial Exhibition, 1918." In *Gaudier-Brzeska: A Memoir,* 136–9. New York: New Directions, 1985.

Selected Letters, 1907–1941. Edited by D. D. Paige. New York: New Directions, 1971.

Selected Poems. New York: New Directions, 1957.

Selected Prose, 1909–1965. Edited by William Cookson. New York: New Directions, 1973.

Social Credit: An Impact. 1935. Reprint. London: Peter J. Russell, 1951.

Rabaté, Jean-Michel. *Language, Sexuality, and Ideology in Ezra Pound's Cantos.* Albany: State University of New York Press, 1986.

Raffel, Burton. *Possum and Ole Ez in the Public Eye.* Hamden, Conn.: Archon Books, 1985.

Redman, Tim. "The Repatriation of Pound, 1939–1942: A View from the Archives." *Paideuma* 8, no. 3 (Winter 1979): 447–57.

Reynolds, Lloyd G. "Economics in History: The Poetic Vision of Ezra Pound." *Yale Review* 75 (Spring 1986): 385–98.

Rorty, Richard. *Contingency, Irony, and Solidarity.* New York: Cambridge University Press, 1989.

Rushing, Conrad L. " 'Mere Words': The Trial of Ezra Pound." *Critical Inquiry* 14, no. 1 (Autumn 1987): 111–33.

Salvatorelli, Luigi, and Mira, Giovanni. *Storia d'Italia nel Periodo Fascista.* Milan: Giulio Einaudi, 1956.

Sanders, Frederick K. *John Adams Speaking: Pound's Sources for the Adams Cantos.* Orono, Maine: University of Maine Press, 1975.

Schafer, R. Murray. *Ezra Pound and Music: The Complete Criticism.* New York: New Directions, 1977.

Selver, Paul. *Orage and the New Age Circle.* London: George Allen & Unwin, 1959.

Sicari, Stephen. "Reading Pound's Politics: Ulysses as Fascist Hero." *Paideuma* 17, nos. 2 and 3 (Fall and Winter 1988): 145–68.

Sieburth, Richard. "In Pound We Trust: The Economy of Poetry/The Poetry of Economics." *Critical Inquiry* 14, no. 1 (Autumn 1987): 142–72.

Smith, Douglas. "Ezra Pound: Poetry and Politics." *Canadian Review of American Studies* 17, no. 4 (Winter 1986): 509–24.

Spiegel, Henry William. *The Growth of Economic Thought.* Rev. and expanded ed. Durham, N.C.: Duke University Press, 1983.

Stock, Noel. *The Life of Ezra Pound.* New York: Pantheon Books, 1970.

Surette, Leon. "Ezra Pound and British Radicalism." *English Studies in Canada* 9, no. 4 (1983): 435–51.

A Light from Eleusis. London: Oxford University Press, 1979.

Terrell, Carroll F. *A Companion to the Cantos of Ezra Pound,* vol. 1. Berkeley and Los Angeles: University of California Press, 1980.

Toniolo, Gianni. *L'Economia dell'Italia Fascista.* Rome–Bari: Gius. Laterza & Figli, 1980.

Torrey, E. Fuller. "The Protection of Ezra Pound." *Psychology Today,* November 1981, 57.

The Roots of Treason: Ezra Pound and the Secret of St. Elizabeths. New York: McGraw-Hill, 1984.

Tytell, John. *Ezra Pound: The Solitary Volcano.* New York: Doubleday, 1987.

Vendler, Helen, ed. *Voices and Visions: The Poet in America.* New York: Random House, 1987.

Vettori, Vittorio. *Ezra Pound e il Senso dell'America.* Rome: ERSI Editrice, 1975.

Watts, Harold H. *Ezra Pound and the Cantos.* London: Routledge & Kegan Paul, 1951.

Wees, William C. *Vorticism and the English Avant-Garde*. Toronto: University of Toronto Press, 1972.

Welk, William G. *Fascist Economic Policy*. 1938. Reprint. New York: Russell & Russell, 1968.

Wilhelm, J. J. *The American Roots of Ezra Pound*. New York: Garland Publishing, 1985.

Zapponi, Niccolò. *L'Italia di Ezra Pound*. Rome: Bulzoni, 1976.

Zuccotti, Susan. *The Italians and the Holocaust*. New York: Basic Books, 1987.

Index

Cambridge Studies in American Literature and Culture

Editor
Albert Gelpi, Stanford University

Robert Lawson-Peebles, *Landscape and Written Expression in Revolutionary America: The World Turned Upside Down*

Robert S. Levine, *Conspiracy and Romance: Studies in Brockden Brown, Cooper, Hawthorne, and Melville*

John Limon, *The Place of Fiction in the Time Of Science: A Disciplinary History of American Writing*

Jerome Loving, *Emily Dickinson: The Poet on the Second Story*

Elizabeth McKinsey, *Niagara Falls: Icon of the American Sublime*

John McWilliams, *The American Epic: Transformation of a Genre, 1770–1860*

Susan Manning, *The Puritan-Provincial Vision: Scottish and American Literature in the Nineteenth Century*

David Miller, *Dark Eden: The Swamp in Nineteenth Century American Culture*

Warren Motley, *The American Abraham: James Fenimore Cooper and The Frontier Patriarch*

Brenda Murphy, *American Realism and American Drama, 1800–1940*

Michael Oriard, *Sporting with the Gods: The Rhetoric of Play and Game in American Literature*

Marjorie Perloff, *The Dance of the Intellect: Studies in the Poetry of the Pound Tradition*★

Tim Redman, *Ezra Pound and Italian Fascism*

Karen Rowe, *Saint and Singer: Edward Taylor's Typology and the Poetics of Meditation*

Barton St. Armand, *Emily Dickinson and Her Culture: The Soul's Society*★

Eric Sigg, *The American T. S. Eliot: A Study of the Early Writings*

Tony Tanner, *Scenes of Nature, Signs of Man: Essays in Nineteenth and Twentieth Century American Literature*★

Brook Thomas, *Cross Examinations of Law and Literature: Cooper, Hawthorne, Stowe, and Melville*★

Albert von Frank, *The Sacred Game: Provincialism and Frontier Consciousness in American Literature, 1630–1860*

David Wyatt, *The Fall into Eden: Landscape and Imagination in California*★

Lois Zamora, *Writing the Apocalypse: Ends and Endings in Contemporary U.S. and Latin American Fiction*

★Published in hardcover and paperback.